Dictatorship and Daily Life in Twentieth-Century Europe

Dictatorship and Daily Life in Twentieth-Century Europe

**Edited by
LISA PINE**

BLOOMSBURY ACADEMIC
LONDON • NEW YORK • OXFORD • NEW DELHI • SYDNEY

BLOOMSBURY ACADEMIC
Bloomsbury Publishing Plc
50 Bedford Square, London, WC1B 3DP, UK
1385 Broadway, New York, NY 10018, USA
29 Earlsfort Terrace, Dublin 2, Ireland

BLOOMSBURY, BLOOMSBURY ACADEMIC and the Diana logo are trademarks of
Bloomsbury Publishing Plc

First published in Great Britain 2023

Copyright © Lisa Pine, 2023

Lisa Pine has asserted their right under the Copyright, Designs and Patents Act,
1988, to be identified as Editor of this work.

Cover design by Jesse Holborn
Cover images: bottom (Adolf Hitler saluting, 1 May 1936),
left (Benito Mussolini Speaking to Crowd, 9 May 1936),
top (Nicolae Ceausescu addresses a civic rally, Romania, circa 1975)
(© Getty Images)

All rights reserved. No part of this publication may be reproduced or transmitted
in any form or by any means, electronic or mechanical, including photocopying,
recording, or any information storage or retrieval system, without prior
permission in writing from the publishers.

Bloomsbury Publishing Plc does not have any control over, or responsibility for, any
third-party websites referred to or in this book. All internet addresses given in
this book were correct at the time of going to press. The author and publisher
regret any inconvenience caused if addresses have changed or sites have
ceased to exist, but can accept no responsibility for any such changes.

Every effort has been made to trace copyright holders and to obtain their permissions for
the use of copyright material. The publisher apologizes for any errors or omissions and
would be grateful if notified of any corrections that should be incorporated in future reprints
or editions of this book.

A catalogue record for this book is available from the British Library.

A catalog record for this book is available from the Library of Congress.

ISBN: HB: 978-1-3502-0901-5
PB: 978-1-3502-0898-8
ePDF: 978-1-3502-0904-6
eBook: 978-1-3502-0907-7

Typeset by RefineCatch Limited, Bungay, Suffolk
Printed and bound in Great Britain

To find out more about our authors and books visit www.bloomsbury.com
and sign up for our newsletters.

Contents

List of figures vii
List of contributors viii
Acknowledgements x
List of abbreviations and glossary xi

    Introduction 1
    Lisa Pine

1. Everyday life in Fascist Italy 15
   Kate Ferris
2. Daily life in Hitler's Germany 51
   Lisa Pine
3. Life in Franco's Spain 75
   Antonio Cazorla-Sánchez
4. Salazar's Portugal: living 'by habit' in an authoritarian regime 101
   António Costa Pinto and Duncan Simpson
5. Transnational totalitarianism and the building of a new public consciousness in Kārlis Ulmanis's Latvia 123
   Jordan T. Kuck
6. Everyday life in the Soviet Union under Stalin 149
   Kees Boterbloem
7. Life in Ceaușescu's Romania 179
   Dennis Deletant

8 Between barbed wire and country garden idyll: dictatorship and everyday life in the German Democratic Republic (GDR) 205
Stefan Wolle

Conclusion 239
Lisa Pine

Index 253

Figures

1.1	A dance party at the Lido, Venice, 1930	26
1.2	Children's summer camp refectory, 1930	36
2.1	The first KdF train, 1934	54
2.2	Mother's Day ceremony with conferment of the Cross of Honour of the German Mother, 1942	59
3.1	General Franco in Seville, 1967	80
3.2	General Franco and his wife at a reception to reward the parents of large families	89
4.1	Salazar giving a speech	102
4.2	Street scene in Torres Vedras, Portugal, 1959	107
5.1	The 1937 Harvest Festival in Jelgava	131
5.2	Ulmanis delivering a celebratory speech at the Victory Clearing in 1936	137
6.1	Communist youths with a huge portrait of Stalin	163
6.2	Architectural contrasts: towering Socialist housing project against old Orthodox church in Moscow	170
7.1	Street scene in Bucharest, 1979	180
7.2	Feleacu village, Cluj county, 1988	184
8.1	Prefabricated buildings in Berlin	223
8.2	Queue at a food shop in East Berlin, 1982	228

Contributors

Kees Boterbloem, a native of the Netherlands, has taught Russian and Soviet History at universities in Canada and the United States for more than a quarter of a century. He is Professor of History at the University of South Florida in Tampa, USA. He has written or edited twelve books and numerous articles on Russian, Soviet and Dutch history, including *Life in Stalin's Soviet Union* (2019), *Russia as Empire: Past and Present* (2020) and *A Forgotten Friendship: The Dutch Republic and Russia* (2021). He is currently working on the history of Tatarstan.

Antonio Cazorla-Sánchez is Professor of Modern European History at Trent University, Canada. He is the author of nine books and dozens of chapters in books and refereed articles. His forthcoming book (in Spanish) is *The Spanish Civil War in 100 Objects*. He is also currently preparing an online museum of the Spanish Civil War. His current research project is a postcolonial analysis of Europe's twentieth-century museums of political and social violence. He was the recipient of the 2020 Trent University Distinguished Research Award, given every three years to a professor in the field of the Humanities.

António Costa Pinto is Research Professor at the Institute of Social Sciences, University of Lisbon. He has been a visiting professor at Stanford University, Georgetown University, a senior visiting fellow at Princeton University, the University of California, Berkeley, and New York University. His research interests include fascism and authoritarianism, political elites and democratisation. He is the author of *The Nature of Fascism Revisited* (2012), *Latin American Dictatorships in the Era of Fascism* (2020) and he co-edited recently (with Federico Finchelstein), *Authoritarian and Corporatism in Europe and Latin America: Crossing Borders* (2019).

Dennis Deletant was Visiting Ion Rațiu Professor of Romanian Studies in the School of Foreign Service at Georgetown University, Washington DC. He is Emeritus Professor of Romanian Studies at University College London and was Professor of Romanian Studies at the University of Amsterdam. Publications include *Ceaușescu and the Securitate: Coercion and Dissent in Romania, 1965–89* (1995), *Hitler's Forgotten Ally: Ion Antonescu and His Regime, Romania, 1940–1944* (2006) and *British Clandestine Activities in Romania During the Second World War* (2016), all being translated into

Romanian. His most recent study in English is *Romania Under Communism: Paradox and Degeneration* (2019).

Kate Ferris is Reader in Modern European History at the University of St Andrews, UK. Her research focuses on Italy and Spain from the late nineteenth to the mid-twentieth century, and especially on questions of subjectivity, agency, practice in everyday life and the lived experience of dictatorship. Her books include *Everyday Life in Fascist Venice* (2012) and (co-edited) *The Politics of Everyday Life in Fascist Italy* (2017). She is Principal Investigator of the ERC-funded research project, 'Dictatorship as experience' (DICTATOREXPERIENCE, 772353) which runs from 2018 to 2023.

Jordan T. Kuck is Assistant Professor of History at Brevard College (Brevard, North Carolina), USA. He teaches European and global history. He has published a number of articles and book chapters on the history of Kārlis Ulmanis, his authoritarian regime and interwar Latvia. He is currently working on a book manuscript on the Ulmanis regime.

Lisa Pine has taught modern History at universities in the UK for more than twenty-five years. She is a graduate of the LSE and obtained her doctorate from the University of London in 1996. She is a Fellow of the Royal Historical Society. Her main research interests are the social history of Nazi Germany and the Holocaust. Her major publications are *Nazi Family Policy, 1933–1945* (1997), *Hitler's 'National Community': Society and Culture in Nazi Germany* (2007, 2017), *Education in Nazi Germany* (2010), *Life and Times in Nazi Germany* (2016), *Debating Genocide* (2018) and *The Family in Modern Germany* (2020).

Duncan Simpson gained his PhD at King's College London. He is the author of one book on the relations between the Catholic Church and the Salazar regime, and has published numerous articles on the Portuguese dictatorship in academic journals in Britain, France, Portugal and Brazil. As a Marie Curie Research Fellow at the Institute of the Social Sciences of the University of Lisbon, he is currently working on a history of the Salazarist political police 'from below', combining the methodologies of quantitative surveying, oral history and archival research.

Stefan Wolle was born in East Germany. He worked in the Department of History at the Academy of Science in East Berlin 1976–89, receiving his PhD in 1984. During 1990–1, he was actively involved in the dissolution of the Ministry of State Security, being appointed Federal Commissioner for the Records of the Stasi. He is a member of the German Research Society. He is now at the Free University of Berlin. In 2006, he was elected Scientific Director of the GDR Museum Berlin. He is the author of many books, and works for newspapers, magazines, television and radio.

Acknowledgements

I would like to thank the proposal reviewers for their positive responses and useful suggestions, which helped me to reconsider the shape of the contents of this book for the better. I am grateful for research funding from the LSS Research Fund at London South Bank University, in the form of two short writing retreats, which allowed me to focus on the draft manuscript without any distractions at crucial moments in its preparation. On that note, I would like to thank Nancy Stevenson for providing a wonderful seaside retreat.

Of course, a volume with multiple authors would be impossible without the hard work and cooperation of the contributors and each one has been assiduous in writing excellent chapters and adhering to deadlines. I am thankful to Marius Turda for his careful reading of my chapter and his suggestions for improvement, as well as other friends and colleagues who have helped me to improve the text. My thanks are due to Michael Fields for agreeing to read the entire manuscript for me, as well as the manuscript reviewer who undertook a reading of the whole text and offered helpful comments. I am very grateful to Sara Hayes for her translation of the final chapter from German into English, as well as to Matthew Jefferies for putting me in touch with her. My thanks are also due to my copy-editor, Sue Littleford, for all her hard work and efficiency.

Together with the publisher, I would like to thank Getty Images for permission to use the majority of the illustrations inside the book, as well as the images on the cover. I would also like to thank the National Archives of Latvia for permission to use the photographs in Chapter 5 and Dennis Deletant for permission to use his photograph in Chapter 7. I have been extremely fortunate to work with my editor, Rhodri Mogford, over the course of many years and several book projects. Once again, I would like to thank him for all his help and encouragement throughout the publishing process.

Lisa Pine
London, 2022

Abbreviations and glossary

4-H	An international youth organisation, based in the US, focused on teaching agriculture and celebrating natural and rural life (replicated in Latvia)
ADN	Archivio Diaristico Nazionale [National Diary Archive] (Italian)
agitprop	agitation and propaganda (Russian)
Aktion T4	'euthanasia' campaign, 1939–41, Nazi Germany (German)
AOI	Africa Orientale Italiana [Italian East Africa] (Italian)
Auslese	selection (German)
Ausmerze	eradication (German)
Bolshevik	communist (Russian)
byt'	everyday existence (Russian)
caciquismo	lit. chieftancy, domination (Portuguese)
Camere del lavoro	Chambers of Labour (Italian)
Carlism	traditionalist political ideology aimed at restoring a different branch of the Bourbon family to the Spanish throne
case del fascio	building housing local branches of the PNF (qv) (Italian)
case del popolo	lit. houses of the people; socialist clubs (Italian)
Case della Madre e del Bambino	mother and child homes (Italian)
Caudillo	leader (Spanish)
CNR	Consiglio Nazionale delle Ricerche [National Research Council] (Italian)
CSS	Council for State Security (Romania)
DDR	Deutsche Demokratische Republik [East Germany] (see GDR in English)
DGS	Direção-Geral de Segurança [Directorate-General of Security] (Portuguese)

Diário de Lisboa	*Lisbon Diary*, a defunct evening newspaper (Portuguese)
Draudzīgais aicinājums	Friendly Challenge, initiative (Latvian)
Duce	leader (Italian)
EIAR	Ente Italiano per le Audizioni Radiofoniche [Italian Body for Radio Broadcasting] (Italian)
Eintopf	one-pot dish (German)
enti	bodies, entities (Italian)
EOA	Ente Opera Assistenziale [Welfare Organisation] (Italian)
Estado Novo	New State (Portuguese)
ETA	Euzkadi ta Azkatasuna [Basque Homeland and Liberty] (Basque)
Falange	lit. Phalanx; the sole political party in Franco's Spain (Spanish)
Fasci femminili	Women's Leagues (Italian)
Fascio, pl. Fasci	League (Italian)
feste del fascio	fascist parties/celebrations (Italian)
FNAT	A Fundação Nacional para a Alegria no Trabalho [National Foundation for Joy at Work] (Spanish)
FRG	Federal Republic of Germany [West Germany]
frontoviki	male army veterans (Russian)
Führer	leader (German)
GDP	gross domestic product
GDR	German Democratic Republic (East Germany)
Gestapo	Secret State Police, Nazi Germany (German)
GIL	Gioventù Italiana del Littorio [Italian Youth of the Littorio; *Littorio* from the Latin for the attendant on the magistrate who carried the fasces in Ancient Rome] (Italian)
Giustizia e Libertà	Justice and Freedom, an anti-fascist resistance movement (Italian)
Gleichschaltung	'streamlining' or coordination of society (German)
GNR	Guarda Nacional Republicana [National Republican Guard] (Portuguese)
Gosplan	Gosudarstvennyy Planovyy Komitet [State Planning Bureau (of the Five-Year Plans)] (Russian)
GULag	Glávnoje upravlénije lageréj [Main Administration of Labour Camps] (Russian)

ABBREVIATIONS AND GLOSSARY

HOAC	Hermandad Obrera de Acción Católica [Workers Brotherhood of Catholic Action] (Spanish)
homines Sovietici	lit. Soviet people (Latin)
INFPS	Istituto Nazionale Fascista della Previdenza Sociale [National Fascist Institute for Social Security] (Italian)
JOC	Juventud Obrera Católica [Catholic Workers Youth] (Spanish)
Junta de Freguesia	parish council (Portuguese)
KdF	Kraft durch Freude [Strength Through Joy] organisation (German)
kolkhoz	collective-farm (Russian)
kolkhozniki	collective-farm workers, men (Russian)
kolkhoznitsy	collective-farm workers, women (Russian)
Komsomol	Kommunisticheskiy Soyuz Molodyozhi [Communist Youth League] (Russian)
lats	unit of Latvian currency, 1922–2014
Lebensborn	lit. Well of Life; Nazi organisation to encourage greater numbers of births (German)
Legião Portuguesa	Portuguese Legion (Portuguese)
Massaie Rurali	Rural Housewives (Italian)
Maurrassian	follower of Charles Maurras, who gave his name to a monarchist political movement
Mazpulki	agriculture-focused youth organisation (Latvian)
MfS	Ministerium für Staatssicherheit [Ministry of State Security], commonly the Stasi (East Germany)
MP	Mocidade Portuguesa, paramilitary youth organisation (Portuguese)
MPF	Mocidade Portuguese Feminina [Portuguese Female Youth] (Portuguese)
musica da ballo	dance music (Italian)
musica leggera	light music (Italian)
MVSN	Milizia Volontaria per la Sicurezza Nazionale [Voluntary Militia for National Security] (Italian)
NCO	non-commissioned officer
NKVD	Narodnyi Komissariat Vnutrennykh Del [People's Commissariat of Internal Affairs] (Russian)
NSDAP	Nationalsozialistische Deutsche Arbeiterpartei [National Socialist German Workers' Party] (German)

NS-Frauenschaft	National Socialist Womanhood (Nazi women's association) (German)
NS-Frauenwarte	*National Socialist Women's Monitor* (magazine) (German)
OECD	Organisation for Economic Co-operation and Development
ONB	Opera Nazionale Balilla [Italian Fascist youth organisation] (Italian)
OND	Opera Nazionale Dopolavoro [National After-Work Body] (Italian)
ONMI	Opera Nazionale Maternità e Infanzia [National Works for Maternity and Childhood] (Italian)
OVRA	Organizzazione per la Vigilanza e la Repressione dell'Antifascismo [Organisation for Vigilance and Repression of Anti-Fascism = secret police] (Italian)
PCI	Partito Comunista Italiano [Italian Communist Party] (Italian)
PCP	Partido Comunista Português [Portuguese Communist Party] (Portuguese)
PIDE	Polícia Internacional e de Defesa do Estado [International and State Defence Police] (Portuguese)
Platte	prefabricated housing (East Germany)
PNF	Partito Nazionale Fascista [National Fascist Party] (Italian)
Podestà	fascist mayor (Italian)
POW	prisoner(s) of war
presente	here I am (Italian)
PVDE	Polícia de Vigilância e Defesa do Estado [Vigilance and State Defence Police] (Portuguese)
Rīts	*Morning*, newspaper (Latvian)
RM	Reichsmark (unit of currency) (German)
sacrarie dei caduti	shrines of the Fallen (Italian)
SD	Sicherheitsdienst des Reichsführers-SS [Security Service, and intelligence agency]
Securitate	lit. Security [political police] (Romanian)
SED	Sozialistische Einheitspartei Deutschlands [Socialist Unity Party of Germany, i.e. the East German Communist Party] (East Germany)
Segreteria Particolare del Duce	Particular Secretariat of the Duce (Italian)

sekretnye sotrudniki	secret collaborators (Russian)
sovversivismo	subversivism (Italian)
SPN	Secretariado da Propaganda Nacional [National Propaganda Secretariat] (Portuguese)
squadrismo, squadristo, squadristi	action squad of the fascist militia (noun and adjective), and its members (Italian)
SS	Schutzstaffeln [Protective Echelon] (German)
Stasi	security police, of the MfS (q.v.) (East Germany)
Strādnieku Avīze	*Workers' Newspaper* (Latvian)
Strēlnieki	40,000 Latvian conscripts into the Russian Imperial Army, 1915
USSR	Union of Socialist Soviet Republics
Uzvaras laukums	Victory Field / Victory Clearing (Latvian)
Vadonis	leader (Latvian)
veglioni tricolori	tricolour balls (Italian)
Volksgemeinschaft	national community (German)
Volkswagen	people's car (German)
vozhd'	boss/leader (Russian)
Weltanschauung	worldview; particular philosophy of life (German)
Wende	turning points (East Germany)
Zemgales Balss	*Zemgale Voice*, newspaper (Latvian)

Introduction

Lisa Pine

This book examines everyday life in the context of European dictatorships in the twentieth century. It brings together historical analyses of daily life in twentieth-century dictatorships in Europe in a single volume, taking a comparative approach to determine commonalities and differences. It explores the impact of dictatorial governments on everyday life, as well as analysing the relationship between the population and the regime in a number of key dictatorships in Europe. The chapters explore the extent to which populations living in these circumstances embraced, appropriated, accommodated or avoided the regime's penetration into daily life. They shed light on nuances in these lived experiences of dictatorship and in the relationship between the population and the government in each case. This introduction to the book consists of three parts. First, it sets out the aims and rationale of the book, explaining the reasons for its overall conception, as well as for the selection of the eight case studies presented. Second, it contextualises the book by exploring what has been written on the history of these regimes and on the history of everyday life in dictatorships so far. Third, it outlines the content of the book, signposting the reader to the crucial questions explored and showing clearly what each chapter covers, in order to ensure that the structure and content – as well as the key areas of focus and investigation – are plain from the outset.

Although particular circumstances and national histories might have been distinctive in the different case studies we are treating, certainly European intellectual, cultural and political traditions had a part to play in the development of conditions in each of these to provide fertile ground for dictatorships to arise when they did, and in some cases to remain in place for several decades. The developments that shaped each of these countries, throughout the course of the nineteenth century and into the twentieth century – within the context of European history – were very significant in determining the paths they took into dictatorship, as political, social and economic circumstances led to the rise of extreme ideologies and autocratic governments. Specifically, modern European history from the Enlightenment onwards set the stage for their emergence and development in a variety of ways. Industrialisation and revolutions (thwarted or not), as well as the rise of new political parties and ideologies of nationalism and racism (and even the levelling aspect inherent in socialism) left their imprint. The establishment of overseas empires (or the incapacity to do so) contributed to the dictatorial impetus. Most acutely, the First World War, its unresolved outcome and the post-war settlements provided fertile ground for extreme ideologies to rise and allowed opportunistic politicians to grab power. Unfavourable economic circumstances heightened the frustration and often desperation among their supporters, as did inequalities between social classes and uneven economic development. For these reasons, this book is restricted to a discussion of the history of dictatorial regimes in Europe's twentieth century, where the circumstances of the development of the dictatorships were different from those of other continents. Limiting the geographical extent to Europe gives coherence to the book, with each case study rooted in the shared history of Europe.

The original concept for this book came from my hearing about the experience of a first-year undergraduate history student at a British university, presented with the essay title 'Was Nazism more similar to Italian Fascism or Stalinism?'. The apparent lack of (up-to-date) secondary sources faced by students like this one to tackle a question of that nature prompted me to consider producing a book to fill this gap. But then it also appeared opportune to expand the remit of such a book beyond these three examples. And so, the case studies selected extend the scope of this book beyond the most obvious 'totalitarian' dictatorships in Fascist Italy, the USSR and Nazi Germany. We examine the Iberian Peninsula, looking at developments in the Franco regime in Spain, as well as the Salazar administration in Portugal, both of which similarly lasted many decades. Ceaușescu's regime in Romania, which lasted from 1965 to 1989 (and was a more extreme version of that of his predecessor, Gheorghe Gheorghiu-Dej), also extended over several decades. Its significant and distinctive social policies towards the family are worthy of discussion in the context of a book that treats the history of everyday life. Beyond that, a coverage of the German Democratic Republic and one of the Baltic states, ensures that whilst this book cannot embrace examples from the whole continent, it does represent a reasonably broad geographical range.

The book covers dictatorships from what are considered to be the extreme left and right of the political spectrum, and one of the intriguing questions it (often implicitly) addresses is whether or not, or how far, daily life in each of these states showed more than superficial commonalities. None of the authors subscribes anymore to the Cold War social-scientific paradigm of totalitarianism, but undoubtedly the European twentieth-century zeitgeist, or, more concretely, at least a shared stage of society's technological development, contributed to the prevalence of often similar conditions of everyday life.[1] As we examine the intersections between the structures of the dictatorships and the citizens who lived under their rule, we see how people attempted to preserve as much of a semblance of normality in their everyday existence as was possible within the context of living under despotic rule.

This book then, examines what happened to people's lives in a political regime characterised by some or all of the following: a one-party state, in which opposition or multiple parties were banned; a cult surrounding the leader; the censorship of the press and other publications; the widespread use of propaganda and political persuasion; and the simmering threat or the actual use of force by the regime and its agents. The chapters investigate crucial questions in relation to life under dictatorships including: What was the impact of censorship on access to news or entertainment? How was leisure time conducted? What was the impact of the regime on working life? What was the potential and scope for dissent and resistance? How much did the regime coerce the population and how much did it attempt to gain popular support? What was the difference for party leaders, comrades and members in terms of the career possibilities and opportunities for social advancement these opened, compared to everyone else in society? In particular, with the shutting down – to a large extent – of civil society and state intrusion into private life, what restrictions were placed on ordinary and day-to-day activities? What happened to religious life and to cultural life and the arts? How were personal choices in aspects of life such as reproduction, education and even food affected by these regimes? What was the impact of different political ideologies on people's way of life – whether fascist, Nazi or communist? In setting out the national histories of each of the different regimes and placing them together in one volume, this book allows readers not only to understand what daily life was like in individual dictatorships, but also to compare them with each other, either singly or severally, as well as allowing a comparison of those based upon left-wing or right-wing ideologies, either together or with each other. This approach helps readers to come to an understanding of the subject and to formulate their own assessments of the dictatorships we cover through comparison and contrast.

It is necessary to contextualise through a brief overview of what has been written, especially recently, on the comparative history of these regimes and on the comparison of the history of everyday life in dictatorships so far to situate the book in the historiography. Some comparative books deal with the machinery of dictatorship or the dictators themselves and make comparisons about those, but none do this in terms of everyday life and the relationship between the regime and the people. The only truly comparable book, edited by Alf Lüdtke, deals with an eclectic selection of cases from across the globe, including two chapters on the Third Reich, one on Italian Fascism, one on Stalinism, two on Korea between 1937 and 1945, one on the German Democratic Republic (GDR), three further chapters on Korea, one on Senegal and one on Ghana.[2] This volume deals with some different cases to his whilst focused solely on Europe. Lüdtke identifies both 'collusion' and its 'crucial flipside: evasion' as the key themes of his book.[3] He notes a range of practices of collusion, as well as 'moments and spaces that allowed evasion of the gazing eyes and listening ears of the authorities and their agents'.[4] These are certainly important themes in the study of dictatorship and daily life. In this book too, we reflect upon the extent to which people made decisions about how to go about their everyday lives within the parameters of the very restricted lifestyles imposed upon them by the governments in question.

A noteworthy comparative study by Glennys Young deals with solely communist regimes.[5] Young's book extends beyond the USSR and Eastern Europe to examine the lives of people across the globe, in China, Korea, Vietnam, Cambodia, Kyrgyzstan, Algeria, Peru, Cuba and elsewhere. It analyses the communist experience, in which people became enthusiasts, reshapers, resisters or victims of the communist ideological project. It is very broad in its coverage, but, as the title already indicates, looks only at communist regimes. In contrast, the comparative volume edited by António Costa Pinto and Aristotle Kallis focuses mainly on the 1920s and 1930s and extreme right-wing examples, so here too the coverage is also not the same as in this book.[6] In addition, it deals with the political or ruling mechanisms of the regimes and with fascist ideology, rather than the history of everyday life. Beyond this, there are some older books that deal with comparisons of Nazism and Stalinism or Nazism and fascism, but precisely therefore, present a narrow comparison between two examples. Richard Bessel's edited book explores Fascist Italy and Nazi Germany.[7] It touches on some aspects of everyday life, such as the experiences of workers and women under these dictatorships but does not treat daily life specifically or comprehensively. Similarly, two important edited books draw direct comparisons between Hitler's and Stalin's regimes, but limit themselves to treat just these two cases.[8] A more recent volume of this kind, edited by Michael Geyer and Sheila Fitzpatrick, published in 2009, comprises four sections – on governance, violence, socialisation and entanglements – comparing different aspects of these two regimes.[9] They explain how 'deeply embedded' the concept of totalitarianism has been in the development of the historiography (which is perhaps a bit of a strawman argument, given the disappearance of the concept from scholarly discourse soon after 1991).[10] In another edited book published in the same year, Paul Corner investigates the popular reactions to totalitarian rule in the Soviet Union, Fascist Italy, Nazi Germany and the communist regimes in Poland and

East Germany after 1945.¹¹ Furthermore, the issue of the public sphere in relation to the private is crucial in these types of political systems. The subject of private spheres, in the USSR and the Third Reich, has started to be investigated in the historiography of these fields.¹² In addition, recent titles on daily life in specific regimes are on a similar theme to this volume, but obviously each of these is devoted to a single dictatorship.¹³ This book incorporates a history of everyday life in several dictatorial regimes in one volume and that is what makes it distinctive.

In Chapter 1, Kate Ferris examines everyday life in Fascist Italy. She shows that Benito Mussolini's formulation, 'Everything in the State, nothing outside the State, nothing against the State', pronounced at a critical juncture in the Italian fascist regime's development – following the declaration of the dictatorship and amidst the dismantling of all vestiges of Italian civil society – signalled Mussolini's intent to revolutionise and regenerate all aspects of Italian society and Italians' lives. It not only pointed to 'ordinary' Italians and their everyday worlds as key recipients of fascism's 'totalising' project, but also tacitly recognised Italians as important potential constructors – and the everyday as a key construction site – of the dictatorship. To this end, in addition to being decreed and imposed from above, the dictatorship was also effectively enacted from below, in the local spaces inhabited and the everyday practices performed day by day, by the people who lived through it. Dictatorial policies and rhetoric were reinterpreted and modified as they were put into effect by representatives and agents of the regime (including local party leaders and members, civil servants, teachers, journalists and midwives) in the local spaces and places that effectively comprised the 'units of experience' of the dictatorship. Individual Italians encountered the dictatorial state not only in official policies, propaganda and rituals, but also in everyday settings, such as the market, the factory, the bar, the street and the home. These venues were sites where the fascist dictatorship could be made, but also potentially 'unmade'.

This chapter explores the everyday, lived experiences of the fascist dictatorship in Italy between 1922 and 1940. (Whilst the fascist regime ruled in Italy until 1943 in southern and central Italy, and until 1945 in northern Italy, this chapter ends its coverage in 1940, at the outbreak of the Second World War in recognition of the substantial changes in lived experience that this wrought.) It examines a range of venues and practices, including urban, rural and colonial spaces, and leisure and consumption practices, as well as differentiated everyday lived experiences of the fascist dictatorship, including those marked by gender, class and race. Whilst Italy's fascist regime may have been the first to declare itself 'totalitarian', and along with the Soviet Union, to envision a radically new social order engineered by the state, to what extent did all facets of Italian life genuinely reside 'within the state'? The chapter investigates the scope of fascism's totalitarian project, as well as its limits. It examines the ways in which violence, coercion and intimidation were combined with enticement, propaganda and the eliciting of support or 'consent', in the regime's attempts to shape Italians' everyday lives. It analyses how the Italians variously negotiated, resisted and exploited the dictates of Mussolini's regime. It investigates the extent to which opportunities existed for Italians to act with agency in their everyday lives.

What emerges is a complex and changing picture in which fascism moved in and out of Italians' lives, as Italians moved in and out of the gaze of state authority, both nationally and locally. To be sure, the dictatorship did interrupt and fundamentally change people's lives, often with violence. However, individuals living under, or through, the fascist regime in Italy did not always feel the impact of the regime at all times and in all aspects of their lives. They could variously – or even simultaneously – be perpetrators and victims, supporters and detractors, participants and evaders. Inevitably, it was impossible for the lived reality of everyday life in fascist Italy to meet fully the expectations of Mussolini's totalitarian formula. By investigating the intersections and mediations between different scales of experience, the dynamic, reciprocal relations between 'above' and 'below', or between 'state' and 'society', Ferris's chapter argues that at different moments, and in a variety of ways, Italians could be 'inside', 'outside' and 'against' the state.

In Chapter 2, I explore the impact of the Nazi dictatorship on German society, the nature of everyday life in the Third Reich and the complex relationship between the Hitler regime and the German population between 1933 and 1945. The first part of the chapter examines the impact on society of mechanisms directed towards the creation of consensus and conformity, including *Gleichschaltung* ('streamlining' or coordination of society) and policies designed to create a cohesive German *Volksgemeinschaft* ('national community'). The complicated relationship between the German people and the Nazi regime was underpinned by both propaganda and policies designed to draw the German population closer to the regime and its goals on the one hand, and the use of terror and coercion on the other hand. The Nazis tried to create their ideal 'national community' in a number of ways through propaganda and policies that brought consensus for their rule and conformity to their ideology. These included Nazi youth groups, women's associations, Strength Through Joy, Beauty of Labour and campaigns such as the *Eintopf* (one-pot dish) that were designed to bring the nation together into uniformity and cohesion. The leadership myth that surrounded Hitler also impacted greatly on the German population and how it interacted with the regime. The Nazi regime underpinned its methods to create consensus for its rule with the threat or use of terror. This chapter examines too, therefore, the role of the Nazi system of terror, particularly highlighting the Gestapo (Secret State Police) and the concentration camp network, in order to illuminate an important aspect of the relationship of the people and the regime. The Gestapo was certainly an institution that instigated fear and terror among the German populace. Its leaders carefully and deliberately adopted the propaganda image of the ubiquitous Gestapo both to intimidate German society and to conceal its own deficiencies. But in reality, the Gestapo was not a completely thoroughgoing mechanism of repression. Instead, it was an understaffed and over-bureaucratised organisation, incapable of comprehensive surveillance. In effect, there were remarkably few Gestapo agents on the ground, and they relied on both amateur and professional helpers. The chapter explores the impact of the Gestapo on German everyday life. In addition, the concentration camps were a hallmark of the Nazi regime and lay at the heart of the Nazis' network of terror. The chapter analyses the effect of these upon the German population.

The second section of the chapter illuminates the impact of Nazi government on the family and private life. To what extent did Nazism penetrate the private life and choices of German citizens, in their family and social settings? How far did Nazi ideology invade the private realm of the family? It was difficult to maintain privacy and personal autonomy in the Nazi dictatorship (although this is an area that has not received as much attention from historians as other aspects of the Third Reich). The negotiation of the separation of aspects of daily life that were private as opposed to public was difficult terrain. For example, radio listening had formerly been a private activity, yet under National Socialism it was one that was encouraged to be public. There was also a tension between other spare time or leisure activities that in normal times were private, but under National Socialism became public, for example, attending art exhibitions. The relationship between the individual and the state was complex.

The final parts of the chapter highlight policies towards food and their impact on different sectors of the German population, especially during the war, as well as the impact of the Nazi regime on different groups in German society – distinctions in the effect of key aspects of Nazi policies of *Auslese* and *Ausmerze* (selection and eradication) on society in terms of education (from Nazi elite schools through to special schools); breeding and eugenics (from Lebensborn and positive population policy to sterilisation and the *Aktion T4* 'euthanasia' campaign between 1939 and 1941). In summary, the chapter presents an analytical overview of key aspects of everyday life in the Third Reich.

In Chapter 3, Antonio Cazorla-Sánchez examines the impact of the Franco regime on everyday life in Spain. He shows that during the dictatorship, the transmission of experiences and of new information was a highly complicated matter. To better understand this, he argues, it is necessary to distinguish between the private and the public spheres. The private realm offered the best possibilities for the intergenerational and intragenerational transmission of information. However, even this dissemination of information was hampered by the perils of exposing children to dangerous ideas that they might repeat outside their homes. This was a risk that many parents – possibly the majority – avoided, thus leaving the children ignorant of key aspects of their own parents' ideas, experiences and hopes. In any case, particularly with regards to the public sphere, people's access to information at the beginning of, during and after the Spanish Civil War, was hampered by censorship and propaganda. Thus, people could only rely on a limited number of resources and experiences to obtain information, and subsequently try to separate out the lies from the truth, amongst the proliferation of repeated rumours, myths and prejudices that were openly available to them.

The lack of an independent media, and the repetition of clichés, outright defamations and lies by official socialisation agencies, such as schools and the mass organisations (including youth groups, unions, the single party and the Church) for the population at large, made it nearly impossible to obtain a clear, well-informed personal and public perspective on both the past and the present. Put differently, even if a subculture of resistance and contestation amongst a minority of the population managed to survive the apparent blanket reality of uniformity, peace and order of Francoism, the majority and least politicised sectors of the population accepted the key aspects of the regime's discourse, including its condemnation of democracy as dangerous for Spaniards. However, this tacit acceptance was made possible only because it coincided with people's actual experiences of political and social strife in the past. From the 1950s, the leading forces behind the growing dissidence in Spain were university students and Catholic activists. Alongside educated university students, new generations of labour and community activists came from the most progressive sectors of the Church (the only major socialisation agency that was independent from the regime), who were mobilised by, or using the means available to, the HOAC (Hermandad Obrera de Acción Católica) and the JOC (Juventud Obrera Católica). Both students and Catholic activists started to connect with the pre-existing cultures of resistance entrenched in the country's large industrial areas where old and new political parties and unions maintained an extremely precarious underground existence until the early 1970s.

Cazorla-Sánchez shows that there were three main factors that determined and arbitrated the realities of Spaniards under the Franco dictatorship, thus conditioning their own analyses of the past, present and future. These three elements were: political, having to do with sympathies chosen and experienced during the Civil War; social class; and the periods through which people had lived. The first two factors were often closely linked. The lower along the socio-demographic scale someone was, the more likely it was that they would have harboured pro-Republican sympathies in the 1930s. During the dictatorship, this translated into antipathy, passive indifference or even partial acceptance, towards the regime. None of those attitudes necessarily excluded the others. Cazorla-Sánchez explains this transition by the fact that working-class people suffered the worst consequences of both the political repression and economic misery imposed by the Franco regime. This prolonged treatment led poor people to become deeply pessimistic about the future and cynical towards public policies. By contrast, middle-class and, particularly, upper-class people, were the main beneficiaries of the regime's imposition of terror on the working class, the destruction of trade unions, the lowering of wages and – importantly and not to be forgotten – the widespread corruption and profiteering that characterised the first decades of the dictatorship. Since these socially privileged groups were also the most fervently Catholic, to them, the dictatorship represented the best guarantee that the social reforms and anticlerical policies of the Republic, the revolution and 'red terror' of the war would never return. As such, the middle and upper classes provided the most enthusiastic and active supporters of the Franco regime. Of course, as Cazorla-Sánchez argues, there were numerous regional differences and other exceptions to this general description. Poor farmers, for example, could hardly be described as middle class, yet were often among the most anti-Republican, pious and pro-Franco people in Spain. Conversely, many members of the middle classes, who had embraced liberal ideas before the Civil War, were amongst the most persistent and better-educated enemies of the regime. And their children, and those of the pro-Franco elites, often became the spearhead of anti-Francoist activities when at university, to the puzzlement, and often contempt, of poor people, terrorised and depoliticised by the regime. In any case, Spanish society greatly changed in sociocultural terms over the course of the dictatorship. The mostly agrarian, poor and illiterate society of 1939 had evolved into a mostly urban, industrial, middle-income and relatively well-educated society by the time of Franco's death in 1975. This meant that the young people of the early 1970s had very different experiences and realities from their parents, and this had an impact upon both their personal and their collective expectations.

In Chapter 4, António Costa Pinto and Duncan Simpson examine daily life in Salazar's Portugal. The Salazar dictatorship (or 'New State') is best defined as a form of hybrid conservative authoritarianism based on the one-party state, the banning of opposition parties, extensive censorship and propaganda, and the use of force by various repressive institutions, such as the political police (PIDE). The regime lasted over forty years, from the early 1930s to the mid-1970s, significantly altering the structures of everyday life in the Portuguese population. In this chapter, the authors analyse the main aspects of this process over time, from the rural social order of the 1930s to the increasingly urban and industrial society of the 1970s. They investigate the following crucial questions and themes of daily life under the 'New State': How was working life affected by the corporatist organisation of society from the mid-1930s onwards? What were the effects of the regime's paramilitary youth organisation (Mocidade Portuguesa) and militia (Legião Portuguesa) in terms of the permeation of everyday life by ideology? To what extent was leisure time altered by state organisations such as the FNAT (National Foundation for Joy at Work)? How did censorship impact the access to news and the development of cultural life and the arts? To what degree did Catholic doctrine affect not only education or public entertainment, but also everyday behaviour and practices? How pervasive was the influence of the PIDE as a factor of demobilisation among the population at large and the minority of active oppositionists? Finally, how did ordinary citizens 'meander' their way through the dictatorial framing of their daily lives? And to what extent did they normalise the institutional set-up imposed by the regime? Costa Pinto and Simpson address these themes diachronically, in order to highlight the various phases in the prolonged existence of the 'New State' and their respective effects on the dynamics of everyday life, from the rise of fascism in the 1930s, to the colonial war which ultimately brought the regime to an end in 1974.

In Chapter 5, Jordan T. Kuck examines Kārlis Ulmanis's regime and the impact of his dictatorship on society in interwar Latvia. He refutes the thesis offered by Aivars Stranga, which contends that the Ulmanis regime was a failure, at least with regard to its stated aims of leading a national revolution. Kuck argues that Stranga cleaves too close to the German and Soviet examples (and definitions) of dictatorship and totalitarianism. He maintains that this view is problematic because Ulmanis did not intend to construct that sort of government. Whereas Adolf Hitler and Josef Stalin both relied strongly on elements of coercion, Ulmanis wanted his rule to be rooted in consent. And whilst it is true that he looked to the German and Italian cases of dictatorship as models to emulate, Kuck argues that Ulmanis did so in a flexible way that necessitates a different model of analysis. Thus, Kuck's chapter employs transnational fascism as the central and strategic approach.

In the main, the chapter focuses on the efforts of the Ulmanis regime to cultivate consent. Because much of the previous historiography has stiffly employed the totalitarian model and because much of the scholarship has focused on urban developments, not enough attention has been paid to the very popular rural-focused projects (and this even though the majority of the population lived in the countryside) initiated by the Ulmanis regime. Hence, the chapter covers Mazpulki (the agriculture-focused youth organisation), land amelioration, the new Harvest Festivals and the so-called Friendly Appeal campaign, all of which were aimed at developing consensus. The chapter concludes with a section on coercion, for the Ulmanis regime did utilise this approach from time to time, though in a mild way in comparison to other interwar dictatorial regimes in Europe. Those who experienced coercion were political opponents (for example, social democrats and communists), as well as ethnic minorities, who found it increasingly uncomfortable to live under a government whose central aim was to create a more Latvian Latvia.

In Chapter 6, Kees Boterbloem explores everyday existence (called *byt'* in Russian) in Stalin's Russia. He demonstrates that whilst this may have had parallels to daily life in other dictatorial regimes in Europe, the Soviet Union remained in other ways a phenomenon *sui generis*. One of its most startling aspects was the almost total lack of a civil society, in which its members could participate in organisations that were not coordinated by the regime. Eventually, even filmscripts, musical compositions and literature slated for publication were personally vetted by the leaders. To be sure, heavy-handed measures were applied to straitjacket people's words and thoughts. However, Boterbloem demonstrates that the limits of imposed uniformity were constantly probed from below. The authorities' means of control, after all, had their limitations in a country as large as the Soviet Union, or even European Russia, in an age that saw a rapid and hardly smooth transition from a premodern to a modern industrialised society. Electricity, telephones and radios were largely absent in the Soviet countryside under Stalin. Shirking from work or other obligations was something difficult to prevent in the collective-farm villages, in which support for the communist cause was more often than not anaemic. Urban intellectuals, too, managed to fake loyalty (or half-heartedly supported the regime) out of self-preservation, writing books 'for the drawer', as the cases of Boris Pasternak or Vasily Grossman show, or having critical conversations out of the reach of secret police agents, or their informers (*sekretnye sotrudniki*).

Boterbloem argues further that in the renewed chaos created by the Nazi-led invasion, Soviet subjects found more agency; no doubt some of the Soviet inhabitants' collaboration with the Nazis (even among the Russians) was not just the result of coercion or a desperate survival instinct. Ostentatiously, the regime managed to recover its hold over its people after May 1945, in part because the Nazis had managed to outdo the Soviet Communists in their malignancy towards their subject peoples. But even so, the regime's level of control over people's daily lives remained far from absolute. Exhausted mentally and physically, the Soviet population was in no state to consider any rebellion after 1945. However, the absurd lengths to which the cult of Stalin's personality was displayed in official discourse appears shrill, and Boterbloem shows that particularly in the countryside, it was reaching a breaking point towards the end of Stalin's life, incapable of meeting absurd economic demands and resisting any further disciplining. The reins needed to be loosened. In the cities, too, the ideals of communism turned into hollow phrases. Especially after 1945, Boterbloem contends, most people who did profess dedication to the cause did so mainly from a wholly instrumental perspective: joining the Party was key to upward social mobility and better living conditions.

In Chapter 7, Dennis Deletant examines everyday life in Ceaușescu's Romania. He explains that it can be tempting to approach communism solely in terms of its repressive nature and its gross denial of human rights. Indeed, the manner in which the political experiment, represented by the ideology and practised by its Soviet masters was imposed upon the countries of Eastern Central Europe, including Romania, exemplified its coercive character. Communism was not elected to power. But once established, its agent, the Communist Party, skilfully employed strategies to maintain itself in power. For that reason, Deletant argues, a cogent study of communism in Romania must be multifaceted. It should include a consideration of the cost–benefit analysis that citizens made in choosing not only to tolerate the regime, but also to demonstrate support for it and for its leader from 1965 to 1989, Nicolae Ceaușescu.

In this chapter, Deletant examines how life went on under dictatorship, even if it was largely mapped out for the individual by the regime. To what extent did the regime intrude into the daily life of the individual? How did the citizen negotiate the challenges placed in his or her path by the state? How important was the role of the political police, the Securitate, in maintaining compliance? To what degree was dissent towards the regime manifested? What restrictions were placed on freedom to travel abroad? To what degree was the moral compass of the person deflected? What role were intellectuals called upon to play in 'validating' the regime? What was the regime's attitude towards religious worship? Why did utopia descend into dystopia under Ceaușescu? In what forms was his personality cult manifested? Deletant's analysis thus addresses crucial questions about the impact of the Ceaușescu regime upon everyday life in Romania.

In Chapter 8, Stefan Wolle analyses everyday life in the GDR, a system of rule that lasted, albeit under different leaders, for four decades from 1949 to 1989. His chapter begins with a discussion of the relationship between the people and the state, especially the Ministry of State Security, or the Stasi. Wolle examines what security meant in the GDR, in terms of both the Ministry of State Security and of security – order, safety and even cleanliness – in everyday life in the expectations and norms of the regime. He analyses the impact of the division of Germany on the citizens of the GDR. This division was set in stone in the form of the Berlin Wall between 1961 and 1989. This engendered a difficult situation for East Germans whose regime pilloried and excoriated everything associated with West German life and politics, but who could not separate themselves from 'the other Germany', West Germany, in so many ways.

The chapter moves on to examine work 'as myth and reality', as a key characteristic of life in the GDR. Work was not only an activity to ensure people's livelihoods, but additionally it was a concept surrounded by a mythical aura, central to the Marxist interpretation of history, with workers portrayed as invincible heroes. Wolle treats not only the significance of work and full employment in the GDR, but also the permanent shortage of personnel and of goods and services. The chapter also contains a section on love in the time of socialism, which examines marriage and the family, and the importance placed by the state on these institutions. Wolle examines relationships between people, sexual education and the impact of the contraceptive pill, as well as population policies designed to support young families and the birth of babies, as well as the role of women in East German society. He considers the role of creches and kindergartens, and after-school care provision, exploring their impact on family life and what everyday lived experiences were like for East German children and for East German women as mothers and as workers. The chapter also examines housing policy and the impact of the *Platte*, the prefabricated building used as housing stock in the Honecker years. In these blocks of flats, uniformity and standardisation was so complete that there was almost no room for diversity or expression. Wolle analyses the experience of consumers and in particular the constant shortages or poor quality of products. He shows how the exchange of goods and services became increasingly commonplace in society and the importance of personal connections in the procurement of essential goods and services on a day-to-day basis.

The conclusion to the book sums up the main points raised by each chapter and in addition provides some comparative analysis of everyday life in these European dictatorial regimes. It examines aspects of similarity and difference between the individual cases treated in the book. It analyses the impact of ideology, the complex relationship between the regimes and their populations, and traces areas of nuance where perhaps unexpected patterns of behaviour found their place. It reflects, too, on the extent of and scope for resistance and dissent or nonconformity in each of these cases. It shows that lived experiences in dictatorships were not uniform and that within each case and between cases, there were differing circumstances for people living in these societies, dependent upon a variety of factors.

Notes

1 Among the standard works were C. Friedrich and Z. Brzezinski, *Totalitarian Dictatorship and Autocracy* (Cambridge, MA, 1956) as well as the still often quoted H. Arendt, *The Origins of Totalitarianism* (New York, 1951). The vanishing of totalitarianism as a concept coincided with the ending of the Cold War. Arendt's continued relevance may have to do with the attention she gives to the impact of 'totalitarianism' on individuals, indeed, on their daily existence. Political scientists such as Brzezinski tended to ignore individual agency, mainly considering the functioning of the system 'from above'. For a good overview of the term's usage, see A. Gleason, *Totalitarianism: The Inner History of the Cold War* (New York, 1995). Of interest in determining the shared roots between European extreme left-wing and right-wing movements is R. Pipes, *Russia Under the Bolshevik Regime* (New York, 1993), 240–81.

2 A. Lüdtke (ed.), *Everyday Life in Mass Dictatorship: Collusion and Evasion* (Basingstoke, 2016).
3 Ibid., 11.
4 Ibid.
5 G. Young, *The Communist Experience in the Twentieth Century: A Global History Through Sources* (Oxford, 2011).
6 A. Costa Pinto and A. Kallis (eds), *Rethinking Fascism and Dictatorship in Europe* (Basingstoke, 2014).
7 R. Bessel (ed.), *Fascist Italy and Nazi Germany: Comparisons and Contrasts* (Cambridge, 1996). In some ways, they go back both to the totalitarian paradigm and even to Alan Bullock. For example, see A. Bullock, *Hitler and Stalin: Parallel Lives* (New York, 1991).
8 H. Rousso (ed.), *Stalinism and Nazism: History and Memory Compared* (Lincoln, NE, 2004) and I. Kershaw and M. Lewin (eds), *Stalinism and Nazism: Dictatorships in Comparison* (Cambridge, 1997).
9 M. Geyer and S. Fitzpatrick (eds), *Beyond Totalitarianism: Stalinism and Nazism Compared* (Cambridge, 2009).
10 Ibid., 2.
11 P. Corner (ed.), *Popular Opinion in Totalitarian Regimes: Fascism, Nazism, Communism* (Oxford, 2009).
12 L.H. Siegelbaum (ed.), *Borders of Socialism: Private Spheres of Soviet Russia* (Basingstoke, 2006) and E. Harvey, J. Hürter, M. Umbach and A. Wirsching (eds), *Private Life and Privacy in Nazi Germany* (Cambridge and New York, 2019).
13 K. Boterbloem (ed.), *Life in Stalin's Soviet Union* (London, 2019); see also K. Boterbloem, *Life and Death under Stalin: Kalinin Province, 1945–1953* (Montreal, 1999); L. Pine (ed.), *Life and Times in Nazi Germany* (London, 2016); J. Arthurs, M. Ebner and K. Ferris (eds), *The Politics of Everyday Life in Fascist Italy: Outside the State?* (Basingstoke, 2017); A. Cazorla-Sánchez, *Fear and Progress: Ordinary Lives in Franco's Spain, 1939–1975* (Chichester, 2010).

1

Everyday life in Fascist Italy

Kate Ferris

Benito Mussolini's pronouncement in October 1925, willing 'everything in the State, nothing outside the State, nothing against the State', three years after the March on Rome had brought his Fascist Party (Partito Nazionale Fascista, PNF) to power in Italy, set the stage for a dictatorship that intended to rule Italians 'totally'.[1] To deliver and maintain the fascist revolution and its promised national regeneration, it would be necessary to permeate and fundamentally reshape all aspects of Italian society and Italians' daily lives. The pronouncement was made just months after the formal declaration of rule by dictatorship in January 1925 and was accompanied by the disassembling of the apparatus of democracy and civil society including the institution of a one-party state, rule by decree, press censorship and the dismantling of trade unions, *Camere del lavoro*, *case del popolo* and other spaces of non-fascist political sociability.

Crucially, though, the maxim that 'everything' must be brought within the purview, and into the service, of the state pointed to 'ordinary' Italians and their everyday worlds as not only key recipients of fascism's 'totalising' project, but also tacitly recognised them as important potential constructors, and the everyday as a key construction site, of the dictatorship. To this end, in the playing out of what we might call the 'actually existing' fascist dictatorship, this was, in addition to being decreed and imposed from above, also enacted 'from below', in the local spaces and everyday practices inhabited and performed day-by-day by the people who lived through it. As they were put into effect, dictatorial policies and rhetoric were (re)interpreted and potentially modified by representatives and agents of the regime, including local party leaders and members, civil servants, teachers, journalists, health visitors and midwives and so on, in the local spaces and places that effectively comprised the basic 'unit of experience' of the dictatorship. Everyday activities and spaces were not the colourful-but-passive backdrop against which the policies, rituals and propaganda of fascism were created and lived; rather, it was exactly in quotidian practices and settings – workplaces, leisure and recreational activities, consumer choices and habits, squares, streets and homes, interactions with friends, family and neighbours – that the dictatorship took shape. These are, therefore, crucial arenas in which to examine the encounters, interactions, ideas and practices that constituted the lived experience of Italy's dictatorship.

This chapter explores the everyday, lived experiences of the fascist dictatorship in Italy between 1922 and 1940, from the March on Rome to Italy's entry to the Second World War. Whilst the fascist regime ruled in Italy until 1943 in southern and central Italy, and until 1945 in northern Italy, this chapter ends in 1940, at the outbreak of the Second World War in Italy, in recognition of the substantial changes in lived experience that this wrought. It is guided by a set of key questions: Mussolini's declared aspiration to 'totalitarian' rule notwithstanding, to what extent did the quotidian facets of Italian life genuinely reside 'within the state'? What was the scope of fascism's totalitarian project, and where were its limits? How did violence, coercion and intimidation combine with enticement, propaganda and the eliciting of support or 'consent', in the regime's attempts to shape Italians everyday lives? And how did Italians themselves variously negotiate, resist and exploit the dictates of Mussolini's regime? How and where, if any, did opportunities exist for Italians to act with agency in their everyday practices? In addressing such questions, the chapter focuses its attention on a select range of venues, practices and interrelations that marked the everyday encounters between 'ordinary' Italians and the regime: the interplay of coercion and persuasion in the state's engagement with Italians; leisure and recreational practices; food consumption; and the intimate and affective networks, interactions and spaces that connected family and friends. All these everyday lived experiences of the fascist dictatorship were themselves conditioned and differentiated by gender, class and race, urban, rural and colonial settings, and other situational and identity-based markers.

The scope of this chapter means that its focus is on the Italian peninsular. That said, it is essential to recognise that lived experiences of Italian fascism did not take place and shape only within its national borders. Many, including the estimated one million Italians – mostly adult men, but also women and children – who, whether as settlers, soldiers, colonial administrators, or opportunists were directly engaged in constructing the Italian empire in North and East Africa (Africa Orientale Italiana, AOI), encountered daily life under the dictatorship outside the metropolitan nation, in Eritrea, Somaliland, Libya, Ethiopia and the Dodecanese islands, or indeed at Italy's edges, as in the case of Istria-Dalmatia and the Alto Adige / Sud Tirol (South Tyrol). Of course, the

Africans and Europeans unwillingly subjected to Italian imperialist rule experienced the double oppression of fascist dictatorship and colonial governance or occupation. The colonial context also gave rise to particular forms of regime intrusion in everyday life and relations, particularly after the Ethiopian War in 1935 motivated the regime to pass increasingly segregationist, racist legislation prohibiting interracial cohabitation, marriage and sexual relations, and denying citizenship and other rights to the many children born of sexual encounters between Ethiopian women and Italian men.[2]

Back on the Italian peninsular, what emerges is a complex and changing picture in which fascism made its presence felt in different aspects of Italians' lives at different times and in different and shifting ways. For their own part, Italians moved in and out of the gaze of state authority, nationally and locally. Of course, the dictatorship did interrupt and fundamentally change people's lives, often with violence. However, individuals living under, or through, the fascist regime in Italy did not always feel the impact of the dictatorship uninterruptedly and evenly. They could be variously, or even simultaneously 'perpetrators and victims, supporters and detractors, participants and evaders'.[3] Inevitably, *in praxis*, it was impossible for the lived reality of everyday life in Fascist Italy to meet fully the expectations of Mussolini's totalitarian formula.

Coercion and persuasion

The relationship between the state and the individual in Fascist Italy rested on the interplay of structures, policies and practices intended to elicit consent for dictatorial rule, through belief, indoctrination, propaganda, education, the assurance (albeit often illusory in reality) of welfare provision and the meeting of material desires on the one hand, and structures, institutions and forms of compulsion, repression, violence and the removal of alternative forms of organisation, protest and redress on the other. Coercion and persuasion went hand in hand, but the connection between the apparatus of repression and structures for building consent was not only one of two faces of fascist policy operating in tandem – one the stick, the other the carrot – to alternately compel and persuade Italians to accept, or at least acquiesce, to the dictatorship. In actuality, there was significant overlap and interplay between the intention to compel and the intention to persuade within the same institutions and structures. For example, many of the institutions and policies established and presented as mechanisms for garnering consent, including those that presented the dictatorship as meeting the population's material needs, like the welfare provision of the Ente Opera Assistenziale (EOA) and the Opera Nazionale Maternità e Infanzia (ONMI), or indeed as meeting growing mass consumerist wants, as did the Opera Nazionale Dopolavoro (OND), also themselves exercised forms of social and political control and carried out functions intended to regulate individual Italians' behaviour and actions, certainly in less violent and overtly threatening ways than the black-shirted MVSN (Voluntary Militia for National Security) and OVRA secret policemen, but in no less effective ways for that. Thus, whilst the section that follows distinguishes in its discussion between the mechanics of repression and the mechanics of persuasion, it is important to recognise that in practice these institutions and their policies operated in overlapping and mutually reinforcing ways.

The apparatus of repression in Fascist Italy combined both ostensibly legal and pseudo-legal means with forms of extralegal violence that functioned, but only technically, outside the state. Fascist authority – and for some its credibility – was sealed both before, during and after the 1922 March on Rome through the violent rampages of the thuggish black-shirted *squadristi*, after the takeover of power corralled into MVSN units, who carried out a campaign of political terror that included murder, the destruction of homes, printing presses, political organisations and social clubs, torture, and ritual humiliations including the infamous forced-ingestion of castor oil, as well as trading pitch battles and occupations with political opponents.[4] The consolidation of the dictatorship and its one-party state, usually dated to 1925–6, involved the suppression of the more indiscriminate and 'intransigent' elements of *squadrismo* violence,[5] though ultimately black-shirted political violence continued to resurface at home and, especially, was redirected to the Italian colonies in Libya and East Africa, to Spain in 1936, and, under renewed licence, towards perceived domestic enemies marked out by the Racial Laws (from 1938) and the outbreak of the Second World War.

In the 'front-line' of what Mussolini termed 'surgical violence' – the selective use of state-sanctioned and institutionalised violence alongside a more widespread climate of repression and fear – were the various branches of the Italian police forces in conjunction with the legal and penal system, which together constructed the fascist 'police state' in the second half of the 1920s. Public Security guards were reconstituted from 1925 and empowered by legal reforms, notably the 1926 Public Security Law, 1930 Rocco Code and 1931 Public Security Code, to investigate and punish 'public order' and 'political' offences, including actions, written- or speech acts newly categorised as criminal, and contained under the umbrella term *sovversivismo* (subversivism). Alongside investigating 'ordinary' crime, responding to emergencies and calamities, issuing permits and licences, the Public Security guards were tasked with an increasing remit of 'political policing' roles, which incorporated the identification and breaking up of underground dissident groups, the seizure of anti-regime material, the monitoring of foreigners and out-of-towners, as well as local Italians deemed potential 'subversives', the surveying of the correct functioning of party organisations, and the prevention and punishment of new or reformulated categories of political crime that included, for example, the procuring of abortion.[6]

At the same time, whilst the police forces were formally integrated into the regime and charged with eliminating political disobedience, the degree to which the police were thoroughly 'fascistised' vacillated significantly and ultimately could only ever be partial. Despite a raft of sackings and forced retirements of police officers between 1924 and the end of the decade 'on the grounds of professional incompetence or political unreliability' as well as influxes of committed fascists into the forces in the 1930s, the Interior Ministry police service, including from 1927 the secret police division, OVRA, which ran networks of informants and infiltrated clandestine anti-fascist groups, was led by career policemen and civil servants.[7] In 1925, at the behest of the then Interior Minister, Public Security police and officials were prohibited from taking up or continuing PNF membership, as were serving Carabinieri (military police) officers, or from joining the fascist syndicate for state employees. In 1932, the ban was reversed, and party membership was made compulsory for all state employees.[8] The incomplete and vacillating harnessing of state police to party interests is reflective of what historian Jonathan Dunnage identifies as the blend of 'political sympathies' towards fascism and 'career opportunism' that characterised the fascist police from its Chief, Arturo Bocchini, down.[9]

The existing penal system was co-opted and adapted to meet the needs of fascist repression. From 1926, the Law for the Defence of the State created Special Tribunals for the trial of the most serious *sovversivismo* cases against the state, reintroduced the death penalty and allowed for severe prison sentences for certain political crimes. Whilst the death penalty was used by the regime relatively rarely, the gamut of punishments and sanctions ranged a wide spectrum from execution, imprisonment and the use of internment camps, through internal exile (*confino di polizia*), restrictions on movement and employment, police probation (*ammonizione*) and warning (*diffida*). The agents of fascist repression deployed infiltration, denunciation, intimidation, violence and torture as means of uncovering political crime. Anyone deemed a potential 'subversive' could expect to be singled out and directly punished, though the police files of the investigation of cases of relatively low-level crimes demonstrate that in addition to being known to have held opposing political views or party membership in the past, holding a certain identity, ethnicity or occupation perceived to lie at Italy's social and racial margins, whether homosexuals, Roma, sex workers, vagrants or alcoholics, would count against the individual and very likely result in harsher punishment.[10]

Because the Italian fascist regime executed far fewer than, for example, did the Soviet Union, Nazi Germany or Francoist Spain, many have been tempted to understand the regime as a comparatively benign dictatorship. However, measuring a regime's repressiveness – a questionably relativising undertaking in any circumstances – solely in terms of how many of its citizens it killed directly does not fully reflect how violence operates in dictatorial societies and, for example, how the impact of violence-done-to-others and the perception and fear of repression can manifest. Mussolini boasted in 1927 of having significantly increased police numbers and under his rule the prisons underwent similar expansion.[11] The number of police arrests, operations against political opponents (reputedly averaging 20,000 per week in 1930), and use of police probation and warnings – Ebner estimates 200,000–300,000 probations were issued – indicates a population under serious surveillance.[12] Torture was deployed to break up clandestine Communist Party (PCI) and liberal Giustizia e Libertà groups, sometimes resulting in unexplained deaths.[13] Prison itself could effectively be a death sentence, as the treatment in custody and ultimate death of Antonio Gramsci, fascism's most famous prisoner, testifies. In all, between the takeover of power, regime persecution, imperialism and war, the fascist regime is held responsible for around one million deaths.[14] As Paul Corner, Michael Ebner and others have pointed out, the Mussolinian regime need not have been as repressive or as violent as its Spanish, German or Soviet counterparts for it still to be recognised as a 'police state'.[15]

The elimination of alternative avenues for expressing discontent or seeking redress from the fascist regime was an integral dimension of the repressive environment. Following the 1924 'Matteotti crisis', when the reformist socialist deputy Giacomo Matteotti was murdered by fascist thugs leading to the subsequent withdrawal from parliament by opposition deputies, Mussolini effectively dismantled the extant political parties, already decimated by *squadrista* violence and regime persecution. Thousands were forced into exile. From January 1926, party headquarters, newspaper and printing presses and offices, and sites of non-PNF political sociability were closed down; in November 1926, a series of 'exceptional decrees' used the excuse of an attempt on Mussolini's life as an opportunity to dissolve all non-fascist political parties and to establish the Special Tribunal and increase police powers.[16] By May 1928, the already de facto one-party state was formalised.

Besides the outlawing of political parties, trades unions were abolished and replaced by a corporatist system of fascist syndicates, each representing different areas of industry, agriculture and economic labour. Venues and organisations of political sociability – that is, spaces that combined political and social functions, wherein people met to socialise as well as to discuss politics, such as working men's clubs, social and welfare associations and other liberal groups – were dismantled. The old *case del popolo* (socialist clubs) were disbanded and were replaced by a strikingly similar fascistised version in the network of *case del fascio* that were constructed as local PNF headquarters and community venues criss-crossing Italian neighbourhoods.[17] Even seemingly apolitical organisations like sporting and amateur dramatics associations were dissolved or subsumed into the fascist after-work organisation, the OND. Finally, the regime censorship apparatus, whose agencies tended to also be those entrusted with propaganda, further pointing to the intentional interplay of coercion and persuasion, carried out first by the Press Office and then by the Ministry for Press and Propaganda (in 1937 renamed the Ministry for Popular Culture), sought to control both press and cultural output in Italy, including the regulation of art, music and cinema.

Through these agencies, structures and policies, the repressive apparatus worked its way through the public and private spheres of ordinary people's everyday lives. Whilst the 'totality' of fascist rule should not be overstated, the perception of widespread surveillance, of a state that gathered information from informants, neighbours and other local figures such that 'it only took the tip off of a passing fascist zealot to get you in a heap of trouble',[18] that imprisoned and meted out violence on those who opposed or disapproved it, and the diminution in alternative spaces and means for expressing and enacting behaviours contrary to the dictatorship all conspired to construct an environment in which dissent, let alone resistance, could seem a very risky prospect indeed.

But the impact of state political violence and climate of repression was manifold and complex. One consequence of the fostering of public cultures of silence and self-censorship for many was the displacement of behaviours or speech acts critical of, or displeasing to, the regime to more intimate, private and familiar spaces. As such, the dictatorship did not eliminate everyday political expression and nonconformity but rather pushed it to spaces such as bars and private homes, which had long played host to forms of political sociability and continued to do so thanks to perceived increased privacy and intimacy and, no doubt, in the case of bars to the effects of alcohol consumed therein.[19] At the same time, it is crucial to recognise that for many Italians who were not necessarily card-carrying fascists or regime supporters, the impact of fascist repressive violence was actually positively received. Luisa Passerini, for example, in her seminal oral history study of *Fascism in Popular Memory* among working-class Turinese, noted the frequent appreciation among interviewees for fascism's 'keeping order [. . .] discipline and security' as a basis of their 'social acceptance' of the regime.[20] More recently, Giulia Albanese demonstrated that the deployment of violence, particularly during the rise of the dictatorship (1919–26), had 'a creative force'.[21] The use of violence helped consolidate the regime's position not just by repressing opponents into submission but also through the courting of positive approval for violence directed towards 'others', deemed political, national or class enemies, which was vital 'in forging the political base of Fascism'.[22]

The regime's apparatus of persuasion and its functioning were similarly complex. The most prominent of the organisations designed to elicit popular approval and acceptance, whilst simultaneously reshaping ordinary Italians into 'new fascist man' and 'new fascist woman' and exerting forms of social surveillance and control, were those run by the single political party, the PNF. The creation of these PNF mass organisations were intended to provide structure, assistance and diversion in Italians' day-to-day lives. Distinct branches guided Italians through the life course, including the Fasci for men, the women's Fasci femminili (incorporating from 1933 the Massaie Rurali for women from rural labouring families), and for children the various ranks of the Opera Nazionale Balilla (ONB) whose divisions for boys and girls aged six to adulthood became a model for the German and Spanish dictatorships. Membership of these party organs was not compulsory until 1937 (from 1932 for state employees) but was central to the negotiation of life under dictatorship for Italians of all ages. Party and syndicate membership acted as a gatekeeper, determining access to certain occupations and workplaces, university places and scholarships as well as to potential networks of patronage and support that could benefit one's everyday life such that in the early 1930s, the regime leadership embarked on a campaign to eradicate the 'superficial careerism' that it believed influenced the decisions of many Italians – especially young Italians – to join the PNF and to participate in its structures and rites.[23]

The regime bodies governing welfare assistance and recreation most readily fulfilled the multivalent functions of simultaneously demonstrating regime benevolence and modern-state competence alongside moulding Italians into fascists. The fascist after-work organisation, the OND, mobilised millions of Italians in its ranks, subsuming pre-existing leisure organisations, and laying on a state-sanctioned portfolio of free or discounted sporting facilities, cinema screenings, touristic activities and folkloric festivals, and facilitating group access to modern recreational technologies including radio sets, phonographs and sewing machines. In the sphere of social assistance, Mussolini claimed to have created one of the most advanced national welfare systems in Europe. Myriad bodies including the EOA, the INFPS (National Fascist Institute for Social Security) and ONMI provided social insurance against illness and unemployment, old age pensions, sanatoria, and assistance to pregnant women and mothers. Undoubtedly, such policies were a source of popular approval and contributed to the regime's intended self-projection as the bearer of order, stability and a degree of well-being. At the same time, significant groups of Italians were actively excluded from social assistance provision, including, as Corner points out *braccianti* (landless rural labourers), domestic servants and, after 1938, 'persons of non-Aryan race'.[24] Fascist health visitors could dispense advice, but they also had the authority to withhold benefits and even to separate children from their parents.[25] Thus, the same institutions and functions intended to entice and elicit Italians' acquiescence to fascist rule operated effectively as instruments of social control, keeping detailed records of families and households, imposing fascism's values, and enacting policies of inclusion and exclusion that distinguished between those deemed politically and morally deserving and undeserving.

The methods through which fascism ruled Italians offered key means for extracting popular support. First, in many respects, fascism presented itself to Italians as a 'political religion', effectively sacralising politics by making it the basis of its appeal to the population, and the relationship that bound Italians to the nation and state, one of faith.[26] To this end the regime adopted religious accoutrements, creating a liturgy and a canon of myths, rituals, martyrs, heroes, feast days and sites of worship, such as the *sacrarie dei caduti* dedicated to those killed in fascism's service, adorned with an eternal flame and the word '*presente!*' on the wall, that were housed in local *case del fascio*, all directed towards soliciting the veneration of the (fascist) state. We might question how far ordinary Italians genuinely believed in and practised the fascist political religion but the evidence suggesting that the regime saw and presented itself as such is compelling. Second, and as part of the fascist political religion, the regime sought to establish a kind of direct connection between Italians and the Duce through a cult of personality. Mussolini and those around him carefully and consciously crafted his image and how this was presented to the population.[27] Portraits of the Duce, dressed in uniform, were hung in local party headquarters, governmental offices and public buildings, schools, workplaces and even homes, making him appear omnipresent and powerful yet accessible. Photographs of him engaging in sport, or working in fields, often bare-chested to emphasise virility and strength, were published in the country's newspapers and magazines, subjected to meticulous curation by the regime censorship office.[28] The cult of personality presented Mussolini as a benevolent and paternalistic figure, who created jobs (through major public work schemes to drain marshland and build new cities) at a time of economic depression, cared for the well-being of his subjects and was the guarantor of order and stability, even against the excesses of other regime elements.

Letters held in the Segreteria Particolare del Duce archive written and sent directly to Mussolini by Italians asking him to intercede personally in difficult individual circumstances, whether a dispute with local officials, personal misery and destitution, or a family member's trouble with the law, in the expectation that Mussolini could and would intervene, suggest that the efforts to present him as the 'father of the nation' resonated with many.[29] There were, though, inevitably limitations to the Duce cult. By presenting Mussolini as above, and somewhat removed, from the 'dirty' end of government, his personal popularity often came at the expense of the party and wider regime. Whilst Mussolini and the regime could exploit this (imagined) division between themselves and the party to build up popular acquiescence for its rule, it also presented something of a loophole to those ordinary Italians who wished to express dissatisfaction or disapproval of the regime in oblique ways. To this end, the frequent 'if only Mussolini knew' refrain could transmute into 'a deliberately confusing combination of loyalty and protest' of the kind that saw protesters in the South make simultaneous declarations of ' "Up with Mussolini" and "Down with the Podestà" (fascist mayor)'.[30]

Going out: leisure and 'free time'

Italians' 'free time', in the sense of time spent out of work or school and away from household tasks and other chores, was not spent entirely 'freely'. The fascist regime sought to bring Italians' leisure activities within the purview of the state through the co-opting of pre-existing organisations, groups and private commercial enterprises and the creation of national-fascist *enti* (bodies), institutes and syndicates covering myriad leisure activities from social dancing to tourism to sports. By far the most important and extensive of the state-run and associated bodies established to regulate, shape and scrutinise free-time and leisure activities was the OND. Established in 1925 as part of the fascist syndicate system and then from 1927 brought under the control of the PNF, the OND replaced or subsumed pre-existing recreational clubs and leisure associations within the umbrella of the OND structure. It provided recreational facilities and activities for its members – often free or at low cost – including football, tennis, skiing, cinema, amateur dramatics, and day trips to notable Italian cities and other tourist sites on specially commissioned so-called 'popular trains'.[31] These took place in on-site workplace facilities as well as in dedicated provincial and neighbourhood OND centres, many of which had their own bar, radio set and even film projector.[32]

As an organisation intended principally to shape the free-time activities of working- and lower-middle-class Italians, the OND mobilised huge numbers of men and women: it amassed 1.5 million members by 1929 and 2.75 million by 1936, at which point 20 per cent of the industrial labour force and 7 per cent of the peasantry were enrolled in its structures.[33] However, crucially, by no means all recreational and leisure structures were drawn into the OND: those remaining outside the fascist organisation included the lay Catholic association, Catholic Action, the Rotary Club, private gentlemen's clubs, nightclubs, dance halls and working-class bars and taverns.[34] Historians often emphasise the extent to which it was the 'free-time' of blue- and white-collar workers and rural labouring classes that were subjected to the 'real political power of the modes of persuasion' and consent-building 'by which fascism [. . .] penetrated every domain of social life'.[35] Undoubtedly, wealthier middle- and upper-class Italians, with the financial means to fund their leisure activities independently, more often engaged in pastimes and social events organised in and by private commercial-cultural enterprises – golf clubs, opera houses, hotel dances and so on – or hosted within social networks by private individuals in their homes.

Nevertheless, whilst socio-economic status and class did demarcate different lived experiences both in terms of the types of recreational and leisure activities engaged in and the extent to which these activities were controlled by the fascist dictatorship, it is important not to overstate this distinction. To take the example of social dancing, whilst wealthy Italians attended dances in varied private or commercial venues including the ballrooms and gardens of luxury hotels, nightclubs and dance halls in the country's capital, industrial centres and fashionable beach resorts, private grand palazzi and more intimate, modest domestic settings, they also attended charitable dances, labelled *feste del fascio* and *veglioni tricolori*, staged in *case del fascio*, OND centres and other party headquarters that became habitual venues for weekend dancing.[36] At the same time, evidence from contemporary diaries and memoirs demonstrate how frequently couple dancing took place in domestic spaces among working-class and rural labouring Italians, with furniture piled and pushed to the edges of the room and music supplied by a radio transmitting EIAR's *musica da ballo* or by 'a gramophone and a handful of discs'.[37] Whilst dancing in private, domestic spaces did not necessarily mean dancing 'outside the state', it did mean dancing outside the strictures of the Interior Ministry's dance licensing system, and its associated Public Security police surveillance. As such, the evidence suggesting that Italians of all classes danced communally in domestic settings placed alongside that demonstrating the regular use of OND centres, *case del fascio* and other regime spaces to host charitable balls – also recognised as prime moneymaking and propaganda-spinning opportunities – aimed at local political and financial elite clientele, offer a useful qualification to the argument that wealth and socio-economic status facilitated the pursuit of leisure and recreational activities outside state structures and which therefore better evaded the dictatorship's regulation and consent-building.

As Victoria de Grazia, the foremost historian of the OND, laid bare, fascist after-work policies fit clearly within regime efforts to create and sustain a 'culture of consent'. The provision of leisure and recreation was conceived as a means of 'improving workers' and rewarding work and productivity – after all, at its 1925 inauguration the OND formed part of the corporatist system of syndicates established for separate trades and professions as supposed

FIGURE 1.1 *A dance party at the Lido, Venice, 1930.* © *Getty Images.*

mediating bodies between employers and employees – as well as a way of meeting Italians' increasing material and consumer desires collectively, in a way that would help tie the population to the state, to its ideology and to its leader, Mussolini, writ in benevolent, paternalistic guise. Simultaneously, it aimed to fulfil the flip side of totalitarian-intent rule, that of comprehensive regulation and surveillance, intended as it did to 'penetrate [. . .] every domain of social life from industrial enterprise and city neighbourhood to rural village'.[38]

Nevertheless, despite the 'decisive support' OND structures offered to the fascist regime's efforts to build consensus for its rule, the would-be totalitarian credentials of the OND were somewhat undermined by the actuality of its functioning and practice. The OND is best understood as a hodgepodge of local organisations, clubs, societies and recreational halls of which approximately half pre-dated the fascist accession to power, approximately one-sixth were run by private companies for their own employees (and thus only came under umbrella of OND indirectly), and only one-third of which were entirely new 'fascist' creations. Because of this, and because of the multiple political, social and cultural aims it juggled – to garner political consent for fascism, to help maintain social cohesion in the absence of the now dismantled liberal and socialist associations which had previously fulfilled this role, and to fulfil the material desires of the population in an era of rising mass consumption – the OND is most accurately viewed as a mediating institution between state and civil society, one that because of its heterogenous components and the often lack of coherence in the way it operated on the ground, in different regions and localities, was constructed as much 'from below' as it was 'from above'.

Crucially, the ability of the regime to dictate Italians' everyday leisure practices and to use these to shape Italians into fascists was limited also by the important impact of leisure and consumer habits and products from outside Italy and the transnational movement of these, which transferred to Italy from cultural capitals like Paris and Hollywood, and which the regime proved unable to either fully mitigate or harness. The dictatorship struggled to compete with and dislodge especially those leisure pastimes and cultural products considered 'American', and thus the epitome of 'modernity', both in regime and popular imaginaries, from cinematic pictures to jazz and social dancing to cocktail parties. Certainly, it tried. The regime-sponsored creation of a national recording and disc distribution company, Cetra, in 1933 and the forbidding, from 1935, of the transmission of 'music in a Negro character' and 'dance music with choruses sung in English' on the national EIAR radio programmes, and the dismissal of foreign and Jewish Italian musicians from both agencies, were intended to break the perceived hegemony of American music and dance styles, especially those associated with African Americans, to enforce conformity with the regime's imperialist-racist and autarkic projects, and to promote instead the 'Italianisation' of *musica leggera* and its associated dance steps.[39] The growing fashionable cachet of drinking cocktails – 'this strange and insidious drink [that] has come from America to Europe' – in Italy's urban centre-north was denigrated by government officials, Italian wine and beer representatives, and the futurist leader Filippo Marinetti alike as 'horrible poisons' that are 'noxious to our race' and a telltale marker of the so-called crisis woman, an archetype popularised in the early 1930s by regime propagandists and cultural producers that characterised urban, middle-class, young women who worked outside the home, did not have children, and followed foreign fashions, as unpatriotic shirkers of the reproductive and home-making priorities the regime expected of Italian women.[40]

Above all, Mussolini sought to dislodge American hegemony in the field of cinema. More than any other new cultural technology or recreational pursuit, cinema represented the new opportunities for mass leisure in interwar Europe. Its communication through a visual, and from 1927 spoken, 'new vernacular' and combination of an aura of exclusivity and luxury – in part because of the kinds of often unattainable material dream worlds it visualised – with the opportunity to engage with audiences as 'individuals within the mass', meant that it was seized by Mussolini as, in his own words, the regime's 'most powerful weapon' for transmitting fascist values and ideals.[41] The OND negotiated ticket discounts with commercial cinemas of between 25–35 per cent for most performances and, in the mid-1930s, mobile cinemas brought moving pictures to rural areas at low or no cost. Some local OND centres established their own cinemas. However, cinema was also the form of leisure pursuit or consumer commodity that provoked the most angst about perceived 'Americanisation'. American films, largely made in the Hollywood studios, were the United States' most financially valuable cultural product in interwar Europe and by the 1930s were only surpassed in terms of circulation by Gillette razor blades and Ford motor cars.[42] Several governmental measures aimed to combat the dominance of Hollywood films in Italy. From 1934, a dedicated directorate for cinema was set up within the Press Office (later morphing into the Ministry for Press and Propaganda and, from 1937, the Ministry for Popular Culture). In 1936 work began on the state-funded Cinecittà studio complex on the outskirts of Rome; completed a year later it churned out half of all the films produced in Italy, amounting to fourteen in 1937, including the directly state-financed *Scipione l'Africano* (1937) whose theme of imperial Roman conquest in Africa matched neatly with contemporary regime priorities in East Africa.[43] In 1938, the Alfieri Law financially incentivised film producers to create scripts that passed censorship laws and a state monopoly on the distribution of films came into effect, prompting (not entirely intentionally) the previously dominant US distributors and studios to boycott the Italian market.[44]

Undoubtedly, the regime's support for domestic producers and temporary withdrawal of US firms boosted the creation of a home-grown studio and star system, as cinema-going was only further entrenched as a regular recreational activity: ticket sales rose from 348 million per year in 1938 to 477 million in 1942.[45] However, even state funding for domestic cinematic productions, censorship and state monopoly on distribution, could not dislodge the primacy of commercial international films, principally emanating from Hollywood. The proportion of Italian-produced films shown after 1935 rose only by approximately 5 per cent, meaning that 80 per cent of films passed by the censors continued to be foreign, mostly American productions. The increase in Italian films was very often of a genre known as 'white telephone', after the aspirational domestic appliance that served as a cipher for the kind of modern, glamourous, materialistic lifestyles depicted in these sentimental comedies. These were Italian copycat versions of American-style films, which effectively aped and validated the '"modern" and cosmopolitan lifestyles' that they presented as 'seductively plausible'.[46] Even in the case of films like *Il Signor Max* (1937), which intended to contrast negatively Hollywood-style material desires with more modest social and cultural aspirations and lifestyles met by fascism through the OND, Italian cinema-goers' recollections of watching such films, which often focused on the more glamorous scenes depicting stylish apartments, fashionable clothes and conspicuous forms of leisure and consumption, revealed the potential gap between regime propagandistic intentions and the actual reception of these.

Eating in the dictatorship: policies and practices of food consumption

Fascist food policy was characterised above all by the principles of autarky, with the aim, as historian Carol Helstosky put it, of bringing about 'alimentary sovereignty' or complete national self-sufficiency in food.[47] Even before the March on Rome (1922), squads of fascist blackshirts patrolled local high streets to police the price and provenance of the staple goods on sale; once in power, from the mid-1920s, the regime moved to bring shopkeepers into the Confederazione Fascista dei Commercianti Italiani (Fascist Confederation of Italian Merchants) and introduced measures to 'discipline commerce', including maximum prices on key goods, temporary shop closures, state-run cooperatives and a licensing system for all retailers, casting the fascist state as the 'protect[or of] consumers from retailers'.[48] Gaining pace through the 1930s, the national-fascist drive for autarky made patriotic consumption and frugality a national duty, especially for women as the assumed controllers of family consumption. Autarky and national self-sufficiency in food were imperatives intricately connected to the regime's imperial and demographic expansion plans: a healthy, virile and sizeable population was essential both to justify colonial expansion and to bring it into being, through war. The conquering of an empire in North and East Africa was further imagined and presented as a means to achieve 'alimentary sovereignty' with the colonised lands in Libya and AOI (Eritrea, Somaliland and, from 1935–6, Ethiopia) envisaged as fertile lands simply awaiting effective cultivation, where the food provisions needed for an expanding empire would be grown. At home, land reclamation schemes – described as a form of internal colonisation – converted marshland into arable farmland to be cultivated by Italian families relocated from elsewhere on the peninsular.

The autarky project sought both to control agricultural production and to shape and restrict consumption through multiple means including production quotas, price regulation and propaganda campaigns. In keeping with its associated foreign policy aims, autarky policies directed at controlling production were couched in military terms, as 'battles' such as the 'Battle for Grain' inaugurated in 1925 to increase national wheat production and end reliance on imported grain, or were styled as folkloristic harvest festivals, in line with the regime's lauding of rural life as authentically Italian and, therefore, fascist. From 1928, celebratory days – or even weeks – were added to the regime calendar, dedicated to certain foods the regime wished to promote: the festival of bread, festival of the grape and the national day of rice.

The regime's propaganda campaigns promoting autarky were ramped up with the invasion of Ethiopia in October 1935 and subsequent imposition of economic sanctions on Italy by the League of Nations from November 1935. The decreeing of sanctions against Italy was seized as an ideal propaganda tool to mobilise Italians on the 'home front', both in support of the colonial war and in support of the regime's autarky drive. The anti-sanctions 'resistance' campaign that sprang up in Italian localities in the form of resistance committees, though heavily encouraged and managed by the centre, directly addressed Italian consumers, now reshaped as 'consumer-combatants'.[49] Italians were instructed variously (and sometimes contradictorily) to buy and eat local or national produce only, to consume home-grown produce where possible, to be parsimonious and frugal, and often to reduce overall food consumption. The state research institution, the Consiglio Nazionale delle Ricerche (CNR) shored up the regime's autarkic line with scientific legitimacy, publishing reports that determined that less meat, less variety and lower consumption in general was better suited to the Italian 'race' and advising that Italian workers engaged in moderate labour needed only 2,500 calories per day, far fewer than contemporary recommendations in other nations.[50] For their part, shopkeepers were instructed to remove foreign foodstuffs from their shops. Local 'price vigilance committees' patrolled stores and market stalls to ensure that merchants were following the maximum price regulations on bread, milk, cheese, eggs and other basic foodstuffs. Other restrictions were imposed, such as the enforced closure of butchers' shops on Tuesdays and the prohibition of the sale (and consumption) of beef, pork and lamb on Wednesdays. Both shopkeepers and (female) consumers found their selling and shopping practices recast as 'patriotic duty'; to infringe the price and other restrictions or to sell or consume foods not considered 'national products' was to act treacherously.[51]

The consumer-focused campaigns were principally aimed at women and at the middle and upper classes. Women were held to be responsible for the purchasing and preparing of food for the family and the middle- and upper classes as those whose means and tastes made them – it was believed – more likely to eat unpatriotically, and to buy foreign and/or luxury foods. Telling workers and labourers to eat locally produced foodstuff, reduce meat consumption, and to grow their own where possible was largely moot to a sector of the population whose diet already consisted largely of bread, vegetables, polenta, rice or pasta and little meat, and which, in the words of one boy from Marghera, the son of a factory worker, 'never set eyes' on a 'piece of steak'.[52]

Cookbooks and other domestic economy literature, such as the monthly magazine, *La Cucina Italiana* (Italian Cuisine/Kitchen), and even 'autarkic cookery' training courses run by Comitati Provinciali Femminili per la Resistenza Contro l'Assedio Economico (Women's Provincial Committees for Resisting the Economic Siege) advised Italian housewives on how to budget carefully and encouraged them to make vegetables and fruit the mainstay of family meals.[53] They offered suggestions for ways of substituting meat and its protein, for example with 'meat broth' or by serving 'a plate of polenta or pasta, garnished with cheese and butter and served with a glass of milk', or ways of eking out meat in meals, for example by serving *la polpa* (meatloaf), thereby treading a careful line between regime-sanctioned assertions downplaying the nutritional value of meat and tacitly recognising how meat consumption operated as a marker of socio-economic status.[54]

The impact of the autarky project was very significant, and largely negative. Whilst the 'Battle for Grain' succeeded in reducing wheat imports to Italy, from an average 22.2 million quintals per year in 1922–8 to 4.7 million quintals in 1937, this left the country unable to profit from the lower international price of wheat due to the combination of an international surplus in wheat and favourable exchange rates. Meanwhile, domestic wheat yields only met the annual national target twice and increased yields varied considerably between regions.[55] Ultimately, less wheat was available to Italian consumers in the 1930s, and what was available was more expensive.[56] Moreover, the giving over of more farmland to grain cultivation came at the expense of other, more appropriate and potentially more profitable (because exportable), crops including citrus fruits and olives, which in turn led to less diversity in the foodstuffs available to Italians.[57]

Accordingly, what Italians consumed changed, especially during the 1930s. Individual consumption of wheat, maize, tomatoes, greens, dried legumes, fresh fruit, dried fruit, most meats, most fats and oils, sugar, coffee, wine, beer and spirits all decreased between the decades 1921–30 and 1931–40, in almost all cases reversing a trajectory of increased and more varied consumption in the preceding decade.[58] Meat consumption, for example, declined from an annual consumption of 18.8 kg per person in 1926–30 to 14.5 kg per person in 1937.[59] Although regional and class distinctions in the foodstuffs and meals eaten by Italians of course persisted, in general terms the trends towards increasing choice and diversification in food consumption that had been underway since the Great War were halted, and even reversed, by fascist autarky. Per capita daily calorie consumption dropped to 2,641.[60]

Italians, predominantly women as the procurers and preparers of family meals, did alter what they bought, cooked and ate in the face of the impact of fascist autarkic policy, but the onslaught of fascist propaganda did not necessarily confirm their enthusiastic 'cooking of consent' for the regime.

Many Italian housewives, as Helstosky put it, 'work[ed] within the limits set by the drive towards self-sufficiency',[61] for example, by differentiating between foods eaten within the family and foods served to guests, as did, for that matter, Italian shopkeepers. In Venice, for example, local fascist leaders repeatedly admonished 'unscrupulous merchants' for not adhering to the maximum price regulations or for engaging in speculative or hoarding activity. Local shopkeepers and market traders were fined, and named and shamed in the local press, for selling basic foods – beef, eggs, fish and radicchio – at prices higher than those stipulated.[62] Furthermore, the already established, often long-standing and, in its way, intimate, client–patron relationship that linked shopkeepers and consumers through relations of credit and trust, could be called upon to evade or circumvent the sanctions resistance restrictions. The Venetian Fascio was sure this was occurring in the case of 'obliging butcher[s]' who were – they speculated – setting aside 'beefsteak or a veal chop' in their icehouses to help clients serve meat on the prescribed meatless days of the week.[63] Nonconformity with regime strictures on autarkic consumption was not necessarily tantamount to resisting, or even rejecting these policies. Rather, the varied, sometimes evasive, responses of Italians to regime efforts to make shopping and the consuming of food politicised and patriotic acts are suggestive of the 'room for manoeuvre' that remained open, in spite of the limits placed by the state, to afford Italian shopkeepers and consumers the possibility to weigh the prioritising of economic and business, consumer preferences, and the performance of class and status identities, alongside politics and supposed patriotic duty in determining what they ate under the dictatorship.

Friends, family, neighbours, domesticity, intimacy

At base, the dictatorship was experienced and lived in and through the spaces and interactions of everyday life. As such, the family, the home, the neighbourhood, and networks of kin and friends were the fundamental units and shapers of experience of dictatorship and, therefore, comprised the basic actions, practices, relations and spaces in which the dictatorship was effectively constituted. Of course, individual Italians' family and community set-ups differed significantly, shaped by gender, age, region, class and occupation, whether one lived in a rural or urban setting and more. In rural peasant families, for example, the household habitually comprised multiple generations and couples living under the same roof, linked to neighbouring farmhouses through economic relations and social practices like the winter evening *veglia* (social gatherings often incorporating multiple households).[64]

Urban working-class Italians might, depending on age, marital status and occupation, live in factory dormitories, *pensione* (guest-house) rooms, or rented tenement apartments in close proximity and connected to other families by balconies and courtyards.[65] Social networks were established and maintained both through work and recreational time spent in cafés and bars for men, and for women, if married and mothers, principally through the interlinked domestic spaces of the neighbourhood.[66] For those that were wealthier, the household might also include domestic servants. Others lived in nuclear family units. Whilst there was significant variance and mobility in family and kin/friendship structures, spaces and networks, all formed vital conduits for the constructing and experiencing of fascism, its policies, values and practices. Their importance was not lost on the regime.

The extent to which the fascist dictatorship sought to, and succeeded in, infiltrating and shaping the everyday relations of families, friends and neighbours and the domestic and neighbourhood spaces in which their interactions took place, might be considered the ultimate barometer of its reach. The PNF secretary, Augusto Turati, declared the family the 'basic cell of the State, the Nation and the people'.[67] In line with Mussolini's statement of totalitarian intent, it was therefore unthinkable that the family unit, and its prime space of operation, the home, be left 'outside the state'. Historians of other dictatorships have similarly accorded significant weight to the relationship between dictatorial regimes and families and the penetration of homes and the most intimate and personal of human relationships: in relation to Nazi Germany, scholars have discussed the extent to which the 'four walls' of the home could offer a 'safe haven' from the dictatorship.[68]

Undoubtedly, in Fascist Italy, the home and family were never insulated, apolitical safe havens. The state sought to scrutinise and enter domestic spaces and to politicise and to dictate the practices and interactions enacted therein. Agents of the state physically entered homes, for example, in the shape of political police officers, investigating potential 'subversive' activities or PNF health visitors (*visitatrici fasciste*) charged with inspecting parenting practices (of predominantly working-class and rural labouring Italians) and advising on infant health under the auspices of the state's developing welfare structures. Women were advised to hang portraits of Mussolini on their walls so that their 'children, tomorrow's soldiers, will learn to love him as he loves them'.[69] In those that that could afford them – 400,000 in 1934 and over one million by the war – the Duce's voice was transmitted directly into middle-class households via radio.[70]

Family roles and relationships, and friendship and acquaintance networks, as well as the most intimate dimensions of individuals' bodies, identity and/or practice, including sexuality, were all key vectors through which the dictatorship assessed individual Italians' political worth and through which individual

Italians' relationship with the dictatorial state were conducted. For both men and women, status was accorded through relational roles, whether as prolific mothers awarded prizes for bearing several children, patriarchal benevolent-disciplinarian-breadwinner fathers, mothers or wives of fallen soldiers or of those 'fallen for fascism', or as consumer-combatant providers of meals prepared from suitably national produce and practitioners of domestic autarky. The same logic that promoted procreation as a national duty dictated that women be prohibited from exerting bodily autonomy and choice: intention or incitement to terminate pregnancy, alongside the carrying out of 'abortive acts' were classified from 1930 as crimes 'against the interest of the nation to ensure the continuity of the race'.[71] Relatedly, within an ideological frame that prized masculine virility, homosexual and effeminate men were denigrated as 'enem[ies] of the "new man" ' and, although homosexual acts were not criminalised in law, they were subjected to police surveillance and, in many cases, persecution through confinement or imprisonment in the penal or asylum system.[72]

At a time when other European and North American states were increasingly intervening in parenting practices, the dictatorial states of interwar Europe took their 'right' to intercede in family life to new limits.[73] Although motherhood was an ideal that had been exalted since Italian unification (and long before), it was under fascism that prolific motherhood became a national duty, fundamentally connected to Italy's national and imperial ambitions.[74] But whilst imagined mothers and fathers were idealised, 'actually existing' Italian parents required intervention. In 1925, ONMI was set up to oversee pre- and postnatal policy and state childcare provision. Under its auspices, paediatric and maternal health clinics, social services, mothers' kitchens and crèches were created: by 1938, the agency boasted, nationwide, 3,500 maternal health clinics, 4,400 infant health clinics, 1,300 kitchens and 190 *Case della Madre e del Bambino*, which brought healthcare, social assistance and propaganda initiatives under one local roof. Unmarried mothers were particularly targeted for assistance.[75] ONMI was a vital tool in the regime's 'demographic campaign', announced in 1927, with aims to reverse the perceived trend towards 'voluntary motherhood', reduce infant mortality and the downward trajectory of the birth rate, which by the early 1930s had dropped to twenty-four births per thousand persons, from a peak of thirty-nine in the late nineteenth century.[76] Additionally, the regime rewarded prolific motherhood – and fatherhood – through myriad means including tax breaks, family allowances and birth prizes for the parents of large families (of more than seven living children).

The dictatorship put pressure on the affective relationships between parents and children as a means to solicit greater political engagement and attachment from both, and at the same time effectively sought to bypass parents entirely and establish a direct relationship between the state and

Italian children. The schooling system and the institution of fascist youth groups, for girls and boys, through the ONB (renamed in 1937 Gioventù Italiana del Littorio, GIL) were the vehicles for both approaches. Until 1937 when membership became compulsory for Italian children, parental permission was required; by tying (from 1928) educational bursaries and prizes, access to university and civil service jobs, and sometimes parents' employment to children's ONB membership, the regime applied social and economic pressures to entice more reluctant parents to sign up their children.[77] Equally, parents often felt pressured to enrol themselves in party groups in order to secure their family's prospects as the well-known alternate meaning of the PNF acronym – not Partito Nazionale Fascista but *per necessità famigliare* (for the needs of the family) – attested.[78]

The regime also sought direct conduits to Italian children that would neatly circumvent Italian parents through the schooling system, ONB and other, ostensibly welfare-focused institutions that brought children under the direct supervision of the state, especially working-class, urban children whose parents were considered the most politically, and morally, suspect. *Colonie estive* (children's summer camps), run by the EOA in invigorating mountain, countryside and seaside resorts, and *recreatori fascisti*, effectively fascist after-school clubs, brought large numbers of working-class children – in 1939, 4,526 summer camps hosted 806,964 children[79] – under the watchful eye of state-employed childcare workers, where they took part in military-type and politically indoctrinating activities and rituals, removed from what the authorities openly deemed 'the tedium of segregation within the family where too often [children] vegetate in restricted and unhealthy environments'.[80] Neither did middle-class parents entirely escape state surveillance and intervention in their parenting practices: as part of the anti-sanctions resistance and autarky campaign and the mid-1930s anti-bourgeois 'custom reform' campaign, they found their (supposed) penchant for foreign-influenced parenting from choice of names, to governesses, to nursery reading material and for purchasing expensive children's clothing instead of making-do and mending, rebranded as unpatriotic.[81]

That some working-class families were seen as an 'unhealthy environment', and some middle-class families as an un-Italian and un-fascist environment for raising children as future fascists, points to the mistrust that the regime evidently harboured for 'actually existing' parents, as well as to some of the boundary limits to the regime's insistence that the family comprised the 'basic cell' of its own idealised society. These limits, at their most destructive with the introduction of the Racial Laws, including 'anti-miscegenation' laws, from 1938, effectively denied the right to exist and dismantled, first in legal terms but also physically, Italian families living on the peninsular and in the empire, including Jewish and mixed-race African ones.[82]

FIGURE 1.2 *Children's summer camp refectory, 1930.* © Getty Images.

The response of parents and children to the intrusions of the state into their affective familial relationships was marked by ambivalence. Of course, some youngsters evidently appreciated the quasi-parental role taken on by the state, enjoying the experience of holiday camps and ONB meetings and especially the opportunities they afforded for diversions with peers. However, evidence also suggests that many Italians resented or tried to ignore fascist intrusions into their parenting choices. Certainly, fascist efforts to increase fecundity were largely disregarded. The birth rate failed to rise and in fact continued to decline throughout the 1930s, especially in the more urban regions of central and northern Italy.[83] Very few Italian couples took out the marriage loans which promised to incrementally cancel the debt owed upon the birth of each successive child.[84]

Individual women's recollections of the period suggest that fascist pronatalist rhetoric had little to no effect on their choices and actions around procreation. Their diaries and memoirs often hint at or explicitly show support for 'conscious maternity' and family planning practices. They reveal the (unsurprising) prioritisation of economic considerations in decisions about reproduction and, at times, starkly illustrate the enormous practical difficulties in raising healthy children in the often cold and unsanitary environments in which poor Italians were compelled to live.[85] In Venice, for example, Vana Arnould recalled her middle-class family's disapproval when news broke in 1933 that her uncle's wife was expecting their third child: 'They had the delicacy to say to E; "better an illness than a pregnancy" '.[86] Just a short walk away from the Arnould family home at Ponte de la Comenda, Rosa d.C, who in 1926 had settled with her family in newly constructed social housing on the island of Sant'Elena, faced the pain of enduring a series of miscarriages, stillbirths and infant deaths in conditions blighted by poverty:

> Not because I wanted to take heed of the 'Duce's orders', but because we wanted to give a little sibling to B, who was always asking us for one, I had a little girl in 1928, whom we called Maria and another in 1930, whom we called Milena. Both died because they were born to me premature and, being born in winter in a house without heating, lived just a few hours and, in the little white box made by my dad, were buried in the cemetery of San Michele.[87]

Laws limiting and outlawing fertility control, including abortion, had been strengthened in 1926, 1927 and 1930 as the coercive 'stick' to complement the propaganda 'carrot' aimed at increasing births through the demographic campaign.[88] Midwives were particularly targeted for 'professionalisation' and state regulation, at least in part because their occupation positioned them to play key roles in helping women to terminate unwanted pregnancies.[89] Nevertheless, and despite the significant prison and *confino* (confinement) punishment that awaited those who were found guilty of procuring or performing abortions, 'abortion continued to exist, just as the midwives who could help procure it and the social networks that made it possible continued to exist'.[90] According to the regime's own figures, recorded abortions increased from 65,676 in 1932 to 91,987 in 1939, estimated to equal approximately 18 per cent of all pregnancies.[91] Such practices were sustained by knowledge-carrying networks, protected by 'code[s] of silence and secrecy' and the difficulty often for state investigators to distinguish an induced abortion from a spontaneous miscarriage, reliant as they were on following hearsay and rumour in the near absence of physical evidence. Among Luisa Passerini's interviewees, many of whom discussed their intimate decisions around birth control and procreation, induced abortion was acknowledged as commonplace:

> Look, I got pregnant again, and I didn't have any money. I didn't want any more, because I had to go to work because there wasn't enough money and he [her son] was three years old, so how was I to manage? [. . .] I borrowed 500 lire and I had an abortion without saying anything to my husband. [. . .] There were 2,000 women where I worked, but you know I saw so many die. Of abortions they carried out themselves.[92]

Historian Alessandra Gissi points out that the complex interplay of sotto voce knowledge, secrecy and rumour, and the difficulty, certainly from the state's perspective, of discerning the 'degree of voluntarism involved in the act', makes it difficult to categorise the multiple individual choices and actions of Italian women with respect to reproduction, certainly in terms of 'resistance'.[93] That said, the procurement of induced abortion amply demonstrates women's continued 'capacity for agency', and the persistent centrality – sitting alongside and within overarching narratives of modernisation – of everyday community webs of knowledge and lived experiences of 'reputation, public hearsay, networks, and relationships' that sustained this agency, which of course carried significant bodily risk, in spite of the heavily criminalised and policed terrain.[94]

Family, friends and acquaintances were crucial in navigating the dictatorship, both as individual mediators and for the networks they created. As Luisa Passerini observed, everyday life in Fascist Italy comprised 'a world of mediations' in which relations and interactions between individual Italians and the fascist authorities (both in Rome and the localities) were very often shaped by intermediaries who, perhaps by virtue of their relational role or position in the community or locality, could effectively form a bridge between the two.[95] Importantly, seeing mediators and mediation as a key analytical tool through which to understand the 'actually existing' relationship between individuals and the state in the fascist dictatorship is particularly useful because, unlike the rather blunter categories of 'consent' and 'dissent', mediation recognises the state–individual relationship as a two-way interaction, one that, albeit significantly asymmetrical, could afford individuals, by way of the intercession of mediators, some agency in shaping how and how far they accepted, rejected or modified state intrusion into their daily life. In addition, what results from understanding these processes as mediatory, rather than as a binary sequence of soliciting and conferring of consent or dissent, is a potentially more complex, multifaceted, reading of the state–individual relationship in which it was possible for individuals to move between different stances at different times or in relation to different aspects of the regime's intrusions, or indeed to hold multiple stances simultaneously. In this way, an individual could exercise tacit approval, what Passerini terms 'pragmatic acceptance', of the regime's policies and expectations of them in one sphere, whilst disapproving or seeking to distance themselves in another. They could, in sum, be 'both perpetrators and victims, supporters and dissenters, participants and evaders' of the dictatorship through their everyday practices.[96] In addition, as Passerini shows, individuals' intentions whether seeking to gain proximity to or distance from regime policies did not always pan out as intended; in practice, mediatory processes embarked upon with the intention to help individuals gain distance from, or even to manifest nonconformity with, regime expectations could, in the end, result in a form of pragmatic acceptance.[97]

There were a variety of roles that placed people in the position to function as mediators between individual and regime, some based on occupation or political rank, including the figure Passerini terms the 'good fascist', a local and usually low-ranking state official or neighbourhood party leader, or a local priest, building concierge, or shop-floor Syndicate representative who used their 'positions of minor power [. . .] to do good'.[98] Conversely, corrupt fascists were also vital nodes in kinship and friendship networks for those seeking to navigating jobs, permits and other dealings with the authorities. Despite regime insistence that it was driving out the clientelism and nepotism that it saw as having characterised the Liberal era, within the PNF, from the top to the bottom of the hierarchy, individuals used family, friendship and acquaintance contacts to call in favours, profit financially or gain political advantage, sometimes through illegal means.[99] In this way, the Fascist *ras* (party boss) of Cremona, Roberto Farinacci could trade in *raccomandazioni* (confidential references) that would help out 'a surgeon looking for a job, [or] a military man faced with an unwanted transfer', or, more politically, might allow individuals 'to avoid categorisation as a Jew, to reverse an expulsion for the Fascist party, to get a son out of prison'.[100]

By far the most prevalent mediators were those acting on their relational roles, as family members or friends. Women were particularly well placed to act as go-betweens or mediators between their husband or children and the regime. In Turin, Luigia Varusco, for example, intervened with the local *Fascio* on behalf of her son in the belief this would allow him to 'save face' in the compromise between regime and personal political belief. Varusco went herself to the local *Fascio* headquarters to request the party card her son needed in order to gain employment at the local factory; her intercession allowed, mother and son believed, the son to maintain 'anti-fascist identity and family dignity' because 'my son went to work with the receipt [but] the card they've still got it there now! Because I never went to get it!'.[101] Conversely, in the San Vitale neighbourhood in Bologna, where the Faggioli family stuck out as being regime supporters when 'everyone on the street was communist', a wife's mediations on behalf of her husband served to keep the family close to the regime. Signor Faggioli, though a 'fascist of the first hour' – the epithet given to those who had joined the fascist movement from its earliest pre-1922 days – was reportedly too 'lazy' to attend regular party meetings at the local *Fascio*; in order to maintain family position and influence and to hear the latest news, in his place, Signora Faggioli 'went and then reported back when she returned home'.[102]

Very often, the outcome of mediations was either not clear cut or could deviate from the originally intended purpose of the intercession. An episode, recounted in the memoir of Lina Cattalini, who was then an eight-year-old schoolgirl living in a village outside Bologna, is a case in point. Cattalini recalled how, when in 1933 her class was instructed to turn up, with their parents, to listen to a speech by some regime 'high-ups' on the promise of a focaccia loaf each in return, following her father's point-blank refusal to attend, her mother interceded and agreed to accompany Lina to the *Casa del fascio*. Whilst the playing on affective child–parent relations and, indeed, the teacher–pupil relationship to ensure attendance at the speech paid off – the hall was 'packed full between children and parents' – the more enduring result of this instance of a mediated state–individual interaction was to seal the family's irreparable distance from the dictatorship. Once the regime 'high-ups' had spoken and left, the local party boss, seated next to the teacher, stood up and announced that, rather than distributing a focaccia loaf per family as had been promised, the loaves 'are not for you. We will offer them to the poor'. Looking around at the impoverished families in attendance, who had 'walked several kilometres' to get there, Lina recalled the 'huge let-down for those poor children' and the certainty that 'my focaccia was definitely eaten by my teacher': 'for us, along with our parents, it was a great disrespect remembered for a lifetime'.[103]

Family ties and 'social capital' could be deployed either to keep the regime at arm's length or to bring individuals closer to the regime, or both, precisely because of the ambivalence of the family vis-à-vis the state. It was the family's 'persistent ambiguity in relation to power' in Passerini's (after Horkheimer) words, that positioned it to function as a 'key site and agent', able to mediate relations between the individual and the dictatorship.[104] As the pronouncements of the PNF secretary Turati made clear, the family was regarded by the fascist authorities as an entity with a public function; it was judged 'the most distant outpost of government power' and was therefore expected to conduct itself with patriotism and in the service of the state.[105] However, it was precisely in the family unit's elision of public and private roles, its ability to move between outward- and inward-facing functions and practices that made it such a potentially useful entity to the fascist state in its pursuit of leaving nothing 'outside the state', whilst it was also the family's fundamental 'ambiguity in relation to power' that meant that it could never be entirely harnessed to the goals of the dictatorship.

The limits to the dictatorship's infiltration and manipulation of Italian families in the service of the fascist state were therefore delineated both by the actions of the regime and by 'family strategies and cultures' that could draw upon 'the peculiar qualities and resources that families have – flexibility, solidarities, networks, well-kept secrets and so on' to exert their own agency in response to fascist family policies.[106] The limits drawn by the state itself were formed of the failures to adequately finance the institutions it charged with enacting family policy, such as ONMI, and the mixed messages it sent out about how families were expected to behave and which families were considered worthy of support. Whilst exalting an idealised vision of the family, and perhaps especially of mothers, the dictatorship demonstrated suspicion of those families whose lifestyles and practices it deemed politically and morally wanting, seeking in some respects to bypass parents altogether and to establish direct relations with Italian children. And it demonstrated outright, destructive hostility, by the late 1930s, towards families that were seen to fall outside the regime's notions of racial purity. In this way, the family unit could never hope to be a secure 'safe haven' from dictatorship, either as a space that might allow for apolitical expression or for the expression of 'oppositional familism'.[107] Nor could it, even on the regime's own terms, furnish a 'basic cell' with which to build a new fascist society. Rather, in multivalent and shifting, elusive ways, the family sat stubbornly both 'inside' and 'outside the state'.

Conclusion

The 'everyday' is a crucial arena in which to examine the functioning of the fascist dictatorship in Italy. With intent and purpose, the regime sought to intrude into the everyday worlds of Italians, their habits and practices, their spaces of interaction, and their relationships, in order to turn these to achieving the dictatorship's principal goals of autarky, demographic growth, national regeneration and imperial conquest, and to turn ordinary Italians into fascists worthy – in the regime's own contorted estimation – of a restored and revitalised Italian nation and empire. To achieve this, by Mussolini's own acknowledgement, it would be necessary to rule Italians with 'ferocious totalitarian will' and to render 'everything' within the purview of the state.

The Mussolinian dictatorship sought to infiltrate, survey and harness all aspects of Italians' day-to-day lives using policies, structures, rhetoric and rituals that purposefully combined the intent to compel with the intent to persuade. Alongside the crude use of *squadrista* violence and the state-led and institutionalised environment of repression and fear that superseded it from the mid 1920s, sat institutions like the OND, ONB, ONMI, and the EOA that were ostensibly intended to fill Italians' 'free' time, provide welfare, promote health and meet material wants and needs, but which also policed Italians' behaviour and practices and created forms of societal inclusion and exclusion in line with fascism's gendered and racist worldview.

Italians' reactions to this overlapping and mutually reinforcing apparatus of coercion and persuasion were multivalent and complicated. Violence elicited fear, retreat, and exile but also shifts in how and where political expression and non-conformist behaviour were given voice and enacted. Spaces like private homes and bars had always been venues for political discussion and action but with the dismantling of non–Fascist Party headquarters, press, and social clubs, they took on renewed importance. Violence could also be for many Italians a source of positive approval who saw in the regime's repression of presumed 'subversives' (a category that included not only political opponents, but also the socially marginalised such as homosexuals, foreigners, sex workers, alcoholics and vagrants) a government that was restoring law and order, stability and discipline to society. For their part, the structures and institutions intended to provide diversion, recreation and assistance were received with similar ambivalence. Undoubtedly for many, the PNF, ONB, OND and welfare organisations were sources of genuine entertainment, enjoyment and support. At the same time and for others, they were structures that were difficult, if not impossible to avoid. Effectively enforced engagement with the party or with Balilla groups was subject to complicated processes of negotiation and mediation, through which ordinary Italians sought to make half-choices and compromises in relation to regime prescriptions and expectations, which, whether they were intended to gain increased distance or proximity to the regime, were always calibrated to benefit oneself or one's family.

Without downplaying the severity of the fascist 'police state' and its ability to intrude into Italians' everyday lives, Mussolini's stated intention to incorporate 'everything within the state, nothing outside the state, nothing against the state' could never fully be realised. There were limits to the regime's intendedly totalitarian reach. These limits were demarcated in part by the regime itself. By failing to thoroughly 'fascistise' the police, by creating a patchwork and heterogenous collation of leisure groups under the umbrella of the OND, by significantly underfunding ONMI and concentrating its provision in the centre and north of the country (rather than in the southern regions where infant mortality was highest), and by sending out often contradictory messages about what the regime expected of Italians in their everyday behaviour, for example in relation to autarkic food consumption, the regime itself reduced its capacity to fully extend its grasp into all aspects of everyday life. In other respects, the limits to the regime's reach were posited by external forces, above all by the lure of the expanding consumer market and the transnational transfer of cultural products, images, mores and habits principally associated with 'America', as Hollywood films, cocktails, jazz music and dancing captured (or so it was feared) the attention of young, urban, middle-class Italians and (again, so it was feared) turned their heads from national and fascist products, pastimes and values. Finally, and crucially, the limits to fascism's reach into the everyday lives of its people were also placed by ordinary Italians themselves. Through their myriad everyday actions, speech acts, practices and interrelations, they found ways and 'room to manoeuvre' towards, around, and from regime impositions (not always with full awareness or as intended), albeit within the restricted parameters of the dictatorship. As such, they were able to use the regime's own differentiation in the Duce cult between the figure of Mussolini and the party to find oblique ways to make fun of, or to criticise, the regime. They could work up to, and occasionally around, the dictatorship's prescriptions on 'alimentary sovereignty', drawing on the relationship of trust between shopkeepers and customers to circumvent the anti-sanctions restrictions on meat consumption or giving primacy to commercial and financial priorities to ignore its maximum price limits on basic goods. They could draw on family, friends, neighbours and local acquaintances, as individual mediators and as nodes in social networks to exert continued, but circumscribed, 'capacity for agency' in shaping their relationship and interactions with the fascist authorities and their day-to-day lives within the dictatorship. As such, the sphere of everyday life is a key arena in which the dictatorship was constituted, wherein the dictatorship as it actually existed – rather than as it was intended, proclaimed or represented – was stitched together and therefore also wherein it might, in limited and ephemeral ways, be modified and unravelled.

Notes

1   B. Mussolini, *Opera omnia*, Vol. 21, ed. Edoardo Susmel and Duilio Susmel (Florence, 1951), 425.
2   G. Barrera, 'Patrilinearity, Race, and Identity: The Upbringing of Italo-Eritreans During Italian Colonialism', in *Italian Colonialism*, ed. R. Ben-Ghiat and M. Fuller (New York, 2005), 97–108.

3 J. Arthurs, M. Ebner and K. Ferris, 'Introduction', in *The Politics of Everyday Life in Fascist Italy: Outside the State?*, ed. J. Arthurs, M. Ebner and K. Ferris (New York, 2017), 1–17.

4 G. Albanese, *La marcia su Roma* (Rome, 2006).

5 M. Ebner, *Ordinary Violence in Mussolini's Italy* (Cambridge, 2011), 12, 41–4.

6 J. Dunnage, *Mussolini's Policemen: Behaviour, Ideology and Institutional Culture in Representation and Practice* (Manchester, 2012), 79–80.

7 Ebner, *Ordinary Violence*, 2; Dunnage, *Mussolini's Policemen*, 37.

8 Dunnage, *Mussolini's Policemen*, 45.

9 Ibid., 49.

10 Ebner, *Ordinary Violence*, 166–214; K. Ferris, 'Everyday Spaces: Bars, Alcohol and the Spatial Framing of Everyday Political Practice and Interaction in Fascist Italy', *European History Quarterly* 52, no. 2 (2022): 136–59.

11 P. Corner, 'Italian Fascism: Whatever Happened to Dictatorship?', *Journal of Modern History* 74, no. 2 (2002): 325–51, 332.

12 The number of police operations is from R. De Felice *Mussolini il duce: Gli anni del consenso, 1929–1936* (Turin, 1974), 83, cited in Corner 'Italian Fascism', 333; Ebner, *Ordinary Violence*, 62.

13 A. Aquarone, *L'organizzazione dello Stato totalitario* (Turin, 1996 [1965]), 108; Corner, 'Italian Fascism', 334.

14 R.J.B. Bosworth, *Mussolini's Italy: Life Under the Dictatorship, 1919–1945* (London, 2006), 4.

15 Corner, 'Italian Fascism', 336–7; Ebner, *Ordinary Violence*, 11.

16 Aquarone, *L'organizzazione*, 97–110; Ebner, *Ordinary Violence*, 44; A. Lyttelton, *The Seizure of Power: Fascism in Italy, 1919–1929* (London, 1973), 297–8.

17 L. Maulsby, 'Case del fascio and the Making of Modern Italy', *Journal of Modern Italian Studies* 20, no. 5 (2015): 663–85.

18 V. Arnould, *Me g'ha contà la nona*, ADN (Archivio Diaristico Nazionale) MP/Adn 202.

19 Ferris, 'Everyday Spaces'.

20 L. Passerini, *Fascism in Popular Memory: The Cultural Experience of the Turin Working Class* (Cambridge, 2009 [1987]), 129–33.

21 G. Albanese, 'Violence and Political Participation During the Rise of Fascism (1919–1926)', in *In the Society of Fascists: Acclamation, Acquiescence, and Agency in Mussolini's Italy*, ed. G. Albanese and R. Pergher (New York, 2012), 63.

22 Albanese, 'Violence', 50.

23 R.J.B. Bosworth, 'Per necessità famigliare: Hypocrisy and Corruption in Fascist Italy', *European History Quarterly* 30, no. 3 (2000): 357–87.

24 Corner, 'Italian Fascism', 342–3.

25 Ibid., 344–5.

26 E. Gentile, *The Sacralization of Politics in Fascist Italy* (Cambridge, MA, 1996).

27 S. Gundle, C. Duggan and G. Pieri, *The Cult of the Duce: Mussolini and the Italians* (Manchester, 2013); L. Passerini, *Mussolini Immaginario: storia di una biografia, 1915–1939* (Rome-Bari, 1991).

28 A. Antola Swan, *Photographing Mussolini: The Making of a Political Icon* (Cham, 2020).

29 C. Duggan, *Fascist Voices: An Intimate History of Mussolini's Italy* (London, 2013).

30 P. Morgan, ' "The Years of Consent"? Popular Attitudes and Forms of Resistance to Fascism in Italy, 1925–1940', in *Opposing Fascism: Community, Authority and Resistance in Europe*, ed. T. Kirk and A. McElligott (Cambridge, 1999), 176.

31 V. de Grazia, *The Culture of Consent: Mass Organization of Leisure in Fascist Italy* (Cambridge, 2002 [1981]).

32 Maulsby, 'Case del fascio and the Making of Modern Italy', 666–8.

33 De Grazia, *The Culture of Consent*, 55.

34 Ibid., 19.

35 Ibid., vii.

36 On the dances held in fascist venues, see A. Tonelli, *E ballando ballando: La storia d'Italia a passi di danza (1815–1996): dal valzer borghese alla macarena dei militanti Popolari* (Milan, 1998), 205–6. See also K. Ferris, 'Dancing Through Dictatorship: Everyday Practices and Affective Experiences of Social Dancing in Fascist Italy', in *Worlds of Social Dancing: Dance Floor Encounters and the Global Rise of Couple Dancing, c. 1910–40*, ed. K. Nathaus and J. Nott (Manchester, 2022), 201–27.

37 Ferris, 'Dancing Through Dictatorship', 212.

38 De Grazia, *The Culture of Consent*, vii.

39 A.H. Celenza, *Jazz Italian Style: From Its Origins in New Orleans to Fascist Italy and Sinatra* (Cambridge, 2017), 110–18; see also Tonelli, *E ballando*, 212 and C. Poesio, *Tutto è ritmo, tutto è swing: Il Jazz, il fascismo e la società italiana* (Milan, 2018), 79–84 on 'Jazz and musical nationalism' and 95–108 on 'Jazz and racism'.

40 K. Ferris, 'Women and Alcohol Consumption in Fascist Italy', *Gender and History* (forthcoming). Available online: https://doi.org/10.1111/1468-0424.12566

41 S. Gundle, *Mussolini's Dream Factory: Film Stardom in Fascist Italy* (New York and Oxford, 2013); J. Hay, *Popular Film Culture in Fascist Italy: The Passing of the Rex* (Bloomington, IN, 1987).

42 V. de Grazia, *Irresistible Empire: America's Advance through Twentieth-Century Europe* (Cambridge, MA, 2005), 288.

43 Gundle, *Mussolini's Dream Factory*, 22–3.

44 Ibid., 29; de Grazia, *Irresistible Empire*, 318–19.

45 On the 'star system' see Gundle, *Mussolini's Dream Factory*; on ticket sales increased see de Grazia, *Irresistible Empire*, 319.

46 The quotations are from Gundle, *Mussolini's Dream Factory*, 72 and Hay, *Popular Film Culture*, 109; see also E. Scarpellini, *Material Nation: A Consumer's History of Modern Italy* (Oxford, 2011), 83.

47 C. Helstosky, 'Fascist Food Politics: Mussolini's Policy of Alimentary Sovereignty', *Journal of Modern Italian Studies* 9, no. 1 (2004): 1–26.

48 J. Morris, 'Retailers, Fascism, and the Origins of the Social Protection of Shopkeepers in Italy', *Contemporary European History* 5, no. 3 (1996): 285–318, 318; K. Ferris, 'Consumption', in *The Politics of Everyday Life in Fascist Italy: Outside the State?*, ed. J. Arthurs, M. Ebner and K. Ferris (New York, 2017), 124.

49 Ferris, 'Consumption', 128–35.

50 C. Helstosky, *Garlic and Oil: Politics and Food in Italy* (Oxford, 2004) 101.

51 Ferris, 'Consumption', 130–5.

52 A. Baldo, *Ricordi di Guerra di un diciasettenne: 1940–1945*, ADN MP/02, 20.

53 P. Willson, 'Empire, Gender and the "Home Front" in Fascist Italy', *Women's History Review* 16, no. 4 (2007): 485–500, 491–2.

54 Helstosky, *Garlic*, 84.

55 Ibid., 76.

56 In 1921–30, wheat availability was 178.5 kg per capita; in 1931–40, this reduced to 164.4 kg per capita. Helstosky, *Garlic*, 76.

57 Helstosky, 'Fascist Food Politics', 5.

58 Scarpellini, *Material Nation*, 5–7.

59 Helstosky, 'Fascist Food Politics', 8.

60 Scarpellini, *Material Nation*, 7.

61 Helstosky, *Garlic*, 81.

62 Ferris, 'Consumption', 136–7.

63 *Gazzetta di Venezia* 20 November 1935, cited in Ferris, 'Consumption', 139.

64 P. Ginsborg, *Family Politics: Domestic Life, Devastation and Survival 1900–1950* (New Haven, CT, 2014), 163, 166.

65 Ibid., 152.

66 Ibid.

67 A. Turati, 'Il partiti e I suoi compiti', 190–1, cited in Bosworth, *Mussolini's Italy*, 245.

68 In the work of Detlev Peukert, an early pioneer of everyday life history, the memory trope of 'withdrawal', 'within the family circle or among close friends' was a notable refrain in individuals' accounts of quotidian life in the Third Reich. D.J.K. Peukert, *Inside Nazi Germany: Conformity, Opposition and Racism in Everyday Life* (New Haven, CT, 1987). Still, as Lisa Pine demonstrates, 'the home was not a safe haven insulated from National Socialism': L. Pine (ed.), *The Family in Modern Germany* (London, 2020), 271.

69 *Gazzetta di Venezia* 17 November 1935; cited in K. Ferris, *Everyday Life in Fascist Venice, 1929–40* (Basingstoke, 2012), 133.

70 The figures refer to the number of subscribers to EIAR, the national radio broadcaster. A significant number of Italians listened to the radio not in their homes but in public spaces including bars, OND centres, and schools – by 1939, 9,000 'collective radios' reached an audience of 850,000 people. J. Tomatis, *Storia culturale della canzone italiana* (Milan, 2019), 34.

71 A. Gissi, 'Reproduction', in *The Politics of Everyday Life in Fascist Italy: Outside the State?*, ed. J. Arthurs, M. Ebner and K. Ferris (New York, 2017), 101–2.

72 L. Benadusi, *The Enemy of the New Man: Homosexuality in Fascist Italy* (Madison, WI, 2012).

73 Ginsborg, *Family Politics*; H. Barron and C. Siebrecht (eds), *Parenting and the State in Britain and Europe c. 1870–1950: Raising the Nation* (Cham, 2016).

74 P. Willson, *Women in Twentieth-Century Italy* (Basingstoke, 2010), 62.

75 P. Willson, 'Opera nazionale per la maternità e infanzia (Onmi)', in V. de Grazia and S. Luzzatto, *Dizionario del fascismo* Vol. 2 (Turin, 2003), 273–7.

76 V. de Grazia, *How Fascism Ruled Women: Italy, 1922–1945* (Berkeley, CA, 1992), 46.

77 T.H. Koon, *Believe, Obey, Fight: Political Socialization of Youth in Fascist Italy, 1922–1943* (Chapel Hill, NC, and London, 1985), 95–6.

78 Passerini, *Fascism*, 140–4; Bosworth, 'Per necessità famigliare', 366–7.

79 Koon, *Believe, Obey, Fight*, 102–3.

80 *Rivista di Venezia*, March 1931 'La scuola comunale a Venezia nel 1930', 112–20.

81 K. Ferris, 'Parents, Children and the Fascist State: The Production and Reception of Children's Magazines in 1930s Italy', in *Parenting and the State in Britain and Europe c. 1870–1950: Raising the Nation*, ed. H. Barron and C. Siebrecht (Cham, 2016), 183–205.

82 G. Barrera, 'Mussolini's Colonial Race Laws and State-Settlers Relations in Africa Orientale Italiana (1935–41)', *Journal of Modern Italian Studies* 8, no. 3 (2003): 425–43; Ginsborg, *Family Politics*, 214–19.

83 De Grazia, *How Fascism Ruled Women*, 46.

84 Willson, *Women*, 66.

85 Indeed, Giuseppe Bottai's own analysis was that the failure of fascism's 'fecund decade' must be ascribed to the elevated levels of economic privation in Italian society; cited in M. Quine 'From Malthus to Mussolini: The Italian Eugenics Movement and Fascist population policy 1890–1938'. PhD thesis, University College London, 1990, 247.

86 Arnould, *Me g'ha contà la nona*, 218.

87 R.d.C. *Mi chiamo R.d.C.*, ADN MP/86, 49.

88 Willson, *Women*, 66–7.

89 Gissi, 'Reproduction', 125.

90 Ibid., 103.

91 Ibid., 114.

92 Cited in Passerini, *Fascism*, 161.

93 Gissi, 'Reproduction', 113; Luisa Passerini did use the category 'resistance to demographic policy' in this context: Passerini, *Fascism*, 150–82.
94 Gissi, 'Reproduction', 115.
95 Passerini, *Fascism*, 138–44.
96 Arthurs, Ebner and Ferris, 'Introduction', 9.
97 Passerini, *Fascism*, 138–44.
98 Ibid., 142–3.
99 Bosworth, 'Per necessità famigliare'; P. Corner, *The Fascist Party and Popular Opinion in Mussolini's Italy* (Oxford, 2012).
100 R.J.B. Bosworth, 'Everyday Mussolinism: Friends, Family, Locality and Violence', *Contemporary European History* 14, no. 1 (2005): 23–43, 29–30.
101 Passerini, *Fascism*, 139.
102 Laura Faggioli, 'Ricordi di Via S. Leonardo e dintorni', ADN MP/98, 3.
103 Lina Cattani, 'Il furto delle mie mucche – Racconti di dolci e amari frammenti di vita vissuta nella prima metà del '900', ADN MP/14, story 18, 'La focaccia', n.p.
104 Passerini, *Fascism*, 139; M. Horkheimer, *Critical Theory: Selected Essays* (New York, 1999), 'Authority and the Family'.
105 Turati, 'Il partiti e i suoi compiti', 190–1, cited in Bosworth, *Mussolini's Italy*, 245.
106 Ginsborg, *Family Politics*, 223–4.
107 Victoria de Grazia used the concept of 'oppositional familism', by which she meant family units who were 'unresponsive, if not resistant, to appeals on behalf of the fatherland'. De Grazia, *How Fascism Ruled Women*, 82. Along similar lines, historian of everyday life under Stalin, Sheila Fitzpatrick, described the 'great resilience' of Russian families in the face of Soviet attempts to fundamentally transform domestic and family life. S. Fitzpatrick, *Everyday Stalinism: Ordinary Life in Extraordinary Times – Soviet Russia in the 1930s* (New York, 1999).

Select bibliography

Albanese, G., and R. Pergher (eds). *In the Society of Fascists: Acclamation, Acquiescence, and Agency in Mussolini's Italy*. New York, 2012.
Arthurs, J., M. Ebner, and K. Ferris (eds). *The Politics of Everyday Life in Fascist Italy: Outside the State?* New York, 2017.
Bosworth, R.J.B. 'Everyday Mussolinism: Friends, Family, Locality and Violence', *Contemporary European History* 14, no. 1 (2005): 23–43.
Bosworth, R.J.B. *Mussolini's Italy: Life Under the Fascist Dictatorship, 1919–1945*. London, 2006.
Corner, P. 'Collaboration, Complicity, and Evasion Under Italian Fascism', in *Everyday Life in Mass Dictatorship: Collusion and Evasion*, edited by A. Lüdtke, 75–93. Basingstoke, 2016.

Corner, P. *The Fascist Party and Popular Opinion in Mussolini's Italy*. Oxford, 2012.
Corner, P. 'Italian Fascism: Whatever Happened to Dictatorship?', *Journal of Modern History* 74, no. 2 (2002): 325–51.
De Grazia, V. *The Culture of Consent: Mass Organization of Leisure in Fascist Italy*. Cambridge, 2002 [1981].
De Grazia, V. *How Fascism Ruled Women: Italy, 1922–1945*. Berkeley, CA, 1992.
Duggan, C. *Fascist Voices: An Intimate History of Mussolini's Italy*. London, 2013.
Dunnage, J. *Mussolini's Policemen: Behaviour, Ideology and Institutional Culture in Representation and Practice*. Manchester, 2012.
Ebner, M.R. *Ordinary Violence in Mussolini's Italy*. Cambridge, 2011.
Felice, R. De. *Mussolini il duce: Gli anni del consenso, 1929–1936*. Turin, 1974.
Ferris, K. *Everyday Life in Fascist Venice, 1929–40*. Basingstoke, 2012.
Ginsborg, P. *Family Politics: Domestic Life, Devastation and Survival, 1900–1950*. New Haven, CT, 2014
Gundle, S., C. Duggan, and G. Pieri. *The Cult of the Duce: Mussolini and the Italians*. Manchester, 2013.
Helstosky, C. *Garlic and Oil: Politics and Food in Italy*. Oxford, 2004.
Passerini, L. *Fascism in Popular Memory: The Cultural Experience of the Turin Working Class*. Cambridge, 2009 [1987].
Scarpellini, E. *Material Nation: A Consumer History of Modern Italy*. Oxford, 2011.

2

Daily life in Hitler's Germany

Lisa Pine

This chapter explores the nature of everyday life in the Third Reich and the complex relationship between the Hitler regime and the German population between 1933 and 1945. It sheds light on daily life in Nazi Germany from an array of different perspectives. The first part of the chapter examines the impact on society of mechanisms directed towards the creation of consensus and conformity, including *Gleichschaltung* (coordination) and policies designed to create a cohesive and obedient German *Volksgemeinschaft* (national community). It analyses the role of the Nazi system of terror, particularly highlighting the Gestapo (Secret State Police) and the concentration camp network, in order to illuminate an important aspect of the relationship between the German people and the Nazi government. The second section of the chapter explains the impact of Nazi dictatorship on the family and private life. It explores the penetration of the Nazi regime into the private life and choices of German citizens, in their family and social settings. It analyses the intrusion of Nazi ideology into the private realm of the family. The third part of the chapter examines Nazi food policy and its strong impact on food choices for the German population, as a crucial aspect of daily life. It demonstrates how the Nazi regime encouraged people to alter their eating habits in order to meet its imperatives, for example suppressing demand for imported goods and encouraging the consumption of ersatz and domestic products. It includes an examination of the government's food campaigns designed to change people's eating habits, such as those for whole-grain bread and the *Eintopf* (one-pot dish). The final section of the chapter explores a small selection of examples that highlight the outcome of the Nazi dictatorship on different groups in Germany – based on the impact of the key Nazi concepts of *Auslese* and *Ausmerze* (selection and eradication) on society in terms of education (from Nazi elite schools through to special schools); selective 'breeding' programmes and eugenics – from Lebensborn (Well of Life) and positive population policy, to sterilisation and the *Aktion T4* 'euthanasia' campaign between 1939 and 1941.

The creation of consensus and the use of terror

The complicated relationship between the German people and the Nazi dictatorship was underpinned by both propaganda and policies designed to draw the German population closer to the regime and its goals on the one hand, and the use of fear and terror intended to coerce into line (actual and potential) resisters and opponents on the other hand. These two aspects of Nazi rule were very closely linked. The Nazis attempted to create their ideal 'national community' in a variety of ways, through propaganda and policies that brought consensus for their rule and conformity to their ideology. The cult of the leader that surrounded Hitler impacted greatly upon the German population and upon how it interacted with the regime. Certainly, the legend and propaganda surrounding the Führer (leader) created widespread support for the regime and for Hitler in particular. As Ian Kershaw has contended, 'there can be no doubt that the penetration of the propagated "Hitler myth" was deep' and appealed particularly – but not only – to the middle class, articulating 'long-standing and pervasive elements of the bourgeois political culture in Germany'.[1] The formation of Nazi youth organisations, the Hitlerjugend (Hitler Youth) and Bund deutscher Mädel (League of German Girls), as well as associations for women, the NS-Frauenschaft (National Socialist Womanhood) and Deutsches Frauenwerk (German Women's Enterprise) played a significant part in the manufacture of consensus for the goals of the Nazi regime. The process of *Gleichschaltung* was designed to bring all aspects of German life under National Socialist state control and to homogenise German society. Richard Evans has noted that 'almost every aspect of political, social and associational life was affected, at every level from the nation to the village'.[2] Within the space of a few weeks of the 'seizure of power', the Nazis took over the federated state governments, in March 1933, appointing Reich Commissioners to replace the existing administrations. By the end of July 1933, all political parties – with the exception of the NSDAP – had been banned or had dissolved themselves and thus a one-party state was established very swiftly. The new regime 'coordinated' the civil service by means of the Law for the Restoration of the Professional Civil Service of 7 April 1933. Other public and state institutions were similarly treated. Between 30 January and 1 May 1933, 1.6 million people joined the NSDAP in order to safeguard their jobs.[3] In addition, the NSDAP destroyed the German trade unions – the most powerful labour movement in Europe – within five months of coming to power. The German trade union movement had been composed of the Free Trade Unions, the Christian Trade Unions and the Hirsch-Düncker Unions. The Free Trade Unions and Hirsch-Düncker Unions were 'coordinated' during the first week of May, and the Christian Trade Unions were banned at the end of June 1933.[4]

'Coordination' of cultural life was achieved by the Reichskulturkammer (Reich Chamber of Culture or RKK), established in September 1933, enabling Joseph Goebbels, Minister of Popular Enlightenment and Propaganda to control all aspects of German arts and culture. The RKK was divided into seven sub-chambers for literature, theatre, music, radio, film, fine arts and the press. Each chamber closely controlled work within its sphere, kept registers of members and issued work permits. It was impossible to work within any of these areas without a permit. Jews and political opponents of the regime were excluded from the RKK and therefore deprived of their livelihood in these areas. The teaching profession was 'coordinated' through the NS-Lehrerbund (National Socialist Teachers' League or NSLB). Jewish teachers – barred from entry into the NSLB – were excluded from their profession. Many business and professional associations and other organisations either voluntarily 'coordinated' themselves with the new regime or dissolved themselves. Forcible 'coordination' ensued, in instances of reluctance or hesitation. This process of 'coordination' or 'streamlining' was designed both to remove the possibility of opposition and to organise society in such a way that people could be imbued with the spirit of National Socialism. Yet the process of 'coordination' – although it was carried out on such a large scale – was imperfect. Membership of the Party or one of its formations did not necessarily imply true ideological loyalty to National Socialism. Indeed, some people who joined the Nazi Party remained committed to ideologies of the political left. They were described as 'beefsteak Nazis' – 'brown' (Nazi) on the outside, 'red' (Communist) on the inside. But *Gleichschaltung* did succeed in eliminating serious public, widespread opposition to the regime and by 1939, as Nicholas Stargardt has noted, two-thirds of the population joined at least one of the Party's mass organisations.[5] In addition, Gellately has shown how those who found jobs after the period of mass unemployment at the end of the Weimar Republic, 'could relish integrating into the community' and belonging to the Nazi project.[6]

Mass tourism and leisure were introduced under the aegis of the Kraft durch Freude (KdF or 'Strength Through Joy') organisation. Shelley Baranowski has stated that the KdF became 'arguably the Third Reich's most popular organisation'.[7] It arranged hikes and sporting activities. Furthermore, it organised subsidised holidays to the Black Forest and other regions of Germany, which were partly designed to reverse German regional particularism by encouraging people to visit other parts of their homeland. This formed part of the process of building the 'national community'. The KdF arranged

FIGURE 2.1 *The first KdF train, 1934.* © *Getty Images.*

steamship tours on the Rhine and the Danube. By 1938, the KdF was organising cruises to Madeira and the Norwegian fjords, as well as trips to other destinations in Europe.[8] By 1939, 43 million Germans had travelled with Strength Through Joy.[9] Julia Timpe argues that the two key goals of the KdF were the creation and stabilisation of the community of all 'Aryan' Germans into the 'national community' and the provision of enjoyment and happiness to those Germans. She describes the activities of the KdF as 'joy production'.[10] As well as a signifier of upward mobility of the working class, the KdF was a significant facet of everyday life – in terms of leisure – under the Nazi dictatorship.

The KdF subsidised tickets for cultural events thereby providing greater access to the theatre, cinema and a range of other activities. Between 1934 and 1938, the number of participants in KdF cultural events increased 'from over nine million to over fifty-four million'.[11] In addition, from August 1938, workers were encouraged to save for a KdF car or Volkswagen (people's car). The scheme entailed a weekly payment of five Reichsmark (RM) over four and a half years for the acquisition of a 'people's car', which made the ownership of an automobile potentially available to every German. This was significant indeed as previously car ownership had been reserved only for the wealthiest members of German society.[12] By 1939, 270,000 people were participating in the KdF car scheme.[13] The Volkswagen was intended as 'a car for free time and leisure' and as a means to shift the German car from the business sector to the private sector as a consumer item.[14] In September 1939, the Volkswagen factory turned to war production and the KdF cars – unproduced – remained 'a blend of propaganda and illusionary politics'.[15]

The Schönheit der Arbeit (Beauty of Labour) department of the KdF played a significant part in influencing the everyday life of German workers.[16] Geraniums were placed at factory entrances to brighten them up, wholesome canteen food was provided and factory hygiene was improved. 'Beauty of Labour' was concerned with the hygiene and the functionality of industrial spaces. It became involved in factory architecture and design, as well as putting into place a variety of campaigns to ameliorate industrial workplaces, including 'Battle Against Noise' (1935), 'Good Light – Good Work' (1935) and 'Hot Food in the Factory' (1938). These measures were designed both to create a sense of attachment of the workers to their workplace and to convince them to accept Nazism. Timpe argues that 'beautification campaigns in both factories and villages were another important element of KdF'S "joy production"'.[17]

The Nazi regime promoted radio ownership and listening in order to create support among the German population. Manufacturers were commissioned to produce two new types of cheap radios, costing RM75 and RM35. During the course of 1933 alone, 1.5 million radio sets were produced and the cheaper version, the Volksempfänger (People's Receiver), could be paid for in instalments. The People's Receiver sets had a limited reception capacity and were unable to receive foreign radio broadcasts. Posters advertising the new, cheap radio sets stated: 'All Germany listens to the Führer with the People's Radio'. By 1939, 70 per cent of German households had a radio. Thus, the Nazi government succeeded in creating a mass radio audience, with a rapid growth of radio ownership across all social classes. Radio became transformed into a medium of mass communication.[18] In addition, the Nazi regime encouraged communal radio listening, in factories, offices and cafés. Loudspeaker columns were set up in city squares and other public places. In this way, Nazi propagandists reached those people who did not possess a radio set. They believed that the popular impact of speeches and rallies broadcast on the radio would be greater in public places than in the private home environment. Communal listening to important announcements and speeches became a significant feature of societal life in Nazi Germany. Radio wardens were responsible for setting up loudspeakers in town squares, in offices and in factories to encourage communal listening. These policies were motivated by the concern to create consensus for the regime. And yet, the relationship between the Hitler government and the German populace was complex. Nathan Stoltzfus has demonstrated how accommodation with the people took a variety of forms and how when the political stakes were high enough, Hitler was willing to compromise with the German population.[19]

The relationship between the Nazi government and its population was indeed complicated. Despite its attempts to do so, the regime could not bring every German into conformity. What were the possibilities for nonconformity in this dictatorship? Detlev Peukert distinguished between four types of dissident behaviour in the Third Reich: nonconformist behaviour, refusal, protest and resistance. Nonconformist behaviour was made up of separate individual acts against the norms and requirements of the state – typically 'grumbling and grousing' – but did not call into question the Nazi system as a whole. These acts usually took place in the private sphere. Refusal was one stage more general and more pointedly directed against the Nazi administration, including acts undertaken in opposition to orders, such as parents not enrolling their children into the Nazi youth groups. Protest was one stage closer to rejection of the regime and more public, but still consisted of actions directed to a specific issue, such as priests sermonising against the 'euthanasia' programme. Resistance included only those forms of behaviour that were rejections of the regime as a whole and sought to overthrow it.[20] To be sure, the regime cracked down on as much of this behaviour as possible.

The Nazi government used fear, terror and force to achieve its ambitions and this formed a central aspect of the relationship between the people and the regime. Within Himmler's vast SS-SD-police complex, the Gestapo, headed by Heinrich Müller, became the crucial link in the system of terror and surveillance in the Nazi state. The Gestapo was certainly an institution that instigated fear and terror among the German populace. However, the popular image of the Gestapo as omniscient and omnipotent is a myth that was instigated by Gestapo leaders and perpetuated in the post-war period by historians who accepted the statements of Gestapo leaders at face value. Klaus-Michael Mallmann and Gerhard Paul have demonstrated that the Gestapo did not have adequate staffing available to be 'omniscient and omnipotent'.[21] Its leaders carefully and purposefully created the propaganda image of the ubiquitous Gestapo both in order to intimidate German society and to conceal its own limitations. In reality, however, the Gestapo was not a completely thoroughgoing mechanism of repression. It was an understaffed and over-bureaucratised organisation, incapable of the comprehensive surveillance of Germans. As there were comparatively few Gestapo agents on the ground, they relied on both amateur and professional helpers. Robert Gellately has argued that the nature of the Gestapo was largely reactive and has described the method developed by the Gestapo as 'a kind of auto-policing, or at least an auto-surveillance system'.[22] With the cooperation of neighbours, friends, acquaintances and family members, the Gestapo was able to infiltrate even the private realm of the home, in order to monitor compliance with the dictates of the regime. Denunciations were the key link in the interactions between the police and the population. Without the help of informers, the Gestapo was not in the position to undertake comprehensive surveillance or perfect repression.

Denunciations were based on mixed motivations on the part of informers, with an array of instrumental or selfish reasons that provided the impetus for denunciations.[23] Informing was used as a way of gaining personal advantage – for example, to settle scores with fellow workers or employers, or even family members, including spouses and siblings. Gellately argues that this demonstrated a growing social consensus and acceptance of the surveillance process, in which the state or its organs were utilised by members of the public to regulate aspects of social life and to settle personal disputes. Eric Johnson notes that despite having limited powers, the Gestapo, as 'the leading organ of terror' in the Third Reich was 'extremely effective all the same'.[24] The complex relationship between the population and the apparatus of the state thus formed a key aspect of the reality of daily life in the Third Reich.

The Nazis established a large and complex camp system. The first concentration camp, Dachau, was established near Munich, in March 1933. Dachau served as a model for the organisation and administration of other concentration camps, with its clearly defined rules for camp behaviour, its classification of prisoners, its graduated system of punishments, its observation towers and barbed-wire electrified fences. The concentration camps lay at the heart of the Nazis' network of terror.[25] Eugen Kogon outlined the function of these camps: 'Their main purpose was the elimination of every trace of actual or potential opposition to Nazi rule. Segregation, debasement, humiliation, extermination – these were the effective forms of terror'.[26] The concentration camp system was designed either to 're-educate' or to eliminate opponents of the regime. Concentration camps were instruments of social terror, first established to isolate and terrorise Communists and Social Democrats. They were used to intimidate all potential enemies of the regime and to have a deterrent effect upon the rest of the population. The SS constructed major purpose-built concentration camps: Sachsenhausen (1936), Buchenwald (1937), Flossenbürg (1938), Mauthausen (1938) and Ravensbrück (1939). Once the elimination of political enemies had been achieved, the concentration camps took in other opponents of the regime, including Jews, Sinti and Roma ('Gypsies'), the 'workshy', homosexuals and Jehovah's Witnesses. In addition, the concentration camp system interned the 'asocial' and 'undesirable' individuals considered by the Nazis to be unproductive and 'inferior'. Hence, everyday life in the Third Reich was differentiated according to the individual and his or her place (or lack of place) in Nazi society. Certainly, belonging to an outsider or enemy group entailed very different circumstances than being a member of the *Volksgemeinschaft*.

Private life and the family

It was not easy to maintain privacy and personal autonomy in the Nazi dictatorship. The negotiation of the separation of private aspects of daily life was difficult terrain. For example, radio listening had formerly been a private activity, yet under National Socialism, as noted above, it was one that was encouraged to be public. There was also a tension between other spare-time or leisure activities that in normal times were private, but under National Socialism, became public, for example, attending art exhibitions, which, as Joan Clinefelter has shown, gave Germans 'the ability to become participating members in the culture-producing *Volksgemeinschaft*'.[27] Moritz Föllmer has contended that the consequences of the Nazi dictatorship for the private realm were 'severe and ubiquitous'.[28]

The subject of private life between 1933 and 1945 has remained relatively unexplored until very recently. New research into this area has extended our knowledge of life under National Socialism by looking at the relationship between people's lifestyles and the requirements of the Nazi government. For example, fresh research into different themes pertaining to private life, such as 'mother happiness' and biopolitics – pregnant women and young mothers in the National Socialist dictatorship; and 'home leave' – soldiers between front, family and the Nazi regime, has started to shed light respectively on the threshold between the private, domestic sphere and the state, and the threshold between the military and civil society. Nicholas Stargardt has shown the importance of the problems and dilemmas faced by individuals in the Third Reich as 'common to that society', stating that the private sphere was at once a fertile and a limited space for moral self-reflection because of a 'bleed through between the public and the private'.[29] In the end, as Föllmer has noted, 'ordinary domesticity' was 'widely desired but notoriously elusive'.[30]

Certainly, the family – usually a private space – was an institution that the Nazi regime was concerned to influence. The main reason for this was that the family could be utilised as means to achieve the population policy goals of the government – to increase the national birth rate. Paul Ginsborg notes the 'extraordinary combination of strategies' that the Hitler government directed at German families.[31] In June 1933, the Marriage Loan Scheme was set up to promote marriages between healthy 'Aryan' partners. A loan of RM1,000 was made to a German couple in the form of vouchers for the purchase of furniture and household equipment. In addition, the loan was only made if the regime considered the political affiliation and 'way of life' of the couple to be acceptable. It was denied to couples if either or both partners had connections with the German Communist Party (KPD), or had had such connections in the past, and it was denied to prostitutes and the 'workshy'. The repayment of the loan was reduced by one quarter for each child born, and was completely

FIGURE 2.2 *Mother's Day ceremony with conferment of the Cross of Honour of the German Mother, 1942. © Getty Images.*

cancelled out with the birth of the fourth child. Between August 1933 and January 1937, some 700,000 marriages were assisted by marriage loans, and by 1939, 42 per cent of all marriages were loan-assisted.[32] However, couples granted a marriage loan had, on average, only one child. The Nazi government attempted to raise the status of motherhood, with a symbolic tribute to prolific mothers in the form of the Cross of Honour of the German Mother. This was awarded to mothers of 'valuable' large families, in bronze, silver and gold – for the birth of four, six and eight children respectively.

Other measures taken to encourage marriages between healthy 'Aryan' partners that would result in large families and increase the nation's birth rate also had an impact on personal decisions and private choices. For example, contraceptives were banned and family planning centres were closed down. In 1941, Himmler's Public Ordinance prohibited the production and distribution of contraceptives.[33] In addition, the abortion laws were tightened up by the reintroduction of Paragraphs 219 and 220 of the Criminal Code, which made provisions for harsher punishments for abortion.[34] Eventually, in 1943, the death penalty was introduced for anyone performing an abortion to terminate a 'valuable' pregnancy, because the regime considered this to be an act of 'racial sabotage' during the crisis of the war.[35]

The Hilfswerk 'Mutter und Kind' (Mother and Child Relief Agency) was a special agency of the *Nationalsozialistische Volkswohlfahrt* (National Socialist People's Welfare), established in February 1934. Its central concern was with the health of mothers and children, in order to preserve 'the immortality of the nation'. Three of the most significant aspects of its work were welfare for mothers, recuperation for mothers and advice centres for mothers. The Nazi regime utilised welfare as an instrument to educate the German nation in the spirit of National Socialism. Welfare, in population policy terms, however, was steered only towards the promotion of the 'racially pure' and 'fit' and was not applied equally across all sections of the German population.

Food policy and food choices

To be sure, food and eating – as essential aspects of everyday life – were profoundly influenced by the Nazi dictatorship. The regime encouraged people to alter their eating habits in order to meet its requirements, for example, suppressing demand for imported goods such as oranges and coffee, as well as foods dependent upon the import of fodder for their production, such as butter and meat, as Germany did not produce enough fodder internally. The Hitler government used propaganda and 'education' to this end. German civilians were asked to develop a 'political stomach'.[36] Grocers, from 1935 onwards, introduced 'coupling transactions', that compelled customers who asked for items in short supply to purchase additional items. Grocers were castigated by the regime for being grumblers and constantly bemoaning unavoidable shortages, instead of re-educating the 17 million housewives with which they had daily contact. In October 1936, Rudolf Hess, Deputy Leader of the NSDAP, made a speech about how women should shop:

> Hardworking and efficient housewives know what they have to do in the service of this great German family – the German people – if it has to overcome temporary small shortages. They simply do their shopping in accordance with the interest of the great German family! They do not attempt to buy expressly that which is in short supply at the time, but instead buy those things which are available in abundance and prepare them in such a way that they look really good and taste really good to their husbands and children. No good German housewife particularly mourns the quarter-pound of pork which, from time to time, she now fails to get.[37]

In September 1938, a newspaper editorial criticised 'those who pretend starvation stares them in the face unless they have their regular supply of vol au vents and whipped cream'.[38]

One of the most widespread campaigns to alter German eating habits was the *Eintopf* 'one-pot dish', promoted by the Winter Relief Agency charity, from October 1933 onwards, in which Germans were asked to eat a one-pot dish or stew on one Sunday each month, and to donate the money they saved against their usual Sunday meal to the state-sponsored charity. Gesine Gerhard notes that 'many housewives responded favorably to the campaign'.[39] One-pot Sundays came to be observed, with magazines publishing recipes and regions developing their own particular variants. One common recipe was a split pea soup, made from dried peas, bacon cubes and potatoes. The Nazi women's magazine *NS-Frauenwarte* included features on and recipes for the *Eintopf*, such as 'fish one-pot dish' and 'macaroni one-pot dish'.[40] The *Eintopf* was intended to symbolise the 'national community', described in a 1934 brochure of the Winter Relief Agency as a 'sacrificial meal as a solemn vow to the unshakeable people's community'. *Eintopf* Sundays changed the drive for autarky into a social ritual that aimed to unite the 'national community' through sacrifice. The Nazi Party leadership was photographed eating the *Eintopf* and *Eintopf* meals held in communal settings, such as town squares, further appealed to the Germans to support the campaign.

One key aspect of Nazi policymaking in relation to consumption was the 'whole-grain bread campaign', instigated by Reich Physicians' leader, Gerhard Wagner. Whole-grain bread was regarded as the food of the 'national community' and consumption of the patriotic loaf increased by 50 per cent by 1939.[41] Wagner attacked 'the recent shift from natural whole-grain bread to highly refined white bread' and advocated a return to whole-grain bread.[42] In 1935, he ordered German bakeries to change over their production to whole-grain bread and launched a campaign to promote this as *Volksbrot* (people's bread). It was a purposeful attempt to change consumption and production patterns. The German whole-grain bread campaign was also partly about strengthening the health of the German *Volk*. Hence, the other significant aspect of Nazi food policies was that eating was not a private matter and the regime was concerned about what people ate in terms of notions of health. Individuals had a duty to be healthy in order for the nation to be great, hale and strong. In 1937, Hans Reiter, President of the Reich Health Office, banned the bleaching of flour. The 'whole-grain bread' campaign was stepped up during the wartime period. On 21 March 1941, Reich Health leader Leonardo Conti made a radio address to the nation, asking people to turn from white bread to whole-grain bread 'for the good of their health and the strength of the nation'.[43] In 1939, only 2,420 German bakeries produced the *Volksbrot*; by 1943, 27,454 bakeries were making whole-grain bread.[44] This was not only a response to Nazi propaganda, but also a pragmatic decision on the part of the bakers, as whole-grain bread was easier to produce than highly refined white bread.

The attempted intervention of the Nazi government in the private lives and homes of its people included instruction, which affected the everyday life, behaviour and decisions of German housewives. The Volkswirtschaft/ Hauswirtschaft (National Economy/Home Economy), a part of the NS-Frauenschaft, distributed educational leaflets and pamphlets (for example, on preserving fruit, sewing, mending and darning clothes), organised cookery demonstrations and ran both courses and advice centres to instruct German women about the use of ersatz products, cooking with limited ingredients and other topics of relevance to their home economy. Women's magazines – which were subject to state censorship and effectively run by the Party – included sections filled with 'practical tips' for 'the clever housewife', such as how to open glass jars and how to clean empty bottles. One Nazi women's magazine gave advice about how to use fresh fruit in winter, including making jams and preserves.[45] Recommendations were given on a wide variety of topics that related to cookery or the household, with a great emphasis on features such as 'Healthy – Tasty – Economical'.[46] For example, there was advice on how to store potatoes correctly and how to peel them properly in order to prevent waste. One magazine gave suggested recipes for lunch and dinner for every day of the month – a typical example was fish soup with potatoes and celery for lunch, followed by semolina and compote, with a spinach bake for the evening meal. Some of the recipes were also offered along with suggestions of what products were especially good to buy each month – for example, beef, spinach, tomatoes, mushrooms, apples and pears were recommended in October. Cooking instructions – for instance, a magazine feature called 'A Vegetarian Week' – demonstrated how meals without meat were not only satisfying, but also cheaper and healthier.[47] *Deutsche Hauswirtschaft* (the magazine of the National Economy/Home Economy agency), was a means of disseminating information and advice to German women. It regularly featured recipes, household tips and exercises for women, as well as seasonal advice, such as what to bake for Christmas. It also contained articles on how to save electricity and gas. The main aim of such features was to discourage squandering and to bring about an awareness of the relationship between the individual household and the national economy. These examples illustrate the extent to which the Nazi government was willing to intervene in everyday life, in order to achieve its aim of influencing people's eating choices and habits.

In particular, the regime educated women about which provisions to buy and how to cook frugal meals in times of national shortage. Housewives were responsible for making sure that their families were getting healthy nourishment, even with the limited availability of some foodstuffs. The National Economy/Home Economy division promoted the consumption of Quark, dark bread and fish. It mounted large campaigns to disseminate its position to German housewives and shoppers, for example, suggesting weekly and monthly menus that reflected the availability of foodstuffs. As Nancy Reagin has explained, 'these menus and lists were then printed in newspapers and magazines, publicised on radio programs, posted in factory floors and marketplaces, and inserted in female workers' pay envelopes'.[48] In addition, the National Economy/Home Economy had 148 advice centres for housewives, which advised women on issues such as recycling, how to use ersatz products and how to preserve foods. The centres had all different types of educational material on view, in the windows, in display cases, on tables and on the walls. Books on display treated topics including the economy, agriculture, home economy, nutrition and cookery, household management, gardening and health. The centres also had educational films on topics such as 'All Kinds of Things from Quark', 'German Grain in the Household', 'Preservation of Fruit and Vegetables' and 'The Preparation of Fish'. In addition, many millions of cookery leaflets were distributed and more than 1.8 million women attended the cookery courses mounted by the National Economy/Home Economy organisation in 1938. Hence, the Nazi regime put considerable effort into such campaigns to influence German consumers. The Nazi women's organisations created cooking demonstrations and exhibitions, across all regions of the land, that were designed to promote 'particular patterns of consumption and housekeeping'.[49] Furthermore, the 'patriotic' diet was also linked to the concept of German 'blood and soil', another favoured theme of the Nazi administration. The regime wanted to bring German women, especially those in the cities, back to a way of thinking that was bound to the German soil. But ultimately, as Hartmut Berghoff argues, Nazi policies consisted of a combination of 'enticement and deprivation' of German consumers, in order to achieve the regime's ideological and political goals.[50] Personal purchasing decisions were closely linked to the needs of the national economy.

The Four Year Plan and policy formulated around Goering's slogan 'guns before butter' meant that food shortages were already present from the mid-1930s onwards. As Reagin has noted, preparations for war 'led to economic policies that often worked against civilian consumers' interests'.[51] For example, by the winter of 1936–7, shopkeepers sold butter only to their regular customers. The quality of butter and cheese declined, and there was an increase in the use of inferior vegetable fats to create new fat compounds. Eating patterns changed. Fish consumption increased by 40 per cent between 1932 and 1938, whilst the consumption of imported fruit decreased by one-eighth during the same period. The regime encouraged the eating of fish instead of meat. It subsidised the fishing industry at all levels, as Reagin notes, 'encouraging investments in fish processing ships, new rail schedules to distribute fresh fish even to inland communities and new technologies to flash-freeze fish fillets'.[52] In conjunction with the fish cookery courses offered by the Nazi women's organisations, this policy contributed to the marked rise in fish consumption between 1934 and 1938. White cabbage and potatoes became increasingly important components of the German diet, whilst consumption of meat decreased. Coffee consumption continued to increase during the 1930s, so that by the late 1930s the demand for coffee exceeded the supply. Goebbels stated quite directly: 'In times when coffee is scarce a decent person simply drinks less or stops drinking it altogether'.[53] During the war, ersatz coffee predominated, but illicit trading in coffee flourished almost from the very start of the war with the introduction of very strict coffee rationing. Black market coffee fetched very high prices. Alcohol was frowned upon by the regime, which equated the consumption of alcohol with degeneracy. At the 1935 Party Congress at Nuremberg, Hitler's speech had made reference to the idea that in the past, 'the ideal German was the man who could handle his beer and hard liquor'. This was no longer the ideal under Nazism. The production of non-alcoholic fruit drinks increased fivefold during the mid 1930s, although people still drank alcohol as well. In 1938, Reiter declared a fruit drink called 'sweet cider' as the official *Volksgetränk* (people's drink). The Nazi regime further discouraged drinking alcohol, both by supporting the production of fruit juices and mineral water and by restricting the sale of beer and wine. During the war, the sale of spirits was proscribed.[54]

During the wartime period, women were urged to grow their own fruit, forage for herbs and to preserve fruits in the winter months. Children were encouraged to gather wild plants, such as rosehips and dandelions for 'German teas'. Even beechnuts, stinging nettles and carnations roots came to have a use. Herbal teas from wild forest plants became more common and coffee substitutes included a malt coffee and a beverage made from oats. To be sure, as the war continued, the demands on the productivity of German farmers became greater and greater. By the winter of 1941–2, farmers were struggling to produce enough potatoes and pork. There were shortages in potato supplies to the cities, reported in Frankfurt am Main, Berlin and Cologne. Whilst farmers had managed to maintain a good grain harvest until 1943, feeding the civilian population, the military as well as all the foreign workers placed huge demands on German agriculture. In 1942, bread, meat and fat rations all had to be cut again, and then decreased further in May 1943. The ration cuts were accepted with grumbles and complaints, but accepted nevertheless. Collingham notes that: 'By 1943–44, an ordinary German civilian was eating 40 per cent less fat, 60 per cent less meat and 20 per cent less bread than in 1939'.[55] As rationing became more widely applied, everyone was supposed to make the same sacrifices for the nation, although pregnant and nursing mothers, as well as workers in heavy industry and, of course, soldiers, did get more provisions and, not surprisingly, foreign workers and prisoners of war fared worst. Even so, miners and workers in war industries clamoured for increased rations. As German farmers were overstretched in terms of supplying the food needed,

Germany looked to its occupied territories to make up for the food deficit, with Goering insisting that hunger should be exported outside the Reich. Minister for Food and Agriculture Herbert Backe was architect of what was known as the Hunger Plan, a policy designed to extract as much as possible out of the occupied territories. The Nazis exploited conquered lands, confiscating food supplies to feed the German army, which in turn, as Reagin has shown, 'reduced the demands for foodstuffs placed on the German domestic economy'.[56] Between 1941 and 1943, occupied Soviet land provided Nazi Germany with 7 million tonnes of grains, 2.7 million tonnes of potatoes, and 325,000 tonnes of edible fat.[57] Yet, as Alice Weinreb has shown, ultimately the Nazi regime 'decreased Germany's available food supplies both by diverting food to industrial and military segments of the population and by reducing food imports', despite its promises of plenty to the German people.[58]

Auslese and *Ausmerze* (selection and eradication)

This final part of the chapter highlights the impact of the Nazi regime on different groups in German society – distinctions in the effect of key aspects of Nazi policies of *Auslese* and *Ausmerze* (selection and eradication) on everyday life. It uses two important examples to illustrate this crucial point: education (from Nazi elite schools through to special schools) and population policy and eugenics (from the Lebensborn breeding programme to sterilisation and the *Aktion T4* 'euthanasia' campaign between 1939 and 1941).

Educational policy during the Third Reich reflected the Nazi regime's fundamental ideological aims, attempting to form 'valuable' young members of the newly ordered German society. After the seizure of power in 1933, educational institutions were swiftly 'coordinated', and those selected to uphold the Third Reich's newly racialised educational community enjoyed considerable power and prestige. They applied extremes of the spectrum of biological selection in education, from the 'positive' biological selection of Nazi elite-school applicants, to the 'negative', eugenic policies applied to supposedly 'abnormal' pupils at the *Hilfsschulen* (special schools).

The Nazi regime established three main types of educational institutions to train the future elite of German society: the Nationalpolitische Erziehungsanstalten (National Political Educational Institutions or Napolas), the Adolf Hitler Schulen (Adolf Hitler Schools or AHS), and the Ordensburgen (Order Castles). These institutions represented a microcosm of the Nazi *Weltanschauung* by fostering the leadership principle, promoting competitiveness and expressing life as a struggle and survival of the 'fittest'.

They encouraged physical prowess, excoriated the 'enemies of the Reich' – in particular the Jews, Communists and Socialists – and emphasised Nordic racial purity, glorified war and fostered militarism. They underlined the necessity for *Lebensraum* ('living space') and had a function in the achievement of a 'greater German empire'.

At the other end of the spectrum was the issue of education for mentally and physically disabled children. The Nazi leadership believed that there was an overabundance of 'special schools' for such pupils.[59] In Nazi education discourse on 'special education', a number of common themes emerge. First, the mentally and physically disabled should be educated separately from normal, healthy children as, if they were educated together, this would slow down the education of the latter and therefore have a negative impact on the *Volksgemeinschaft*. Second, a combination of eugenic policies – especially sterilisation, which would prevent the births of 'inferior' children in future – and educational efforts for 'abnormal' children in special schools was considered to be a suitable way forward. Third, in giving special care to 'abnormal' children in 'special schools', consideration had to be given to the economic efficiency of this and the question of whether the resources spent upon it were worthwhile. Fourth, this type of 'special education' would only be tolerated if on exit, 'usefulness' to society afterwards was a possibility. Heredity and genetics had to be taken into account in order to achieve in the healthy survival and advancement of the *Volk*. The Nazi regime considered it an economic waste to spend time and money on the education and upbringing of 'feeble-minded' children.[60]

Similarly, the concepts of *Auslese* and *Ausmerze* applied to breeding and eugenics in the Third Reich too – exemplified by the Lebensborn programme on the one hand, and Nazi policies of sterilisation and 'euthanasia' on the other. The Lebensborn agency was set up in December 1935. Its aims were to support 'hereditarily-biologically valuable, *kinderreich* (child-rich) families', to care for 'racially valuable and hereditarily healthy mothers-to-be',[61] to look after the children born from such mothers and to care for the mothers after the delivery of their babies. It established maternity homes in which single women could give birth to illegitimate children, in a comfortable environment, away from their own homes, and thus without the knowledge of their neighbours, relatives and priests. Himmler pronounced these homes to be: 'primarily [. . .] for the brides and wives of our young SS men, and secondarily for illegitimate mothers of good blood'.[62] The prerequisite for access, of course, entailed fulfilment of the SS's criteria regarding race and hereditary health. The Lebensborn did not serve mothers who had been involved in 'indiscriminate relationships' that would lead to the birth of 'racially inferior' or 'hereditarily ill' children.[63] Indeed, of nearly 3,000 applications by unmarried mothers-to-be, less than half were accepted.

The Lebensborn saw its chief task as 'the support [. . .] of mothers-to-be of good blood'.[64] It played a part in the struggle against abortions, by providing discreet delivery homes for illegitimate births and thereby preventing a number of pregnant girls and women from feeling the necessity to terminate their pregnancies. For if the mother and the father of the baby were both 'hereditarily healthy', the child would be 'valuable'.[65] Hence, the Lebensborn provided practical protection for such mothers-to-be in its delivery homes, of which six were established in the first two years of its existence. By 31 December 1938, 653 mothers had used the Lebensborn delivery homes. The infant mortality rate in these homes was 3 per cent, which was half that of the national average. The Lebensborn homes were unpopular with many ordinary German citizens, especially in rural, Catholic areas, where people were disgruntled with the official condonement and even encouragement of the birth of children out of wedlock. As a result, all types of rumours were perpetuated about the Lebensborn homes. These included allegations that the Lebensborn homes employed permanent 'procreation helpers' or that they were 'stud farms' for the SS. The fact that the homes were set up in secluded areas and shrouded in secrecy fuelled such rumours.

Himmler took a keen interest in the administration of the Lebensborn homes. He advised them about the correct diet for the women, promoting the importance of porridge and wholemeal bread. He also ensured that the homes received priority treatment during the war, in terms of rations of luxury items such as fresh fruit. To prepare the mothers for their future responsibilities, Himmler made sure that Reichsmütterdienst (National Mothers Service) courses were held in each Lebensborn home, to train mothers in all aspects of household management and childcare. In addition, the SS was responsible for the 'ideological education' of the women, which it achieved by holding lectures, film screenings and discussion evenings. In the homes, mothers had the chance to relax during their free time and to form friendships with the other women. According to a Lebensborn pamphlet, a sense of camaraderie developed between the mothers as each was giving a German baby a life. Once she had given birth, a mother who was not in a position to take her baby with her could leave it to be looked after in the home for one year. If, after that time, the mother was still unmarried or not able to take care of the child, it was given out to foster parents, usually to SS leaders who were childless or who had just one or two children.

In contrast, sterilisation was the main method employed by the Nazi regime to prevent people it considered to be eugenically 'undesirable' from having children. On 1 January 1934, a compulsory sterilisation order, the Law for the Prevention of Hereditarily Diseased Offspring, came into effect. It called for the mandatory sterilisation of anyone that suffered from 'congenital feeble-mindedness, schizophrenia, manic depression, hereditary epilepsy, Huntington's chorea, hereditary blindness, hereditary deafness, serious physical deformities' and 'chronic alcoholism'.[66] Between January 1934 and

September 1939, approximately 320,000 people (0.5 per cent of the population), were forcibly sterilised under the terms of this law.[67] The majority of them were of German ethnicity, but they were considered to be 'hereditarily ill' or to be 'feeble-minded' by the regime and its eugenic experts.

To be sure, the Nazi government did not want to continue spending money on those individuals it considered to be 'incurable' and the question of eliminating the 'burden' of the 'unfit' continued to be raised. For example, in a discussion on the subject with Dr Gerhard Wagner, the Reich Physicians' leader, Hitler said that the question of 'euthanasia' would be taken up 'in the event of war', as it would be more easily solved in wartime. Indeed, Stefan Kühl has shown that once war broke out, influential eugenicists such as Otmar von Verschuer, Eugen Fischer, Fritz Lenz and Ernst Rüdin 'saw the necessity not only for an economic and military mobilisation, but especially for a biological one [. . .] The killing programme was the symbiosis of an economic, military and race hygienic mobilisation at the "home front"'.[68] The 'euthanasia' campaign (code-named *Aktion T4*) was implemented at six killing centres – Bernberg, Brandenburg, Grafeneck, Hadamar, Hartheim and Sonnenstein.

The mentally ill and physically disabled were stigmatised as 'hereditarily ill', 'unproductive' and ultimately 'unworthy of life'.[69] The 'children's euthanasia' programme claimed the lives of at least 5,200 children, including adolescents, but the total number of victims may have been as many as 6,000. The adult 'euthanasia' campaign claimed 70,273 lives. Michael Burleigh has argued that the 'euthanasia' programme was 'a carefully planned and covertly executed operation with precisely defined objectives'.[70] Its practitioners believed that they were carrying out a necessary task for the benefit of the *Volk*.[71] They also justified their work in terms of benefiting the patients' families. Whilst some parents may have wanted to remove the burden of handicapped children – either so that they could give more attention to their other healthy children or because they wanted to eliminate any blemish such offspring had on their family's value – the 'euthanasia' murders had a tragic impact upon countless families. Finally, the impact of Nazi policies directed at Jews and at Sinti and Roma ('Gypsies') – as well as other outsiders, dissenters and resisters – brings us back to the point that everyday life was not the same for all groups in German society under the Hitler dictatorship and that Nazi terror was meted out to particular parts of German society for a variety of reasons. Certain sectors of society were ultimately marked out for first exclusion and then extermination – most notably the Jews and the Sinti and Roma. Their experience of everyday life was completely different from that of the majority of German citizens, but an examination of life in the Third Reich cannot exclude mention of these groups who were considered by the Nazi regime to be outside the *Volksgemeinschaft*.[72]

In summary, the impact of the Nazi dictatorship upon daily life in Germany was extremely wide-ranging and complex. This chapter has analysed aspects of the Nazi policies aimed at the creation of consensus and conformity and a cohesive German *Volksgemeinschaft*. It has examined the use of terror by the Nazi regime, especially highlighting the role of the Gestapo and the concentration camp network in the Third Reich, in order to shed light on a crucial aspect of the relationship between the German people and the apparatus of the state. The chapter has analysed the impact of Nazi government on family life and private life, examining the way in which it penetrated into the personal lives and decisions of German citizens. It has explored Nazi food policy and its impact on food choices for the German population, as a significant part of everyday life. The last part of the chapter has examined examples that demonstrate the outcome of the Nazi dictatorship on different groups in German society – the impact of key aspects of the Nazi policies of *Auslese* and *Ausmerze* on society in terms of education and eugenics. Daily life in the Third Reich was not the same right across German society – Nazi policies to 'select' those it considered to be 'valuable' and to 'eradicate' those it deemed 'inferior' created an additional layer of complexity to this.

Notes

1 I. Kershaw, *The 'Hitler Myth': Image and Reality in the Third Reich* (Oxford, 1989), 254.
2 R. J. Evans, *The Coming of the Third Reich: How the Nazis Destroyed Democracy and Seized Power in Germany* (London, 2004), 381.
3 R. J. Evans, *The Third Reich in Power: How the Nazis Won Over the Hearts and Minds of a Nation* (London, 2006), 14.
4 P. Brooker, *The Faces of Fraternalism: Nazi Germany, Fascist Italy, and Imperial Japan* (Oxford, 1991), 136.
5 N. Stargardt, *The German War: A Nation Under Arms, 1939–45* (London, 2015), 9.
6 R. Gellately, *Hitler's True Believers: How Ordinary People Became Nazis* (Oxford, 2020), 319.
7 S. Baranowski, 'A Family Vacation for Workers: The Strength Through Joy Resort at Prora', *German History* 25, no. 4 (2007): 539–59, 542.
8 M. A. Merritt, 'Strength Through Joy: Regimented Leisure in Nazi Germany', in *Nazism and the Common Man: Essays in German History (1929–1939)*, ed. O.C. Mitchell (Washington DC, 1981), 74–5.
9 K. Semmens, 'A Holiday from the Nazis? Everyday Tourism in the Third Reich', in *Life and Times in Nazi* Germany, ed. L. Pine (London, 2016), 143.
10 J. Timpe, *Nazi-Organized Recreation and Entertainment in the Third Reich* (London, 2017), 3.

11 Baranowski, 'A Family Vacation for Workers', 542.
12 Merritt, 'Strength Through Joy', 86.
13 W. König, 'Adolf Hitler vs. Henry Ford: The *Volkswagen*, the Role of America as a Model, and the Failure of a Nazi Consumer Society', *German Studies Review* 27, no. 2 (2004): 249–68, 258. On this, see also, B. Rieger, *The People's Car: A Global History of the Volkswagen Beetle* (Cambridge, MA, 2013).
14 König, 'Adolf Hitler vs. Henry Ford', 258.
15 Ibid., 260. See also Evans, *The Third Reich in Power*, 327–8, 338.
16 On Beauty of Labour, see S. Baranowski, *Strength Through Joy: Consumerism and Mass Tourism in the Third Reich* (Cambridge, 2004), 75–117.
17 Timpe, *Nazi-Organized Recreation*, 192.
18 U.C. Schmidt, 'Der Volksempfänger: Tabernakel moderner Massenkultur', in *Radiozeit: Herrschaft, Alltag, Gesellschaft (1924–1960)*, ed. I. Marssolek and A. von Saldern (Potsdam, 1999), 136–59.
19 N. Stoltzfus, *Hitler's Compromises: Coercion and Consensus in Nazi Germany* (New Haven, CT, and London, 2016).
20 D.J.K. Peukert, *Inside Nazi Germany: Conformity, Opposition and Racism in Everyday Life* (London, 1987), 81–5.
21 K.-M. Mallmann and G. Paul, 'Omniscient, Omnipotent, Omnipresent? Gestapo, Society and Resistance', in *Nazism and German Society, 1933–1945*, ed. D.F. Crew (London, 1994), 166–96.
22 R. Gellately, *The Gestapo and German Society: Enforcing Racial Policy, 1933–1945* (Oxford, 1990), 258.
23 R. Gellately, *Backing Hitler: Consent and Coercion in Nazi Germany* (Oxford, 2001), 193.
24 E. Johnson, *Nazi Terror: The Gestapo, Jews, and Ordinary Germans* (London, 2000), 485. See also, E. Johnson and K.-H. Reuband, *What we Knew: Terror, Mass Murder, and Everyday Life in Nazi Germany* (London, 2005).
25 On the history of the concentration camps, see N. Wachsmann, *KL: A History of the Nazi Concentration Camps* (London, 2016).
26 E. Kogon, *The Theory and Practice of Hell: The German Concentration Camps and the System Behind Them* (London, 1950), 30.
27 J. Clinefelter, 'Representing the *Volksgemeinschaft*: Art in the Third Reich', in *Life and Times in Nazi Germany*, ed. L. Pine (London, 2016), 195.
28 M. Föllmer, *Individuality and Modernity in Berlin: Self and Society from Weimar to the Wall* (Cambridge, 2013), 131.
29 N. Stargardt, 'Private and Public Moral Sentiments in Nazi Germany', in *Private Life and Privacy in Nazi Germany*, ed. E. Harvey, J. Hürter, M. Umbach and A. Wirsching (New York, 2019), 101.
30 Föllmer, *Individuality and Modernity in Berlin*, 179.
31 P. Ginsborg, 'The Family Politics of the Great Dictators', in *Family Life in the Twentieth Century*, ed. D.I. Kertzer and M. Barbagli (New Haven, CT, and London, 2003), 175.

32 L. Pine, *Nazi Family Policy, 1933–1945* (Oxford, 1997), 18.
33 P. Ginsborg, *Family Politics: Domestic Life, Devastation and Survival, 1900–1950* (New Haven, CT, and London, 2014), 380.
34 Pine, *Nazi Family Policy*, 20.
35 J. Stephenson, *Women in Nazi Society* (London, 1975), 69.
36 R. Grunberger, *A Social History of the Third Reich* (London, 1991), 263.
37 Speech by Rudolf Hess, cited from the *Völkischer Beobachter*, 13 October 1936, in N. Frei, *National Socialist Rule in Germany: The Führer State, 1933–1945* (Oxford, 1993), 165.
38 *Schwarzes Korps*, 22 September 1938.
39 G. Gerhard, *Nazi Hunger Politics: A History of Food in the Third Reich* (Lanham, MD, 2015), 34.
40 *NS-Frauenwarte*, 1935–6, Issue 16, 525.
41 L. Collingham, *The Taste of War: World War Two and the Battle for Food* (London, 2011), 354.
42 R. Proctor, *Racial Hygiene: Medicine under the Nazis* (Cambridge, MA, and London, 1988), 235.
43 Ibid., 237.
44 Ibid.
45 *NS-Frauenwarte*, 1935–6, Issue 3, 86.
46 *NS-Frauenwarte*, 1935–6, Issue 20, 652.
47 *NS-Frauenwarte*, 1935–6, Issue 9, 288.
48 N. Reagin, 'Comparing Apples and Oranges: Housewives and the Politics of Consumption in Interwar Germany', in *Getting and Spending: European and American Consumer Societies in the Twentieth Century*, ed. S. Strasser, C. McGovern and M. Judt (New York, 1998), 256.
49 N. Reagin, '*Tischkultur*: Food Choices, Cooking and Diet in Nazi Germany', in *Life and Times in Nazi Germany*, ed. L. Pine (London, 2016), 26.
50 H. Berghoff, 'Enticement and Deprivation: The Regulation of Consumption in Pre-war Nazi Germany', in *The Politics of Consumption: Material Culture and Citizenship in Europe and America*, ed. M. Daunton and M. Hilton (New York, 2001), 165–84.
51 Reagin, '*Tischkultur*', 22.
52 Ibid., 28.
53 *Völkischer Beobachter*, 11 March 1939.
54 On alcohol in Nazi Germany, see J. Lewy, 'Vice in the Third Reich? Alcohol, Tobacco and Drugs', in *Life and Times in Nazi Germany*, ed. L. Pine (London, 2016), 50–4.
55 Collingham, *The Taste of War*, 164.
56 Reagin, '*Tischkultur*', 38.
57 A. Weinreb, *Modern Hungers: Food and Power in Twentieth-Century Germany* (Oxford, 2017), 69.

58 Ibid., 86.
59 L. Pine, *Education in Nazi Germany* (Oxford, 2010), 29.
60 Bundesarchiv Berlin NS 12/825, 'Gutachten zur Übersteigerung der Anormalen-Erziehung', 25 November 1934, 4.
61 Bundesarchiv NS 48/29, 'Satzung des Vereins "Lebensborn" e.V.', 24 December 1937, 1.
62 Bundesarchiv NS 48/31, 'Bemerkungen des Reichsführer-SS zum Vortrag "Zwei Jahre Lebensborn-Arbeit" ', 7.
63 Pine, *Nazi Family Policy*, 40.
64 Bundesarchiv NS 48/31, 'Zwei Jahre Lebensborn-Arbeit', 1–13. Cited in Pine, *Nazi Family Policy*, 40.
65 Ibid.
66 'Gesetz zur Verhütung erbkranken Nachwuchses von 14 Juli 1933', *Reichsgesetzblatt*, I, 529–30.
67 Pine, *Nazi Family Policy*, 13.
68 S. Kühl, 'The Relationship Between Eugenics and the So-Called "Euthanasia Action" in Nazi Germany: A Eugenically Motivated Peace Policy and the Killing of the Mentally Handicapped During the Second World War', in *Science in the Third Reich*, ed. M. Szöllösi-Janze (Oxford, 2001), 203–4.
69 For a more detailed discussion of this, see G. Aly, P. Chroust and C. Pross, *Cleansing the Fatherland: Nazi Medicine and Racial Hygiene* (Baltimore, MD, and London, 1994), especially 22–98.
70 M. Burleigh, *Death and Deliverance: 'Euthanasia' in Germany 1900–1945* (Cambridge, 1994), 4.
71 On this, see H. Friedlander, 'The T4 Killers: Berlin, Lublin, San Saba', in *The Holocaust and History: The Known, the Unknown, the Disputed, and the Reexamined*, ed. M. Berenbaum and A. Peck (Bloomington, IN, 1998), 243–51.
72 For a more detailed discussion on these topics, see L. Pine, *Hitler's 'National Community': Society and Culture in Nazi Germany*, 2nd edn (London, 2017), 145–212.

Select bibliography

Evans, R.J. *The Coming of the Third Reich: How the Nazis Destroyed Democracy and Seized Power in Germany*. London, 2004.
Evans, R.J. *The Third Reich in Power: How the Nazis Won Over the Hearts and Minds of a Nation*. London, 2006.
Gellately, R. *Backing Hitler: Consent and Coercion in Nazi Germany*. Oxford, 2001.
Gellately, R. *The Gestapo and German Society: Enforcing Racial Policy, 1933–1945*. Oxford, 1990.
Gellately, R. *Hitler's True Believers: How Ordinary People Became Nazis*. Oxford, 2020.

Gerhard, G. *Nazi Hunger Politics: A History of Food in the Third Reich*. Lanham, MD, 2015.
Harvey, E., J. Hürter, M. Umbach, and A. Wirsching (eds). *Private Life and Privacy in Nazi Germany*. New York, 2019.
Kershaw, I. *The 'Hitler Myth': Image and Reality in the Third Reich*. Oxford, 1989.
Peukert, D.J.K. *Inside Nazi Germany: Conformity, Opposition and Racism in Everyday Life*. London, 1987.
Pine, L. *Hitler's 'National Community': Society and Culture in Nazi Germany*, 2nd edn. London, 2017.
Pine, L. (ed.). *Life and Times in Nazi Germany*. London, 2016.
Stoltzfus, N. *Hitler's Compromises: Coercion and Consensus in Nazi Germany*. New Haven, CT, and London, 2016.
Timpe, J. *Nazi-Organized Recreation and Entertainment in the Third Reich*. London, 2017.
Wachsmann, N. *KL: A History of the Nazi Concentration Camps*. London, 2016.

3

Life in Franco's Spain

Antonio Cazorla-Sánchez

The Franco regime had a very long and complex life. The dictatorship came into being in 1939, when the forces of fascism swept a continent in which both poverty and intolerance were the norm. It ended in 1975, just after the closing of the longest period of economic and social improvement in Europe's history, with democracy deeply rooted in the Western part of the continent, and when many traditional values had been deeply undermined.[1] In spite of its relative isolation and economic backwardness, Spain shared those changes with one very important exception: the nature of its political regime. This exception was not an isolated aspect of the country's life with a limited effect on the overall evolution of society. On the contrary, politics had a deep impact on the daily lives of Spaniards, making their experience in many ways unique – even more than in other contemporary dictatorships such as Portugal and Greece – in the context of post-war democratic Europe.[2] In the following pages we shall see how Spaniards and regime interacted. First, we will see the political repression applied by the dictatorship on people. Second, we will explore how popular opinion evolved. Next, we will describe the overall social changes. And last, we will analyse the political dilemmas that Spaniards faced in the last years of the regime.

A cruel peace, 1939–52

The key to understanding the evolution of Spanish society under the dictatorship is the Civil War (July 1936 to March 1939). Franco's regime emerged from the war, but so did many deep cleavages in Spain that have yet to fully close.[3] However, Spain was not simply divided simply between winners and losers. This would be a rather simplistic categorisation. No doubt, members of the regime enjoyed a monopoly of political power and well-being while the fate of their defeated counterparts could be resumed in many combinations of the following words: prison, exile, execution, social ostracism and economic penury.[4] But for the majority of the population – from those who openly supported the new regime for whatever reasons to those who secretly opposed it, and the many millions in the grey areas in between – the war had been an unwanted and unexpected traumatic experience that had brought collective pain and incertitude. For them, the experience of the war constituted a social trauma that forged a widely shared desire, or value, that 'never again' should such a confrontation take place among Spaniards.[5] In this, Spain was not dissimilar (but perhaps only a more evident case) to other Western countries that went through civil wars in the twentieth century or many societies that underwent the worst horrors of both world wars. What the Spanish case proves is that pacifism can also grow under a dictatorship.

Had Franco's regime been an inclusive, democratic one, such as those in France, Italy or the Netherlands after the Second World War, the trauma of the war could have been used to reunite the nation around a series of convenient national myths that, while betraying the historical record (such is the case of the role of the Resistance in these three countries), would have made it possible to overcome deep social fractures, at least on the surface. But this was not the intention of the Spanish dictatorship. On the contrary, the regime made the victory of a self-proclaimed true Spain over a false one the cornerstone of its political legitimacy. In this way, while peace for most Western Europeans meant a link between national unity and democracy, in Spain it entailed social segregation and dictatorship. The high priest and main beneficiary of this formula was Franco, who in this way successfully locked the political future of the country to his own lifespan. Among those who paid most dearly for this arrangement were not only the political opponents of the regime, but also those who having economic, social or even cultural grievances, were deprived of the right to express them, let alone to act to address their problems. Politics in Franco's Spain determined everybody's daily life, but for most people they only accentuated, for better or for worse, their social and economic reality.[6]

Terror commenced the first day of the Civil War and ended only after the regime's demise. It was very intense in the first years and milder and subtler in the final ones; but the threat of massive violence was present during the whole dictatorship. Franco often spoke to Spaniards about peace. It was one of the favourite topics in his speeches and the motive of two major propaganda campaigns (the rather austere Twenty Years of Peace in 1959 and the more bombastic Twenty-Five Years of Peace in 1964).[7] But when he mentioned peace, everybody understood he was talking about the threat of war and violence if his power was ever challenged.[8] In this sense too, Spain's post–Civil War peace meant something different from Europe's post–World War peace. Spain's peculiar peace meant officially forgetting and/or insulting the memory of the regime's victims, including the at least 130,000 people who had been executed (most of whom lay in unmarked mass graves), 400,000 exiles and the hundreds of thousands who, at one point or another populated the regime's prisons and camps.[9] For those people and their relatives, the regime offered only contempt. For them there were no pensions, no compensation, no pardon. Their families also suffered disproportionately the hunger and widespread misery that characterised the very long post-war period. The 'reds' and their families were officially and often socially ostracised. However, if a person was a former Francoist combatant, or victim or relative of a victim of the Republicans, the regime made sure that official recognition and material compensation ensued. However, these two very different situations, of both the clear winners and the persecuted losers, did not directly affect most of the population except in one aspect: they could not express their opinions and memories in public and they had to go along with the official narrative and realities imposed by the dictatorship. This policy was very different from the policies of reconciliation, reintegration, forgiveness and national unity followed elsewhere in Europe after the Second World War, and particularly since the 1950s.

Francoism captured public discourses by reducing civil society to a minimum. The regime limited political participation to a single party, the Falange, which controlled most of what was left of the now tightly controlled and censored media after the purging and destruction of liberal and leftist newspapers and radio stations.[10] The single exception to this policy was the Church's controlled outlets. The Church had a privileged position and power superior to that in Portugal and Italy, and perhaps similar to Dollfuss's Austria, or the brief murderous wartime regimes of Tiso's Slovakia or Pavelić's Croatia. Most civic organisations were suppressed by, intervened in by, or put under the control of, the Falange, again with those attached to the Church being the exception. The regime not only manipulated and misinformed Spaniards, but also made sure children would grow up ignorant and contemptuous of democratic and humanistic values. The school system was purged of both liberal teachers – a quarter of them suffered dismissal or lesser sanctions – and democratic ideas. Instead, loyal but generally ill-paid educators instilled ultra-Catholic and authoritarian thinking into students. This was the situation for the luckiest pupils. The regime had minimal interest in the education of the masses and accordingly invested very little in the public school system. Consequently, millions of poor children received a most cursory instruction, one that in most cases ended only after very few years of schooling or even never started. The dictatorship thus prolonged Spain's old problem of illiteracy, total or functional, that the Republic had tried to eradicate between 1931 and 1936. The main beneficiary of this situation was the Church which, catering to the affluent sectors of society, greatly expanded its network of schools, making big inroads in the then very elitist secondary education. With those policies, Francoism imposed authoritarianism, selective ignorance and class discrimination on Spanish society.[11]

This reactionary sociocultural project complemented an economic model that was both highly regressive and shockingly inefficient. At the base of this model was autarky.[12] Franco himself, who fancied that he knew about everything, including economics, was convinced that autarky would soon make Spain great again and, like Germany and Italy, capable of confronting the detested 'plutocratic' democracies of France and the UK. He continued to believe this long after the demise of his admired Axis powers, and thus autarky was not completely abandoned until 1959. From the end of the Second World War until then, while the Western world entered the long period of economic renaissance known as the Golden Age, the Spanish economy continued to decline. Autarky was a disaster that cut off Spain from world markets, hurting its most dynamic economic sectors. It impoverished the Spanish economy and in a context of officially sanctioned wage reductions condemned people to hunger. Workers' diets went back to where they had stood at the beginning of the century, and in many of the poorer sectors of society to even further back, as famine – as we shall see shortly – not known in the country since the mid-nineteenth century, came back.

Behind this flawed economic thinking was a mix of militarism and social revenge. The pillar of the post-war governments was the Army, whose leaders sincerely believed that they knew better than civilians how to run the country.[13] Their socio-economic project included permanently dominating and subjugating the working classes, both in the cities and in the countryside, which they deemed responsible for subverting the natural social order during the Republic. Saving Spain implied reducing workers' wages to a third of what they were in 1936 (agrarian salaries did not surpass their pre-war purchasing power until 1962), destroying independent unions and making sure they would not protest or go on strike again.[14] These policies became deadly, simply because poor people could not afford to buy food at real market prices.

The Civil War meant the triumph of capital over labour, and those who had the first, even if it was a modest business or some land, did much better than the rest; while those who had only their hands went hungry, and more. Approximately 200,000 Spaniards starved between the end of the Civil War and 1945. This was a unique case in Western Europe where famine in the twentieth century had been a product of defeat against a foreign power (in the case of central Europe after the First World War) or foreign occupation (in the case of France, the Netherlands or Greece under the Nazis in the Second World War). The only other example of a ruler starving his own people was that of Stalin during the grand Ukrainian famine of the early 1930s. Perhaps this is no coincidence since both Franco and Stalin did not consider the victims as their own people, but as enemies. Starvation in Spain, like in the Soviet Union, was the product of misguided economic policies, state intervention in the market, official corruption, and indifference. The rationing system in Spain was insufficient (and too corrupt) to provide the minimum amount of food to save the poor from the regime's laws, reduced wages and inept management of the food supply. Moreover, it was never intended to fully supply the population with the calories and vitamins it needed but to complement their diet. Since workers' salaries were too low, rationing could not save the poor from starvation.[15]

Rationing existed from 1939 until 1952. The intervention of basic food stuffs such as olive oil and wheat lasted well into the next decade and produced two main results: permanently high food prices and a vast black market that made the rich richer thanks to the impunity with which they conducted their corrupt deals. This money was channelled into banks and the stock market, for which the 1940s were years of big profits. Put differently, the poor's daily hunger fed the financial system. This sweet deal for capital, abetted by censorship, allowed many Spaniards not to notice that workers literally fell exhausted to the shop floor, that landless peasants died of pellagra, that their children too often died in infancy or grew sickly or too slowly, and that in any case they could not attend school because they had to help their parents to obtain some food to allow for the family's survival. This situation would last until the country's economic boom in the early 1960s. It was an experience very different from that of most European countries, where governments were democratically elected and had to respond to their citizens' demands. Unlike those countries, in Spain (and in Portugal) there was no social pact between governments, unions and employers to promote growth policies that would share their resources in a minimally equalitarian way. And therefore, Spaniards continued to live in misery for two decades after the end of their Civil War, while beyond the Pyrenees fellow Europeans started to taste the fruits of economic and social welfare, not to mention freedom, after the Second World War.

The people and the regime, 1939–59

With the near suppression of civil society, Spaniards had to deal with the power of officially sanctioned institutions. Above them all stood the Catholic Church. After having suffered the killing of nearly 7,000 clerics at the hands of the Republicans during the war, the post-war Church was in a belligerent mood, and it formed a close alliance with the dictatorship. The Church blessed Franco and his regime paid the Church, supporting it both financially and symbolically. As a result, Spaniards, regardless of their beliefs, were forced to respect and follow Catholic doctrine in both their private and public lives. People were expected to attend mass, Easter processions, take sacraments, etc. Civil marriages were annulled, divorces too, and children born of those unions were considered illegitimate. People living in free unions were forced to marry, children were baptised or had to take their first communion. In school, they had to pray, and they were forced to attend religious instruction. Nothing that people read, heard on the radio, saw in the theatre or in the cinema escaped clerical censorship. Priests and nuns were embedded in charity centres and in the Army. They became figures of authority, whose approval could help people to obtain official favours or vice versa. Spain was officially Catholic, and it would remain so until the end of the dictatorship.[16] However, in spite of the regime's and the Church's efforts, in reality, millions of Spaniards did not go to mass, or they attended only some specific ceremonies such as marriages or funerals. While they had to conform externally and be very careful about their opinions, they also had a more or less deep contempt for the institution and its representatives.

Franco created a political system that suited his own needs. Up to 1945 it had clear fascist trappings that were toned down after the defeat of the Axis power. From then on, the dictatorship would insist that it was essentially an anti-communist, Christian regime adapted to Spain's own idiosyncrasy. Political activity was in theory controlled by the single party, the Falange,

FIGURE 3.1 *General Franco in Seville, 1967.* © *Getty Images.*

which had been created in April 1937. But the power of the Falange was always marginal. Real power lay in the hands of Franco himself who, thanks to the passing of three 'prerogative laws' in 1936, 1938 and 1939, was above any other law: he was the ultimate source of authority of all the state's powers. Franco's Spain never had a constitution, but instead a few 'organic laws' that addressed the dictator's circumstantial political needs.

Franco was never a Falangist, but a reactionary opportunist who often showed contempt for the organisation that he considered (in private) to be little more than a bunch of sycophants with a penchant for violent macho attitudes. However, he saw the convenience of channelling political life at the medium and low levels through the party, while reserving the high powers of the state for the different groups that composed the regime's different political families (including the Army, Catholics, conservatives, Falangists, Carlists and technocrats). The role of the Falangists was dealing with ordinary people.[17] Their main function was to run the official unions and their associated organisations; that is, to discipline the masses. They were not popular. Falangists had a well-deserved reputation for corruption, incompetence and ruthlessness. In the case of workers, this meant to force them to accept their dreadful labour conditions and miserable salaries. Spain was officially a union-based fascist state, but the Falange-controlled single unions developed very slowly, particularly in the countryside (they did not reach the whole country until the late 1950s). In any case, the unions made little difference since they were established to impose the regime's socio-economic policies, not to protect workers who, of course, had no legal means to collectively demand reforms or improvements to their situation. The Falangists also ran the mass organisations for the youth, which never managed to enrol more than 30 per cent of children, and the very inadequate and ill-funded welfare organisations. They also controlled most of the press, which of course was nothing more than the dictator's propaganda mouthpiece. The fact that everybody knew that the press was there to propagate lies combined with the low educational levels and the general poverty, resulted in the 1940s and 1950s in Spain having one of the lowest rates of newspaper readership in the West.

Because of the disaster of autarky, the state provided Spaniards with very limited resources in terms of health, pensions, housing or education. It did not help that there was minimal taxation of the rich who, for example, paid no income tax. The Francoist state gave little but demanded a lot. Both the defeated in the war and the poor learned almost immediately that the state was no friend. The regime imposed policies that benefited capital over labour, it disciplined the latter, and it always threatened, and occasionally exercised, repression. People thus avoided (when they could) dealing with the state, or to use it only for their interests. For example, they utilised the unions' official channels to address a grievance, but they were very careful to employ

Falangist and Catholic rhetoric, and to praise Franco in their petitions. By submitting to the regime's logic and formally recognising its legitimacy, workers pressed the authorities to deliver the promises of justice that their own discourses contained. It was a classic weapon of the weak, that sometimes worked, but most times did not. Another way of manipulating the system was to look for people of influence who could help in getting a favour from the authorities. This was possible because behind the legal and institutional facade of Falangism functioned a clientelist system that worked for those with political contacts but that, at the same time, created a dependency or clientele among those at the bottom.[18]

Despite their best efforts, there were instances when people could not avoid dealing with the state. Normally this happened in their contacts with the unions and the regime's welfare system. In addition, for men, the almost unavoidable contact happened when they were drafted to serve in the armed forces for an average of two years. It was too often a daunting experience. This was not a citizens' military. The dictatorship's Army was as large as it was inefficient and corrupt. It was conceived for the internal occupation of the country, that is, to control the population, rather than to combat external aggression. Officers and NCOs treated the recruits very poorly, and physical violence was the usual response to real or perceived infringements of norms. Soldiers were very deficiently housed, dressed and fed, in part because their superiors took the best food for themselves and their families, or for side dealing. This was hardly a novelty. Franco made his first millions during the war after appropriating and selling the coffee and tobacco sent by sympathetic foreign dictators to reward his troops.[19]

Repression, hunger, corruption, inefficiency and cruelty were the trademarks of the regime, and most people resented this. But more than the dictator, they blamed his officials, the single party or even the Army. In fact, although it suffered ups and downs, Franco's personal popularity remained relatively high among large sectors of the population, and eventually rose further as the regime stabilised in the late 1940s and the worst of the economic misery eased in the 1950s. It is impossible to know exactly – there were no free opinion polls – what people felt about the dictator and what percentage of the population supported him or not but, not unlike other contemporary dictators such as Mussolini, Stalin or Hitler, historians have clear indications that Franco was more popular than his regime and that eventually his figure came to a certain degree to be detached in the popular imaginary from the worst aspects of reality and associated with the better ones.[20]

The differentiation between dictator and dictatorship in the popular imagination started during the first months of the Civil War. The image of the militant 'people' of Spain resisting fascism is as powerful as it is misleading. True, millions of Spaniards backed the Republic, but millions too supported the rebel side. But at the same time, less politically committed Spaniards just wanted the war to end as quickly as possible, and they increasingly pinned their hopes on the winning side, which by the late summer of 1937 was clearly Franco's.[21] The dictator himself was lavishly praised by the new regime's propaganda machine even before he became the rebel side's indisputable leader on 1 October 1936. The military successes of the colonial troops he commanded contributed decisively to his increased prestige. Once in control of the rebel side, the main message of the propaganda was to praise his figure as a providential one in the country's history, and the result of a divine intervention. The Church's hierarchy backed this message.

Both the dramatic circumstances – a civil war – in which the myths surrounding Franco's personality cult developed, and their sanction by official Catholicism, contributed to the dictator's image becoming increasingly separate from that of his regime. This fork between dictator and regime in popular perceptions grew in the harrowing post-war years as hunger, scarcity, economic shocks, and repression became daily realities. In those circumstances, with no external references such as a free press that could have explained the reality and checked facts, people deposited their faith in the remote man that so many sources said was good and wise, while directing their contempt at the local authorities who they could see for themselves were corrupt, negligent and cruel. As in other contemporary dictatorships, the leader was assumed not to know what terrible things his minions were doing, he was continuously misled by those who surrounded him, and it was believed that had he known what reality was, he would have righted the situation immediately and, no doubt, punished those responsible.

The cementing of Franco's popularity, which now went beyond the initial supporters of the regime, took place during the Second World War. Spain was close to becoming involved in the war several times, mostly because of Franco's ambition and negligence. When France fell in June 1940, Franco changed Spain's official position from neutrality to non-belligerence. It was an ominous gesture because this was the same disposition adopted by pro-Germany Mussolini in September 1939 prior to Italy's entry in the war. (Spain continued this position until October 1943, right after the fall of Italy.) Crucially, in October 1940, Franco and Hitler met in Hendaye (France) and fortunately for Franco – who was eager to enter the war at the last minute but wanted huge territorial gains at minimal risk – there was not an agreement. In Hitler's opinion, the Spanish dictator offered very little while asking for too much (Franco wanted Hitler to carve up France's North African empire and give it to him). Luckily too, Hitler never made good on Franco's offer to enter the war when the German dictator so decided. In June 1941, Franco again overplayed his hand by sending the Blue Division to fight alongside the Axis forces in the Soviet Union. He was fortunate once more that the Allies did not declare war on Spain for this, or for the abundant evidence of his collaboration with the Nazi war machine. He was lucky again that when the Allies counter-attacked in November 1942 in the North Africa and in July 1943 in Sicily, they decided not to intervene in Spain. When the war came to an end in May 1945, the victors condemned his regime but did not force him to step down. Shortly afterwards, the Cold War first and then the United States' new strategic interests in Spain, all but guaranteed his regime's survival.[22]

These events threatened to plunge the country into what most Spaniards dreaded the most: another war. Any military foreign intervention was certain to cause more misery to ordinary Spaniards, and perhaps would ignite another civil war. Spaniards did know that the regime's propaganda machine continuously praised the Axis and excoriated the Allies. They also had doubts about Franco's true intentions. But in the end, the reality is that Spain did not enter the war and the majority of people considered – and the propaganda machine hammered this home – that this was Franco's doing. This conviction was reinforced by the news that came from abroad. For example, Spaniards were informed of the horrors that fell on Italy after September 1943, and they were grateful that, unlike the Duce, the Caudillo had not taken the country to war and ruin. Furthermore, in the last months of the conflict, the regime adopted a balanced tone towards the Western Allies, while attacking the Soviets, and eventually it even condemned Japan. Britain preferred to maintain the Peninsula's political status quo, and in this, its Iberian ally, António de Oliveira Salazar, logically concurred (perhaps ignoring that a few years before Franco had planned to invade Portugal as soon as the UK was out of the war).[23] As soon as the Second World War ended, Germany and Italy's contribution to the rebels' victory in the Civil War was forgotten by Franco's propaganda, which now presented the Caudillo just as a good Christian warrior who had fought communism before any other leader. His only 'fault' was that he had seen the red danger and acted too early, in 1936, while the West slept or erroneously focused on fighting fascism.

The dictatorship's opportunistic turn did not fool the Allies, but it coincided with what most Spaniards wanted to believe. So, when the newly created United Nations condemned Franco's Spain, the regime was able to manipulate such ineffectual declarations and to present them to an anxious population as a threat to the country's peace. Most Spaniards rallied behind the dictator. It did not help the anti-Francoist cause that many of those United Nations declarations were put forward by the Soviet Union and/or its new satellite regimes, whose credibility as defenders of freedom was not high among the population. To see, for example, Communist Poland arguing that Franco's Spain was a threat to world peace was not only ridiculous, but also a gift to the regime's propaganda machine at a time when the Western world was increasingly adopting an anti-communist rhetoric not too dissimilar from

Spain's. In those circumstances, most Spaniards felt that, for all its shortcomings, Franco's rule was there to stay. Only the passing of the dictator, decades afterwards, would finally untangle this very complex knot. But this does not mean that during the dictatorship people ignored the depth of social cleavages and injustices in the country. It simply meant that Spain's abnormality (like Portugal's) among the Western nations was the new normality, and that there was no feasible, peaceable alternative in sight. Spain was accepted into the United Nations in 1955. Franco's Spain was never a regime fully rehabilitated internationally, but its close cooperation with the United States (even before the 1953 Treaty by which the Americans got military bases in Spain in exchange for aid), the backing of the Vatican and other Catholic states, mostly in Latin America, and the benevolent attitude of Britain first and later France, would suffice for the regime to survive.

For most Spaniards, Franco had preserved peace. This was a myth, but it helped him to extend his popular appeal beyond his hard-core supporters. The Spanish population progressively became more 'Francoicised' in the 1940s. People adjusted to a reality they could not change. They had lives to live, and most Spaniards lived their lives mostly divorced from politics, either pro- or anti-regime ones.[24] As a result, conservative, authoritarian and individualistic (or at least limiting solidarity to one's family) values made new inroads in society. People concentrated on surviving the daily terrible social and economic situation, often taking a second job. (This would have a lasting impact on Spaniards' eating habits: now people waited until leaving the first job, at 2–3 pm, to have lunch before heading back to their tasks.) At the same time, the regime largely abandoned fascist mobilisation in 1945. Not many regretted this. The Falangists kept doing their rituals and their ceremonies, most of them copied from Italian fascism (mass parades of men in uniform, cult of the dead, display of banners, singing of solemn songs, etc.). They ran the unions and the welfare services with incompetence and arrogant manners, while people who badly needed those services pretended that they respected them.

For their part, as the 1940s progressed, fewer and fewer Republican Spaniards dared to challenge the regime. Opposition politics was too dangerous for them and too costly for their families. A few thousand tried to maintain the torch only to be almost inevitably apprehended by the police, tortured, condemned to lengthy prison sentences and occasionally killed, although this became rarer as the 1940s progressed. While they fought and lost, their spouses and children lived in poverty and were continuously harassed by the police. An ill-fated attempt by the Communist Party to wage a guerrilla war in the second half of the decade ended in an abysmal and costly failure. It only managed to prolong the regime's terror in the countryside and to leave behind more militants (and policemen and soldiers) dead. In those circumstances, most militants just gave up fighting, went home and tried to keep a low profile until, they hoped, in a distant future, conditions for change would emerge.

A particular group of resisters were those who, speaking a different language from Spanish, felt that their culture was despised or simply suppressed by the regime's centralising policies and its concept that the true soul of Spain was its Castilian heritage. Those policies denied the multinational character of Spain. Accordingly, instruction in the country's other languages such as Catalan, Galician or Basque was banned and the cultural activities in those languages either forbidden or reduced to anecdotal and marginal forms. Civil society organisations that had promoted those different cultures in the liberal and Republican past were closed or taken over by sympathisers of the regime, which in the process eviscerated both their nature and many of their objectives. Dissent took refuge in private reading or writing in those languages; little else could be done. With this, Francoism appropriated the concept of Spain and associated the national identity to its own repressive and narrow concept of it. This would have lasting consequences once democracy was restored, as many felt that Spain, and not just the dictatorship, had been and continued to be the true enemy of their national identity.[25]

One last group of political dissidents were the exiles. After the war, nearly 400,000 Spaniards ended up in French territory, mostly in camps in Southern France or in Algeria. From there, tens of thousands found their way into Latin America, mainly to Mexico and Argentina. This last group was the better educated among the exiles and often did well, as they were received with open arms and allowed to continue with their professional or business careers. Those who remained in France were often less educated and suffered more. The French camps were hard places. When they were offered freedom, men were drafted into the French Army's auxiliary services or the Foreign Legion. Others were pressed to go back to Spain where a vindictive Franco awaited them. When France fell in June 1940, some 10,000 Spanish Republicans again ended up in camps, but now in the Nazi ones. (The first train of deportees from France to the camps was composed of Spanish Republicans.) Around 7,000 perished there, most of them in Mauthausen.[26] Others joined the Resistance or General Leclerc's Free French Army in North Africa and contributed to the liberation of the country. But since the Allies decided that Spain was not to be liberated, they ended up staying in France, where they built their lives, mostly around Paris, or in Toulouse and other parts of the south.

The future for most of the population inside Spain had nothing to do with any political projects. Everything was about survival or, in the best cases, material progress. For those at the bottom of society, life in the 1940s was mainly about not starving, and in the 1950s it was about managing with very little. Since the state offered next to nothing, and civil society all but disappeared, they resorted to the only institution that remained intact and at their service: the family. The concept of family then meant extended family, in which different generations and branches of the same kinship group often lived together – the housing deficit in Spain was abysmal until the 1970s – and even more frequently shared their meagre resources. When people were out of work, or the salary was insufficient, they had a pot from which to eat a hot meal at least once a day. When they lost their house or a spouse, or they married, there was always a little corner in a room, sometimes already cramped, to place a mattress for the night. This solidarity sometimes extended to some trusted neighbours or godchildren and their parents. The family group offered consolation and support when a relative was shot or put in prison, or when, as happened so often in the post-war years, a child died. This mechanism allowed people not only to survive but also, sometimes, accumulate a modest capital to start again, to rent a house on their own, buy furniture or open a small business.

Of course, such circumstances created frequent conflicts within the family group, but people had few other options. Women, who ran the day-to-day operations of the family, were essential in maintaining its precarious emotional and resource-distributing mechanisms. They could work outside the home too, but their familial obligations were many and their salaries very small. Men were supposed to be working the whole day (in those days the working week was six days) and contributing the bulk of their salary to their wives or mothers. But then, on Saturday evening and even on Sunday, they would go out with their friends to drink and forget about their daily miseries. Women, on the contrary, stayed home after work. When not attending school (for very few years), foraging for food and, in the case of girls, helping in the domestic chores, children played in the streets; if they were very lucky perhaps from time to time they obtained enough money to go to the cinema.

Another crucial mechanism for survival among the poor was resorting to the black market. The same system that facilitated the accumulation of great fortunes among the rich and well connected also allowed humble people, mainly women, to obtain a meagre income by buying or bartering products in the countryside and, after a perilous journey in which the police could apprehend them, resell their modest cargo in the cities. Only the poor suffered the regime's draconian laws against black marketeering. The other side of the coin was that in their efforts to survive they also contributed to the corruption and social inequalities of the country. The products they sold were often too expensive for other poor people to buy. Their main clients were often middle-class families who, in this way, complemented their diets. If the poor were very poor, the standard of living of the Spanish middle class in the late 1940s and 1950s was well below that of their European counterparts, except for one aspect: since workers' salaries were so low, they often could employ female servants for next to nothing. Even in their relative poverty, they still had plenty of fellow Spaniards below them. Scarcity only exacerbated social cleavages as it divided the country between those who had nothing and those who, having something, felt both privileged and consequently that they had more to lose if the regime came to an end. Misery, in sum, made Spaniards more generous in the private sphere, but at the same time more socially conservative and sceptical of the common good. It was a victory for the regime that left a lasting imprint in Spanish society.[27]

An evolving society, 1939–70

The society that emerged from the war was full of class prejudice against the poor, who were expected to remain in their current state while, at the same time, being thankful for the charity that the state, the Church and their social betters offered them. Those three institutions and groups believed that the root of social problems was the lack of morality among the poor. Accordingly, reforms should start by changing the habits and values of the culprits. In this mission the Catholic Church, with the full support of the regime, was to play a crucial role. Seeing itself as a perfect society, the Church blamed both progressive ideologies and social resentment for its suffering during the Republic and the Civil War. Therefore, it focused on imposing Catholic values on society and obtaining, if not the sincere conversion, at least the submission of the ample social sectors that had abandoned obedience to its teachings during the previous decades. Post-war Spain saw massive religious ceremonies and pilgrimages, forced marriages and baptisms, constant propaganda campaigns, censorship of the arts and in particular of books, films and plays, and even conversion missions in which whole towns were taken over by clerics during a few days. Those activities had a very limited impact on actual true conversions but set the public tone of what was admissible and what was not. The new school curriculum, whose content was vetted by the Church, had more impact. Children were taught to accept the latter's moral values as the natural and truly Spanish ones and were kept ignorant of dissenting interpretations.[28] Not surprisingly, many youngsters felt the call to priesthood. Vocations rose vigorously and stayed strong from the 1940s until the late 1960s. However, towards the end of this last decade, vocations experienced a dramatic fall while, at the same time, a massive secularisation of priests took place.[29]

One of the key sets of values reinforced by this alliance between Church and the Francoist state was sexism. Spanish women had achieved improvements in their legal and real situation during the Republic: the rights to vote and divorce, more protection against sexual and physical aggression, full rights for children born out of wedlock, well-paid careers in teaching, access to highly placed public jobs and even, very briefly, the right to abortion. Those rights were taken away and replaced by a stronger subjugation of women to men, which started as soon as they entered the school system (if they were schooled at all) as co-education was banned by the new authorities. Parts of the school curriculum differed for boys and girls (for example, the latter had specific courses to teach them house management). Women were considered legal minors again.[30] They were targets of a set of values that placed on their shoulders the weight of what morality was, which gyrated around a very narrow and repressive concept of sexuality. Women, unlike men, were expected not to feel sexual desire, to be chaste and to have no more personal goals than becoming good wives and mothers. If they wanted to go beyond that, they depended on the will of their legal tutors, their fathers or elder brothers. For most working-class and peasant women, this meant a life of hard work both at home and outside that started in infancy, followed by a strictly codified engagement, and crowned by the 'blessing' of a marriage and children. They were supposed to be stuck in unhappy or even violent

FIGURE 3.2 *General Franco and his wife at a reception to reward the parents of large families.* © *Getty Images.*

marriages. Middle-class women would escape the hardships of heavy work, but their ultimate fate was also to run their households for the happiness of their families.[31] This life and those values might not be very different from those in which other European women lived at the time, particularly in Catholic and rural countries such as Ireland or most of Italy, but what is most striking about Spain is that there was neither the possibility to criticise such policies nor to propose alternatives. Last, in Franco's Spain, like in all Western countries, homosexuals (mostly men) were legally persecuted, criminalised and both publicly and privately ridiculed.

Social values started to change very slowly in the 1950s. One reason for this was a certain modernisation of the Church's teachings, not so much in what the Spanish Church itself preached, as in the new ideas that came from Rome and from more enlightened Catholic circles, mainly in France and Germany. Spanish Catholic Action was the main means of spreading the new ideas that, among other things, gave women a bigger credit as independent thinkers and encouraged them to pursue professions (while not forgetting their 'natural' duties). At the same time, the concept that behind every social problem was a moral one was progressively replaced by a less socially prejudiced view. Crucial in this process was the role of the Workers' branch of the Catholic Action (HOAC) that by the early 1950s had become very critical of both the regime's policies and the structural fault lines of Spanish society. As we shall see, the HOAC became an indispensable actor in the reconstruction of anti-Francoist parties and unions in the 1960s and early 1970s.[32]

Another, perhaps even far greater, factor in the changes in social values was migration. Like all European countries, communist ones included, Spain experienced an enormous internal migration from the countryside to cities in the three decades that followed the end of the Second World War. By 1970, one in three Spaniards lived in a different municipality from the one of their birth. With migration from the countryside, thousands of villages disappeared and many more saw their population both shrink and become more aged. People escaped the harshness of tilling the land and the lack of services in the rural areas, mostly in the impoverished south, west and north-west of the country.[33] They went to the cities – particularly Madrid and Barcelona – and the Basque Country where an expanding industrial and services economy offered better opportunities. Old values eroded more rapidly in the cities and were replaced by new ones that were less constrained by group and family norms. The slow increase in educational levels, particularly since the 1960s, accelerated this process of cultural transformation. Women, particularly young ones, found paid jobs in the cities, and with this they acquired a new sense of empowerment that would eventually transform their own self-perception and personal expectations. But not everything was rosy. Migration was a daunting transition because the state did not provide the housing, educational and health services migrants needed. People often ended up living in shantytowns on the peripheries of the big cities. Living in the cities was also more expensive than in their original towns, and salaries were not much higher. Their children – particularly those of the landless peasants and workers who were the first to emigrate in the late 1940s and 1950s – frequently left school too soon and were thus condemned for life to low-paid jobs. The families of the small and medium-sized farmers who migrated in the 1960s in general fared better, but they still suffered the serious shortcomings of city life imposed by a negligent state.

More than two million Spaniards migrated to Europe during the 1960s, mostly to Germany, France, Switzerland and the Benelux Countries.[34] In the main, those people either went without their families or planned to return to their places of origin after a few years of intensive work and, hopefully, with some savings. This migration abroad was good business for the regime. It provided hard currency that financed the country's development. The state gave little back in exchange. The reason for this was Spain's peculiar tax and wealth distribution system. Since there was no income tax and property taxes were very low, there was little to distribute in the form of services and pensions that constitute a welfare state. In 1965, public expenditure in Spain was 15 per cent of the GDP, less than half of the OECD average, which stood at 31 per cent.[35] This is what lay behind both the lack of services in the cities and the lack of investments in the country's poor regions that provided the bulk of the migrants.

The deficit in services in the poorer and working-class areas of the cities where immigrants settled led, in the second part of the 1960s and particularly in the 1970s, to the rise of a new phenomenon that augmented the country's social capital: the creation of neighbourhood associations. These associations were tolerated by the regime as long as they maintained an apolitical appearance. However, they soon became very combative in their demands on local authorities. Francoist unelected municipal governments were very inefficient and openly corrupt, and they frequently failed to significantly improve the neighbourhoods' situations. This led to a growing political radicalisation of the associations. Quite often the leaders of those associations were left-wing Catholics (sometimes even the local parish priests and worker-priests), and other progressives who were also connected to the illegal unions and political parties that were slowly emerging. The workers' branch of Catholic Action played a crucial role in this process.[36] Left-wing militants and their persecuted organisations found protection in the HOAC and among friendly priests. This movement took inspiration in the change of the Church's relation with modern social and political problems since the Second Vatican Council (1962–5). The encyclicals by John XXIII and Paul VI stressed the need for social reforms and the defence of human rights, and by extension of democracy. In Spain, as the regime understood all too well, this meant a rejection of the dictatorship.[37]

In this new context, progressive Catholics and non-believing progressives buried old divisions and prejudices from the Civil War and started working together to bring democracy and social justice back to Spain. Nowhere was this collaboration more evident than in the neighbourhood associations and in the banned unions. Catholic language also was very appropriate for protesting legally since it confronted the officially Catholic regime with its own shortcomings: if the Church in Rome spoke of social justice and freedom, how could the Catholic Franco regime refuse both to Spaniards? The growing distance between ordinary Catholics and the dictatorship moved up into the ranks of the Spanish Church as Pope Paul VI started to appoint progressive bishops when the old pro-dictatorship ones retired. By the early 1970s, the Franco regime knew that a large section of the official Church wanted democracy restored. It could persecute Catholic militants, arrest priests and even harass the most outspoken bishops, but it could go no further than that without infuriating Rome.[38]

Neighbourhood associations and other tolerated civic associations such as cultural associations, housewives' associations or even groups of parents with children with disabilities, became schools of democracy.[39] There, unlike in official institutions, people voted directly on who was going to manage the organisation. The same happened in the outlawed unions and parties. This created a set of alternative views of society that were not only beyond the regime's control, but also opposed to it. In those associations, people with different backgrounds met and discovered that, contrary to what the dictatorship said, democracy could work for Spaniards. Furthermore, people had already noticed that democracy had worked very well in the rest of Western Europe, where its citizens were not only freer, but also more prosperous than in Spain. They could see this reality in films, on television, in their trips abroad (to work, to study or as tourists) and in their interactions with the millions of foreign visitors who came to Spain every year, and whose more relaxed habits and better socio-economic situation was evident to all. Most Spaniards understood that the country's political system and its relative socio-economic backwardness were an exception, and many wondered if that could be changed, and how. A growing number of Spaniards, mainly the young ones, concluded this would never be achieved under the dictatorship's rules or by reform. This, in part at least, explains the growing opposition to the regime among university students, who by the 1960s were widely mobilised (and repressed) in their quest to overthrow Francoism.[40] They were joined in the early 1970s, by ample, but still minority sectors of Spanish society, such as workers, civic activists, artists and members of the liberal professions who had become hostile to the regime. Many among those groups embraced the ideas of the New Left, usually in the form of radical Marxism.

While a minority was embracing opposition politics, a large majority lived a new reality: consumerism. This was possible because of the sudden, spectacular economic growth that started in Spain in 1961. The reason for this was the definitive abandonment of autarky in 1959 with the adoption by the government of the OECD-sponsored Stabilisation Plan. Economic liberalisation attracted massive foreign investment to a country where salaries were very low and workers were tightly controlled. In addition, migrants to Europe and tourists to Spain poured huge amounts of hard currency into the national economy. Spain finally benefited, about fifteen years late but ultimately very strongly, from Europe's long post-war economic miracle.[41] But the redistribution of wealth via taxation and services that most Europeans enjoyed was still greatly curtailed in Spain by the regime's very regressive fiscal and social policies. This meant that behind the Spanish version of the miracle stood also a disproportionate economic exploitation of the poor who still had meagre incomes and very limited public assistance to help them out.[42]

In any case, with an annual growth average in GDP of nearly 8 per cent, the general population, first the middle classes and, later in the decade, the working classes, experienced a general increase in their purchasing power not seen since the Republic. This dramatic economic expansion allowed Spaniards to acquire the new products and to adopt the habits that characterised the post-war European consumer boom: cars, home improvements, electric appliances, music, a more protein-rich diet, new hygienic habits, paid holidays, etc. People now watched TV programmes at home, some of which were made abroad and showed strange values, often at odds with traditional Catholic morality. Spaniards now mingled with tourists on the beaches and, as a result, men started to wear shorts and women bikinis.[43] Young people also quickly adopted the new musical tastes – the Beatles first toured Spain in 1965 – clothes, language and, in many cases, sexual habits that were very far from the traditional ones. Young women, now better educated than ever before, also developed a new consciousness about their rights and a minority learned about feminism. In sum, society was becoming modern and the debates about culture or gender relations that took place in Spain were not much different from those in other strongly Catholic, albeit democratic, countries such as Italy or Ireland, where there was also moral censorship in the media and deep intergenerational cultural differences. After all these socio-economic and cultural changes, by the mid-1970s, Spain was almost a normal Western European country.[44] But there was still one very significant difference: Spain was still a dictatorship in the middle of a mostly free continent.

The end: between fear and freedom, 1970–5

European youth took to the streets in 1968 to demand change, but they meant many, often contradictory, things by this. In Spain, however, these demands meant one very clear thing: opposition to the dictatorship. In that year, the Basque ETA terrorist group committed its first deliberate murder. The phenomenon of terrorism was hardly unique to Franco's Spain. It happened almost simultaneously in other European countries such as the UK, Italy, Germany and France. The Spanish dictatorship was very harsh in repressing it, but not necessarily much more so than the British government. However, the effect of ETA's actions went beyond that of the other contemporary terrorist groups. This is because ETA contributed to both the poisoning of Spanish public life and to accelerating the falling apart of the dictatorship. ETA's actions commenced when Franco's personal prestige among the Spanish population was at its highest. But his reaction to this and other challenges to his rule presented by opposition forces started a steady decline in his popularity on the one hand and the growing perception that his regime was increasingly adrift and bound to disappear once the dictator died, on the other.

Born in 1892, in the late 1960s, Franco was approaching 80 years old. By then he had built a public image of a paternal figure that looked after Spain's newly found prosperity. Most Spaniards saw him as a benevolent, but also misinformed ruler.[45] Beyond student circles, sectors of the working class, intellectuals and peripheral nationalist groups, opposition was very weak. At most, not even a third of the total population was anti-Francoist, but they were either silent or very cautious about their opinions. What is clearer is that Franco's prestige was much higher than that of his regime. The Falange had lost almost any capacity to mobilise the population, which was mostly apolitical. This does not mean that people had no social grievances, opinions and memories of the past that contradicted the official version of events. People remembered but preferred both not to share their ideas beyond their closest circle of family and friends and not to take part in politics, either in favour of the regime or against it. The regime's decomposition was appearing even at the top. There were open divergences among the elites that had permeated to the public. Corruption and cronyism (in which some members of the Franco family were involved), which people suspected or experienced in person, were rife.

For most Spaniards, life was better than ten years before, but still it was hard. When people protested – and students and workers protested more and more frequently – and ignored the official mechanisms set by the Falange to control them, the authorities' response was force. This was effective in the short term, but it undermined one of the main pillars of Francoism's self-proclaimed legitimacy: its capacity to maintain peace. When ETA attacked and the police reacted with extreme violence, often against innocents or just mere sympathisers of Basque independence, most Spaniards sided with the police but at the same time wondered if their own future offered more violence. When students protested and the police beat them, ordinary citizens had more doubts about the authorities' response. And when workers or neighbours from poor areas protested and they were beaten, incarcerated or dismissed, most people sided with the workers.[46] According to the very imperfect popular opinion data from the period, more and more people were becoming attracted to the side of political liberalisation. However, to the growing dissent in the country the dictatorship offered nothing but violence; and this was something that made most Spaniards very nervous.[47]

By 1973 Franco's health was failing fast. He suffered from Parkinson's disease and, as Spaniards could see on television, his hand trembled and his speech became increasingly slurred. Exhausted, that June the dictator promoted his long-time right-hand man, Admiral Luis Carrero Blanco, to the position of prime minister. ETA killed him in December. Uncertainty about the future grew even stronger both within the regime and among the general population. Franco's appointed successor, Prince Juan Carlos de Borbón, was mostly unknown and unloved by some of the regime's main supporters, particularly among the Falangists. The sense of the end of an epoch increased when, in April 1974, the Portuguese regime fell to a military coup that restored democracy. In December the same happened to the other last Western dictatorship, Greece. To add more misery and uncertainty, the economic crisis unleashed in the Western world suddenly questioned the Francoist economic model (and ended the post-war European Golden Age), as unemployment and inflation spiralled. In response, workers' unrest in the form of strikes grew to dimensions not experienced in Spain since the Republic. By then, the official unions had been widely infiltrated at their lower levels by opposition members and employers were negotiating directly with those genuine workers' representatives and bypassing the Falangist bureaucrats. In these circumstances, the opposition started to coordinate forces and to establish contacts with the reformers inside the regime. Prince Juan Carlos, very subtly, did the same. For its part, the United States encouraged change, albeit limited to a partial restoration of political diversity and not to a full democracy.[48]

In this complex and often confusing situation came a rapid succession of dramatic events. In September 1975, Franco's regime executed five members of the opposition accused of terrorist acts. Whether they agreed or not, Spaniards were anguished. Violence was again between them and the future, and this time Franco, who had confirmed the death sentences, was clearly responsible. The executions were met with a widespread popular, and even governmental, rejection in most Western countries. The regime was more isolated than since the early 1950s. Furthermore, Franco fell gravely ill in

October. Taking advantage of this, in early November Morocco launched a military–civil march to occupy the Spanish colony of the Western Sahara. The possibility of another war, in this case foreign, loomed on the immediate horizon. Franco died on 20 November 1975. According to a poll never made public, about half of Spaniards felt saddened. The rest had a variety of opinions. But contrary to what many, inside and outside Spain expected, there was no violence. Nor was there a foreign war as Spain ceded the Western Sahara to Morocco. Juan Carlos became king and, helped both by able insiders and encouraged by France and Germany, he started a relatively swift process of reform that, in June 1977, resulted in the first democratic elections in the country since February 1936. The centre-right and the centre-left forces won those elections with a landslide majority. In December 1978 Spain had a new constitution, the first since December 1931. In the meantime, government and opposition forces negotiated reforms, while most Spaniards indicated that they wanted a better future without violence. They had rejected both the calls from the regime's hardliners to support the dictatorship and those from the sectors of the opposition that preached revolution. Voting for reforms and for moderate parties, normal people told the political elites what the margin for manoeuvre was. A consensus around peace and freedom had prevailed over radical or populist discourses. Despite the violent practices by both a still-authoritarian tainted police and terrorist groups, Spaniards found that peace and freedom signalled their way to a better future. They had many memories and opinions to tell now that they were free from their terrible past.

Spaniards entered a new chapter of their history with the political transition to democracy. But the people still faced very serious problems. The international economic crisis that started in 1974 hit Spain very hard. Both inflation and unemployment were rampant. One million migrants came back from elsewhere in Europe, after they lost their jobs, to a country that was not prepared to receive them. On top of that, terrorism, instead of declining, grew in its deadly intensity. For ETA, the worse the situation was in Spain, all the better for its independence cause. Democracy had many enemies in the Army and the state apparatus. However much besieged by very deep socio-economic woes, terrorism and the barely hidden evidence of right-wing military conspiracies, most Spaniards hoped for a better, freer life.

Notes

1   T. Judt, *Postwar: A History of Europe Since 1945* (New York, 2005).
2   An overview in A. Cazorla Sánchez, *Fear and Progress: Ordinary Lives in Franco's Spain, 1939–1975* (Chichester, 2010).

3   P. Aguilar Fernández, *Memory and Amnesia: The Role of the Spanish Civil War in the Transition* (New York, 2002). Also, A. Cazorla, 'Democracy and the Legacies of Extremism', in *Ruptura: The Impact of Nationalism and Extremism on Daily Life in the Spanish Civil War, 1936–1939*, ed. C. Hernández Burgos (Brighton, 2020), 235–54.

4   M. Richards, *A Time of Silence: Civil War and the Culture of Repression in Franco's Spain, 1936–1945* (New York, 1998).

5   A. Cazorla Sánchez, 'Surviving Franco's Peace: Spanish Popular Opinion During the Second World War', *European History Quarterly* 32, no. 3 (2002): 391–411.

6   F. Sevillano, *La cultura de guerra del 'nuevo Estado' franquista: Enemigos, héroes y caídos de España* (Madrid, 2017).

7   A. Castro and J. Díaz (eds), *XXV Años de Paz franquista: Sociedad y cultura en España hacia 1964* (Madrid, 2017).

8   A. Cazorla Sánchez, *Franco: The Biography of the Myth* (Abingdon and New York, 2013).

9   P. Preston, *The Spanish Holocaust: Inquisition and Extermination in Twentieth-Century Spain* (New York and London, 2012).

10 J. Matthews (ed.), *Spain at War: Society, Culture, and Mobilization, 1936–44* (London, 2019).

11 M. Richards, *After the Civil War: Making Memory and Re-making Spain Since 1936* (Cambridge, 2013).

12 J. Catalan, *La economía española y la Segunda Guerra Mundial* (Barcelona, 1995).

13 A. Cazorla-Sánchez, 'Family Matters: Ministerial Elites and the Articulation of the Francoist Dictatorship', *Portuguese Journal of Social Science* 3, no. 2 (2004): 73–90.

14 J. Babiano Mora, *Paternalismo industrial y disciplina fabril en España (1938–1958)* (Madrid, 1998).

15 M. Ángel Almodóvar, *El hambre en España: una historia de la alimentación* (Madrid, 2003).

16 W.J. Callahan, *The Catholic Church in Spain, 1875–1998* (Washington DC, 2000).

17 C. Molinero, *La captación de las masas: política social y propaganda en el régimen franquista* (Madrid, 2005).

18 A. Cazorla Sánchez, *Las políticas de la victoria: la consolidación del Nuevo Estado franquista, 1938–1953* (Madrid, 2000).

19 Á. Viñas, *Sobornos: De cómo Churchill y March compraron a los generales de Franco* (Barcelona, 2016).

20 O. Figes, *The Whisperers: Private Life in Stalin's Russia* (New York, 2007); I. Kershaw, *The 'Hitler Myth': Image and Reality in Nazi Germany* (Oxford, 1987); L. Passerini, *Mussolini immaginario: storia di una biografia, 1915–1939* (Bari, 1991).

21 J. Cervera Gil, *Madrid en Guerra: la ciudad clandestina, 1936–1939* (Madrid, 2000).

22 D.W. Pike, *Franco and the Axis Stigma* (Basingstoke, 2008).
23 R. Wigg, *Churchill and Spain: The Survival of the Franco Regime, 1940–45* (Abingdon and New York, 2005).
24 A. Cazorla-Sánchez, 'Beyond They Shall Not Pass: How the Experience of Violence Re-Shaped Political Values in Early Franco Spain', *Journal of Contemporary History* 40, no. 3 (2005): 503–20.
25 F. Molina Aparicio, ' "La reconstrucción de la nación": Homogeneización cultural y nacionalización de masas en la España franquista (1936–1959)', *Historia y Política* 38 (2017): 23–56.
26 D.W. Pike, *Spaniards in the Holocaust: Mauthausen, the Horror on the Danube* (Abingdon, 2014).
27 A. López Pina and E. López Aranguren, *La cultura política de la España de Franco* (Madrid, 1976).
28 C.P. Boyd, *Historia Patria: Politics, History, and National Identity in Spain, 1875–1975* (Princeton, NJ, 1997).
29 A. Cazorla-Sanchez, 'A Different Path? National Catholicism, Laicization and Dechristianization in Spain, 1939–1975', in *The Sixties and Beyond: Dechristianization in North America and Western Europe, 1945–2000*, ed. N. Christie and M. Gauvreau (Toronto, 2013), 351–66.
30 M. del Rosario Ruiz Franco, *¿Eternas menores? Las mujeres en el franquismo* (Madrid, 2007).
31 A.G. Morcillo, *True Catholic Womanhood: Gender and Ideology in Franco's Spain* (DeKalb, IL, 2000).
32 B. López García, *Aproximación a la historia de la HOAC, 1946–1981* (Madrid, 1995).
33 J.L. Leal, J. Leguina and J.M. Naredo. *La agricultura en el desarrollo capitalista español, 1940–1975* (Madrid, 1975).
34 G. Díaz-Plaja, *La condición del emigrante: los trabajadores españoles en Europa* (Madrid, 1974).
35 M. Crespo Garrido, 'La historia del impuesto sobre la renta de las personas físicas en España a través de sus dos siglos de existencia', *Documento de trabajo, Serie A, no. 2* (Madrid: Universidad de Alcalá, Escuela Universitaria de Turismo, 2002), 1–34.
36 R. Pàmpols, L. Anoro, J. Farras, A. Nolan and P.H. Kolvenbach, *Curas obreros: entre la Iglesia y el Reino – Evaluación, perspectivas* (Barcelona, 1987).
37 M. Ortíz Heras and D.A. González (eds), *De la cruzada al desenganche: la Iglesia española entre el franquismo y la transición* (Madrid, 2011).
38 A. Brassloff, *Religion and Politics in Spain: The Spanish Church in Transition, 1962–96* (New York, 1998).
39 P.B. Radcliff, *Making Democratic Citizens in Spain: Civil Society and the Popular Origins of the Transition, 1960–78* (Basingstoke, 2011).
40 M. Ángel Ruiz Carnicer, *El Sindicato Español Universitario (SEU): la socialización política de la juventud española en el franquismo* (Madrid, 1996).

41 L. Enrique Alonso and F. Conde, *Historia del consumo en España: una aproximación a sus orígenes y primer desarrollo* (Madrid, 1994).

42 D. Casado, *La pobreza en la estructura social de España* (Madrid, 1976).

43 S.D. Pack, *Tourism and Dictatorship: Europe's Peaceful Invasion of Franco's Spain* (Basingstoke, 2006).

44 N. Townson (ed.), *Spain Transformed: The Late Franco Dictatorship, 1959–1975* (Basingstoke, 2007).

45 Cazorla Sánchez, *Franco*.

46 X. Domènech, *Clase obrera, antifranquismo y cambio político: Pequeños grandes cambios, 1956–1969* (Madrid, 2008).

47 R. López Pintor, *La opinión pública española del franquismo a la democracia* (Madrid, 1982).

48 E. Lemus, *Estados Unidos y la Transición española. Entre la Revolución de los Claveles y la Marcha Verde* (Madrid, 2011).

Select bibliography

Aguilar Fernández, P. *Memory and Amnesia: The Role of the Spanish Civil War in the Transition*. New York, 2002.

Boyd, C.P. *Historia Patria: Politics, History, and National Identity in Spain, 1875–1975*. Princeton, NJ, 1997.

Callahan, W.J. *The Catholic Church in Spain, 1875–1998*. Washington DC, 2000.

Cazorla Sánchez, A. *Fear and Progress: Ordinary Lives in Franco's Spain, 1939–1975*. Chichester, 2010.

Morcillo, A.G. *True Catholic Womanhood: Gender and Ideology in Franco's Spain*. DeKalb, IL, 2000.

Pack, S.D. *Tourism and Dictatorship: Europe's Peaceful Invasion of Franco's Spain*. Basingstoke, 2006.

Pike, D.W. *Spaniards in the Holocaust: Mauthausen, the Horror on the Danube*. Abingdon, 2014.

Preston, P. *The Spanish Holocaust: Inquisition and Extermination in Twentieth-Century Spain*. New York and London, 2012.

Radcliff, P.B. *Making Democratic Citizens in Spain: Civil Society and the Popular Origins of the Transition, 1960–78*. Basingstoke, 2011.

Richards, M. *A Time of Silence: Civil War and the Culture of Repression in Franco's Spain, 1936–1945*. New York, 1998.

Townson, N. (ed.). *Spain Transformed: The Late Franco Dictatorship, 1959–1975*. Basingstoke, 2007.

Wigg, R. *Churchill and Spain: The Survival of the Franco Regime, 1940–45*. Abingdon and New York, 2005.

4

Salazar's Portugal

Living 'by habit' in an authoritarian regime

António Costa Pinto and Duncan Simpson

In 1938, António de Oliveira Salazar, the de facto leader of the self-styled dictatorial Estado Novo (New State), told one of his foreign admirers, the Maurrassian Henry Marris, that his aim was 'to make Portugal live by habit'.[1] By this he meant that the Portuguese were to be realigned – if necessary, by force – with their 'genuine' socio-historical trajectory, as defined by the conservative authoritarian regime in direct reaction to a century of 'foreign-imported' liberalism. Though the expression is often taken as a mere bon mot, Salazar would in fact prove remarkably successful at achieving his aim. The Estado Novo arguably came closer than any of the European dictatorships born in the interwar years to embodying the ideal type of an 'organic' society based on the affirmation of traditional hierarchies, the pervasive imposition of a conservative social and moral 'order', and the political demobilisation of the population. For over four decades, Portuguese society was effectively forced to 'live by habit'.

This chapter highlights the institutional mechanisms and sociopolitical structures that made this possible and examines their practical effects on the daily lives of individual citizens. It focuses on the main, intertwined processes that fashioned everyday life in Salazar's Portugal. The first is the regime's ability to build on the predisposition of Portuguese society in the first third of the twentieth century, namely as an essentially rural, poverty-stricken national community marked by deeply entrenched local systems of power relations.

FIGURE 4.1 *Salazar giving a speech.* © *Getty Images.*

The second consists in the regime's apparatus of repression and ideological inculcation, which ensured the persistence of an immutable social 'order' and conditioned the possibility of any coordinated, large-scale opposition movement. Finally, there was also a measure of 'normalisation' of Salazarist rule among the population, which gradually assimilated the institutions of the Estado Novo as the natural framework of their daily lives. Studying the experience of everyday life in Salazar's Portugal requires a brief preliminary analysis of the regime's repression and co-optation institutions and its value system.

The Estado Novo and its repressive and co-optation institutions

Portugal experienced a right-wing dictatorship that lasted from 1926, the year in which a military *coup d'état* overthrew the First Republic, until 25 April 1974, when the dictatorship was overthrown by another military coup. The first years of the dictatorship were of crises, revolts and military conspiracies and movements led by republican military officers calling for the restoration of liberal order; however, at the governmental level, a more cohesive group of conservative generals consolidated around General Óscar Carmona, who was elected president in a fake plebiscite in 1928.[2] In the wake of a major financial crisis, António de Oliveira Salazar was named finance minister, subsequently gaining a wide range of powers over the other ministries. Salazar was a conservative Catholic politician and university professor who remained Portugal's dictator until he was incapacitated in 1968.[3] One of the first political institutions created by the new regime was the single party, the National Union, which was legally established in 1930 as an 'anti-party party' uniting all the civilian forces that supported the new regime.[4] In 1933, a new constitution declared Portugal a 'unitary and corporatist republic', in which the liberal and corporatist principles of representation were balanced. The former, however, were eliminated through subsequent legislation, whilst the latter were limited to the point of insignificance. Institutionalised during the 'era of fascism', Salazar's Estado Novo survived the Second World War and a substantial part of the Cold War.

The 1933 Constitution retained a directly elected head of state and a parliament to which deputies were elected from a single list prepared by the National Union, and introduced a corporatist chamber. The result was a dictatorship headed by a prime minister and a national assembly dominated by the National Union through non-competitive elections. To avoid any loss of power, even to a parliament dominated by the government party, the executive was made almost completely autonomous. Censorship eliminated any suggestion of political conflict and censors devoted their attention to the left-wing opposition as well as to the fascist minority led by Rolão Preto.[5] The political police was reorganised and used with remarkable rationale. All this was done from above, and with little fascistic demagoguery. It was a process that depended more on generals and colonels than on lieutenants, and more on the Interior Ministry than on 'the mob'. By 1934, liberalism had been eliminated and the old republican institutions replaced.

With the consolidation of the dictatorship, political repression came under the auspices of the political police, the Vigilance and State Defence Police (PVDE), which was formed in 1933 by the merger of police forces inherited from the military dictatorship. With a strong military presence from the outset, the PVDE received technical assistance from the Italian Fascist regime and established a network of informants. In later years, the PVDE would twice be rebranded for cosmetic reasons – in 1945 as the International and State Defence Police (PIDE), in an effort to overcome associations with the 'era of fascism', and in 1969 as the Directorate-General of Security (DGS), in the context of the post-Salazar 'Marcelist Spring'. Despite these name changes, Salazar's political police force maintained a constant presence and was not abolished until the restoration of democracy in 1974.[6] Whilst formally under the control of the Interior Ministry, its independence increased and it dominated the investigation and presentation of cases to the political courts.

The political police became the spine of the system of repression, and was responsible for arresting, torturing and, occasionally, murdering the regime's opponents. In addition to imprisonment, the dictatorship also gave itself the legal tools to purge the civil service, allowing it to remove all civil servants who expressed opposition to the government 'either in the course of their duties or in their private life'. There were several such purges, particularly in the aftermath of legal and clandestine demonstrations. From 1931, those seeking employment in the civil service had to make a declaration involving 'the active repudiation of communism and of all subversive ideals'.[7]

Following the consolidation of the dictatorship in the second half of the 1930s, some characteristics of political repression remained constant throughout the duration of the Estado Novo: political repression affected both pro-democratic activist and organised clandestine groups, in particular the Portuguese Communist Party (PCP). There is a strong correlation between the waves of anti-dictatorship political activism and subsequent repression. According to the report published by the semi-official commission created in the 1970s, from 1932 to 1945, 13,663 individuals were detained or imprisoned for political reasons.[8]

The Estado Novo experienced some institutional alterations with the end of the Second World War, and periods of 'limited pluralism' within the regime were permitted during election campaigns, when opponents of the dictatorship were allowed to operate legally and media censorship was relaxed. The political amnesties that had been granted since the 1930s were now made more extensive. In 1945, the regime established the exceptional application of habeas corpus; however, the political police's authority was strengthened as its monopoly over the trials and 'security measures' continued to allow them to prolong imprisonment indefinitely.[9]

Salazar was replaced by Marcello Caetano in 1968.[10] The new leader reformulated some of the regime's institutions and allowed a relaxation of censorship and political repression during the first year of his premiership and the opposition leader, Mário Soares, and others were authorised to return from exile. However, by 1969, after non-free and non-competitive elections had been held, it was clear that Salazar's successor had set out on a process of 'liberalisation without democratisation'. Regardless of other institutional changes introduced in the late 1960s, there was a continuity in the succession of conjunctures of an increase of 'limited pluralism', namely during 'election' periods, followed by waves of repression. One example is the presidential electoral campaign in 1958, when the dissident General Humberto Delgado obtained significant results, illustrating some disaffection toward the dictatorship from urban segments of Portuguese society. Here, the Portuguese case is an example of how dictatorships within the framework of an 'economy of terror' are able to achieve an optimum result. As Hermínio Martins has pointedly argued in his seminal analysis of Salazarist repression, 'with a small number of political murders and arrests [. . .] it [. . .] succeeded in politically atomising the underlying population and paralysing the elite opposition'.[11]

The value system: 'God, Fatherland, Family, and Work'

The selective nature of censorship reflected the 'organic' ideal of a conflict-free society. Because conflict had theoretically been abolished, nothing was published that might testify to its existence. The censors were ruthless when it came to compulsory 'social peace'. The regime did not ban or systematically dissolve opposition publications – they survived throughout the 1930s and beyond – but they reached only an isolated or reduced intellectual readership that was allowed to engage in debates on such themes as the social significance of art for example, as long as such debates stayed strictly inside Lisbon's cafés and well away from the working class. Salazar did not have to worry about his rural and provincial bastions because he trusted traditional structures, such as the Church, notables and the bureaucracy to ensure social control. As he put it, 'politically speaking, only what the public knows to exist, exists'.[12]

Salazarist ideology was based on the four-part doctrine of 'God, Fatherland, Family, and Work', propagated through various instruments of ideological inculcation. It shaped teachers' lives in particular. Mandatory school textbooks were issued and special classroom decorations were created, including the affixing of crucifixes and portraits of Salazar and the incumbent president of the republic. The values of resignation and obedience, as well as the concepts of an 'organic' and politics-free society, dominated primary-school teaching. Christianisation was another official obsession that affected everything from classroom decorations to school rituals.[13] The influence of traditional Catholicism and the Church both limited fascistisation in the 1930s and increasingly came to represent the dictatorship's most powerful weapons.[14] When the regime's ideological vitality began to fade after 1945, the vitality of the Catholic organisations took over. In the early 1940s, Catholic Action organisations had almost 70,000 members, mostly in the youth organisations; by 1956, its membership had risen to 100,000.[15]

Salazar also tenaciously consolidated and 'popularised' the idea of a 'national regeneration'.[16] This idea was based on the colonies, the empire, national independence and the discoveries that had made Portugal small in Europe, but large globally. The reconciliation between traditional Catholicism and corporatism – a 'national tradition' nearly destroyed by 'imported' liberalism and secularisation – also became important elements of this vision. Catholicism was linked with the nation's formation, whilst rituals and official discourse reinforced Portugal's medieval birth in the reconquest from the Moors. The movement to 'reinvent the past' experienced an effective qualitative leap. School socialisation, cultural propaganda and a policy of national monument restoration proceeded apace. Any memory of Moorish culture and cultural diversity (already weak in any case – even in the south) was silenced. The north – in particular the town of Guimarães, capital of the medieval kingdom – was upheld as the 'Christian cradle of nationhood'. The preservation of national monuments led to the reconstruction of 'Christian reconquest' symbols, with the restoration of castles and military fortresses. The 'heroes' of the nation's founding or the maritime conquests were mythologised graphically, cinematographically and – literally – monumentally. The regime used all the propaganda of the 'age of the masses' to promote this new vision of the nation.[17] In addition the National Propaganda Secretariat (SPN), founded in 1932, sought to promote an official political culture for the masses and the elites, restoring (or building) most of the national monuments, introducing popular 'historical' cinema, and 'reinventing' Portuguese folklore.[18] Official competitions for 'the most Portuguese village in Portugal', for example, aimed to 'develop in the Portuguese the cult of tradition'. These competitions expressed the Estado Novo's traditionalist nationalism. The village was seen as a microcosm of a traditional conflict-free society, based on harmonious social relations between God-fearing individuals who were immune to urban vices.[19] Such propagandistic rhetoric, however, masked the altogether different experience of daily life for the bulk of the population, particularly in rural areas.

The politics of subsistence in rural Portugal

For most of the duration of the Estado Novo, the everyday experience of the majority of the population was marked by rurality. Between 1930 and 1950, half of the active population, both male and female, worked in the primary sector. Only in 1960, as Portugal entered the logic of Kuznetsian modern economic growth, did the number show any sign of diminishing (43 per cent), although to a level still abnormally high in the Western European context.[20] The overwhelming majority were landless agricultural labourers who sold their labour to large landowners, in particular in the extensive latifundia region of the Alentejo (roughly the southern half of Portugal), or small landowners or land-renters, many of whom were also forced to seasonally migrate to the latifundia in order to complement their meagre incomes. The large corpus of neorealist novels published from the late 1930s onwards provides a graphic, documentary-like insight into their living conditions.[21] Everyday life for the common rural dweller was particularly bleak, limited in effect to mere subsistence. Among its many practical effects, poverty reflected in malnourishment, rudimentary clothing, high natality rates and deficient housing conditions. In 1970, 61 per cent of housing in the northern district of Bragança still had no running water, electricity or bathroom facilities.[22] The rural population also suffered particularly from the persistent state of nationwide under-education, reflected in the high illiteracy rates (42 per cent in 1950). Even as the number of schools increased in the 1960s, and as compulsory attendance was raised from three to six years, the experience of schooling represented 'for the vast majority an episode limited in time', 'burdensome' and 'interspersed by other urgencies (work, support in domestic tasks) that interfered with regular class attendance'.[23] Rural communities continued to form a self-contained world, rooted in superstition, traditional values and the pervading influence of the Catholic Church – including through the 'Christianisation' of school curricula in 1936.[24] Poverty, however, was not

FIGURE 4.2 *Street scene in Torres Vedras, Portugal, 1959.* © *Getty Images.*

only the result of unequal land distribution, but also of deeply entrenched mechanisms of social control at the local level.

For the average rural labourer, everyday life meant being trapped in a rigidly hierarchical social order whose defining features long predated the existence of the Estado Novo – though the dictatorship, as we shall see, worsened their effects on the small peasantry. In this system, which in its modern form had taken shape in the final decades of the liberal constitutional monarchy (1834–1910),[25] rural labourers were dependent on the goodwill of locally prominent individuals (or *caciques*) for subsistence. As dispensers of favours, local large landowners, political individualities (at the municipal *Junta de Freguesia* level) and clergymen, who usually cultivated close relations between one another, could enable or deny the concession of credit, access to land and to work itself. In return for such favours, the small peasantry were expected to accept their servile condition and, at election time, cast their votes in favour of their respective patrons, in accordance with the logic of political clientelism.[26] The First Republic (1910–26), in spite of its positivist rhetoric and equalitarian ideals, prolonged the existence of traditional local power networks not only by limiting the franchise,[27] but also by maintaining systems of electoral clientelism of its own and ultimately keeping decision-making in the hands of a small group of politicians in Lisbon.[28] By the time Salazar had consolidated his position as undisputed leader of the Estado Novo in 1933, the bulk of the population had long been trapped in the mental prison of rural subsistence and the asymmetrical power relations between client and patron, which all but removed them from any potential role as autonomous political actors.[29]

In a political regime whose ideological precepts included the glorification of country life, 'honourable' poverty, and work as a form of sacrificial redemption conducive to the 'moral regeneration' of the nation,[30] the condition of the rural masses was unlikely to improve. The Estado Novo in fact reinforced the established hierarchical structures through a combination of legal and administrative measures.[31] These included the drastic reduction of the franchise, which excluded landless rural labourers from the electoral process at both the local and national levels. As a consequence, their sole source of leverage in the unequal relation with local patrons effectively ceased to exist.[32] Ever more frequently reduced to offering bribes or free labour in return for favours or assistance in negotiating their way through the increasingly complex bureaucratic system, their general state of dependency intensified.[33] A further complicating factor was the fact that the functionaries of the municipal *Juntas de Freguesia* tended not to operate according to the Weberian rational-bureaucratic logic in their relation with the rest of the community, instead pursuing their personal benefit whenever public and private interests conflicted.[34] Even more important in terms of its negative effects on the daily lives of the small peasantry was the fact that at the core of the Estado Novo's approach to peripherical powers lay the co-optation of the local oligarchy within the state's gradually expanding reach into country life, whether through the expansion of the public administration, the local structures of the National Union – which has aptly been defined as 'an organisation of provincial caciquism'[35] – and the gradual deployment of the corporatist apparatus.[36] Local patrons and influential notables were successfully integrated into the state's administration and institutions, whose mechanisms they then used to continue to manoeuvre the contest of interests and clientelist exchanges, in turn strengthening 'the power of the local elites over the small peasantry and rural labourers'.[37]

Faced with such asymmetrical relations of power, rural dwellers were left with few options to break out of their position as social subordinates. Most simply submitted to the established social order, occasionally engaging in small acts of daily resistance. These tentative efforts to oppose the status quo were limited to the infra-political realm, that is, in James C. Scott's definition, to 'the vague cultural struggle and political expression of subordinate groups who ha[d] ample reason to fear venturing their unguarded opinion'.[38] This included stealing acorns and olives, poaching and livestock trespassing, or simply feigning ignorance of the many laws regulating country life.[39] Open confrontation, when it did occur, in the form of hunger riots or strikes involving the underground cells of the PCP, rarely tended to extend beyond isolated episodes in response to local social conditions, such as in the aftermath of a poor harvest or the lowering of daily wages (or *jorna*). One exception was the conquest of the 'eight-hour day' in 1962, as a result of strikes in the Alentejo and Ribatejo (until then, rural labourers were made to work 'from sunrise to sunset').[40] The established authorities could also count on the support of the National Republican Guard (GNR), which typically sided with the local notables, and the political police, whose agents were dispatched on site if deemed necessary.[41] For the unsubmissive rural dweller, the threat of physical violence was thus very much a reality of everyday life. In addition to the thousands of injured, the police were directly responsible for forty-one deaths among the rural labourers involved in demonstrations, strikes or hunger riots over the duration of the regime.[42] The shooting at point-blank range by the GNR, in May 1954, of the rural labourer (and communist militant) Catarina Eufémia, figurehead of the strike movement in Baleizão (Alentejo), was paradigmatic of the potentially illimited violence faced by recalcitrant rural labourers.

In response to the favourable context provided by the post-war economic boom, and further enticed after March 1961 by the unappealing prospect of being conscripted to fight in the colonial war, emigration also became an increasingly appealing option for rural dwellers desperate to escape a fate of poverty and social subordination.[43] Between 1957 and 1974, over 1.5 million Portuguese citizens effectively voted with their feet by migrating – the majority of which illegally and in perilous conditions[44] – to the more prosperous Western European nations, in particular France. There, in addition to the gradual economic and social ascent enabled by the *Trente Glorieuses* (thirty-year period of economic growth), they acquired the experience of democratic practices, contributing on their return to the social diffusion of the cultural conditions that would make the Carnation Revolution possible.[45]

Many rural dwellers also opted to migrate internally toward the growing urban centres, namely Porto and, especially, Lisbon. Between 1960 and 1970, the capital's suburban areas, such as Damaia and Odivelas, expanded dramatically, respectively by 136.43 per cent and 169.99 per cent.[46] Rural exodus and the consequent process of urbanisation resulted from the process of rapid industrialisation and tertiarisation of the economy, leading between 1960 and 1973 to the period of fastest economic growth in the country's history (an average of over 6.5 per cent increase of national income per capita).[47]

Urban life: repression, 'room for manoeuvring', and the normalisation of rule

From the early 1960s, increased investment in the economy, education and social support schemes opened the way for the improvement of living conditions.[48] In practical terms, however, its effect on daily life was slow, in particular for the lower social classes. Urban life between 1960 and 1974 continued to be defined by enduring continuities both in terms of entrenched inequalities and hierarchical social structures. The most visible elements of continuity were the living conditions of the influx of rural migrants, who moved directly from their squalid provincial homes to the 'mushrooming' shanty towns (*bairros de lata*) of suburban Porto and, especially, Greater Lisbon – most of which were without running water or electricity.[49] Mass rural exodus worsened the pre-existing infrastructural deficiencies in both cities, as was dramatically highlighted by the floods that hit Lisbon in November 1967, killing over 500 people, the majority from the poor neighbourhoods on the outskirts of the capital.[50]

Whilst the rapid tertiarisation of the economy benefited primarily (though not exclusively) the educated elites, urbanisation, coupled with industrialisation, contributed to the growing proletarianisation of Lisbon's 'plebeian' core population,[51] whose professional activity was increasingly defined by factory work in large industrial units, such as the Companhia União Fabril on the south bank of the Tagus. In addition to these developments, the important social and cultural changes brought about by the process of urbanisation – such as improved access to education, information channels and modern forms of sociability – also meant that in the long term the urban and suburban population would increasingly come to act as an 'agent of social and political intervention'.[52]

This particular point should not be overemphasised, however. Individual politicisation – let alone active oppositionism – remained the attribute of a small minority, in particular segments of the social elites with access to higher education, increasingly receptive to the influence of Marxism or progressive Catholicism.[53] In contrast, the overwhelming majority of Portuguese youth remained undereducated and were consequently 'rapidly integrated into the labour market', mostly in isolation from any of the focal points of politicisation.[54] To a certain extent, the 1960s process of material modernisation itself – in particular the rapid growth in ownership of radios and television sets[55] – carried developments which 'positively emphasised the individualised private sphere' to the detriment of engagement in public affairs.[56] More importantly, widespread depoliticisation was also the result of the regime's coercive apparatus. The political police proved effective in stifling the small minority of active oppositionists, unleashing against them its arsenal of 'punitive violence', including physical and psychological torture.[57] Its effect on the rest of the population, long accustomed to political disengagement and lacking in any practical experience of democracy, was more ambiguous than is commonly recognised, however – though it certainly served as a further 'preventive' deterrent to mobilisation. According to a recent survey directed at 400 citizens who had lived under the dictatorship in its final two decades, over two-thirds of respondents (69.9 per cent) either 'agreed' or 'strongly agreed' with the statement that 'Providing you did not get involved in politics, it was possible to lead a perfectly normal life without having to worry about the [political police]'.[58] In fact, the overwhelming majority appeared to have done just that, as over three-quarters of participants (76.5 per cent) reported having had either 'little' or 'no' interest in politics during the Estado Novo. If steering clear of politics was to a large extent a long-internalised disposition among the population, it was also perceived as the easiest means of gaining both some 'room for manoeuvring' and space for 'evasion' from the dictatorship's most coercive institution.[59] Such results also raise valuable questions as to the potential normalisation of the regime's institutions by the population. The concept of normalisation is here envisaged as a mechanism of change over time. Its definition by Mary Fulbrook, in her study of power and society in the GDR, adapts well to the Portuguese dictatorship. One may indeed argue that the exceptional longevity of the Estado Novo allowed for a significant period of 'stabilisation [. . .] and the associated [. . .] routinisation of institutional structures and regular patterns of behaviour'. As 'processes of political, economic, and social change t[ook] place in which people's changing experiences affect[ed] their attitudes and patterns of behaviour', the public 'adapt[ed] to new circumstances and s[ought] to realise their interests in changing socio-political environments, in the process also changing their own conceptions of "normality" '.[60] The avoidance of politics by the bulk of the Portuguese population was one aspect of this internalised 'normality', which in turn removed the potential threat posed by the political police. The normalisation of the political police itself, as part of the accepted framework of everyday life, is further emphasised by the number of ordinary citizens who sought to instrumentalise it for their own purposes – in line with the logic of *Eigensinn* (obstinacy) – whether to further a personal agenda (through letters of denunciation), to satisfy basic necessities (through petitions), or as an economic resource (through 'spontaneous application letters').[61] Thus in February 1964, the inhabitants of a small semi-rural locality on the fringes of Greater Lisbon, A-da-Beja, successfully petitioned the PIDE official António Faria Pais, who had rented a property in the village, to obtain the installation of public street lighting in the municipality. In January of the same year, a teacher at the seminary in Ermesinde, having been dismissed from his functions, wrote to the PIDE to falsely accuse a member of the seminary's administrative staff of carrying out 'subversive activities', in what was tantamount to the instrumentalisation of the PIDE as an instrument of private conflict resolution.[62]

Communist militants and sympathisers were the principal victims of the Estado Novo's repressive apparatus. The cultural intelligentsia, established mainly in the capital, was another prime target. Strict censorship of periodical publications, such as the daily press, had been instituted in the Constitution of 1933 and thereafter succeeded in preventing the formation of an informed public opinion. In 1936 censorship was extended to the publication of books. Prominent writers, most of whom were directly associated with the opposition (be it democratic or communist), were kept under the watchful eye of the political police.[63] If censorship severely hampered both artistic and intellectual production, not least in the field of historiographical production,[64] literary authors were nevertheless able (and, to an extent, allowed) to form a relatively autonomous space for reflection and even exercise a (narrow) margin of freedom to criticise the regime – a further example of 'room for manoeuvring' within the Estado Novo. The extensive body of neorealist works published between the 1930s and 1960s, at the core of which was the (albeit implicit) Marxist criticism of the social structures generated by Salazarism, emphasises the fact. A (controlled) measure of freedom of expression was also granted to the pro-democratic press, such as the *Diário de Lisboa*, during the periods of post-1945 'semi-authorised' electoral campaigns. Such governmental concessions stemmed from pragmatism rather than liberalising benevolence. The authorities were indeed well aware of the diminutive impact of such literary works in Portugal, whose influence was limited mostly to a small readership among the cultivated urban elite. The fact that the regime had failed to generate its own literary school or to attract the most prominent authors of the time to its cause merely accentuated the need for a pragmatic stance.[65]

It was also in Portugal's urban areas that the regime's instruments of ideological inculcation exerted the most influence on the daily lives of the population, in particular the Portuguese Youth (Mocidade Portuguesa, or MP). Membership of the MP was compulsory for all children between the ages of seven and fourteen years. Created in September 1936 in the context of civil war in neighbouring Spain – and the incurring ideological radicalisation of the Estado Novo – it was originally designed to fashion youth along the principles of nationalism, anti-communism, respect for authority, physical vigour and the cult of Salazar.[66] From 1940 onwards, however, its fascistic pretentions were abandoned as the Catholic Church successfully asserted its presence in the organisation, adding to its own rapidly growing social influence through the Portuguese Catholic Action groups.[67] In 1937, the MP's influence was further expanded through the creation of Portuguese Female Youth (Mocidade Portuguese Feminina, or MPF), which served essentially as a form of primary conditioning for school-age girls, membership being compulsory up to the age of fourteen. The MPF was designed to provide them from an early age with first-hand experience of the 'abilities' expected of a devoted housewife, and to socialise them into the virtues of the 'sweet subjection of a wife to her husband'.[68] It also explicitly sought to inculcate the values of female 'humility' and 'decency', as well the 'sane' moral principles defined by Catholic doctrine.[69] Although compulsory membership was in both cases abandoned in 1970 – by which time the movement had effectively been downgraded to mere 'sporting associations',[70] its legitimacy increasingly contested by its own 'affiliates'[71] – participation in the MP's Saturday morning activities was a central component of the weekly routine for generations of Portuguese school pupils. Its effect was to further accentuate the already thoroughly ideological nature of the national education system along increasingly religious (Catholic) lines.

Salazarist gender politics: the subordination of women

In a society subjected to the effects of the alliance between the Estado Novo and the Catholic Church, aimed at achieving an idealised (and failed) programme to 're-Christianise' the nation, conservative Catholic principles of morality permeated not only the established moral norms but also much of the regime's social legislation.[72] This was particularly apparent in the legislation designed to define the allocated role of the female population in society. Salazar himself, in a series of interviews given in 1932, had outlined the 'functions' attributed to women, namely as 'mothers', 'educators of [their] children' and dedicated housewives.[73] A series of decree laws gradually instituted the dictator's vision into fact, as women were increasingly subjected to both economic dependence and gender submission in relation to men. These included conditioning the obtention of a passport (and thus the possibility of travelling abroad) or the opening of a bank account to the authorisation of their husbands.[74] Certain professions were simply forbidden to women by law. These included the judicial career, the diplomatic corps, the police and the armed forces.[75] Women were also effectively excluded from the franchise – unless they could demonstrate their status as 'head' of the family unit and the payment of a minimal amount of fiscal contributions to the state. Not until 1968, under Marcello Caetano, were all women given the right to vote (though not in municipal elections), under the assumption that 'women were more conservative than men' and consequently less of an electoral risk.[76]

In addition to legislation that effectively turned women into second-class citizens, the Estado Novo also counted upon the action of its organisations of ideological inculcation aimed at socialising the female population according to the subordinate role expected of them. In particular, the action of the regime's Female Youth organisation was complemented by the Mothers' Work for National Education (Obra das Mães para a Educação Nacional, or OMEN), created in 1936, whose stated aim was to 'better prepare the female generations for their future maternal, domestic, and social duties'.[77] Led by female members of the aristocracy and the wives of prominent figures of the regime, the OMEN undertook primarily to habilitate mothers for their contribution to 'the education of the family', namely in their ascribed role in fomenting 'among their children the taste for domestic tasks'. In addition to the organisation of social assistance and natality campaigns, it also actively promoted the 'return of women to the household' through the institution of a 'family salary'.[78]

In social terms, women also faced a situation of systematic subordination. Women, especially in rural Portugal but also in urban areas, were particularly prone to illiteracy. In 1960, 36.7 per cent of women were illiterate, compared to 24.9 per cent of men.[79] The so-called 'return to the household' also signalled their marginalisation on the labour market. Those who did work were often relegated to menial positions. The paradigmatic – if extreme – example is provided by the daughters of the newly arrived rural migrants (and of the remaining rural population), commonly employed as domestic maids by the wealthier families of Lisbon and Porto.[80] Whilst a law was passed in 1966 that sought to address gender inequality in salaries, women also continued to receive lower pay than their male counterparts in all sectors of the economy.[81]

The indivisible nature of religious matrimony, instituted in the Concordat of 1940, was also often the cause of further economic minorisation for women, whilst the legal prohibition of abortion also exposed women – in particular those from the poorer social classes – to the dangers of illegal abortion.[82]

Conclusion

Everyday life in Salazar's Portugal was systematically and persistently marked by the effects of the system of social control and repression either established by the Estado Novo itself, or predating its existence and subsequently reinforced by it. For the bulk of the rural population, which until the 1960s represented the majority of the population at the national level, daily life consisted primarily in designing strategies of survival within an immutable, rigidly hierarchic social order whose mechanisms were strengthened by the action of the dictatorship. Both the small peasantry and rural labourers effectively remained trapped in a clientelist relation of client to patron that condemned them to economic dependence (at subsistence level), social subordination and political demobilisation. Whilst infra-political acts of daily resistance were frequent, the mechanisms of deeply ingrained local power relations combined with the increasing capillarity of Salazarist repression – through the GNR and the political police – to ensure that no mass dissident movement was ever likely to develop, still less to threaten the stability of the regime or lead to significant changes in the daily lives of rural dwellers. The (gradual) weakening of this system of provincial control came only as a result of the decision to emigrate to the more prosperous Western European nations or to migrate internally towards the country's main centres of urbanisation, as happened from the late 1950s. The consequent tertiarisation of the economy benefited primarily the educated elites, though the increasing proletarianisation of the 'plebeian' core of the main urban areas of Lisbon and Porto was not entirely devoid of opportunities for economic and social betterment. In political terms, however, popular disengagement was a long-internalised practice. Oppositionist activism remained limited to a minority intelligentsia and some industrial areas associated with the clandestine Communist Party. Whilst these succeeded in creating limited spaces of evasion, as well as some 'room for manoeuvring' within the institutional structures of the dictatorship (largely conceded by the regime), their limited connection with the bulk of the undereducated population meant that their action remained, if not inconsequential, at the very least limited in a society marked by pervasive conformism. By the 1960s, a significant part of the population seemed indeed to have normalised the institutions imposed by the regime as the framework for their daily lives.

Notes

1. J. Medina, *Salazar em França* (Lisbon, 1977), 50.
2. L. Farinha, *O reviralho: revoltas Republicanas contra a ditadura e o Estado Novo, 1926–1940* (Lisbon, 1998).
3. For a biography in English, see F.R. de Meneses, *Salazar: A Political Biography* (New York, 2009).
4. M.B. da Cruz, *O partido e o Estado no Salazarismo* (Lisbon, 1980).
5. A.C. Pinto, *The Blueshirts: Portuguese Fascists in the New State* (New York, 2000).
6. On Salazar's political police, see M. da Conceição Ribeiro, *A polícia política no Estado Novo, 1926–1945* (Lisbon, 1995); and I.F. Pimentel, *A história da PIDE* (Mem Martins, 2007).
7. See Ribeiro, *A polícia política no Estado Novo*, 18.
8. A.C. Pinto and F. Raimundo, 'Die Opfer der Salazar-Diktatur: Der Umgang mit den Opfern Tätern in Demokratische Portugal' [The Victims of Salazar's Dictatorship: Dealing with Victims and Perpetrators], in *Nach den Diktaturen: Der Umgang mit den Opfern in Europa*, ed. G. Heydemann and C. Vollnhals (Göttingen, 2016), 81–106.
9. A.C. Pinto and F. Raimundo, 'Violence, Repression and Terror in Mass Dictatorships: A View from the European Margins', in *The Palgrave Handbook of Mass Dictatorships*, ed. P. Corner and J.H. Lim (London, 2016), 105–17.
10. F.C.P. Martinho, *Marcello Caetano and the Portuguese 'New State': A Political Biography* (Brighton, 2018).
11. H. Martins, 'Portugal', in *European Fascism*, ed. S.J. Woolf (New York, 1968), 329.
12. A.O. Salazar, *Discursos e notas políticas, 1: 1928–1934* (Coimbra, 1935), 259.
13. A. Nóvoa, 'A "Educação Nacional" (1930–1974)', in *Portugal e o Estado Novo (1930–1960)*, ed. F. Rosas (Lisbon, 1992), 458–60.
14. A.C. Pinto and M.I. Rezola, 'Political Catholicism, Crisis of Democracy and Salazar's New State in Portugal', in *Clerical Fascism in Interwar Europe*, ed. M. Feldman and M. Turda (Abingdon, 2008), 141–56.
15. M.I. Rezola, 'Breve panorama da situação da Igreja Católica em Portugal, 1930–1960', in *Portugal e o Estado Novo (1930–1960)*, ed. F. Rosas (Lisbon, 1992), 238.
16. On this topic, see R.W. Sousa, *The Rediscoverers: Major Writers in the Portuguese Literature of National Regeneration* (University Park, PA, 1981).
17. N.G. Monteiro and A.C. Pinto, 'Cultural Myths and Portuguese National Identity', in *Contemporary Portugal: Politics, Society and Culture*, ed. A.C. Pinto, 2nd edn (New York, 2011), 55–72.
18. D. Melo, *Salazarismo e cultura popular, 1933–1958* (Lisbon, 2001).
19. J.P. Brito, 'O Estado Novo e a aldeia mais portuguesa de Portugal', in *O Fascismo em Portugal: actas do Colóquio realizado na Faculdade de Letras*

de Lisboa em março de 1980, ed. Faculdade de Letras de Lisboa (Lisbon, 1982), 508; see also, Melo, *Salazarismo e cultura popular*.

20 A. Garrido, 'Um retrato da sociedade portuguesa no salazarismo (1930–1960)', in *História social contemporânea: Portugal 1808–2000*, ed. A.C. Pinto and N.G. Monteiro (Lisbon, 2020), 184–5. The figures stood at 51 per cent in 1930, 52 per cent in 1940, and 49 per cent in 1950.

21 See, in particular, A. Redol, *Gaibéus* (Lisbon, 1939); M. da Fonseca, *Cerromaior* (Lisbon, 1943); and the memoirs of the country doctor, F. Namora, *Retalhos da vida de um médico* (Lisbon, 1963).

22 S.M. Pereira, 'Cenários do quotidiano doméstico: modos de habitar', in *História da vida privada em Portugal: os nossos dias*, ed. A.N. de Almeida (Lisbon, 2011), 32.

23 M.M. Vieira, 'Aprendizagem, escola e pedagogização do quotidiano', in *História da vida privada em Portugal: os nossos dias*, ed. A.N. de Almeida (Lisbon, 2011), 174.

24 M.F. Mónica, *Educação e sociedade no Portugal de Salazar: a escola primária salazarista, 1926–1939* (Lisbon, 1978).

25 See P.T. de Almeida, *Eleições e caciquismo no Portugal oitocentista (1868–1890)* (Lisbon, 1991).

26 A particularly insightful analysis of clientelism as a means of social control from the perspective of political ethnography is provided by J. Auyero, *Poor People's Politics: Peronist Survival Networks and the Legacy of Evita* (Durham, NC, 2001).

27 P.T. de Almeida, *Legislação eleitoral Portuguesa 1820–1926* (Lisbon, 1998), 733.

28 J. Serra, 'O sistema político da Primeira República', in *A primeira república Portuguesa*, ed. A.C. Pinto and N. Teixeira (Lisbon, 2000), 111–12.

29 On the apoliticism of the small peasantry, see J.F. Riegelhaupt, 'Os camponeses e a política no Portugal de Salazar: o estado corporativo e o "apoliticismo" nas aldeias', *Análise Social* 15, no. 59 (1976): 505–23, 510.

30 On Salazarist ideology, see L.R. Torgal and A.C. de Homem, 'Ideologia salazarista e "cultura popular" – análise da biblioteca de uma casa do povo', *Análise Social* 72/74 (1982): 1437–64, 1438–39.

31 For case studies carried out across Portugal from an anthropological perspective, see J. Cutileiro, *A Portuguese Rural Society* (Oxford, 1971); M.C. Silva, 'Camponeses nortenhos: "conservadorismo" ou estratégias de sobrevivência, mobilidade e resistência?' *Análise Social* 23, no. 97 (1987): 437–45; and J.M. Sobral, *Trajectos: o presente e o passado na vida de uma Freguesia da Beira* (Lisbon, 1999).

32 Decree Law 2015, of 28 May 1946, essentially limited the franchise to the literate male population or to citizens able to demonstrate property rights and a minimal fiscal contribution to the State. See A.S.M. Ferreira, 'O sistema eleitoral no Estado Novo', *História* 9, no. 2 (2019): 62–86, 67–8. By 1965, the right to vote remained limited to 14.9 per cent of the population, see da Cruz, *O partido e o Estado no Salazarismo*, 204.

33 P. Silveira e Sousa, 'Caciquismo e poder local na literatura sob o Estado Novo', in *História dos municípios e dos poderes locais*, ed. C. Oliveira (Lisbon, 1996), 337–8.
34 Ibid., 340.
35 Da Cruz, *O partido e o Estado no Salazarismo*, 243.
36 An insightful analysis of the intertwining of statist and peripherical powers is provided by R. Ramos, 'O Estado Novo perante os poderes periféricos: o governo de Assis Gonçalves em Vila Real (1934–39)', *Análise Social* 22, no. 90 (1986): 109–35.
37 Silveira e Sousa, 'Caciquismo e poder local na literatura sob o Estado Novo', 333.
38 J.C. Scott, *Domination and the Arts of Resistance: Hidden Transcripts* (London and New Haven, CT, 1990), 184.
39 On the infra-politics of rural labourers in the latifundia-based south, see J.A.R. Cardeñoso, 'Weapons of the Weak in Portugal During the early 20th Century: The Example of the Central Alentejo', *e-Journal of Portuguese History* 16, no. 2 (2018): 24–41.
40 On the 1958–62 period of social unrest, which followed the presidential electoral campaign of General Humberto Delgado for the opposition, see D.P. Cerezales, *Portugal à coronhada: protesto popular e ordem pública nos séculos XIX e XX* (Lisbon, 2011), 304–16.
41 For a detailed analysis of resistance and repression in the village of Couço, at the limits of the Ribatejo and Alentejo, see P. Godinho, *Memórias da Resistência Rural no Sul – Couço (1958–1962)* (Oeiras, 2001).
42 D.P. Cerezales, 'Joao Madeira (coord.), *Vítimas de Salazar*. Lisboa: Esfera dos Livros, 2007' [review], *Análise Social* 42, no. 185 (2007): 1128–35, 1130.
43 The regime's obstinate refusal to adapt to the 'wind of change' eventually led to war with the African liberation movements in Angola (March 1961), Guinea (January 1963) and Mozambique (September 1964). The conflict ended only in the aftermath of the downfall of the regime in April 1974.
44 On the experience of clandestine emigration networks in the north of Portugal, see M.N. Silva, *Os trilhos da emigração: redes clandestinas de Penedono a França (1960–1974)* (Lisbon, 2011).
45 V. Pereira, *La dictature de Salazar face à l'émigration: l'état portugais et ses migrants en France (1957–1974)* (Paris, 2012), 412.
46 J. Mattoso (ed.), *História de Portugal, sétimo volume: O Estado Novo (1926–1974)* (Lisbon, 1994), 425.
47 A. Barreto, 'Democratização e mudança social (1960–2000)', in *História social contemporânea: Portugal 1808–2000*, ed. A.C. Pinto and N.G. Monteiro (Lisbon, 2020), 218–19.
48 R. Ramos (ed.), *História de Portugal* (Lisbon, 2009), 687–90.
49 For a graphic description of the *bairros de lata* of the 1960s–1970s, see Pereira, 'Cenários do quotidiano doméstico', 20–1.

50 For a good, albeit journalistic treatment of the event, see: https://www.publico.pt/2017/11/12/sociedade/reportagem/a-noite-do-fim-do-mundo-1791985 (accessed 12 May 2021).

51 J.A. França, *Lisboetas no século XX: anos 20, 40 e 60* (Lisbon, 2005), 73.

52 F. Rosas, *História de Portugal, sétimo volume: O Estado Novo (1926–1974)* (Lisbon, 1994), 426.

53 On the movements of student opposition to the regime, see M. Cardina, 'Movimentos estudantis na crise do Estado Novo: mitos e realidades', *e-cadernos CES* 1 (2008). Available online: https://doi.org/10.4000/eces.101 (accessed 11 May 2022).

54 L. Pappámıkail, 'Juventude: entre a fase da vida e o tempo de viver', in *História da vida privada em Portugal: os nossos dias*, ed. A.N. de Almeida (Lisbon, 2011), 215–16.

55 A. Barreto (ed.), *A situação social em Portugal, 1960–1995* (Lisbon, 1996), 146.

56 D.J.K. Peukert, *Inside Nazi Germany: Conformity, Opposition and Racism in Everyday Life* (London, 1993), 78.

57 F. Rosas, *Salazar e o poder: a arte de saber durar* (Lisbon, 2012), 190–210.

58 D. Simpson and A. Louceiro, Everyday Life Under the PIDE: A Quantitative Survey on the Relations Between Ordinary Citizens and Salazar's Political Police (1955–1974)', *International Journal of Iberian Studies* 34, no. 3 (2021): 195–216.

59 On the concepts of 'room for manoeuvring' and 'evasion', see A. Lüdtke, 'Ordinary People, Self-Energising, and Room for Manoeuvering: Examples from 20th Century Europe', in *Everyday Life in Mass Dictatorship: Collusion and Evasion*, ed. A. Lüdtke (New York, 2016), 13–34. Lüdtke's influential analytical framework has barely been used for the study of everyday life in Salazar's Portugal. The sole, and insightful, exception is the work of Beatriz Valverde Contreras and Alexander Keese on the societal reactions to the presence of the political police in the Azores: B.V. Contreras and A. Keese, 'The Limits of Authoritarian Rule at the Periphery: The PIDE, the American Airbase, and Social Control on Teirceira Island, Azores, 1954–1962', *Journal of Social History* 52, no. 4 (2019): 1307–29.

60 M. Fulbrook, 'The Concept of "Normalisation" and the GDR in Comparative Perspective', in *Power and Society in the GDR 1961–1979: The 'Normalisation of Rule'?*, ed. M. Fulbrook (Oxford: 2008), 14–15.

61 D. Simpson, 'Approaching the PIDE "From Below": Petitions, Spontaneous Applications and Denunciation Letters to Salazar's Secret Police in 1964', *Contemporary European History* 30, no. 3 (2021): 398–413. On *Eigensinn*, or 'adherence to one's own agenda' in a dictatorial setting, see A. Lüdtke (ed.), *Histoire du quotidien* (Paris, 1995).

62 On each of the cases, see Simpson, 'Approaching the PIDE "From Below" ', 402–3, 408.

63 On the cases of Miguel Torga and Fernando Namora, see R. Nunes, *Miguel Torga e a PIDE: a repressão e os escritores no Estado Novo* (Coimbra, 2007);

and P.M. da Silva, *Fernando Namora por entre os dedos da PIDE: a repressão e os escritores no Estado Novo* (Coimbra, 2009).

64 L.R. Torgal, 'A história em tempo de "ditadura" ', in L.R. Torgal, J.M.A. Mendes and F. Catroga, *História da história em Portugal: Sécs. XIX–XX* (Lisbon, 1996), 241–75.

65 Silveira e Sousa, 'Caciquismo e poder local na literatura sob o Estado Novo', 328.

66 See S. Kuin, 'A Mocidade Portuguesa nos anos 30: anteprojectos e instauração de uma organização paramilitar da juventude', *Análise Social* 28, no. 122 (1993): 555–88. For a critical assessment of the regime's attempt to promote a fascistic 'New Man', see R.A. de Carvalho and A.C. Pinto, 'The "Everyman" of the Portuguese New State During the Fascist Era', in *The 'New Man' in Radical Right Ideology and Practice, 1919–45*, ed. J. Dagnino, M. Feldman and P. Stocker (London, 2018), 131–48.

67 D.A.H. Simpson, *A Igreja Católica e o Estado Novo Salazarista* (Lisbon, 2014), 94–7.

68 In I.F. Pimentel, *Mocidade Portuguesa Feminina: educar para ser boa esposa, boa mãe, católica e obediente* (Lisbon, 2007), 63.

69 See A. Cova and A.C. Pinto, 'Women Under Salazar's Dictatorship', *Portuguese Journal of Social Science* 1, no. 2 (2002): 129–46; and Pimentel, *Mocidade Portuguesa Feminina*, 133–53.

70 A.C. Pinto (ed.), *Contemporary Portugal: Politics, Society and Culture* (New York, 2011), 45.

71 J. Vieira, *Mocidade Portuguesa* (Lisbon, 2008), 257.

72 Simpson, *A Igreja Católica e o Estado Novo Salazarista*.

73 A. Ferro, *Salazar: o homem e a sua obra* (Lisbon, 1933).

74 E. Guimarães, 'A mulher portuguesa na legislação civil', *Análise Social* 122, no. 92/93 (1986): 557–77, 568.

75 Barreto, 'Democratização e mudança social', 229.

76 A. Cova and A.C. Pinto, 'Women Under Salazar's Dictatorship', 134.

77 See I.F. Pimentel, *História das organizações femininas do Estado Novo* (Lisbon, 2001).

78 I.F. Pimentel, 'Obra das Mães para a Educação Nacional', in *Dicionário de história do Estado Novo*, Vol. II, ed. F. Rosas and J.M. Brito (Venda Nova, 1996), 675–6.

79 Cova and Pinto, 'Women Under Salazar's Dictatorship', 132.

80 I. Brasão, *O tempo das criadas: a condição servil em Portugal (1940–1970)* (Lisbon, 2012).

81 Cova and Pinto, 'Women Under Salazar's Dictatorship', 132–3.

82 I. Freire, *Amor e sexo no tempo de Salazar* (Lisbon, 2010), 255.

Select bibliography

Almeida, A.N. de (ed.). *História da vida privada em Portugal: os nossos dias*. Lisbon, 2011.
Barreto, A. (ed.). *A situação social em Portugal, 1960–1995*. Lisbon, 1996.
Brasão, I. *O tempo das criadas: a condição servil em Portugal (1940–1970)*. Lisbon, 2012.
Cardeñoso, J.A.R. 'Weapons of the Weak in Portugal During the Early 20th Century: The Example of the Central Alentejo', *e-Journal of Portuguese History* 16, no. 2 (2018): 24–41.
Cutileiro, J. *A Portuguese Rural Society*. Oxford, 1971.
Freire, I. *Amor e sexo no tempo de Salazar*. Lisbon, 2010.
Godinho, P. *Memórias da resistência rural no Sul: Couço (1958–1962)*. Oeiras, 2001.
Lüdtke, A. (ed.). *Everyday Life in Mass Dictatorship: Collusion and Evasion*. New York, 2016.
Lüdtke, A. (ed.). *Histoire du quotidien*. Paris, 1995.
Melo, D. *Salazarismo e cultura popular, 1933–1958*. Lisbon, 2001.
Pimentel, I.F. *História das organizações femininas do Estado Novo*. Lisbon, 2001.
Pinto, A.C. (ed.). *Contemporary Portugal: Politics, Society and Culture*. New York, 2011.
Pinto, A.C. and Monteiro, N.G. (eds). *História social contemporânea: Portugal 1808–2000*. Lisbon, 2020.
Pinto, P.R. ' "Everyday Citizenship" Under Authoritarianism: The Cases of Spain and Portugal', in *Civil Society Activism Under Authoritarian Rule: A Comparative Perspective*, edited by F. Cavatorta, 13–33. London, 2012.
Ramos, R. 'O Estado Novo perante os poderes periféricos: o governo de Assis Gonçalves em Vila Real (1934–39)', *Análise Social* 22, no. 90 (1986): 109–35.
Riegelhaupt, J.F. 'Os camponeses e a política no Portugal de Salazar: o estado corporativo e o "apoliticismo" nas aldeias', *Análise Social* 15, no. 59 (1976): 505–23.
Silva, M.C. 'Camponeses nortenhos: "conservadorismo" ou estratégias de sobrevivência, mobilidade e resistência?', *Análise Social* 23, no. 97 (1987): 407–45.
Silveira e Sousa, P. 'Caciquismo e poder local na literatura sob o Estado Novo', in *História dos municípios e dos poderes locais*, edited by C. Oliveira, 325–41. Lisbon, 1996.
Simpson, D. 'Approaching the PIDE "From Below": Petitions, Spontaneous Applications and Denunciation Letters to Salazar's Secret Police in 1964', *Contemporary European History* 30, no. 3 (2021): 398–413.
Simpson, D. and Louceiro, A. 'Everyday Life Under the PIDE: A Quantitative Survey on the Relations Between Ordinary Citizens and Salazar's Political Police (1955–1974)', *International Journal of Iberian Studies* 34, no. 3 (2021): 195–216.
Sobral, J.M. *Trajectos: o presente e o passado na vida de uma Freguesia da Beira*. Lisbon, 1999.

5

Transnational totalitarianism and the building of a new public consciousness in Kārlis Ulmanis's Latvia

Jordan T. Kuck

Introduction

Few terms in the field of modern European history are as debated and politically fraught as fascism and totalitarianism. Since the terms first emerged in Italy in the early 1920s, scholars have been debating their meanings and usefulness as categorical ontologies. Thus, Aivars Stranga made a bold and controversial historiographical claim when, in a recent work, he claimed that the Kārlis Ulmanis regime, which ruled Latvia from 1934 to 1940, saw itself as both fascist and totalitarian. Stranga writes, 'In 1939, when the fifth anniversary of the regime was celebrated, both fascism and totalitarianism were inseparable from the regime's self-definition'.[1] Stranga concludes, however, that in the end the Ulmanis regime 'fell short of its self-ascribed fascist totalitarianism' and therefore should instead be remembered as a 'chaotic autocracy that was devoured by the real totalitarian polities it took [. . .] as models'.[2]

This chapter aims to debate Stranga's polemical thesis. The approach taken here is multifaceted. First, this work contends that if we are going to use a controversial term like totalitarianism, then it is imperative that we explicitly define the term and use it in a way that avoids essentialism or teleological thinking. Thus, the first section of the chapter deals with the history of the term totalitarianism, making clear what interwar actors on the far right meant when they employed it.³ When intellectuals and political leaders used the term totalitarianism in the 1920s and early to mid-1930s, they typically did not use it to connote aspirations of total control or total power. And at that point in history, the term certainly did not immediately conjure up in the minds of the average European citizen images of a concentration camp or gulag camp. In other words, those well-known post–Second World War theories of totalitarianism espoused by Hannah Arendt, Carl Friedrich, Zbigniew Brzezinski and others are actually of little value in terms of helping us to understand its contemporary use in the 1920s and early 1930s.⁴ If we return to the primary sources of that time and avoid the teleological thinking that comes from our knowledge of the later outcomes (e.g. the Holocaust or Stalin's gulag system), then it becomes clear that totalitarianism referred to the 'spirit' of far-right politics, which strove to remove the boundary between politics and everyday private life. Perhaps no one better explained totalitarianism – at least in its early stages – than the Italian philosopher Benedetto Croce. A critic of fascism who ultimately broke off relations with his friend and fellow philosopher Giovanni Gentile (who of course became an ardent supporter of Benito Mussolini and ghostwrote *The Doctrine of Fascism*), Croce believed that totalitarianism was ultimately about the creation of a new 'governmental morality', whose tenets were to circumscribe and animate private lives.⁵ The Ulmanis regime understood totalitarianism in a very similar fashion – not as total control or total power or absolute nihilistic destruction, as Arendt argued, but as a novel form of politics and political practice that aimed to supplant individualism and what Fritz Stern famously labelled 'cultural despair' with collective values and action.⁶

After clarifying the origins of the term totalitarianism and what members of the Ulmanis regime meant when they utilised it, this chapter proceeds to investigate whether in fact the Ulmanis regime's practices fell abysmally short of its own aims, as Stranga has argued. To do this, it examines two scenes of life in Ulmanis's Latvia to uncover what sort of totalitarian-governmental morality the regime sought to develop. This approach to analysing fascist totalitarianism *in practice* is partly derived from the recent book *Visualizing Fascism*, in particular Ruth Ben-Ghiat's fascinating chapter 'Five Faces of Fascism'.⁷ Of course, this approach also borrows from earlier studies of fascism as an ideology of spectacle.⁸

In total, the chapter posits that Stranga somewhat missed the mark with his claim that the Ulmanis regime fell substantially short of its totalitarian aims and intentions. That contention would be true if we were to hold the Ulmanis regime to the standards of totalitarianism outlined by Arendt and Brzezinski, or if we compare the Ulmanis regime to those of Adolf Hitler or Josef Stalin. Indeed, this is apparently what Stranga has done, though he does not clarify his use of the term totalitarianism. But that standard is anachronistic, and those comparisons are anathema to how totalitarianism was understood and practised in the interwar period. One could also make the claim that Arendt and others failed to see that even in 'classic cases' of totalitarianism, the dictators never had total, absolute power. For example, Nathan Stoltzfus has convincingly shown how often Hitler had to compromise or deviate from plans due to public sentiment.[9]

In many ways, totalitarianism is just like fascism: as it was adopted across the borders of nation states, practitioners tweaked it (both as a term and as a concept) and appropriated specific aims unique to their particular cultures and national circumstances. Thus, just as scholars have argued in favour of using the term 'transnational fascism',[10] so too must we shift our analysis of totalitarianism to that of 'transnational totalitarianism'.[11] What then of Ulmanis's successes or failures? This chapter maintains that if we analyse the Ulmanis regime as an example of transnational totalitarianism, then we cannot confidently conclude that it was a failure. Rather, it seems that the regime was well on its way to achieving most of its aims when Ulmanis's rule was abruptly ended following the invasion of the Soviet Red Army in June 1940.

A brief overview of the Ulmanis regime

From a biographical standpoint, Kārlis Ulmanis was a most unusual European dictator. Born in 1877 in the westernmost part of the Russian Empire, Ulmanis did not come from a prominent family, and he did not rise to national prominence through the military or business. Rather, Ulmanis was a farmer's son who spent the formative years of his adult life in the American Midwest, where, living in political exile due to his journalistic involvement in fomenting the 1905 Russian Revolution, he worked in menial agricultural jobs while attending classes at the University of Nebraska. Ulmanis remained in Nebraska until 1913, when, following Tsar Nicholas's declaration of a general amnesty, he decided to return home. There Ulmanis found employment as an agronomist and agricultural journalist, a position which led him to become a nationalist leader in the Farmers' Union (*Zemnieku savienība*) party. In 1918, following Latvia's declaration of independence, he was elected as the first prime minister of Latvia. However, despite his earlier democratic convictions and experiences, including three stints as prime minister, on the night of 15 May 1934, Ulmanis took over in a bloodless *coup d'état*, becoming the authoritarian Vadonis (leader) of Latvia. As Vadonis, Ulmanis eliminated all semblances of parliamentary rule. For instance, all political parties were banned – even the Farmers' Union. While Ulmanis talked about rewriting Latvia's constitution, ultimately this project was never completed. Instead, Ulmanis ruled via a corporative chamber system that was developed according to the Italian model. Also borrowed from abroad was the concept of fascist rebirth – the regime called post–15 May Latvia 'renewed Latvia' (*atjaunotā Latvija*) – and a new national calendar, with 15 May serving as the most trumpeted holiday. Ulmanis remained in power until June 1940, when he was deposed by Josef Stalin's forces and shipped to a prison in present-day Turkmenistan, where, it is believed, he died in 1942.[12]

Totalitarianism and transnational totalitarianism

In his chapter in the edited volume *Dictatorship in History and Theory: Bonapartism, Caesarism, and Totalitarianism*, Peter Baehr calls out his fellow scholars' uncritical use of terminology. He writes, 'Modern historians are still obliged to show that they understand the mercurial quality of the terms with which they are working. Even for the best historians, this is not always the case'.[13] David D. Roberts expresses a similar sentiment in his newest book, *Totalitarianism*.[14] Heeding Baehr and Roberts's call for more critical and nuanced use of scholarly terminology, this section offers a brief overview of the early history of the term totalitarianism and seeks to clarify both the general meaning of the term in international interwar dialogue, as well as what precisely the term meant when it was deployed within the confines of Latvian interwar politics.

Although Benito Mussolini and the Fascists popularised the term totalitarianism, they did not in fact coin it. That honour goes to Giovanni Amendola, a journalist and politician who was bitterly opposed to fascist rule. In May 1923, Amendola penned a scathing article against the Fascists' proposed change to how seats in the parliament would be distributed following national elections (Mussolini's proposal was to give two-thirds of all seats to the single party that won the most votes). He warned readers that the Fascists were attempting to destroy democratic majoritarian rule in favour of what he called '*sistema totaliaria*' (a totalitarian system). A few months later, in an article published on the anniversary of the March on Rome, Amendola for the first time used the term totalitarian in reference to fascism as a whole. He wrote:

Actually, the most salient characteristic of the fascist movement [. . .] remains its 'totalitarian' spirit. This spirit will not allow any new day to dawn that has not rendered the fascist salute, just as it does not allow the present era to know a conscience that has not bowed the knee and confessed: 'I believe'. This remarkable 'war of religion', which has been raging for over a year in Italy [. . .] denies you the right to possess a conscience – of your own, not one imposed by others – and burdens the future with a mortgage heavy as lead.[15]

For the first two years of the term's existence, as Abbott Gleason highlights in his study of totalitarianism, it referred rather specifically to the Fascists' unique political 'spirit' – Amendola and other anti-Fascists regularly described that spirit using adjectives like 'wild' and 'ferocious' – and to their commitment to create a new public morality or conscience that usurped that of the individual. However, as the frequency in use increased in 1924, some anti-Fascists began to use the term to refer to the wanton authoritarian power that the Fascists were accumulating. For example, the socialist Lelio Basso argued that, '[a]ll the organs of the state, the crown, Parliament, the law [. . .] the armed forces [. . .] are becoming instruments of a single party that makes itself the interpreter of the people's will, of undifferentiated totalitarianism!'.[16] Thus, by 1925, the term had developed two interrelated but nonetheless bifurcated meanings: one version referred to a *style* of politics while the other focused on authoritarian *aims and motivations*.

By the middle of 1925, the Fascists themselves appropriated the term. For instance, during a speech in June, Mussolini used the term in reference to the Fascists' will to action:

> We want the Italians to make a choice [. . .]. We have conducted the struggle in so open an arena that there can be only a clear For or Against. And furthermore: we will pursue what has been called our fierce totalitarian will [*la nostra feroce volonta totalitaria*]. We want to make the nation fascist, so that tomorrow Italians and Fascists [. . .] will be the same thing.[17]

As for why Mussolini and the Fascists decided to adopt what had been a term of abuse lobbed at them and use it as 'a motif of self-definition', Gleason assumes that they must have liked the term's 'extremist ring', for it 'sounded "modern," supporting fascist claims to have created new state and social forms appropriate to the present and breaking decisively with the decadent, liberal past'.[18] What is more, this appropriation is yet another telling example of just how much Italian fascism and transnational fascism writ large were syncretic movements whose vocabulary, to say nothing of their political platform, was borrowed from both the left and right.

Mussolini's repeated use of the terms totalitarian and totalitarianism resulted in their entering the international lexicon of the interwar period. In the case of Latvia, the Italian *totalitaria* was rendered into Latvian as *totalitārs* (totalitarian) and *totalitārsms* (totalitarianism). According to a search of interwar periodicals on Periodika, the Latvian National Library's digital repository,

Latvians first encountered the terms, at least in print, in January 1926, when the term *totalitārsms* appeared in an article on international politics in the Social Democratic daily paper, *Strādnieku Avīze*.[19] In this instance, the term was used in reference to the complete fascistisation of the Italian state. Although first used in 1926, the terms totalitarian and totalitarianism very rarely appeared in the Latvian press – and this is true of both the Latvian- and German-language press – until 1933. At that point, Hitler's ascension to power resulted in new coverage of totalitarianism as an international phenomenon. For example, the first instance of the term's use in the German-language press in Latvia came in August 1933 in *Rigasche Rundschau*. Thereafter, it appeared in a translation of Mussolini's speech about the emergence of two civilisations in Europe.[20] Articles in the Latvian language also discussed Hitler's regime becoming 'totalitarian', especially after the killing of Ernst Röhm, Gregor Strasser and others during the Night of the Long Knives.[21] However, it should be noted that the total number of times that the terms totalitarian or totalitarianism appeared in the Latvian press prior to Ulmanis's coup in May 1934 remained very low. And when the term was sparingly used, it referred to fascist authoritarianism and, by summer 1934, to the emergence of a fascist-authoritarian political movement in Europe.

Following Ulmanis's coup on 15 May 1934, a state of emergency was declared, and as part of that decree, the Ministry of Internal Affairs was granted the authority to suspend any press, trade or associational publication that was deemed a threat to public order. Thus, almost immediately following the coup, the Ministry of Internal Affairs shut down some fifty publications. By the end of June 1934, that number had ballooned to ninety-nine, though some were later permitted to resume publication. Many of the organisations and publications targeted were, unsurprisingly, left-leaning, but there were also a handful of prominent conservative publications, such as *Latvis*, that were pulled from circulation. Finally, the Ministry of Internal Affairs also began censoring the press immediately after the coup. Originally censorship occurred prior to publication, but as the ministry could not keep up, in November 1934 censorship was transferred to post-publication.[22]

During the so-called 'Ulmanis Times' (*Ulmaņa laiki*),[23] the terms totalitarian and totalitarianism appeared with increasing regularity in reference to international affairs. To be sure, there was much coverage of the emergence of a bitter divide in Europe between liberal, individualistic-minded states and authoritarian, fascist or totalitarian states (these three terms were often used interchangeably). In contrast to coverage of global politics, these terms were very rarely used in reference to domestic politics and the Ulmanis regime itself. For his part, Ulmanis never publicly used the terms in reference to his own authoritarian rule. Furthermore, a search of the terms in contemporary periodicals (via Periodika) yields less than ten articles that promoted the

Ulmanis regime as an example of totalitarianism. Does this mean that the Ulmanis regime did not see itself as part of the wider political trend? The answer is very clearly no; there is a plethora of archival evidence that proves that Ulmanis was an ardent student of politics who modelled his rule on fascist 'best practices'.[24] What the scarcity of use might mean, then, is that as a conservative ultranationalist, Ulmanis chose not to slavishly borrow 'foreign' vocabulary. In this sense, totalitarianism is not unlike fascism, for as Reto Hofmann has shown in his work on fascism in Japan, the challenge of transnational fascism was 'how to bring about fascism without fascism'.[25] In other words, members of the transnational network of the far right had to take concepts and vocabulary from the international realm and adopt and appropriate them within their respective national spaces in a way that did not overtly violate the calling card of their political movement: nationalism.

Thus, when members of the Ulmanis regime did use the terms totalitarian or totalitarianism, they were careful to reinterpret them through the lens of Latvian culture and nationalism. The most articulate and elongated explanation of the Ulmanis regime's connection to totalitarianism came in an August 1936 article, written by Professor Kārlis Dišlers, that was published a few days after the annual 'Festival of Workers' that was attended by approximately 150,000 people. Pairing stirring images of the large crowd at the event with his text, Dišlers, a specialist in administrative law who served multiple stints as dean of the faculty at the University of Latvia, argued that totalitarianism is a mere extension of authoritarianism – and that both are often incorrectly believed to be opposed to democracy. Explaining the nature of 'the new state', he wrote, 'The most frequently mentioned and most characteristic designation of the new state is – the authoritarian state. However, this term is often misunderstood; chiefly, the concept of an authoritarian state is perceived as the opposite of the concept of a democratic state. This is wrong'.[26] What the new authoritarian state is against, Dišlers continued, is not democracy but the 'parliamentary state', which is 'usually weak and unstable because it is dependent on the parliament, which itself is made up of many political party factions often led by power-hungry party leaders [*godkārigiem partiju līderiem*] who try to impose on the government both their personal demands as well as those of their faction'. A true democratic state, Dišlers claimed, is one wherein the government pursues the collective interests of the nation, as opposed to personal or party interests. Latvia has such a state, he assured readers, because under Ulmanis 'the current government', and here he quoted Ulmanis directly, 'is not a government of parties and in fact is not even a government of a single party'.[27]

As for totalitarianism, Dišlers explained that whereas authoritarianism means that all political interests are subjugated by the authoritarian state, in a totalitarian state that is true not only of political interests but of '*all* [my emphasis] interests that are of significance to the state or nation'. Offering specific examples, he noted:

> An important significance is placed on economic interests, which is particularly understandable in the context of the crisis of recent years. As a good example of the interests included in the government programme of a totalitarian state, one can mention the agricultural cultivation of marshes (in Italy), the management of construction and state beautification (in Latvia), or even the regulation of church life (in Germany).[28]

As a well-known academic and professor of law, Dišlers became the most-cited theorist in Latvia on the phenomenon of totalitarianism. Clearly, he did not associate it with a monolithic and uniform approach to top-down rule – to what historian David D. Roberts has termed 'the straw man of "total domination" '.[29] Instead, Dišlers theorised totalitarianism as a novel form of interaction between political leaders and the masses, with the end goal of collectively working on matters of mutual importance. What this means, then, as he indicated with his choice of examples, is that each respective nation would appropriate totalitarianism in a unique way. Therefore, when we talk about interwar totalitarianism, we must not fall into the trap of essentialism, assuming that all instances of 'successful' totalitarianism should mirror the Italian, German or Soviet cases. As David D. Roberts has powerfully argued, interwar totalitarianism should not be examined using an either/or model, for doing so 'obscures the dynamic relationships of the time and thus fails to account for the novelty of these movements and regimes'.[30] Hence, the best way to make sense of the ideology of the Ulmanis regime – and to evaluate Stranga's claim – is to adopt the new analytical model of transnational totalitarianism.

Transnational totalitarianism: two scenes on the building of public consciousness

As is true of all of the interwar dictatorships, the Ulmanis regime relied on both coercion and consensus. The former took place mostly during the early months of authoritarian rule. Arguably the two most noteworthy examples are the temporary internment of 369 mostly left-leaning national politicians in a prison camp in Liepāja in far western Latvia, well away from the centre of power in Rīga, and the dismissal of some local government workers for reasons of 'political unreliability'.[31] However, beyond these two very public and visible instances of coercion and repression, Ulmanis focused on cultivating consensus. That meant that everyday life in Ulmanis's Latvia was framed by ideology and spectacle. Most telling is mass participation in public events.[32] This was arguably the lynchpin of transnational totalitarianism in Latvia. The regime placed great priority on these events because they were fundamentally important to building consensus and conformity. Shared experiences would lead to shared values and worldviews – or so the regime believed. Big public events were also vital to the regime's legitimacy, for, as Vita Zelče has concluded, an individual's participation served as collective and very visual 'mobilising acts', suggesting that the people and the government were in lockstep.[33] To highlight the use of public events as a predominant aspect of everyday life and the building of a new totalitarian public consciousness and morality, this section considers two scenes: the Harvest Celebrations (*Pļaujas svētki*) and the Victory Clearing (*Uzvaras līdums*). The intent is to show how the Ulmanis regime used these public events to promote values like unity, modernism, optimism, ambition and efficiency.

Harvest Celebrations

The three national Harvest Celebrations in 1935, 1936 and 1937 were the most widely attended public events in the history of the Ulmanis regime.

FIGURE 5.1 *The 1937 Harvest Festival in Jelgava.* © *Courtesy of the National Archives of Latvia, LNA_KFFDA_F1_10_14817.*

However, they have received scarce attention from scholars – as is also true of the Reich Harvest Thanksgiving Festival (*Das Reichserntedankfest*).[34] This is a major gap in the historiography because these events tell us much about the regime's ideology, as well as the public's reaction to it. Each of the celebrations lasted for a week (and sometimes longer) and the schedule comprised agricultural and industrial exhibits, livestock shows, competitions, amusements etc. On the final day, a Sunday, Ulmanis and other top government officials arrived for the closing ceremonies, where Ulmanis always delivered the much-anticipated keynote speech, followed by the so-called 'Work Parade'.

It is important to note that the idea of a harvest celebration was not new to Latvians. Rather, it had been a part of Latvian rural culture for centuries. However, as one author explained in his article drumming up support for the First Harvest Celebration, which took place in October 1935 in Koknese, this ancient tradition was 'repressed and disparaged' by centuries of life under serfdom, as well as in recent times by foreign ideas that 'confused Latvians' free actions and preached disunity', an obvious reference to the principle of individualism inherent in liberal democracy.[35] What made the Harvest Celebrations different from the ancient custom, then, and why it was publicly understood to be symbolically representative of 'renewed Latvia' as a whole, was that for the first time it was organised by the state and was intended for all citizens, not just local, rural residents who celebrated the end of harvest in their area.

The promotion of modern agricultural practices was also an addition to the old tradition. As the primary organiser (along with the Ministry of Public Affairs), the Latvian Chamber of Agriculture (*Latvijas lauksaimniecības kamera*, or LLK) naturally used the exhibition portion of the Harvest Celebration to educate farmers about new work methods, seed varieties, machinery and so on. In fact, the LLK agronomist Viļums Skubiņš, who oversaw a number of the Harvest Celebrations, once clarified that the exhibition portion was intended to be a sort of 'agricultural people's college'.[36]

To that end, Skubiņš organised, in the case of the Second Harvest Celebration in Rēzekne, an exhibition that was more than five hectares in total size. Working with at least 1,159 companies and persons who applied and paid by the cubic foot for a booth at the exhibition, Skubiņš grouped them into eleven thematic sections, including, for instance, on metal work and machinery, textiles, woodworking and furniture, housekeeping, and agriculture, which was far and away the most popular as a result of the tractor demonstrations.[37] As for the celebration of Ulmanis and the progress of 'the regime of 15 May', there was a special section of the exhibition on 'The Unity of the Nation', and the focal point was a huge painting of Ulmanis that was adorned with wreaths of grain and a draping of Latgalian cloth. Above the painting was a huge placard reading: 'Belief in the Leader – the Nation's Strength'.[38] Finally, the entertainment during the exhibition period (the Monday–Saturday portion of the festival) offered a main event each day. Sometimes it might be a lecture as, for instance, during the first day of the festival when there were talks on 'history and the idea of the national state', while other times it involved Mazpulki (Latvian 4-H) competitions, horse races or scenic bus tours through the beautiful Latvian countryside.[39]

One of the most popular events at the Harvest Celebrations was the bonfire party. This always occurred on the night prior to the closing ceremonies, and it mimicked *Līgo* (traditional midsummer solstice festivities), the most beloved Latvian holiday. At the First Harvest Celebration in Koknese, for example, festivalgoers gathered around two huge bonfires adjacent to the old castle ruins and Daugava River, where they spent the evening singing folk songs and dancing. Of course, such activities worked up an appetite, so the organisers also kept the beverage and food tents open all night.[40]

In addition to all the other fun and educational opportunities that were afforded throughout the week, certainly the most highly anticipated portion of the Harvest Celebration was the closing day, when Ulmanis and other dignitaries made their grand appearance. In fact, put together, more than 480,000 people – in a country of only two million – attended the concluding events of the three Harvest Celebrations. Attendance at the closing ceremony was not mandatory at any level, though certainly the regime greatly propagandised the event and arranged for discounted travel and lodging in the hopes of boosting the turnout.[41]

In the instances of the Second and Third Harvest Celebrations, the day's festivities began around noon with the arrival of the special government train. From the train station all the way to the festival field on the outskirts of town, festivalgoers lined up to wave and cheer as Ulmanis passed by. Often, Ulmanis would stop at the festive gates to greet particular people or groups. For instance, after passing through a festive gate reading 'The People's Leader, Take Our Hands and Hearts' and another saying 'Latgale Welcomes the United Country's Saimnieks [Husbandman]', Ulmanis stopped to say hello to Mazpulki members, who greeted him with flowers and a song.[42] In the case of the First Harvest Celebration, they touched on Ulmanis's image as the *Saimnieks*, singing a short song whose refrain instructed, 'We are all one family /We all have one Saimnieks'.[43]

The use of the term *saimnieks* is interesting. The approximate translation of 'husbandman' does not fully convey the various uses and meanings of *saimnieks*. The root of the word, *saim-*, comes from *saime*, meaning family or household. So, in one way, the word can be understood as the patriarch of the family and household – and at times Ulmanis was indeed described as the father of the nation.[44] Additionally, the term was also historically used to refer to a free, landed farmer – as opposed to a feudal serf engaged in unfree labour – and thus prior to Latvian independence, when few Latvian farmers owned land, this specific use of the term connoted great prestige and was a marker of personal initiative and individual standing. Thus, the use of *saimnieks* can be seen as an example of the Latvianisation of the fascist leadership principle, for this term surely sounded more culturally authentic than Vadonis (the Leader).

Once Ulmanis and his entourage had slowly made their way through the streets lined with thousands of people and hundreds of Latvian flags and arrived at the festival grounds, the afternoon of speeches commenced, as did the live radio broadcast. From local farmers and mayors to heads of government chambers, one speaker after another offered their perspective on the meaning of the Harvest Celebration, always ending by thanking 'the country's mighty Saimnieks [. . .] for peace and harmony amid the nation, and for the land's bounties and blessings'.[45] Wanting very much to include the perspective of the capital, so as to show unity between town and country, the organisers invited Rīga's mayor, Roberts Liepiņš, to speak. His remarks at the Second Harvest Celebration are particularly striking. He began by noting that since 15 May the harvest festival tradition has grown in many ways, and the phrase *Pļaujas svētki* (Harvest Celebrations) took on a connotation of the nation's successes, not only in the countryside, but also in the cities. Indeed, Liepiņš pointed out that Ulmanis had created a place for everyone at the communal festival table, because 'for as much as he has focused on agriculture, he has also paid close attention to the beautification, the modernisation, and to all of those affairs tied to the Latvianisation of our city'.[46] By uttering the line 'Latvianisation of our city', Liepiņš was referring to Latvian nationalists' desires to overturn centuries of 'foreign influence' in Rīga, which was established by Germans in 1201 and later became a major hub of international trade.[47]

By mid-afternoon, it was Ulmanis's turn at the microphone. Each year he gave a rather long address, typically at least an hour in duration. Ulmanis crafted each of the speeches around the themes of joy and gratitude. Speaking to the ancient tradition of celebrating the harvest, Ulmanis pointed out at the First Harvest Celebration that the primary element of joy comes from knowing that one's hard work has paid off, that the crops cared for 'during sweltering days and through thunderstorms' has 'been harvested and the granary is full of new grain'.[48]

Ulmanis then turned to the other obvious source of gratitude and joy – freedom. This most precious joy, Ulmanis explained, comes from the recognition that 'this country, this land of ours, has given its fruits to us, and to no one else', a line referencing the bitter history of serfdom, which drew applause from the crowd. Continuing on, Ulmanis stated:

Today with complete justification we can say that this land is our land. But for a long time foreign feet have walked over this land, and it groaned under the oppression of those foreign feet. Back then our farmers could not be happy about their produce, about their harvest, about the fruits of their labour. During those years and throughout that long timespan, this land has now and again been heavily inflicted. We know and have learned that there has been a time when travelling through open stretches one did not see for ten kilometres a single building, home, or barn, nor even a living person. Today we say that now and again there have been overlords over us who told us what to do [. . .] Those days in our country have been experienced and lived through, and now our land has come into our hands. Now this land is cultivated by our hands. This land has given its fruits under the drone of our own footsteps.[49]

Another portion of his remarks at the First Harvest Celebration were on the joy and gratitude derived from unity. Recalling the rancour and dysfunction of parliamentary politics, Ulmanis instructed his listeners to be grateful that the government's actions are no longer bogged down 'by the demands and constraints of parties'. Likewise, Ulmanis admitted that he personally appreciated that:

> the government is not encountering any opposition from the side of urbanites when it wants to come to the aid of the farmers or to support agriculture. Everyone understands that from the land, from the farmer's work comes the first initiative, the first spark that drives the wheels of our economy and intellectual life, and which sustains the system. [Therefore] all of the farmers themselves must know that the rest [of the nation] are prepared to give them a helping hand, and they truly need to take note of that. We need to understand that it is good [. . .] to be ready to come to each other's aid.[50]

Finally, gazing out over the crowd of roughly 150,000 people from all walks of life, Ulmanis concluded his speech by talking about the joy and gratitude inherent in the organic unity shown at the event. He closed, saying:

> The sea of people and the forest of flags before our eyes give evidence not only of festivals of joy and gratitude, but also, in the fullest sense of the word, a festival of unity, of an unrivalled and unbreakable unity. The physical labourer meets here with the intellectual and everyone understands each other. This unity among us wasn't experienced earlier in the era of party wrangling: in those times of discord, it simply wasn't imaginable. 15 May has brought this unity to us, and that is the greatest benefit of this new era

of 15 May. May this unity remain our most precious possession, because it gives us strength, it teaches us to truly understand the people, the nation and the state, and why we must love our nation and state. This unity will make our oak-tree sons into true sons of the fatherland and our linden-tree daughters into hardworking maidens, into caring housewives, and the bearers, protectors and nurturers of the next generation [. . .] This unity teaches us and gives us the courage and strength to take on and carry out each of our responsibilities, whether big or small, and it teaches us and gives us the courage to accept the duty so that we can stand one for all and all for one [. . .] We will all live and work together for one goal and one duty![51]

Following Ulmanis's speech, there was an intermission to prepare the stage for the Work Parade. In the meantime, Ulmanis took the opportunity to converse with the journalists present, including, at the Second Harvest Celebration, journalists from England, France, Italy, Germany, Poland, Bulgaria, Hungary, Czechoslovakia, the United States and the Soviet Union.[52] The always-popular Work Parade thus began by late afternoon. This particular event was especially well liked because it told the story of progress as participants marched across the stage to the accompanying music of the orchestra and the choir. In other words, the parade was by far the most sensory experience of the whole festival.

For example, the 1935 iteration at the First Harvest Celebration involved 2,000 people representing various trades, jobs and tasks. Participants were assembled in two ways. First, their order in the parade was determined by the work calendar so that, for example, the ploughers and sowers came before the harvesters. Second, the marchers were also organised according to a teleological narrative of progress. Consequently, the ploughers, for instance, would begin with a ploughman driving a horse and wooden plough. Then, as the parade progressed, each subsequent group of ploughers marched across – always turning to face and salute Ulmanis, who was seated in the benches arranged above the parade platform, with an arm raised in the fascist style – with sequentially more advanced tools and equipment, so that in this case the group of ploughers ended with ploughmen driving across brand-new tractors and large, shiny steel ploughs.[53]

Victory Clearing

Late in the afternoon on a cool, damp September day in 1936, Kārlis Ulmanis strode to the microphone to address the citizens of Latvia amid the most unusual of backdrops – a marsh. Accompanied by the calls of cranes, the song

FIGURE 5.2 *Ulmanis delivering a celebratory speech at the Victory Clearing in 1936. © Courtesy of the National Archives of Latvia, LNA_KFFDA_F1_11_9_A39.*

of the forest shrike birds and the sounds of the rustling birch and pine forests, Ulmanis approached the podium, bedecked in an oak-leaf garland, that was framed by three Latvian red-white-red flags hoisted aloft by the winds of change. Indeed, Ulmanis had come to this staged event to celebrate a dramatic change: the transformation of a marsh into fertile farmland. A miracle of modern scientific progress and agricultural ingenuity, Ulmanis called the project 'Victory Clearing'.[54]

After a long list of formal greetings to those various groups of people who were among the approximately 1,000 citizens in attendance, and after he had thanked those tuning in to listen via the radio broadcast, Ulmanis commenced his remarks. 'We are gathered here today with feelings of joy and anticipation in our hearts', he began, 'because today we have assembled here to see and learn about the project that in our land [. . .] is entirely new'.[55] Wanting to frame for his listeners the importance of the work being done in the Olaine-Tireļa marsh – which was located approximately halfway between Rīga, the capital city, and Jelgava, the fourth largest city in Latvia and the home of the Latvian Chamber of Agriculture – Ulmanis discussed the Latvian nation's long struggle to find arable land amid the soggy lowlands of the Daugava River and its many tributaries. Having laid out the history of that endeavour, Ulmanis then instructed the audience that his government's work was the cause for a newfound hope, for, as he put it, 'Today we see here the first fruition [of the belief] that it is possible to conquer the land, to recapture the unsuitable, infertile land by making it suitable and productive'.[56] Moreover, he pointed out that such work 'has again stirred and awakened in a new way' our 'ancient homesteaders' spirit, that spirit of work and persistence'. Finally, as he came to a close, he urged his listeners to learn the lesson of how 'human work and ingenuity have transformed the thousand-year-old marsh into suitable fields, meadows, and forests [. . .] making our land beautiful and rich'.[57] After the speech and the solemn singing of the national anthem, Ulmanis and the other government officials present then walked under the specially erected festive gate reading 'We Welcome the Great Leader to the Land Reconquered from the Marsh!' and participated in placing the cornerstone for the first of eighteen planned farmhouses, all of which were later given to landless *Strēlnieki* and Latvian National Army veterans of the Great War and subsequent War of Liberation (1918–20).[58]

As David Blackbourn has shown so brilliantly in the case of Germany, nations have long striven to 'conquer' nature in the name of national progress and in pursuit of certain national characteristics.[59] This was the case, too, in interwar Latvia. While certainly the regime appreciated the practical benefits of draining marshes to create more farmland and boost domestic agricultural output, really the project was an ideological one. By transforming the marsh, the regime hoped to concurrently transform collective identity and values. Historically, Latvians' collective identity had been tied to the countryside, rather than to cities like Rīga, due to the cultural legacy of serfdom and the urban dominance of Baltic Germans and other 'foreigners'.[60] Consequently, for many Latvians the estimated 650,000 hectares (1,606,185 acres) of marshland in the countryside in the mid-1930s was not just an agricultural impediment; these lands also represented the Latvian nation, and thus while people appreciated the marshland for its pristine beauty, many progressive-minded citizens also viewed it as a sign of national inferiority and backwardness, as indeed something to be overcome and conquered – hence Ulmanis's decision to call the resulting farmland 'Victory Clearing'.[61] Thus, while the project had pragmatic intentions, like making more arable land available to family farmers, it was clearly understood through an ideological-nationalist lens as well.

Although the Olaine-Tīreļa marsh was far from the only land amelioration project,[62] the Ulmanis regime chose to highlight Victory Clearing because it was located just off what was typically the busiest road in all of Latvia: the highway between Rīga and Jelgava. In fact, in 1936 the government estimated that some 1,200 vehicles used the road each day.[63] Certainly, then, the Ulmanis regime seems to have wanted to turn Victory Clearing into a tourist destination – just one of many locales that comprised a new ideologically oriented domestic tourism culture – where one could go to see first-hand the remarkable transformations taking place under Ulmanis's leadership. Another noteworthy example was the Ķegums Dam and hydroelectric station.[64]

Among other 'photo-op' or propaganda-focused activities at the celebration, Ulmanis assisted in the placing of the cornerstone for the first of the eighteen planned houses. The Victory Clearing was propagandised as yet another effort to help the Latvian farmer and to heal the urban–rural divide. Yet, what made this project doubly powerful and impactful in terms of public relations potential is that it also involved veterans of the wars. In 1936, the government invited veterans to submit applications to receive one of these new farms at Victory Clearing. To be eligible the men had to have served in the *Strēlnieki* or in the Latvian National Army during the War of Liberation. They also had to have a family and had to be currently farming rented land or working as a hired hand. In total, 329 veterans filed applications for these farms. The Ministry of Agriculture's Central Land Survey Committee cooperated with the Ministry of Defence in selecting the recipients.[65]

In the years that followed, the Latvian press continued to report on the progress of the new farms at Victory Clearing. For example, the local newspaper *Zemgales Balss* reported that on 7 September 1937, Minister of Agriculture Jānis Birznieks witnessed the beginning of the first ever grain harvest at Victory Clearing.[66] The next week the state-wide newspaper *Rīts* ran an article on Jānis Alksnis, the owner of Avoti Farm at Victory Clearing. Alksnis had just harvested the first oats to be cultivated there, and as a gesture of gratitude he sent Ulmanis a small sample of his harvest. It was reported that Ulmanis in turn sent a thank you note, in which he congratulated Alksnis and his family for having 'awakened the slumbering marsh to new, productive life'.[67] Not to be overlooked, Victory Clearing also became a favoured charity cause as part of Ulmanis's so-called Friendly Challenge (*Draudzīgais aicinājums*) initiative, which encouraged Latvians to donate money and items to schools and organisations, and for projects like Victory Clearing and Victory Field, the new multipurpose amphitheatre and parade grounds in Rīga that opened in 1938.[68] To give but one illustrative example of the publicised donations for Victory Clearing, in 1937 the company A/S Kaļķis gave 17,000 kilograms of lime for the farms at Victory Clearing in order to honour Ulmanis on the occasion of his sixtieth birthday.[69]

In his remarks at the celebration of the Victory Clearing in 1936, Minister of Agriculture Jānis Birznieks pointed out that Victory Clearing was only one part of the larger project aimed at, as he put it, 'freeing the land of water, stumps, shrubs, and rocks' in order to make it possible to use 'easier and more modern forms of cultivation'. He went on, 'Here, in this place, we have made great efforts to show that it is truly possible with human capabilities to reconquer the marshes that have dominated for centuries'.⁷⁰ While that might have indeed been the case, what Birznieks might just as well have said is that Victory Clearing was also part of a larger initiative to transform nature in the hope of 'conquering' Latvian minds: to do away with Latvians' pessimism and innate inferiority complex, both of which were rooted in the cultural heritage of serfdom. In other words, beyond the mere practical benefits of the Victory Clearing, or for that matter even the Ķegums Dam, this and other similar projects were immensely popular because people understood that these were about far more than the celebration of the farmer or even the achievements of the Ulmanis regime. Victory Clearing was really about proving that Latvians, too, were forward-thinking and capable of the type of progress that had long been part of the drive toward modernity in the Western world. In short, as a spectacle-like scene of public morality, Victory Clearing was about promoting confidence, positivism and a will to action.

Conclusion

The Ulmanis regime was absolutely determined to bring about a new Latvian consciousness. As one proponent of the regime put it, this 'new consciousness' must be 'that of the winner, the consciousness of the ruler, the consciousness of the people crowned by glory and success'.⁷¹ To give an indication of just how pervasive this ideological effort was, in 1939 the regime passed a law that encouraged Latvians to change the spelling of their surnames. Advocates of the law complained that Latvians used too many diminutives – and in the case of surnames too many diminutive suffixes. This was seen as hindering the effort to develop a new national consciousness because '[f]amily names like Ozoliņš (Little Oak), Avotiņš (Little Spring), and Akmentiņš (Little Stone) actually imply inferiority and complaint warm-heartedness'. Summarising the intent of the law, the author quipped, 'Certainly, family names will not change the national character, but due to their frequent use in everyday communication, they still have a certain educational role'.⁷²

In his August 1936 article on authoritarianism and totalitarianism, Kārlis Dišlers noted that an excellent example of totalitarianism is the agricultural cultivation of marshes. In the article, he cited Italy as the foremost example of this (of course, Mussolini had transformed the Pontine marshes near Rome to great popular acclaim). The date of publication of Dišlers's article is important because the celebratory event at Victory Clearing took place just a few weeks later. Thus, it is safe to assume that the regime was inviting the public, as part of the effort to develop a new consciousness and public morality, to make transnational comparisons – and to see that 'renewed Latvia' was every bit as advanced as the 'big powers' of Europe.

In his closing remarks at the 1935 Harvest Celebration, Ulmanis had called the event a 'festival of unity'. The festivities brought together town and countryside. As Ulmanis put it, the physical labourer and the intellectual congregated together. To be sure, the last refrain in that speech summarises well the ideological purpose of the Harvest Celebrations: 'We all live together for one goal and one duty!'. 'Renewed Latvia' was to be a reunified Latvia, and the regime regularly talked about the need to rekindle the unity that had been felt in 1918, when, in the midst of war and uncertainty, Latvians had had the courage and initiative to declare their national independence.

Undeniably, the Harvest Celebrations were also part of a wider effort to rehabilitate Latvian history, which had previously been dominated by the experience of serfdom and '700 years of German oppression'.[73] As Education Minister Jūlijs Auškāps explained, 'Not so long ago some people were still ashamed of the fact that Latvians were called the peasant people'. But now, he continued, 'we are proud that we are farmers or at least feel close to the land'.[74]

It was noted at the outset that Aivars Stranga sees the Ulmanis regime as a 'chaotic autocracy' that failed to meet its own fascist and totalitarian aims. For their part, Deniss Hanovs and Valdis Tēraudkalns have posited that Ulmanis was merely a conservative authoritarian leader whose ideology was rooted in traditionalism.[75] This scholarship has not accurately captured the dynamic and fluid nature of totalitarianism in the interwar period, as well as the way in which it was reinterpreted in the Latvian case. Ulmanis's goal was never to develop total control or brutal dictatorial rule. Yet he was also not just a 'traditional' strongman. Certainly, he did embrace traditional Latvian values, but he did so while employing *modern* political concepts, such as, in the words of Amendola, fascism's 'totalitarian spirit'. That spirit animated a novel form of politics that sought to meld together public and private life – as well as state and society – to blur the line between politics and everyday life.

In 2014, a lecture series on Ulmanis was held in Latvia. The series was titled 'Reassessing Vadonisms in Latvia: Kārlis Ulmanis in History, Culture and Memory'. In her fascinating talk, Vita Zelče examined the historical memory of the 'Ulmanis Times'. The starting point for her presentation was a look at a 2010 public survey. In the survey, respondents were first asked about their opinions of all the noteworthy eras of Latvian history, from ancient times to the present day. Tellingly, respondents ranked the 'Ulmanis Times' (1934–40) as the best, most positive era. Roughly 65 per cent of survey-takers responded that they had a good view of the period. In contrast, about 35 per cent of respondents had positive opinions about the second era of Latvian independence (1991–present).[76] Also noteworthy is the response to this question: 'Based on your opinion, please name the most positive person in twentieth-century Latvian history'. Ulmanis received four times more votes than the next closest historical figure, Jānis Čakste, who served as the first president of Latvia. These statistics suggest that the Ulmanis regime is not viewed by the present-day average Latvian citizen as a chaotic failure. Similarly, as noted above, the enthusiastic turnout for the Harvest Celebrations suggests that Latvians who lived through the Ulmanis Times also did not see the regime in such a way. Rather, they mostly responded positively to Ulmanis's novel form of politics, which can be seen as an example of transnational totalitarianism. Perhaps most telling of all, there was no substantial dissent or resistance to Ulmanis's regime. This fact tells us just how successful Ulmanis was in developing a new public consciousness, whose legacy is still evident today.

Notes

1. A. Stranga, 'The Political System and Ideology of Karlis Ulmanis's Authoritarian Regime: May 15, 1934–June 17, 1940', in *War, Revolution, and Governance: The Baltic Countries in the Twentieth Century*, ed. L. Fleishman and A. Weiner (Boston, MA, 2018), 58.
2. Ibid., 75.
3. This work only analyses the term totalitarianism. For a similar investigation of the term fascism, particularly in the context of Latvian interwar politics, see J.T. Kuck, 'The Blurring of Lines: Democracy, *Vadonisms*, and Latvia in Transnational Context', in *Latvijas ārlietu simtgade: Pasaules doma un Latvija*, ed. A. Sprūds, V. Ščerbinskis and K. Bukovskis (Rīga, 2019), 60–78; 'The Dictator Without a Uniform: Kārlis Ulmanis, Agrarian Nationalism, Transnational Fascism, and Interwar Latvia' (PhD diss., University of Tennessee, Knoxville, 2014); and 'Renewed Latvia: A Case Study of the Transnational Fascism Model', *Fascism* 2, no. 2 (2013): 183–204.
4. In particular, see H. Arendt, *The Origins of Totalitarianism* (New York, 1951); C.J. Friedrich and Z.K. Brzezinski, *Totalitarian Dictatorship and Autocracy* (Cambridge, MA, 1956).
5. For an excellent overview of Croce's views and the wider development of totalitarianism as a term and theory, see especially A. Gleason, *Totalitarianism: The Inner History of the Cold War* (Oxford and New York, 1995). For the quote about totalitarianism as governmental morality, see 18.
6. F. Stern, *The Politics of Cultural Despair: A Study in the Rise of the Germanic Ideology* (Berkeley, CA, 1974).
7. R. Ben-Ghiat, 'Five Faces of Fascism', in *Visualizing Fascism*, ed. J.A. Thomas and G. Eley (Durham, NC, 2020), 94–110.
8. Classic studies on this include Walter Benjamin's 1936 essay 'The Work of Art in the Age of Mechanical Reproduction'. Available online: https://www.marxists.org/reference/subject/philosophy/works/ge/benjamin.htm (accessed 27 May 2021). More recent works of import are S. Falasca-Zamponi, *Fascist Spectacle: The Aesthetics of Power in Mussolini's Italy* (Berkeley, CA, 2000);

J.T. Schnapp, *Staging Fascism:* 18 BL *and the Theater of Masses for Masses* (Stanford, CA, 1996).

9   N. Stoltzfus, *Hitler's Compromises: Coercion and Consensus in Nazi Germany* (New Haven, CT, 2016). Of course, such an interpretation of Hitler as weak and prone to compromise began with the scholarship of Hans Mommsen.

10 Scholarship on transnational fascism is now rather vast. Particularly insightful are: A. Bauerkämper and G. Rossoliński-Liebe (eds), *Fascism Without Borders: Transnational Connections and Cooperation Between Movements and Regimes in Europe from 1918 to 1945* (New York, 2017); D.D. Roberts, *Fascist Interactions: Proposals for a New Approach to Fascism and Its Era, 1919–1945* (New York, 2016); A. Kallis and A.C. Pinto (eds), *Rethinking Fascism and Dictatorship in Europe* (Basingstoke, 2014); S.H. Goodfellow, 'Fascism as a Transnational Movement: The Case of Inter-war Alsace', *Contemporary European History* 22, no. 1 (2012): 87–106; A.C. Pinto (ed.), *Rethinking the Nature of Fascism: Comparative Perspectives* (Basingstoke, 2011).

11 To the author's knowledge, this is the first scholarly use of the term, though Federico Finchelstein seems to have embraced a similar transnational perspective in his use of the phrase 'global totalitarianism'. See F. Finchelstein, *Transatlantic Fascism: Ideology, Violence, and the Sacred in Argentina and Italy, 1919–1945* (Durham, NC, 2010), especially Chapter 5. And certainly, David Roberts has encouraged a critical, international approach to understanding totalitarianism. See in particular, D.D. Roberts, *Totalitarianism* (Cambridge, 2020).

12 For a biography of Ulmanis, see especially A. Bērziņš, *Kārlis Ulmanis: cilvēks un valstsvīrs* (New York, 1974); E. Dunsdorfs, *Kārļa Ulmaņa dzīve: ceļinieks, polītiķis, diktātors, moceklis* (Stockholm, 1978). On Ulmanis's coup and regime, see V. Zelče et al. (eds), *Reiz dzīvoja Kārlis Ulmanis* (Rīga, 2007); V. Ščerbinskis and Ē. Jēkabsons, *Apvērsums: 1934. gada 15. maija notikumi avotos un pētījumos* (Rīga, 2012); D. Hanovs and V. Tēraudkalns, *Laiks, telpa, Vadonis: autoritārisma kultūra Latvijā, 1934–1940* (Rīga, 2012).

13 P. Baehr, 'Max Weber and the Avatars of Caesarism', in *Dictatorship in History and Theory: Bonapartism, Caesarism, and Totalitarianism*, ed. P. Baehr and M. Richter (Cambridge, 2004), 157.

14 Roberts, *Totalitarianism*, 4.

15 Quoted in Gleason, *Totalitarianism*, 14.

16 Ibid., 15.

17 Ibid., 16.

18 Finchelstein, *Transatlantic Fascism*, 143; Gleason, *Totalitarianism*, 19.

19 See 'Pasaules politika', *Strādnieku Avīze*, no. 8, 12 January 1926, 2.

20 'Zwischen zwei Zivilisationen', *Rigasche Rundschau*, no. 18, 14 August 1933, 5.

21 For example, see 'Rehms noschauts', *Pēdēja Brīdī*, no. 152, 2 July 1934, 1; 'Likvidēts triecinnieku apversuma mēģinājums', *Latviajs Kareivis*, no. 142, 3–4.

22 V. Ščerbinskis, 'Leaders, Divided Society and Crisis Leaders, Divided Society and Crisis: The Coup d'État of 1934 in Latvia, Its Causes and Consequences',

in *Forgotten Pages in Baltic History Diversity and Inclusion*, ed. M. Housden and D. Smith (Amsterdam, 2011), 200.
23 This is a colloquial phrase used in reference to the period of Ulmanis's authoritarian rule.
24 I have covered this fact at length in two of my works: 'The Blurring of Lines'; and 'The Dictator Without a Uniform'.
25 R. Hofmann, *The Fascist Effect: Japan and Italy, 1915–1952* (Ithaca, NY, 2015), 137.
26 Prof. K. Dišlers, 'Autoritāra, totālitāra, korporātiva valsts', *Aizsargs*, no. 7, 15 August 1936, 475.
27 Ibid.
28 Ibid., 476.
29 D.D. Roberts, *The Totalitarian Experiment in Twentieth Century Europe: Understanding the Poverty of Great Politics* (New York, 2006), 16.
30 Roberts, *Totalitarianism*, 7.
31 On the prison camp, see especially V. Ščerbinskis, 'Liepājas koncentrācijas nometne un tās režīms: 1934. gada maijs-1935. gada marts', *Latvijas Arhīvi*, no. 1 (2009): 66–88. On the 'purging' of local government workers, see V. Ščerbinskis, 'Leaders, Divided Society and Crisis', 187–209.
32 I very much agree with Paul Corner, who has argued that mass participation in public events was the single most defining trait of Italian Fascism. See, 'Collaboration, Complicity, and Evasion Under Italian Fascism', in *Everyday Life in Mass Dictatorship: Collusion and Evasion*, ed. A. Lüdtke (New York, 2016), 75–93.
33 V. Zelče, ' "Bēgšana no brīvības": Kārļa Ulmaņa režīma ideoloģija un rituāli', in *Reiz dzīvoja Kārlis Ulmanis*, ed. V. Zelče et al. (Rīga, 2007), 325.
34 Hanovs and Tēraudkalns are the only other scholars who have discussed these events, but they only devote a mere eight pages to the celebrations in their work. See *Laiks, telpa, Vadonis: autoritārisma kultūra Latvijā, 1934–1940*. Surprisingly, there is not a single monograph-length book in English on the Reich Harvest Festival. Two works that do cover it at some length are: R. Gellately, *Hitler's True Believers: How Ordinary People Became Nazis* (Oxford, 2020) and G. Gerhard, *Nazi Hunger Politics: A History of Food in the Third Reich* (Lanham, MD, 2015).
35 Ž. Gībietis, 'Vienības zelta Pļaujas svētki', *Rīts pielikums: Darbs un arodorganizācijas*, 12 October 1935, 2.
36 'Tās noguruma nepazīst: atklāja lielo izstādi', *Brīvā Zeme*, no. 202, 7 September 1936, 9.
37 Latvian State Historical Archives (LVVA), 1690. f., 4. apr., 1598. l., 1.-4. lp.; LVVA, 1690. f., 4. apr., 1695. l.; LVVA, 1690. f., 4. apr., 1969. l., 13. lp.
38 'Ministri lielās izstādes apskatē', *Brīvā Zeme*, no. 202, 7 September 1936, 13.
39 *Brīvā Zeme*, no. 200, 4 September 1936, 1. Mazpulki, or Latvian 4-H, was established in 1929 at the urging of Ulmanis, who first encountered 4-H while living in Nebraska; 4-H is a youth organisation that historically has focused on teaching agriculture and celebrating natural and rural life. But after 1934,

Ulmanis transformed Latvian 4-H into a fascist-style youth organisation. On this topic, see Kuck, 'The Dictator Without a Uniform', especially Chapter 4.

40. '130.000 apmeklētāju lielajos pļaujas svētkos', *Rīts*, no. 283, 14 October 1935, 4; 'Tas jāzina visiem pļaujas svētku apmeklētājiem', *Rīts*, 11 October 1935, 8.
41. Kuck, 'The Dictator Without a Uniform', 333–5.
42. 'Fanfaras vēsta Prezidenta ierašanos', *Brīvā Zeme*, 14 September 1936, 4.
43. 'Gavilēšana valsts prezidentu, ministru prezidentu un valdību sagaidot', *Rīts*, 14 October 1935, 4.
44. For example, one 1936 article is titled 'Dr K. Ulmanis Is a Real Family Man – Strict and Fair'. Quoted in I. Lipša, 'Nation Building and Gender Issues in Interwar Latvia', in *War, Revolution, and Governance: The Baltic Countries in the Twentieth Century*, ed. L. Fleishmann and A. Weiner (Boston, MA, 2018), 35.
45. R. Dzērve, 'Varpu zelta vaiņags: Pļaujas svētki – himna radošam darbam', *Brīvā Zeme*, no. 206, 11 September 1936, 1.
46. 'Galvas pilsētas sveiciens: Rīgas pilsētas galva uzrunā Prezidentu', *Brīvā Zeme*, 14 September 1936, 4.
47. For a history of Rīga, see K.C. O'Connor, *The House of Hemp and Butter: A History of Old Riga* (Ithaca, NY, 2020); A. Kolbergs, *The Story of Riga: History of Riga Old Town* (Rīga, 1998). Hanovs and Tēraudkalns cover the Ulmanis regime's effort to 'Latvianise' Rīga in Chapter 7 of their book, *Laiks, telpa, vadonis*.
48. 'Ceļš uz valsts varenību: Ministru prezidenta lielā runa pļaujas svētkos', *Rīts*, no. 283, 14 October 1935, 5.
49. Ibid., 4–5.
50. Ibid.
51. Ibid., 5.
52. 'Tauta ar valdību: Prezidenta uzruna žurnālistiem', *Brīvā Zeme*, 14 September 1936, 13; 'Galvas pilsētas jaunākie notikumi', *Brīvā Zeme*, 11 September 1936, 15.
53. '2000 zemes kopēju darba parāde', *Rīts*, 14 October 1935, 10.
54. This detailed description of the event is based on newspaper and journal accounts and photos.
55. 'Uzvaras līdums', *Jaunākās Ziņas*, 1936, 1.
56. 'Vecais līdumnieku', *Brīvā zeme*, 1936, 1.
57. 'Uzvaras līdums', 1.
58. 'Vecais līdumnieku', 3. The *Strēlnieki*, or Latvian Riflemen as the term is typically rendered in English, was a group of roughly 40,000 men who in 1915 were conscripted by the Imperial Russian Army into all-Latvian units to fight against the Germans. Following the Bolshevik Revolution, the *Strēlnieki* broke into numerous factions, with some fighting with the Whites while the majority broke into two more camps: those supporting the Bolsheviks and those supporting the idea of an independent Latvia.
59. D. Blackbourn, *The Conquest of Nature: Water, Landscape, and the Making of Modern Germany* (New York, 2006).

60 For excellent discussions on the emergence of Latvian national identity and the importance of the countryside, see especially K.Z.S. Schwartz, ' "The Occupation of Beauty": Imagining Nature and Nation in Latvia', *East European Politics and Societies* 21, no. 2 (2007): 259–93; I. Ijabs, 'Another Baltic Postcolonialism: Young Latvians, Baltic Germans, and the Emergence of Latvian National Movement', *Nationalities Papers* 42, no. 1 (2014): 88–107; I. Zake, 'Inventing Culture and Nation: Intellectuals and Early Latvian Nationalism', *National Identities* 9, no. 4 (2007): 307–29.

61 'Uzvaras līdums', *Meža dzīve*, 1936, 4846.

62 For example, in addition to Victory Clearing, by 1936 the government had also initiated amelioration work along the shores of Lake Lubāns, the largest lake in Latvia. The goal was to convert 50,000 hectares (123,553 acres) of marshland along the lake into farmland. And as proof of how serious the Ulmanis regime was about such undertakings, by 1936 the government had already invested more than 1,000,000 lats into amelioration projects. See, 'Cilvēka spēki uzvarējuši purvu', *Brīvā Zeme*, 1936, 6.

63 'Kā izveidos Rīgas-Jelgavas autoceļu', *Zemgales Balss*, 1937, 1.

64 On the topic of tourism, see especially A. Purs, 'One Breath for Every Two Strides: The State's Attempt to Construct Tourism and Identity in Interwar Latvia', in *Turizm: The Russian and East European Tourist Under Capitalism and Socialism*, ed. A. Gorsuch and D. Koenker (Ithaca, NY, and London, 2006), 97–115. On the dam, see R. Andersone, *Ķeguma hidroelektrostacija: laiki, notikumi un cilvēku likteņi* (Rīga, 2004) and *Ķeguma apvidus vēsture* (Lielvārde, 1999).

65 'Sadalīs Uzvaras līdums', *Zemgales Balss*, 1936, 4.

66 'Kulšana Uzvaras līdumā', *Zemgales Balss*, 1937, 9.

67 'Prezidenta novēlējums', *Rīts*, 1937, 1.

68 For a good summary of *Draudzīgais aicinājums*, see J. Graudonis, 'Ministru prezidenta Kārļa Ulmaņa Draudzīgais aicinājums', in *Kārlim Ulmanim 120*, ed. A. Caune et al. (Rīga, 1998), 137–46. On the history of *Uzvaras laukums/parks*, see M. Ruks, *Spridzinātāji* (Rīga, 2011).

69 'Ziedojums Uzvaras līdumā', *Zemgales Balss*, 1937, 1.

70 'Uzvaras līdumā iesvētīti', *Jaunākā Ziņas*, 1936, 3.

71 Quoted in Lipša, 'Nation Building and Gender Issues in Interwar Latvia', 35.

72 Ibid., 34.

73 Aldis Purs offers an excellent overview of the nationalist trope of '700 years of German oppression' in his book *Baltic Facades: Estonia, Latvia and Lithuania Since 1945* (London, 2012).

74 Lipša, 'Nation Building and Gender Issues in Interwar Latvia', 34.

75 D. Hanovs and V. Tēraudkalns, 'The Return of the Gods? Authoritarian Culture and Neo-Paganism in Interwar Latvia, 1934–1940' in *Latvia – A Work in Progress? 100 Years of State- and Nation-Building*, ed. D.J. Smith (New York, 2016), 91–106 and *Laiks, telpa, Vadonis* (Rīga, 2012).

76 V. Zelče, 'Kārlis Ulmanis Latvijas Sociālajā Atmiņā', 14 May 2014, https://www.youtube.com/watch?v=h-JwKsnHCOA (accessed 26 May 2021).

Select bibliography

Arendt, H. *The Origins of Totalitarianism*. New York, 1951.
Baehr, P. 'Max Weber and the Avatars of Caesarism', in *Dictatorship in History and Theory: Bonapartism, Caesarism, and Totalitarianism*, edited by P. Baehr and M. Richter, 155–74. Cambridge, 2004.
Bauerkämper, A. and Rossoliński-Liebe, G. (eds). *Fascism Without Borders: Transnational Connections and Cooperation Between Movements and Regimes in Europe from 1918 to 1945*. New York, 2017.
Ben-Ghiat, R. 'Five Faces of Fascism', in *Visualizing Fascism: The Twentieth-Century Rise of the Global Right*, edited by J.A. Thomas and G. Eley, 94–110. Durham, NC, 2020.
Corner, P. 'Collaboration, Complicity, and Evasion Under Italian Fascism', in *Everyday Life in Mass Dictatorship: Collusion and Evasion*, edited by A. Lüdtke, 75–93. New York, 2016.
Falasca-Zamponi, S. *Fascist Spectacle: The Aesthetics of Power in Mussolini's Italy*. Berkeley, CA, 2000.
Finchelstein, F. *Transatlantic Fascism: Ideology, Violence, and the Sacred in Argentina and Italy, 1919–1945*. Durham, NC, 2010.
Friedrich, C. and Brzezinski, Z. *Totalitarian Dictatorship and Autocracy*. Cambridge, MA, 1956.
Gleason, A. *Totalitarianism: The Inner History of the Cold War*. Oxford and New York, 1995.
Hanovs, D. and Tēraudkalns, V. *Laiks, telpa, Vadonis: autoritārisma kultūra Latvijā, 1934–1940*. Rīga, 2012.
Hanovs, D. and Tēraudkalns, V. 'The Return of the Gods? Authoritarian Culture and Neo-Paganism in Interwar Latvia, 1934–1940', in *Latvia – A Work in Progress? 100 Years of State- and Nation-Building*, edited by D.J. Smith, 91–106. New York, 2016.
Kallis, A. and Pinto, A.C. *Rethinking Fascism and Dictatorship in Europe*. Basingstoke, 2014.
Kuck, J.T. 'The Blurring of Lines: Democracy, *Vadonisms*, and Latvia in Transnational Context', in *Latvijas ārlietu simtgade: Pasaules doma un Latvij*, edited by A. Sprūds, V. Ščerbinskis and K. Bukovskis, 60–78. Rīga, 2019.
Kuck, J.T. 'The Dictator Without a Uniform: Kārlis Ulmanis, Agrarian Nationalism, Transnational Fascism, and Interwar Latvia', PhD diss., University of Tennessee, Knoxville, 2014. Available online: https://trace.tennessee.edu/utk_graddiss/2895/ (accessed 12 May 2022).
Kuck, J.T. 'Renewed Latvia: A Case Study of the Transnational Fascism Model', *Fascism* 2, no. 2 (2013): 183–204.
Lipša, I. 'Nation Building and Gender Issues in Interwar Latvia', in *War, Revolution, and Governance: The Baltic Countries in the Twentieth Century*, edited by L. Fleishmann and A. Weiner, 30–55. Boston, MA, 2018.
Roberts, D.D. *The Totalitarian Experiment in Twentieth Century Europe: Understanding the Poverty of Great Politics*. New York, 2006.
Roberts, D.D. *Totalitarianism*. Cambridge, 2020.
Ščerbinskis, V. 'Leaders, Divided Society and Crisis: The Coup d'État of 1934 in Latvia, Its Causes and Consequences', in *Forgotten Pages in Baltic History: Diversity and Inclusion*, edited by M. Housden and D.J. Smith, 187–209. Amsterdam, 2011.

Ščerbinskis, V. and Jēkabsons, Ē. *Apvērsums: 1934. gada 15. maija notikumi avotos un pētījumos*. Rīga, 2012.
Stranga, A. 'The Political System and Ideology of Karlis Ulmanis's Authoritarian Regime: May 15, 1934–June 17, 1940', in *War, Revolution, and Governance: The Baltic Countries in the Twentieth Century*, edited by L. Fleishman and A. Weiner, 56–75. Boston, MA, 2018.
Zelče, V. ' "Bēgšana no brīvības": Kārļa Ulmaņa režīma ideoloģija un rituāli', in *Reiz dzīvoja Kārlis Ulmanis*, edited by V. Zelče et al., 325–50. Rīga, 2007.
Zelče, V. 'Kārlis Ulmanis Latvijas Sociālajā Atmiņā', filmed May 2014 at Kārlis Ulmanis Lecture Series. Available online: https://www.youtube.com/watch?v=h-JwKsnHCOA (accessed 26 May 2021).

6

Everyday life in the Soviet Union under Stalin

Kees Boterbloem

Totalitarian *byt'*?

Exploring everyday existence (a concept called *byt'* in Russian) in Stalin's Soviet Union may show parallels with daily life in other contemporary dictatorial regimes in Europe, but the Union of Socialist Soviet Republics (USSR) was in many ways a phenomenon *sui generis*, rather than an example of a species of interwar and wartime European dictatorships. Indeed, scholars no longer place mid-twentieth-century dictatorships under the common denominator of 'totalitarianism', a term most famously conceptualised by Hannah Arendt (albeit coined long before her 1958 treatise). Historians reject the existence of twentieth-century regimes in total control of their subjects, as has been graphically depicted in the dystopias conjured up by writers such as Evgenii Zamiatin, Aldous Huxley, George Orwell or Margaret Atwood.[1]

The concept of totalitarianism might still be useful as a heuristic tool, however, if it is conceived as a Weberian *idealtypus* rather than an actual historical manifestation. If seen from such a perspective, one might suggest that Hitler, Lenin or Stalin *strove* to achieve total control with every means at their disposal, but, given the limitations of the tools they wielded, they did not accomplish this goal, even when acquiring such power was their ultimate aim.

Nonetheless, Stalin, Hitler, Mussolini and Franco did not exert totalitarian control over their societies in actuality. In the right-wing dictatorships, for example, the continued independent operation of the churches significantly undermined the effort to create an all-powerful state, while the army, even in Germany, was another key institution that maintained a considerable measure of independence (at least until late 1941). And significant differences between the dictatorships can be detected in terms of their efforts at acquiring unrestricted control over their subjects. Despite its ominous sound, for instance, Nazi *Gleichschaltung* ('coordination') did not amount to the same sort of absolute control over social organisations that the Soviet regime imposed during the 1930s.

Indeed, among the European dictatorships of the age it was the Soviet one that may have progressed furthest on the path to total control. In its heyday around 1950, the USSR was a country in which the government's power over its population appeared to know no limitation. Startlingly, the country almost totally lacked any trait of a civil society: no independent organisations existed in which members could participate in activities that were not coordinated by the regime. By the late 1930s, even filmscripts, musical compositions or works of literature slated for publication were personally vetted by the country's leaders.

In addition, the Soviet regime was unlike its counterparts in that it lasted far longer – three-quarters of a century – than any other twentieth-century European dictatorship: on the right of the political spectrum, Portugal's was the longest lasting (1926–74), while on the left each of the various People's Republics of East-Central Europe lasted fewer than 45 years. But even Stalin was ultimately nowhere near exerting totalitarian power over his people, as his subjects still carved out a private life, harboured dissenting thoughts, uttered criticism about his regime and acted in defiance of its precepts.

The brutal context of daily life

While it is justified to make a distinction between the first dozen years of communist rule under Lenin (1917–29) and Stalin's personal dictatorship (1929–53), and between Stalin's period and his successors' terms (1953–91), these three timespans within the history of the Soviet Union are not entirely distinct. Before 1929, V.I. Lenin (1870–1924) and his lieutenants (who already included Stalin) set up most of the main components of Stalin's subsequent regime, while after 1953 Nikita Khrushchev (1894–1971) and those who succeeded him tinkered with the manner in which Stalin's state operated, rather than changing it to any profound degree.

The crucial difference between the Stalin years in Soviet history and the other periods is the amount of bloodshed and suffering unleashed by the dictatorship on its own population *in peacetime*, as well as the staggering loss of life the country suffered during the Second World War. Adding Golfo Alexopoulos's estimates that 6 million camp inmates (political and criminal convicts) died to other scholars' calculations that between 1.5 to 2 million people were executed outright under Stalin, 7 to 8 million Soviet citizens died at the orders of the regime, while several more *additional* millions succumbed because of famines that could have been avoided.²

In terms of its peacetime killing of its own population, only a few other twentieth-century dictatorial regimes can be compared to Stalin's: those of Mao Zedong in China, Pol Pot in Cambodia, and – as much as we can tell – Kim Il-sung in North Korea. In Europe, only Franco and Hitler may have unleashed a terror on their own population that resembles anything near the intensity of Stalin's efforts, but Franco did so mainly in the course and immediate aftermath of a civil war, while Hitler's genocide of Jews and mass murder of other marked peoples truly began after 1 September 1939 (and especially 22 June 1941), after his declaration of war on Poland. The famine that laid low five million people in 1932 and 1933 as well as Stalin's mass terror of 1937 and 1938 were unleashed when the USSR was at peace; both even returned in a sort of echo effect after 1945, when peace had once again descended on his country. Upon his death in 1953, several million convicts (approximately 2 per cent of all adults in the country) were released by the GULag (Main Administration of Labour Camps) from the Soviet labour-camp system, indicating that until the very end, political protests – and even minor crimes – were met with harsh repercussions from the authorities.

Astonishingly, the massive extent of this state terror was easily surpassed by the 25 to 28 million deaths during the Second World War. Globally, no fewer than half of the total deaths during this conflict may have been of people who resided in the Soviet Union before 22 June 1941. This wartime death toll merged with the suffering the Soviet population underwent at the hands of its own regime in peacetime, blurring the entire period of Stalin's autocracy into a nightmare of relentless pain in the minds of those who lived through it and survived it.

Another difference from Europe's other contemporaneous dictatorships was that the Soviet Union's territory was incomparably vast; of course, its larger part was situated in Asia (even if four-fifths of its population lived west of the Urals and north of the Caucasus, that is, in Europe as it is most commonly defined by geographers). This, too, made the Soviet dictatorship a distinctive beast from its European counterparts. Despite this difference of scale, the Soviet regime under Stalin nevertheless shared numerous traits with other contemporary dictatorships in Europe. Long before Stalin was hailed as its peerless leader, its leaders introduced the prototype of the one-party state that became the standard for the extremist regimes of both left and right everywhere. Already in 1921, the highest bosses of the Soviet Communist Party banned opposition even *within* its ranks. Its leadership cult, which began in truth with Lenin's death in January 1924, resembled that of the interbellum's right-wing dictatorships, even if it echoed in part the worship of the tsar that had been common in pre-revolutionary Russia. Its severe censorship of the printing press and other media was likewise similar to that of other authoritarian regimes in Europe.

The Communist Party's systematic use of propaganda to indoctrinate its population was another trait the Soviet Union had in common with other European dictatorships: Years before the Bolsheviks (Communists) took power in October 1917, Lenin had begun to hammer home the importance of agitation and propaganda (*agitprop*). Once the Communists were in power, *agitprop*'s presence became all-pervasive in Soviet society, harnessing the country's greatest creative minds into its service. It involved 'political education', which became an obligation for all. To explain the current political situation at home and abroad, as well as the leadership's policies, to low-level Party members and the population at large, cells (the Communist Party's lowest-level organisations) held regular meetings, while *agitprop* workers routinely addressing shopfloor workers and collective-farm meetings. School curricula at all levels required study of Marxism-Leninism. Stalin's subjects were guided by canonical texts such as *The History of the All-Union Communist Party (Bolsheviks): Short Course*, edited by the 'Boss' (*Vozhd*') himself, which was the world's best-selling book during the 1940s.[3] Secret-police agents, or their informers (*sekretnye sotrudniki*), closely watched the populace's compliance with the Party line, a phenomenon not unknown in other dictatorial states.

The secret police and its world

The Soviet secret police began to enforce communist law and order in December 1917. The organisation was created some six weeks after the Bolshevik takeover of power that autumn. Its goal was to combat political and economic crime, loosely defined in laws that allowed a very wide net to ensnare people for even the pettiest of crimes. And, especially because formally a state of emergency prevailed throughout Stalin's rule, the secret police could apprehend suspects through emergency-decree authorisation. Before Stalin unleashed his 'Great Leap Forward' ('Great Turn' or *Velikii Perelom*) in 1929, the secret police already systematically collected data on the popular mood across the Soviet Union. The intent of the reports (*svodki*) based on these findings was not yet deliberately aimed at persecuting political dissenters, but the information they contained about them was carefully preserved. Those denounced in such reports in the 1920s ended up incarcerated in the 1930s.

From 1929 onward, a direct threat of arrest for falling foul of the authorities enforced conformity.[4] Different damning labels were applied to alleged opponents of the regime when prosecuted, but for most of those arrested the outcome was the same, that is lengthy sentences in labour camps in horrible conditions. Few of the accused were ever found innocent by the courts (some of which were 'extraordinary', while others were part of the more regular judicial system), as even the slightest or most ancient utterance of political disagreement with the regime might be spun into grandiose anti-Soviet conspiracies by the NKVD (Narodnyi Komissariat Vnutrennykh Del or People's Commissariat of Internal Affairs, the secret police's name during its grimmest phase in the 1930s). Since they were themselves exposed to brutal torture while routinely their families were threatened, the suspects mostly confessed to the imaginary crimes of which they stood accused. Until 1945, the death rate in the 'corrective labour' camps for convicts was so high, that one of its former inmates, Aleksandr Solzhenitsyn, with good reason called them 'destructive-labour' camps.

It is not wholly clear how much 'those on the outside' knew about this 'GUlag Archipelago' (again Solzhenitsyn's term, 'Archipelago' indicating the vast number of camps dotting the Soviet map, resembling an island archipelago in the sea).[5] Countless 'free' Soviet inhabitants, even in the cities, witnessed convicts working on various projects. Most of the camp inmates worked in remote areas, however, felling trees, digging ore in gold and uranium mines, or building railroads in the Artic north or Siberia. Even if one did not oneself meet convicts detailed to urban construction projects or canal building, given the number of people apprehended, some awareness of a brutal penal system for those falling foul of the authorities can be assumed for everyone. The historian Steven A. Barnes plausibly suggests that 'some 18 million people passed through the prison and camps of the Gulag' within the quarter century of Stalin's rule.[6] That amounts to 10 per cent of the population.

The regime pretended that only hard-core delinquents served time in the camps, hiding the vast extent of the system to the outside world. But given the proportion of the population that was confined in the camps (which was even higher among grown-ups, as virtually all of the camp population consisted of [largely male] adults), the threat of incarceration was visceral for most. As Alexopoulos writes, meanwhile, 'declassified Gulag archival documents fail to tell the whole story'.[7] In other words, there may have been more than 18 million inmates in the Gulag. Their mortality was significantly higher than the official currently available statistics suggest.

As in other dictatorships, the role of internal security forces was crucial in enforcing communist rule. Voluntary or coerced informers were expected to denounce any nonconformists. The merciless attitude towards political opposition was underlined by the authorities' trumpeting of public trials (often known as show trials) that were staged against alleged 'enemies of the people'. Judges condemned the accused – hauled before these kangaroo courts – to the death penalty, or to endless years of imprisonment in the 'corrective labour camps', as the concentration camps of the GULag were officially termed.[8]

Thus, heavy-handed measures (which also included mercilessly combating crimes committed by people often living at, or even below, subsistence levels) were applied to straitjacket popular behaviour, words and thoughts. No doubt Soviet denizens behaved with utmost caution toward each other, even within their own households, but the effort to make everyone into committed, or even zealous, Soviet citizens by 'atomising' them never quite succeeded. Orwell in *Nineteen Eighty-Four*, or Arthur Koestler in *Darkness at Noon* have their protagonists convert to the cause, but historians have found that not a great many Russians, Ukrainians, Georgians, Jews, Tajiks and so on became convinced *homines Sovietici*.[9]

Such new Soviet men and women could be encountered on the lifeless pages of socialist-realist prose, but the fictional tales about these cardboard characters hardly passed the muster of popular taste. This distaste showed how few among the Soviet public identified with such socialist heroes, even if the quality of the writing may be partially faulted for the tepid readers' response. Rare was the loyal Soviet writer who matched the craft of Maksim Gor'kii (1868–1936), whose work served as a model for socialist-realist literati. Indeed, the voracious reading appetite of much of the Soviet population preferred characters from a different era who spoke to the imagination: One could always turn to the Russian nineteenth-century classics such as Lev Tolstoy or Fyodor Dostoyevsky (even if the reading of the latter's work was often discouraged).

The Great Turn and the Great Terror

Within the period of Stalin's twenty-five-year autocracy, the historian can identify three phases, in which the life of his subjects unfolded within dramatically different contexts: 1929–41; 1941–45; and 1945–53. This is a bit of a crude division, of course: in 1939 and 1940, significant territories in the west were added to the USSR, whose populations only then encountered Soviet rule for the first time, and their history's timeline is therefore different.[10] The more than three months of armed conflict with Finland (the so-called Winter War) in 1939 and 1940 not only affected the Leningrad region on the Finnish borders directly, but also saw hundreds of thousands of soldiers enter combat. After May 1945, western territory lost in 1941 was regained. This led to a renewed strenuous effort to impose Soviet order, which was met with armed resistance in a number of areas; after much bloodshed, this guerrilla war was only suppressed towards 1950. And Ukrainians and others suspected of being anti-Soviet were deported in their tens of thousands to the GULag.[11] Even before the war, ethnic deportations had seen entire population groups (such as the Korean community of the Far East) deported from their homelands;

during the war, those deportations increased, as peoples such as the Crimean Tatars and Chechens were accused of collaboration with the Nazis. For all of them, then, the history of Stalin's time unfolded with a rather different chronology.

For the majority of the Soviet population, nonetheless, the three stages fit. The first phase that began in 1929 was that of the 'Great Turn', the effort to transform a still largely rural economy with a labour force predominantly occupied in agriculture into a modern industrialised country of urban workers.[12] This process was steered by the heralded Five-Year Plans and led to a massive migration from the countryside to the cities to work in the quickly swelling labour force of the mushrooming factories. Additionally, this migration was a consequence of the severe pressure from the authorities in forcing peasants to discard private farming to join collective farms, uprooting traditional village society. In these farms, the 'means of production' (tools, draught animals) became property of the village community, while crops, dairy foods and meat were collectively produced.

Or so was the plan. Collectivisation did not work as efficiently in reality as when the concept was thought up in the planning offices in Moscow. Collective farmers received little remuneration for the food they produced that the state obliged them to deliver. The government never offered the collective farms enough payment in exchange for the products it procured from them. Rather than raising workers' wages, Stalin's regime tried to keep its crazed industrialisation drive rolling by offering factory workers cheap basic foodstuffs extracted at nominal cost from the socialised sector of the farms.

Most farmers were forced to survive on private plots through the crops they grew and the small animals that they were allowed to keep outside the socialised sector of the collective farm. Eventually, collective farmers discovered the optimal balance between doing the required labour for the collective and working for themselves on their plot without being sanctioned. This did mean, however, endless workdays for the *kolkhozniki* (men) and *kolkhoznitsy* (women). Few on the farms wholeheartedly broke their backs for the communist cause, sacrificing everything they had to meet state-imposed production targets; energy needed to be husbanded to work on the private plot to ensure survival.

The impossibly high production targets in industry and agriculture developed by the State Planning Bureau (Gosplan) for the Five-Year Plans were nowhere near met, even if the regime's propaganda announced otherwise. The massive famine that broke out in Ukraine, southern Russia and Kazakhstan at the end of the First Five-Year Plan in the autumn of 1932 showed the disastrous consequence of collectivisation. Hunger may have killed five million people. Instead of admitting to this debacle, Stalin 'doubled down'. While the Second Five-Year Plan (1933–7) was more realistic and overall results were better,

Soviet industry continued to be plagued by massive problems such as wastage, industrial accidents, supply shortages and production stoppages, while agricultural results remained anaemic.

The attempt to transform people's mindset through a concomitant 'cultural revolution' meanwhile also faltered, with many stubbornly adhering to cultural traditions, not least their ancestral religion.[13] Stalin became enraged when he found out about this persistent religiosity through a census in early 1937 in which more than half of respondents professed to be believers (undoubtedly, many additionally pretended not to be religious even when they were). Religion, Karl Marx's 'opium of the people', was expected to wither away as a 'relic of the past', but little headway had apparently been made twenty years after the great revolution of 1917. Such a conservative mindset, from Stalin's Marxist perspective, might also indicate that the road to traverse before communism would be reached was still quite lengthy, since the so-called superstructure (mindset) was a reflection of the base in the Marxist analysis. The radical transformation of the Soviet economy, society and culture on which Stalin had embarked in 1929 proved a much slower process than anticipated.

All the problems encountered with the execution of his grandiose plan to remake Soviet life, Stalin blamed on everyone but himself. Undoubtedly, his anger about the failed transformation informed the Great Terror that he unleashed in the course of 1937, in which well-nigh 700,000 people were executed in a year and a half, with at least another 1.5 million incarcerated. By November 1938, he decided that everyone had been taught their lesson and enough anti-Soviet elements, counter-revolutionaries, enemies of the people, and saboteurs had been eliminated, ordering the NKVD to end the mass purge.

But his subjects gained little respite. War was in the offing. A localised undeclared war with Japan was fought out in the Far East in 1938 and 1939. Nazi aggression was temporarily deflected by the Molotov–Ribbentrop Pact of August 1939, but preparations for war were stepped up while the Soviet Army marched into eastern Poland in the following weeks. The war with Finland (December 1939–March 1940) led to an unexpectedly high level of casualties and placed a further strain on the Soviet economy. Finally, the Nazi-led invasion of the Soviet Union on 22 June 1941 abruptly ended the first period of Stalin's rule.

The Great Patriotic War

The second period of Stalin's reign that radically changed people's daily existence was the Great Patriotic War, the name under which the Second World War became known in the USSR. It killed one in six of its people, while the lives of those who survived, whether on occupied territory, near the frontline or in the hinterland, were wholly uprooted. The destruction of housing, transport, industrial plant and so on was immense. No one will ever be able to accurately estimate the massive trauma the war caused, but in countless ways its effect can still be felt even in our own time.

All of Ukraine, Belarus and the recently (June 1940) annexed Baltic Soviet republics, as well as a considerable part of European Russia fell for a while under Nazi occupation. Despite initial hope among some for a less oppressive regime than Stalin's, the Nazis showed even less mercy than the Soviets to the inhabitants of these occupied regions. They murdered all those identified as ethnic Jews or as card-carrying communists, while the lives of most eastern Slavs (Russians, Ukrainians, Belarusyn) were spared only to be put to work in slave-like conditions producing food for the Nazi Reich or in German industry (*Ostarbeiter*), replacing German men who served in the army or SS (*Schutzstaffel*, German death squads). The agricultural peons and those assigned to factory work were beaten, malnourished, poorly housed and suffered from a variety of illnesses without access to adequate medical aid.

The fate of those living in European Russia who avoided Nazi occupation varied. In Leningrad, the second city of the Soviet Union, which for more than two-and-a-half years was almost wholly encircled by enemy forces, a famine may have killed a million people in the autumn, winter and spring of 1941–2. The Soviet leaders understood too late that the city might be threatened, and evacuated merely several tens of thousands of Leningraders before enemy encirclement made any efforts to flee the city well-nigh suicidal. Elsewhere, millions did succeed in evacuating or fleeing before the Nazi forces arrived, but this massive population movement caused chaos behind the front in the autumn of 1941. Once the Nazi advance was halted by the late autumn of 1941, however, a certain stability was restored. Minutely allocating everything and everyone to the war effort, the planned economy, in a sense, worked best in wartime. Perhaps, too, stability prevailed since almost everyone determinedly defended their homeland, ignoring any doubts they might harbour about the Soviet system or Stalin.

Rationing, already a feature during much of the 1930s, was reintroduced in 1941 and guaranteed urban dwellers at least a bare minimum of basic foodstuffs. Anything additional might be bought at the legal *kolkhoz* (collective-farm) markets, bartered (legally or not) or purchased on the black market. Illegal traders may have enjoyed slightly more freedom to manoeuvre from the authorities than prior to or after the war, and sometimes prevented acute shortages of key commodities. Meanwhile, town-dwellers tried as much as possible to cultivate garden plots on the outskirts of their town. Of course, this indicates that shortages were common, and that nourishment was more often than not insufficient. Few enjoyed anything near a balanced diet.

While staunch support for the motherland was universal on the Soviet side of the front, it was far lower on occupied territory. In the first six months of the war (from July to December 1941), with one Nazi victory following another, many concluded that the Soviet regime was finished. Those who fell under Nazi rule tried to adjust to the New Order, that is, if they survived the sifting carried out by the Nazis and were not slaughtered as communists or Jews. In the vast expanse of European Russia, Ukraine and Belarus, some managed to escape Nazi surveillance and joined the Soviet partisan movement sabotaging the German war effort behind the frontline. Partisan resistance in this early phase of the war was slight, with the population reeling from the initial onslaught. When it became apparent that the Nazis might not defeat the Soviet Army easily, though, partisan units gradually increased in number and size and began to truly sabotage the German war effort. Retributions were harsh, and the Nazis routinely engaged in mass executions of hostages in retaliation for partisan actions. Given such savagery, it is understandable that many hesitated to join the resistance.

The motives of most of those who aided the enemy were decidedly mixed, rather than a consequence of their inveterate hatred of the Soviet order of things.[14] Most often, collaborators did so out of pure desperation, as the Nazis would kill them if they did not render them support. Collaboration often occurred because former Soviet citizens (not least POWs) tried to evade starvation and abuse at the hands of the Germans. POW camps for Soviet captives were deathtraps, as they were not monitored by neutral observers representing international organisations such as the Red Cross, which the Soviet regime had refused to join. Therefore, probably more than half of Soviet POWs died after capture (including several tens of thousands who were the first victims of mass gassing at Auschwitz). To avoid such a fate, many Soviet POWs joined the Nazi-led military forces as volunteers, while others actively aided the SS-led persecution and killing of Jews and other 'undesirables'.

The war's unfolding indicates that one of the main goals of the Great Terror had been largely missed. Speaking as a pensioner in the 1960s, Stalin's sidekick V.M. Molotov (1890–1986) declared that the Terror had a prophylactic aim, which was to purge Soviet society of those people who might turn against communist rule in times of crisis (such as war). Countless thousands of Stalin's pre-war subjects, however, collaborated with the Nazi occupiers and their Finnish, Romanian or Hungarian allies during the war. Clearly, not all potential turncoats had been weeded out in 1937 and 1938. Despite the extent of such collaboration, though, it cannot be denied that most Soviet denizens ultimately preferred Stalin over Hitler, even in much of Ukraine, which had seen so much misery under Soviet rule in the dozen years before war's outbreak.[15]

Trauma

The war, given its utter devastation, was of course a watershed in everyone's life. Few did not lose a relative, while the depth of the trauma generated by the war for its survivors is impossible to fathom. After the war's conclusion, the demobilisation of the regular armed forces happened in three waves after May 1945, the last of which only concluded in 1947. Most young men (and a considerable number of young women, even if they only saw combat duty in the air force) thus spent the early years of their adulthood in uniform on active duty, and many older men also served for years. It might be said that their army service in the war for most of them became the defining moment of their life.

Veterans' reintroduction into civilian life may have been as difficult as it was elsewhere. The regimented nature of life in Stalin's country, however, did resemble in some ways the strict rules and regulations of army life (with similar draconian penalties for violating them), perhaps easing such adjustment. The emotional scars of many survivors seem to have mainly been drowned in alcohol. Heavy drinking was a tradition among the male Slavic population pre-dating the foundation of the Soviet Union, and had been encouraged in the army, where soldiers received two shots of vodka per day as part of their ration. After the war, drinking bouts were probably heavier than before it, albeit limited by the amount of alcohol available for consumption in the lean post-war years. In 1948, laws against the illegal distillation and sale of moonshine (*samogon*) were sharpened, because such practices had spread in recent times. A high demand was not met by the alcohol produced by the state monopoly, which was sold in limited amounts and at high prices.

The war (and this was not unlike the early post-war years elsewhere in Europe) was not elaborately celebrated after the initial victorious euphoria, and veterans' benefits were not particularly generous.[16] The most tangible advantage enjoyed by those who returned from the war might be a somewhat higher position in the labour force than they had occupied before their call-up (especially if they had joined the Communist Party's ranks during their army service). Regular *kolkhoz* workers, for example, might be appointed as team brigadiers or farm chairs upon their return, while factory workers or miners might be named foremen. Physically disabled veterans were not particularly well cared for, although a good number of such war wounded managed to find a position in which their physical challenges did not stop them from working.

Post-war

The third and final period of Stalin's dictatorship began in May 1945 and ended with his death in March 1953 (the Soviet Union briefly went to war with Japan in August 1945, but the effect of this war on most of the country was rather ephemeral). This was a period of reconstruction that took its cue from the feverish planning of the 1930s (the fourth Five-Year Plan started in early 1946). Apart from recovery from the wartime devastation, Stalin decided that a key priority was the development of a Soviet nuclear bomb to face down the American atomic challenge in the early Cold War. The Soviet bomb project perhaps involved one million (incarcerated and free) labourers.[17] It came to fruition in August 1949 with the detonation of the first Soviet atomic bomb, but the means and people dedicated to it were diverted from rebuilding the country in general.

In 1946 and 1947 another famine raged, killing perhaps 1.5 million people.[18] After it, living conditions remained spartan, right up until Stalin's death. Within months after his demise in March 1953, his successors changed a number of policies, raising state prices for agricultural products and releasing most of the millions who languished in the Soviet penitentiary system. Soon an extensive building programme commenced in the cities as well, which drastically improved housing. For the first time since the late 1920s, life in the USSR became liveable again for the mass of its population.

Resist and adapt

Still, somehow people did survive the time of Stalin. We have already seen how many in the countryside learned to calibrate their behaviour to the demands of the dictatorship. The limits of the uniformity imposed from above were constantly probed from below. The authorities' means of control, after all, had their limits in a country as large as the Soviet Union, in an age that witnessed a rapid and rocky transition from a premodern to a modern industrialised society. Despite the lofty goals of mechanisation and the diffusion of technology, electricity, telephones and radios remained largely absent in the Soviet countryside under Stalin, for example.

Shirking from work or other obligations, a widespread phenomenon in the countryside, was something difficult to prevent in the collective-farm villages in which support for the communist cause was more often than not anaemic.[19] In urban settings, enthusiasm was often token, even if the 1930s and 1940s were not yet hallmarked by the notorious adage of later Soviet times, which had workers mockingly declare that 'we pretend to work', while 'they [the Communist chiefs] pretend to pay us'. A particularly fine illustration of the level of political participation and enthusiasm among the urban population may be found in Serhy Yekelchyk's work on post-war Kyiv, Soviet Ukraine's capital.[20] He suggests that the city's population (largely made up of Russians and Ukrainians, with a sprinkling of those few Jews who had survived the war) endeavoured to show their loyalty to the cause with a sort of mixed motivation: the people of Kyiv professed loyalty and dutifully voted for the Party's (and singular) candidate at the regularly staged elections and marched earnestly in parades. Boundless enthusiasm was hard to come by, however, as wretched living conditions (shoddy housing, food scarcity and so on) made the communist utopia seem a pipe dream. But Kyiv's inhabitants also realised that demurring might only lead to unpleasant consequences, while an outwardly positive outlook could aid one's career prospects.

Generally, an appreciation of the Soviet ideals of human equality and patriotism could be encountered among (aspiring) Communist Party members, as Edward Cohn has charted.[21] No doubt, the higher one stood on the social ladder, the greater the support for the system; without unwavering loyalty, the ambitious could not make a career. But a certain stoicism, perhaps even cynicism, can be noticed among those who hit a ceiling beyond which they could not rise, especially among the mostly male army veterans (*frontoviki*).[22] This might have been the consequence of a lack of education or patronage network to aid one to move further up the ladder, while some were so traumatised by the war that they could barely put in a token effort on their job while fighting their demons (often through heavy drinking).[23]

Gender relations

Differences of class, gender or ethnicity were to dissolve in the communist future according to the Marxist-Leninist blueprint. From October 1917 onwards, full ethnic equality was promulgated, even if Russian was the central state's and Communist Party's language of communication, and Russians and their culture were ever more favoured over other Soviet languages and cultures after 1929. The Soviet Union professed to be a classless society, or a society in which the distinction between social classes was rapidly disappearing because the means of production were collectively owned. In practice, however, Soviet discourse still distinguished two different classes, those of the workers (employed in factories and mines, etc.) and of the peasants (working on collective and state farms), while a sort of substratum of white-collar employees (more or less the same group as what was called 'Soviet intelligentsia') was also recognised. In effect, though, there was a privileged ruling class (mainly the members of the Communist Party), which lorded it over everyone else employed in services, manufacturing or agriculture. A classless society appeared still a while away in Stalin's day.

Frequently, the return of demobilised men in the post-war era had the effect of demoting women to rank-and-file jobs, which illustrates one of the many ways in which women suffered discrimination in a country that had professed gender equality since its inception.[24] Women under Stalin faced distinctive challenges compared to men, because of gender differences that refused to disappear in Soviet practice. Whether in Russia or Kyrgyzstan, whether in the Communist Party or outside of it, whether atheist, Christian or Muslim, women faced different challenges from men, and did not achieve legal, political, economic or social equality with men in any meaningful fashion.

Traditional Eastern Slavonic or Russian culture was probably no less misogynist than other cultures that could be encountered in the tsar's empire.[25] In the Muslim cultures of the Caucasus or Central Asia, women's domain was primarily the private sphere, with men monopolising the public arena. Across the tsar's empire, women did not enjoy the same amount of access to formal education as men, even if this varied, with for example Tatar women in the Volga region being better educated than their Russian counterparts before 1917. Meanwhile, women everywhere shouldered part of the burden in agriculture, while in the industrialising areas many took factory jobs (textile mills employed a majority of women for example). More women found their way into the factories during the First World War, replacing conscripted men.

While virtually all women were employed, they did not usually occupy the more senior positions in their workplace before 1941. After 1929, many women chose to become professionals, for example by taking a medical or teaching degree. But after completing their studies, female doctors usually became lower-paid general practitioners rather than specialists, while female teachers were paid as much, or as little, as skilled (and often male) blue-collar workers. Equally significant gender differences can be charted in Soviet academe, with few women for example occupying full professorships. According to the 1936 constitution, one-quarter of the members of the Supreme Soviet, the country's lower legislative house, had to be female, but this was a rubber-stamp parliament. In the Communist Party, in whose higher echelons any meaningful decisions were made, women did not play more than a token role. Few government ministers or members of the Party's leading Central Committee were women.

Altogether, then, the gender gap that existed before 1917 was not overcome before Stalin's death, even if women's fate may have improved, not least by becoming literate. This was reflected everywhere in the labour force, with women often serving in subordinate roles in factories, offices, shops or collective farms. It is true that only a select few women did not have a job, but that was not primarily because women proudly defended their right to work. It usually resulted from sheer economic necessity, as families could not survive on one income.

Education, socialisation, town and country

After the civil war had quietened down in the early 1920s, girls began to attend school as much as boys. In Stalin's time, all girls nominally enjoyed a measure of formal education, that is, completed the minimal four-year curriculum (still, in 1937 only two-thirds of all women were literate, against almost 90 per cent of men). In the mid-1930s, seven years of obligatory education in urban areas became the norm, but in the villages this length of schooling was only introduced after 1950. Schools, until 1943, were co-educational. In that year in the cities single-sex schools were introduced, a practice that ended soon after Stalin's death.

In the civil war, the Communist Youth League (Komsomol) started as a training ground for teenagers and young adults who wanted to join the Communist Party. The Party's membership was only open to a select few, who were often scrutinised by their Party units (cells) for ideological soundness and exemplary behaviour. Because of this ideological puritanism, initially the Komsomol was a rather select affair itself, which only true zealots joined, who usually had an eye on future Party membership. But whereas the Party during the war experienced a sudden large influx of front soldiers who lacked much

FIGURE 6.1 *Communist youths with a huge portrait of Stalin.* © *Getty Images.*

ideological training (and not just replenished its ranks replacing those who had fallen, but significantly increased its size in absolute numbers), the Komsomol became a true mass organisation even before the war. It bundled the drummed-up mass enthusiasm among Soviet boys and girls for Stalin's 'socialist construction'. In the cities, especially, by the late 1930s only a rare few between the ages of fourteen and approximately twenty-five did not join the youth league. And, as a sort of answer to the popularity of the boy scouts and girl guides (or girl scouts) of Western capitalism, children younger than fourteen met at the weekends or in the evenings in the Young Pioneer movement, which also became quite large in the course of the 1930s. The Komsomol focused mainly on political education, but the Pioneers engaged in physical exercise, singing and dancing as well, and participated in summer camps and Soviet jamborees. Both youth organisations and the Party itself were less popular in the countryside, confirming the convictions of Marx himself already expressed in *The Communist Manifesto* (1848) that rural life was 'backward'. Rural dwellers were not often held to be ripe to join the ranks of the 'proletarian vanguard' of Communists.

Indeed, in the countryside most children fully worked alongside their parents from the age of twelve onwards, once they had completed their primary education. Except for winter, they therefore did not have much time for Komsomol or Pioneer activities. And the adults on the collective farms were in the vast majority women, ever more so during and after the war, since millions of men departed for, and never returned from, the front. Since female membership of the Communist Party was proportionally far lower than male, this reinforced the already low ratio of rural dwellers among Party members.

After 1945, many young men who left for military training usually did not return to their villages after completing it, using the various skills they had learned in the army to find employment in the towns (which also faced a severe labour shortage). If *frontoviki* did return after 1945, they often replaced women in leading roles on the farms, as directors, brigadiers (team leaders) or bookkeepers. Other men with military experience became mechanics or operators on the regional Machine Tractor Stations that rented out mechanised equipment (combine harvesters, tractors, etc.) to the farms.[26]

Because village homes were usually made of wood, and new structures or attachments could be easily built, finding housing in the Soviet countryside was less of a challenge than in the cities, but household chores were far more onerous, and fell on women's shoulders. Villages usually lacked a connection to the electrical grid, and their water supply was usually provided by wells, while sewers were absent. But the more ample floorspace available did lead to Soviet families in the countryside being larger than in the towns, as they had sufficient room available to accommodate more children.

Initially, Soviet law had made divorce straightforward. If either husband or wife wanted to leave their union, nothing stopped them from doing so. But the shortage of men contributed to the issue of a decree in the summer of 1944 that made divorce far more difficult (not least by making it expensive). Before this law came into force, men were apparently often wont to abscond and wholly abandon their spouses and children.[27] And during the war, even if their husbands returned from the front, women might eventually end up as single parents. Married or not, Soviet women faced a triple burden in daily life, of working, doing almost all of the household chores, and raising their children. If they had a mother who was able-bodied, then some of their childcare might be covered, while women in some jobs (especially when employed in factories) might be able to use day-care facilities.

The regime tried to organise day care that could look after younger children and set up some after-school facilities, but their use often remained limited to those employed in urban environments. Day-care facilities were frequently of dubious standards in terms of hygiene or nutrition. As a result, even in the cities many women turned to their mother or mother-in-law to care for the children while they were at work. Meanwhile, women (rather than men) were not only seen as primary caregivers for their children, but also were expected to tend to the household. This meant that they were responsible for all the shopping (no mean feat in a country where shortages were rampant and queues long), cleaning and cooking.

Health and welfare

Even after the war, several local epidemic outbreaks (diphtheria, dysentery) broke out in the USSR. They might have had less of an impact on the villages, which often benefitted from their remote location in avoiding widespread infection. Nevertheless, healthcare was poor in the villages, which normally at best might have a residing nurse (*feld'sher* or *akusherka*) rather than a doctor serving them. In emergencies, doctors might travel to the collective farms from a somewhat larger settlement (in which they might be employed in a clinic or hospital), but that could be a challenge because of the state of the (often unpaved) roads. Roads might be traversed by motorcars or motorcycles, but, especially in muddy season (*rasputitsa*), this was treacherous. Often, sleighs or horses still provided the physician with transportation. Penicillin came into widespread use in the Soviet Union during the war, which reduced the level and severity of infections, but the villages had less access to antibiotics. Thus, as much as villagers were more prone to remain religious (and were less subject to anti-religious campaigns), as much did they turn to traditional healers and healing methods based on folk wisdom.

Practical obstacles (the lack of medical care, the impossibility of hiding a pregnancy in a close[d] community) may have been just as important as religiously driven objections to make the incidence of abortions in the countryside far lower than in the towns. In the cities, meanwhile, women often underwent multiple abortions. Before 1936, abortions were legal in the Soviet Union, and in the absence of contraceptives (a very low priority for Gosplan), turned into the means used to practise birth control.[28] After 1936, abortions were outlawed except for acute medical problems, but seem to have been performed regardless, since raising large families (which was also costly, of course, for it might force women to stop working) remained exceedingly difficult in Stalin's realm. To a considerable degree, urban women ended pregnancies because housing conditions made it very difficult to raise more than two children. Families or single mothers had at best two-room apartments available to them, with each room no larger than twenty square metres. Indeed, before 1953 more families lived in so-called *kommunalka*s than in separate apartments, that is, they resided in single rooms with kitchen and bathroom shared with a number of other households. Even that was a step above the barracks-style housing young factory workers often used, with several men or women sleeping on bunk beds. By 1956, abortions were once again legalised. The regime tacitly admitted defeat with regards to its efforts to stimulate population growth by banning abortion.

The regime did introduce a fairly young age at which people (in the cities) could retire from the labour force, sixty for men and fifty-five for women. But the harsh life most had endured (besides everything else, especially among men for whom chain smoking and heavy drinking was the norm) did not allow a great number of people to enjoy retirement, many dying before reaching pension age. Meanwhile, the government, even if encouraging disabled veterans to rejoin the work force in fitting occupations, did not always live up to its billing as a government by and for the toilers, ignoring the appalling circumstances in special facilities for those who were in need of constant care. Even after the war begging occurred, as did crimes such as burglaries, muggings or street fights. Highwaymen sometimes raided collective farms in the early post-war years. Before the war, a clampdown had been undertaken against the high number of homeless or delinquent children and teenagers, but not all were rounded up and placed in orphanages and youth homes, and the wartime dislocation caused a re-emergence of street youth.

Stalin's cult and popularity

Still, the Stalinist Soviet Union was not wholly a facade upheld by coercion and rank hypocrisy. After 1950 in particular, a growing segment of the Soviet population joined in the spoils, finding better housing that included the use of a variety of modern amenities in their home (such as running water, toilets and electric light), broadening leisure options (including the reading of newspapers and books) or consuming goods that would have been of unimaginable variety and refinement to their – mainly rural – ancestors. Although the quality of healthcare remained uneven, for the great majority of children, educational opportunities improved dramatically from the 1920s onwards. All such things engendered support for the regime, and, even if these spoils were largely limited to material comforts, many people persuaded themselves to believe in the 'radiant future' of communism long after Stalin's death in 1953. Stalin was often celebrated as the man who had overseen the road to modernity that increasingly generated this improved standard of living, and who had steadfastly stood at the helm when the country witnessed its darkest hour in the Second World War. Indeed, it was in the villages, in which living circumstances improved little (if at all) under Stalin, where he was also least popular.[29]

Contemporary foreign observers and Russian émigrés frequently recognised traditional overtones in the cult of Stalin that was assiduously propagated by the vast *agitprop* apparatus developed by the Communist Party. In other words, Stalin was said to be a 'Red Tsar'. This then might combine with essentialist suggestions of 'Russians' (rather than various Soviet peoples) being historically conditioned to autocratic rule, and therefore incapable of living in a democratic society. Although such verdicts are simplistic and veer towards racism, the Soviet authorities (Stalin had been instrumental in creating a cult of Lenin in the 1920s) sometimes deliberately tried to fill the void left by their prohibition of the worship of Christian or Islamic deities with Stalin's cult. Stalin's image was everywhere, on posters and banners, in newspapers and books, and his every uttering in public speeches or in writing was depicted as a fount of wisdom.

A good number of Soviet women and men resisted this deification of the leader, but a quarter of a century of the incessant propagation of Stalin's infallibility and farsightedness and his omnipresent image did rub off on many people. Even some of the so poorly treated rural dwellers displayed a framed picture of Stalin in their living rooms in front of which they burned a candle in the evening, as if it was an Orthodox icon. Remarkably few questioned Stalin's fumbling immediately before and at the beginning of the Great Patriotic War, although its outbreak and early days wholly contradicted Stalin's declarations before 22 June 1941 that no such war was in the offing, while his public silence about the unexpected turn of events until July should have raised eyebrows, too. And when he died in March 1953, many Soviet citizens were shaken to their core. The cause for this worship may be sought in more than just religious feelings to which the cult certainly appealed. The almost total lack of agency the regime had cultivated among its subjects prevented the consideration of a life without (or after) the helmsman, who had become the all-Soviet patriarch not least in a psychological sense as well. The death of their father in 1953 left his children feeling orphaned.

Subversive behaviour

Meanwhile, the outside rigour projected by the system was not as sturdy as it appeared. The post-war stoicism or cynicism of some of the *frontoviki* might also be observed among teenagers and young adults after 1945.[30] Initially subdued in the utterly difficult immediate post-war years, toward 1950 a more vocal and restless cohort can be identified, especially in urban areas, no longer accepting the blunting of personal initiative. This younger generation was no longer satisfied either with the rather bare-bones material conditions with which those who previously came of age in Stalin's realm had been content.

Despite the Young Pioneers or Komsomol, post-war Soviet youth sometimes chafed against its academic and political schoolwork and the bleak prospects of selfless work and duty for the motherland that awaited it thereafter. These were the years that the later political leaders Boris Yeltsin (1931–2007) and Mikhail Gorbachev (b. 1931) came of age, as well as many other future nonconformists, among whom were the filmmaker Andrei Tarkovsky (1932–86), the painter Ilya Kabakov (b. 1933), and the writers Vasily Aksyonov (1932–2009), Fazil' Iskander (1929–2016), and Vladimir Maksimov (1930–95). The poet and folksinger Vladimir Vysotsky (1938–80), the poet and prose writer Bella Akhmadullina (1937–2010), and the poet and Nobel laureate Joseph Brodsky (1940–96) were teenagers in those years. Clearly, these were restless souls, whose subsequent creative output shows how they were anything but bridled by their experience of Stalinism in their teens and twenties.

Civic life: civil society?

And certain cultural traditions pre-dating the Soviet era persisted in Stalin's reign; among urban Russian youth, for example, the age-old custom existed of long walks in search of excitement, especially during long summer evenings. Sometimes such *guliane* might amount to no more than meeting members of the opposite sex, but at other times scuffles might break out. Some male village youths continued to seek out those of other villages to engage in fist fights, an underlining of masculinity that perhaps was entangled with traditional courtship rituals and the complicated route to exogamous marriages.

Although the overtly religious side of certain traditional holidays may have been muted as it might cause problems with the authorities (if they found out about them), in the countryside certain celebrations, as at Shrovetide (*maslenitsa*), continued to be observed. If circumstances allowed it, this Mardi Gras sort of party lasted several days, during which a great amount of eating and drinking took place. Of course, in Stalin's time, more often than not, the villagers were starving, and this and other traditional feasts might be rather lean occasions. In the towns, such traditional feasts were actively discouraged by the regime's watchful zealots. The Soviet state did not recognise religious marriage, but it tried to compensate with a sort of ritualised civil ceremony during weddings before the state official registering the union. Likewise, an effort was made to replace Christmas with a more elaborate New Year's celebration. Other new holidays were introduced such as festive election days (for the rubber-stamp legislatures at local, regional or union-wide levels, all of which were staged every four years), when most people enjoyed a day off work. At the same time, voting was mandatory, and the regime kept close tabs on the very few who refused to do so (usually out of religious convictions).

Religion

The advance of atheism or agnosticism progressed more in the traditionally Christian than the Islamic parts of the USSR, but whether the regime's anti-religious policies (which included the rounding up of bishops, priests and mullahs) were truly effective is not readily apparent, as the 1937 census results show. The League of Militant Atheists (its name is telling) was too blunt an instrument, too often crudely ridiculing religion and probably counterproductive in many cases. It seems rather that the spread of education and the general weakening of religious faith in modernising (urbanising, industrialising) societies were mainly responsible for the erosion of beliefs. Still, the absence of religious teachers and dignitaries may have led to more people questioning their faith than if the heavy-handed persecution had not made the clergy vanish.

The First Five-Year Plan had also given birth to an attempt to end the seven-day week, although more out of a concern for greater economic productivity than as a part of the anti-religious drive (by eliminating Sunday as a traditional day of rest as well as a day to worship for the Orthodox). But the five- or six-day week failed to become popular. Families, for example, often had leisure

FIGURE 6.2 *Architectural contrasts: towering socialist housing project against old Orthodox church in Moscow.* © *Getty Images.*

days on different days. Ultimately, the Soviet Union reverted to the seven-day calendar in 1940.

Intelligentsia

Some free-spirited urban intellectuals faked loyalty (or half-heartedly supported the regime) out of self-preservation, writing books 'for the drawer', as the cases of Boris Pasternak or Vasily Grossman show, or having critical conversations at locations out of the reach of the ears of secret-police agents or their informers.[31] After the invasion of 22 June 1941, the renewed chaos created by the Nazi-led invasion allowed Stalin's subjects more agency; some of the Soviet inhabitants' collaboration with the Nazis (even among the Russians) was not the result of coercion or a desperate survival instinct, but of a hope for greater freedom. And at the other side of the frontline, Stalin, momentarily, felt necessitated to relinquish some of his tight control over his subjects. Religious organisations were given a measure of freedom, leading to the reopening of churches and mosques, in exchange for resolute support of the war effort by the worshippers. In literature, the reins were loosened, allowing a few writers (such as Mikhail Zoshchenko) to publish satirical works that did not quite meet the rigid requirements of socialist realism, while works by several others were published for the first time after having been ostracised for years (such as by the poet Anna Akhmatova). Foreign journalists from allied countries traversed the country to report on the Soviet war effort, and were allowed to interview Soviet citizens without too many constraints. Soviet visitors travelled abroad to elicit support for their country's war effort, among Orthodox, Jewish and other immigrant communities in the allied countries. This freedom proved merely temporary, and was wholly curtailed by late 1947.

Hoping against hope, some of this 'Soviet intelligentsia' thought at the time of the victory over the Nazi bloc that the regime might loosen the reins more permanently. After all, the dictatorship should have become confident of the steadfast loyalty of its subjects, who had been unwavering in fighting the invaders, while no immediate foreign threat further loomed.[32] Some of Stalin's pronouncements in May and June 1945 fuelled this fire. But such hopes were quashed; Stalin was set in his ways. He ultimately decided that the victory was due to the barracks' socialism he had imposed after 1929, not to an erupting popular patriotism during wartime. Writers, philosophers, musicians and scientists were taken to task in public campaigns, muffling any independent voices.[33] The campaigns were, then and for some time after, considered the handiwork of Andrei Zhdanov (1896–1948), but it is now abundantly evident that he did Stalin's bidding. Indeed, the campaigns continued after Zhdanov's death.

The survival and adaptation of popular and elite culture

The regime managed to recover its hold over its people after May 1945 in some part because the Nazis had managed to outdo the Soviet Communists in their malignancy towards their subject peoples in Eastern Europe. But the Soviet regime's level of control over people's daily life remained far from absolute, even if it superficially appeared otherwise. Exhausted mentally and physically, the great majority of the Soviet population was in no state to consider any sustained and coordinated opposition, let alone rebellion after 1945. Still, in the Baltic states and western Ukraine, which had been ruled only briefly by the Soviet regime in the immediate pre-war years, armed resistance against the Nazis often transformed into a guerrilla war against Soviet dictatorship, after the Red Army had reoccupied those territories.

The absurd lengths to which the cult of the personality was displayed in official discourse appears shrill after 1945. Some evidence shows that the countryside in particular was reaching a breaking point towards the end of Stalin's life, incapable of meeting absurd economic demands and resisting any further disciplining. The reins needed to be loosened, the remuneration of farm labour increased. In the cities, too, the ideals of communism turned into hollow phrases: after 1945, especially, most who did profess dedication to the cause did so mainly from a wholly instrumental perspective. Joining the Party was key to upward social mobility and better living conditions for oneself and one's family. In a thought-provoking work, Vera Sandomirsky Dunham suggested that the regime struck a deal after the war with the country's social elite of ranking Party members, economic managers (such as factory directors), scientists, military officers and so on, in a sort of 'big deal', which bought their silence in exchange for perquisites and greater access to scarce consumer goods or services.[34] Dunham's claim may be overstated, for the political, scientific and cultural intelligentsia both across the USSR and in specific republics was subject to a number of hostile campaigns from 1945 to 1953 that seem to have been intended as deliberate reminders of the 1930s witch-hunts. But many among these groups were lucky enough to escape retribution and plucked the fruits of their hard work, holidaying in spas in the Caucasus or at the Black Sea coast, being driven around in cars by chauffeurs, living in spacious apartments, attending the theatre in smart outfits, consuming foods not available to others and retreating to well-endowed country residences (*dachas*) at the weekends. These were very much akin to the creature comforts the 'odious' bourgeoisie of the capitalist world enjoyed at the same time in the West.

These were far removed from the sort of collective pastimes that had been the more traditional form of socialist entertainment (in the 1930s parades and large-scale sporting manifestations, such as collective gymnastic exercises, had been the rage), and the more mundane amusements the masses enjoyed. But workers and farmers equally carved out a private space: they went to the cinema, attended an amateur play (as actors or spectators), played musical instruments or sang in a choir, read library books and magazines, played cards or chess, or just simply chatted around the dinner table with drinks and bites to eat (*zakuski*). Sport was popular as well, although not to the same extent as football games were in Europe or Latin America. The Soviets did not join the Olympic Games until 1952, and the pre-war Spartakiad never rivalled it. But many participated in sport as players, or attended football and other ball games, swimming in lakes, ponds and rivers, playing ice hockey and racing in skating meets, etc. Others escaped their daily sorrows by going fishing, at all times of year, even on the ice in wintertime. The radio became a common feature in most urban households after the war, which allowed for the enjoyment of musical performances at home (while some even had gramophones).

Such leisure activities were less available in the villages, where people also had less free time to engage in pastimes. Nonetheless, collective farms tended to have some sort of place for cultural activities (often using a space in which meetings were held or lectures delivered by *agitprop* visitors to double as a stage for amateur performances), with a small library in which political texts, newspapers, magazines and literary works were shelved. Occasionally, itinerant operators, equipped with projectors and movable screens, even visited the farms to show films. Radios and telephones were rare on the collective farms, although after the war some radio programmes were broadcast with the help of a public address system. It is also evident that many *kolkhoznitsy* and *kolkhozniki* visited the nearest towns to sell whatever surplus they might have produced on their private plot and to buy consumer goods that they did not produce themselves and were rarely on offer in the mostly empty village stores that were poorly supplied through the state-distribution system. These visits, too, were an outing of sorts.

Concluding remarks

Daily life under Stalin was nonetheless an extraordinarily bleak affair. For most, it amounted to a genuine struggle for survival, every day traversing a treacherous terrain without much prospect of any brighter future. Sheer luck was required to avoid falling victim to the meat grinder, before, during and after the war. Massive famine, arrests and violent deaths were common occurrences. Those who survived were heavily scarred by their experiences. The Soviet Union's browbeaten population remained tranquil for a generation after Stalin's death before contemplating in earnest another, perhaps more humane, historical path than that imposed by Stalin and his acolytes such as Nikita Khrushchev, Leonid Brezhnev or Yuri Andropov.

Notes

1. H. Arendt, *The Origins of Totalitarianism* (New York, 1951). See also A. Gleason, *Totalitarianism: The Inner History of the Cold War* (New York, 1995); E.I. Zamiatin, *We* (New York, 1924); A. Huxley, *Brave New World* (London, 1932); G. Orwell, *Nineteen Eighty-Four* (London, 1949); M. Atwood, *The Handmaid's Tale* (Toronto, 1985).
2. See G. Alexopoulos, *Illness and Inhumanity in Stalin's Gulag* (New Haven, CT, 2017), 243–4.
3. See Marxists Internet Archive, *History of the Communist Party of the Soviet Union (Bolsheviks): Short Course* (New York, 1939; J.V. Stalin Archive, 2008), available online: https://www.marxists.org/reference/archive/stalin/works/1939/x01/ (accessed 9 June 2020).
4. V. Izmozik, *Glaza i ushi rezhima: gosudarstvennyi politicheskii kontrol za naseleniem Sovetskoi Rossii v 1918–1928 godakh* (Saint Petersburg, 1995).
5. A.I. Solzhenitsyn, *The Gulag Archipelago: An Experiment in Literary Investigation* (New York, 1974–8); see also S. Barnes, *Death and Redemption: The Gulag and the Shaping of Soviet Society* (Princeton, NJ, 2011).
6. Barnes, *Death and Redemption*, 1.
7. Ibid., 238.
8. Alexopoulos, *Illness and Inhumanity*, 232–43.
9. A. Koestler, *Darkness at Noon* (London, 1940); Orwell, *Nineteen Eighty-Four*. Illuminating in this regard are further A. Zinov'ev, *Gomos sovetikus; moi dom – moia chuzhbina* (Moscow, 1991); L.Z. Kopelev, *The Education of a True Believer* (New York, 1980); A.I. Solzhenitsyn, *In the First Circle, a Novel: The Restored Text* (New York, 2009); J. Hellbeck, *Revolution on My Mind: Writing a Diary Under Stalin* (Cambridge, MA, 2009); V. Garros, N. Korenevskaya, and T. Lahusen (eds), *Intimacy and Terror: Soviet Diaries of the 1930s* (New York, 1997); and J. Scott, *Behind the Urals: An American Worker in Russia's City of Steel*, enlarged edn (Bloomington, IN, 1989).
10. J.T. Gross, *Revolution From Abroad: The Soviet Conquest of Poland's Western Ukraine and Western Belorussia*, rev. edn (Princeton, NJ, 2002 [1988]).
11. P. Polian, *Against Their Will: The History and Geography of Forced Migrations in the USSR* (Budapest, 2003); N.F. Bugai, *L. Beriia – I. Stalinu: Soglasno Vashemu ukazaniiu* (Moscow, 1995); A. Nekrich, *The Punished Peoples: The Deportation and Fate of Soviet Minorities at the End of the Second World War* (New York, 1978).
12. Far more is available in English about developments in the European part of the USSR than elsewhere in this regard, but see A. Khalid, *Making Uzbekistan: Nation, Empire, and Revolution in the Early USSR* (Ithaca, NY, 2015), 342–89.
13. See S. Fitzpatrick, *Cultural Revolution in Russia, 1928–1931* (Bloomington, IN, 1978) and S. Fitzpatrick, *The Cultural Front: Power and Culture in Revolutionary Russia* (Ithaca, NY, 1992).

14 I. Deák, *Europe On Trial: The Story of Collaboration, Resistance, and Retribution During World War II* (London, 2018); K. Slepyan, *Stalin's Guerrillas: Soviet Partisans in World War II* (Lawrence, KS, 2006).

15 K. Berkhoff, *The Harvest of Despair: Life and Death in Ukraine Under Nazi Rule* (Cambridge, MA, 2008).

16 See K. Boterbloem, 'Soviet GIs or Decembrists?: The Reintegration into Postwar Soviet Society of Russian Soldiers, POWs, Partisans, and Civilians Who Lived under German Occupation', *War and Society* 25, no. 1 (2006): 77–87.

17 D. Holloway, *Stalin and the Bomb: The Soviet Union and Atomic Energy, 1939–1956* (New Haven, CT, 1996).

18 V.F. Zima, *Golod v SSSR 1946–1947 godov: Proiskhozhdenie i posledstviia* (Moscow, 1996).

19 See F. Abramov, *The New Life: A Day on a Collective Farm* (New York, 1963).

20 S. Yekelchyk, *Stalin's Citizens: Everyday Politics in the Wake of Total War* (Oxford, 2014).

21 E. Cohn, *The High Title of a Communist: Postwar Party Discipline and the Values of the Soviet Regime* (DeKalb, IL, 2015).

22 See E. Fraser, *Military Masculinity and Postwar Recovery in the Soviet Union* (Toronto, 2019).

23 See J.W. Jones, *Everyday Life and the 'Reconstruction' of Soviet Russia During and After the Great Patriotic War, 1943–1948* (Bloomington, IN, 2008); M. Edele, *Soviet Veterans of World War II: A Popular Movement in an Authoritarian Society* (Oxford, 2009); A. Weiner, *Making Sense of War: The Second World War and the Fate of the Bolshevik Revolution* (Princeton, NJ, 2001).

24 See E.T. Ewing, *Separate Schools: Gender, Policy and Practice in Postwar Soviet Education* (DeKalb, IL, 2010).

25 O.S. Tian-Shanskaia, *Village Life in Late Tsarist Russia*, ed. D. Ransel (Bloomington, IN, 2008).

26 See for more Fraser, *Military Masculinity*.

27 K. Boterbloem, *Life and Death Under Stalin: Kalinin Province, 1945–1953* (Montreal, 1999), 196–7.

28 Ibid., 69–71.

29 Ibid., 144–51, 206–31.

30 See J. Fürst, *Stalin's Last Generation: Soviet Post-War Youth and the Emergence of Mature Socialism* (Oxford, 2012).

31 See B. Pasternak, *Doctor Zhivago* (London, 1958); V. Grossman, *Life and Fate: A Novel* (New York, 1985); V. Grossman, *Forever Flowing* (New York, 1972).

32 E. Zubkova, *Russia After the War: Hopes, Illusions and Disappointments, 1945–1957* (London, 1998); M. Gefter, *Iz tekh i etikh let . . .* (Moscow, 1991).

33 See K. Boterbloem, *The Life and Times of Andrei Zhdanov, 1896–1948* (Montreal, 2004).

34 V.S. Dunham, *In Stalin's Time: Middleclass Values in Soviet Fiction*, rev. edn (Durham, NC, 1990).

Select bibliography

Alexopoulos, G. *Illness and Inhumanity in Stalin's Gulag*. New Haven, CT, 2017.
Barnes, S.A. *Death and Redemption: The Gulag and the Shaping of Soviet Society*. Princeton, NJ, 2011.
Berkhoff, K.C. *The Harvest of Despair: Life and Death in Ukraine Under Nazi Rule*. Cambridge, MA, 2008.
Boterbloem, K. *Life and Death Under Stalin: Kalinin Province, 1945–1953*. Montreal, 1999.
Boterbloem, K. *The Life and Times of Andrei Zhdanov, 1896–1948*. Montreal, 2004.
Cohn, E. *The High Title of a Communist: Postwar Party Discipline and the Values of the Soviet Regime*. DeKalb, IL, 2015.
Dunham, V.S. *In Stalin's Time: Middleclass Values in Soviet Fiction*, rev. edn. Durham, NC, 1990.
Edele, M. *Soviet Veterans of World War II: A Popular Movement in an Authoritarian Society, 1941–1991*. Oxford, 2009.
Ewing, E.T. *Separate Schools: Gender, Policy and Practice in Postwar Soviet Education*. DeKalb, IL, 2010.
Fitzpatrick, S. *The Cultural Front: Power and Culture in Revolutionary Russia*. Ithaca, NY, 1992.
Fitzpatrick, S. *Cultural Revolution in Russia, 1928–1931*. Bloomington, IN, 1978.
Fraser, E.L. *Military Masculinity and Postwar Recovery in the Soviet Union*. Toronto, 2019.
Fürst, J. *Stalin's Last Generation: Soviet Post-War Youth and the Emergence of Mature Socialism*. Oxford, 2012.
Gleason, A. *Totalitarianism: The Inner History of the Cold War*. New York, 1995.
Gross, J.T. *Revolution From Abroad: The Soviet Conquest of Poland's Western Ukraine and Western Belorussia*, rev. edn. Princeton, NJ, 2002 [1988].
Hellbeck, J. *Revolution on My Mind: Writing a Diary Under Stalin*. Cambridge, MA, 2009.
Kopelev, L.Z. *The Education of a True Believer*. New York, 1980.
Marxists Internet Archive. *History of the Communist Party of the Soviet Union (Bolsheviks): Short Course*. New York, 1939. J.V. Stalin Archive, 2008. Available online: https://www.marxists.org/reference/archive/stalin/works/1939/x01/ (accessed 9 June 2020).
Nekrich, A.M. *The Punished Peoples: The Deportation and Fate of Soviet Minorities at the End of the Second World War*. New York, 1978.
Polian, P. *Against Their Will: The History and Geography of Forced Migrations in the USSR*. Budapest, 2003.
Scott, J. *Behind the Urals: An American Worker in Russia's City of Steel*, enlarged edn. Bloomington, IN, 1989.
Slepyan, K. *Stalin's Guerrillas: Soviet Partisans in World War II*. Lawrence, KS, 2006.

Solzhenitsyn, A.I. *The Gulag Archipelago: An Experiment in Literary Investigation.* New York, 1974–8.
Weiner, A. *Making Sense of War: The Second World War and the Fate of the Bolshevik Revolution.* Princeton, NJ, 2001.
Yekelchyk, S. *Stalin's Citizens: Everyday Politics in the Wake of Total War.* Oxford, 2014.
Zubkova, E. *Russia After the War: Hopes, Illusions and Disappointments, 1945–1957.* London, 1998.

7

Life in Ceaușescu's Romania

Dennis Deletant

Introduction

It is tempting to approach communism solely in terms of its repressive nature and its gross denial of human rights. Indeed, the manner in which the political experiment, represented by the ideology and practised by its Soviet masters, was imposed upon the countries of Central Europe, including Romania, exemplified its coercive character. Communism was not elected to power. But once established, its agent, the Communist Party, skilfully employed strategies to maintain itself as the sole political force.

For that reason, a cogent study of communism in Romania must be multifaceted. It should include a consideration of the cost–benefit analysis that citizens made in choosing not just to tolerate the regime, but also to demonstrate support for it and for its leader from 1965 to 1989, Nicolae Ceaușescu.[1] This chapter examines how life went on under dictatorship, even if it was largely mapped out for the individual by the regime. To what extent did the regime intrude into the daily life of the individual? How did the citizen negotiate the challenges placed in his or her path by the state? How important was the role of the political police, the Securitate, in maintaining compliance? To what degree was dissent towards the regime manifested? What restrictions were placed on freedom to travel abroad? To what degree was the moral compass of the person deflected? What role were intellectuals called upon to play in 'validating' the regime? What was the regime's attitude towards religious worship? Why did utopia descend into dystopia under Ceaușescu? In what forms was his personality cult manifested? These are some of the questions addressed in this analysis.

While doing so, it is instructive to examine the economic achievements of the regime. In 1938, Romania's population stood at almost nineteen million, of whom 80 per cent lived on the land in villages that were poorly served by transport and communications. Few villages had piped water or electricity, and health services were primitive, especially in the more backward regions of Moldavia and Bessarabia.[2] In such conditions, it is hardly surprising that with infant mortality, at 17 per cent of live births, Romania had the highest such rate in Europe.[3] Under communism, major strides were taken to introduce universal education, a health service accessible to all and improvements in the supply of piped water to villages. Romanians began to enjoy the rise in living standards which the whole of Eastern Europe, except Albania, experienced in the late 1960s and the first half of the 1970s. Car ownership increased significantly as the Romanian version of the Renault 14, named Dacia, began to roll off the assembly lines at a newly built factory in Pitești; the number of cars sold annually jumped from 9,000 in 1965 to 25,000 in 1970, and 45,000 in 1975. Sales of television sets, refrigerators and vacuum cleaners, most of them Romanian-made, also soared.[4] Although caution must be exercised in accepting all of these figures at their face value, in view of the propensity of factories to inflate production figures, they do reflect a trend which was evident to the population.

Yet this progress was made at the cost of repressive single-party rule. Romania shared a level of economic development in 1938 with that of Greece and therefore a comparison of the growth of gross domestic product (GDP) of

FIGURE 7.1 *Street scene in Bucharest, 1979.* © *Getty Images.*

the two countries between that year and 1989 is eloquent. Greece's GDP in 1938 stood at $19.3 billion and that of Romania at $19.4 billion. In 1989, the respective figures were $79.2 billion and $42.1 billion.[5]

The role of the political police, the Securitate

The task assigned to the communist political police, defined under its founding decree no. 221 of 30 August 1948, was to 'defend the democratic conquests and to ensure the security of the Romanian People's Republic against the plotting of internal and external enemies'.[6] Defence of the 'democratic conquests' meant the maintenance of the Communist Party in power and thus the new People's Republic officially certified itself a political police state. In the building of the People's Democracy the Securitate was called upon to eradicate existing political institutions and social structures. Police coercion and intrusion in the late 1940s and 1950s became part of everyday life and a feature of existence that generated a pervasive fear, a state of mind that revolutionised not just society's structures, but also personal behaviour. The animated conversation gave way to the furtive whisper or parable, suggestion replaced open discussion, and the simplest of messages was often wrapped in a code.

Ceaușescu's short-sighted economic policies and their negative impact upon the living standards of Romanians at the end of the 1970s fuelled increasing internal discontent. In order to contain it, Ceaușescu turned to the Securitate.[7] While not relying on the extremes of repression pursued during the early years of communist rule in Romania, Ceaușescu showed that his rule was capable of resorting to the practices of the past in order to maintain his dominance of Romanian society. The institutions and legal codification of coercion remained unchanged. Some provisions of the penal code remained dormant until he found it convenient to resuscitate them; such was the case with the decree requiring the registration of typewriters with the police which was revived in a decree that came into force in April 1983, and with a provision of Ceaușescu's predecessor Gheorghiu-Dej, introduced in 1958, which made failing to report a conversation with a foreigner a criminal offence (decree no. 408 of December 1985). Photocopying machines were a rarity, and the few that were available in national libraries were closely supervised and special permission was required for their use. The materials and number of copies made were carefully recorded by a librarian.

The degree of Ceaușescu's intrusion into the lives of individuals was most potently illustrated by measures of family planning. Abortion on demand had been legalised in 1957 and became the principal means of family planning. When the 1966 birth rate dropped to fourteen per thousand people (much the same as in Britain), thereby heralding a decline in the workforce and a threat to the pace of the country's industrialisation, the law was adjusted to allow abortion only to women over forty, mothers of four or more children, victims of rape and incest, and in cases of possible foetal abnormality. After the 1966 law went into effect, the abortion-related mortality rate among Romanian women increased to a level ten times that of any other European country. Since contraceptives, while not illegal, were virtually unobtainable, many women used abortion as the main method of birth control and were forced to obtain it illegally.

From a peak of twenty-one per thousand people in 1969 the birth rate showed an annual decline thereafter, due both to the increase in the number of illegal abortions and the fall in living standards in the late 1970s. Figures for 1981 showing the birth rate at six per thousand people led Ceaușescu to insist that steps be taken to reverse this trend. Prime Minister Constantin Dăscălescu took up this theme in a speech in September 1983. In March 1984, Ceaușescu issued a summons before a gathering of National Women's Councils in Bucharest to 'breed, comrade women, it is your patriotic duty'.[8] At the same time he issued one of his notorious unpublished orders that women of childbearing age were to be subjected to compulsory gynaecological examination to check that they were not breaking the law by using contraceptive devices. Women doctors were required to conduct monthly examinations of factory women in Bucharest and to ask each one of them if she was pregnant, and if not, why not. In fact, the doctors often falsified records in the patients' favour and sold contraceptive pills to them which they had obtained from other East European countries.[9]

To bolster the drive to increase the birth rate, Ceaușescu introduced punitive tax measures, introducing additional taxation for all childless couples over 25. In 1986, he raised the minimum age for women to be allowed an abortion from forty to forty-five and lowered the age at which women could marry from sixteen to fifteen. Although the birth rate did rise between 1986 and 1988, it fell again in 1989 to sixteen per thousand. But the measures led to tragedy. There was a dramatic increase in backstreet and self-induced abortions, especially among young working women, despite the harsh penalties given to those involved in them. Doctors risked fines and imprisonment if they gave medical help without legal authorisation when self-induced abortions went wrong, and the delays in securing this often led to fatalities. Securitate officers were assigned to every maternity hospital to ensure that the provisions of the abortion law were strictly observed although in some cases they turned a blind eye.

The figures for deaths among Romanian women resulting from the anti-abortion law are the single most powerful indictment of the inhumanity of Ceaușescu's regime. In the twenty-three years of its enforcement, it is estimated that the law caused the death of over 10,000 women from unsafe abortion. The majority died from post-abortion haemorrhage and blood poisoning.[10] The black irony of this tragedy is that it took place in a country whose 'First Lady', Elena Ceaușescu, was lauded in its media as the 'Woman-Mother'.[11]

Compliance

A feature of public attitudes in Romania towards Ceaușescu was compliance. His ability to garner support for his regime from intellectuals by using the 'nation' as his constant point of reference in defining his policies was equally efficacious when applied to many creative writers and historians.[12] The corollary of Ceaușescu's achievement in this respect was a virtual absence of intellectual dissent or, expressed otherwise, a monotonous compliance by intellectuals with the regime. Some Romanian émigrés and Western observers have sought an explanation for this compliance or acquiescence in the Romanians' past, in a long-entrenched Ottoman tradition of dissimulation, and in deep-rooted practices of corruption, nepotism and bribery.[13] They also point to the absence of a focal point of opposition in post-war Romania. The weakness of the pre-war Romanian Communist Party, which was proscribed between 1924 and 1944, may explain the few challenges to the communist regime from within Marxist circles. Other analysts, and these include native Romanian writers themselves, ascribed this compliance to opportunism. The prospect of financial and material gain by accommodating oneself with the regime proved irresistible to many individuals and the resulting prevalence of opportunism amongst creative intellectuals was recognised by the poet Ana Blandiana (1942–) as a blight on Romanian society and culture.[14]

However, the blandness of dissent amongst the creative intelligentsia is merely one aspect of the compliance that characterised the Ceaușescu era. The reasons for this docility on the part of intellectuals must be examined in the context of the relative absence of major challenges to the Ceaușescu regime from any group in society. That absence of challenge can be ascribed in part to the efficiency of the Romanian Communist Party machine and its insinuation into the public domain. Party membership was a passport to job security and advancement in professional life. Successful acceptance into the Union of Communist Youth (Uniunea Tineretului Comunist) for candidates under the age of twenty-two, and promotion to membership of the Romanian Communist Party above that age, was a cause for celebration similar to that of a birthday or name-day. Party membership signalled loyalty to the regime; without it, professional advancement was virtually impossible.[15] Self-interest, therefore, dictated conformity and compliance.

Any analysis of compliance under Ceaușescu must also consider the condition of the rural and urban workers, of the technical intelligentsia of engineers, economists and managers, and of the Church. Although the Romanian urban worker had a lower standard of living than his Hungarian or Polish counterpart, it was higher than that of a Romanian villager or peasant. Given the fact that in the early 1980s over 60 per cent of the urban workforce in Romania came originally from the village, the point of comparison for industrial workers was their birthplace. Wage differentials between the agricultural and urban sectors remained considerable throughout the Ceaușescu period. In 1965, the wages of a villager working on a cooperative or state farm were only half of the average income, and while they had risen by 1979 to 66 per cent of the average industrial wage, there was still obviously a marked discrepancy. As a result, a low status was associated with agricultural labour, which in its turn prompted migration to the towns and the factory. At the same time, this low status generated low expectations.[16] The bulk of the peasantry had little knowledge of living standards in other parts of the communist bloc.[17] With low expectations went a suspicion of authority, and a conviction of impotence. These attitudes were inherited by those industrial workers who originated from the village. The significance of this peasant background in determining the outlook of industrial workers was highlighted

FIGURE 7.2 *Feleacu village, Cluj county, 1988. © Author's photograph.*

by the calculation in 1982 that almost 30 per cent of Romania's urban workforce commuted from the village. Such a high proportion of commuting workers led to the creation of a semi-urban society in which the village and the ritual of the Orthodox Church remained very strong, and around which family reunions and feast days were celebrated.[18]

The conviction of impotence which field work by Western scholars on the Romanian peasantry revealed merits closer examination for an understanding of compliance towards the regime. The proverb *'capul plecat nici sabia nu-l taie'* ('the sword will not sever a bowed head') is often invoked as emblematic of Romanians' attitude to authority. This submissiveness can be derived from what the Romanian philosopher Mircea Vulcănescu (1904–52) called 'the Romanian dimension of existence' which is characterised by its fatalism.[19] This acceptance of fate, which is determined by a belief in a spiritual eternity, can be equated in a political context with an acquiescence in temporal authority and recognition of the futility of resisting it. Such a conviction produced in some citizens a perverse pride in lamenting their personal plight: during the late 1980s, when austerity measures led to the introduction during the winter of heating restrictions in apartment complexes fuelled by a communal generator – common in those built in the 1960s in cities and towns – some citizens compared with a form of demonic pleasure the low temperatures in which they spent their 'leisure' hours.

Not only could the Securitate count upon passivity from the population, it also derived benefit from its ability to deflect the moral compass of the citizen by cultivating informers. The motives for collaboration with the Securitate were multiple. One was fear. Fear was a great labour-saving device, and it was a mark of the success of the Securitate in instilling that fear that Romanians came to hold the widespread belief that the visible presence of so many engaged in 'collaboration' with the secret police represented but a drop in the ocean of a ubiquitous network of officers and informers. The Securitate was as much a state of mind as the instrument of state terror. It was only after the 1989 Revolution that access to the Securitate's archives allowed scholars to give authoritative figures of the Securitate's strength. The total number of its personnel on 22 December 1989 was 38,682 of whom 23,370 were in the security troops command (the population of Romania was approximately 23 million). Of the remaining figure of 15,312 there were 6,602 in the national directorates and special units, 2,426 in the Foreign Intelligence Department, 6,059 in the county offices and 225 in the schools.[20] Police approval was required for a citizen to move his or her residence to another location in the country and restrictions were placed on travel abroad, especially to non-communist countries. The issue of a passport was a privilege, not a right. Thus, all those who were granted passports were adjudged to have made concessions to the Securitate, either in the form of accepting a *misiune*, a 'mission' in the form of reporting on the activities of Romanian relatives and friends abroad, or of informing on them at home, for which the favour of a passport was the reward. This was certainly the case with many Romanians who were allowed to travel in the communist era, but it was unlikely to be true of all. The Securitate were selective in their interest in Romanians wanting to travel abroad and it is doubtful whether they had the resources to charge every traveller with a mission. Even if they did, we cannot be sure that everyone so ordered actually complied.

Connection through family or friendship with an officer in the Securitate could be a guarantee of preferment in all state institutions, irrespective of personal merit, and the Securitate used this system of patronage to great effect. The advantages were reciprocal, for in return for the support of an officer, the collaborator was expected to pass back information. The second form involved branch officials of the Communist Party. In every institution there was a local Party organisation whose secretary Securitate officers would regularly interview, although they were required to obtain permission from the local Party secretary.

There were other, more basic, motives for collaboration with the Securitate which we can ascribe simply to human weakness; blackmail by the Securitate; a personal grudge or jealousy against an individual; the desire to feel part of a privileged group; or insurance in times of difficulty. The institutionalisation of police control itself made forms of collaboration a legal requirement. Every block of flats was required to nominate from amongst its residents a 'caretaker' who would not only be responsible for the upkeep of the building but also for keeping a register of all tenants and visitors who spent more than twenty-four hours in a flat. Every fortnight the register would be inspected by the local Securitate officer in whose 'beat' the block fell. After the 1989 Revolution some 'caretakers' were unfairly vilified as collaborators by their fellow tenants. Similarly, some figures were castigated as Securitate officers in cases where the position they occupied was designated *post facto* by Ceaușescu as one that could only be held by a Securitate officer, and hence the incumbent was judged to have been recruited into the agency.

Virgil Măgureanu, head of the post-communist security service, the Serviciul Român de Informații (Romanian Intelligence Service; SRI), stated that the number of informers in the records of the Securitate in 1989 was 400,000.[21] How many were active is not clear. A reliable network of informers is crucial to the success of any security service and the Securitate had no qualms about squeezing as much information as possible from its resource. The numbers of informers grew steadily over the years and although a nationwide figure has yet to be revealed, the publication of details from the Sibiu county inspectorate of the Securitate gave some idea of the scale of informing. The number of informers in the records of the latter in 1989 was

10,500, of whom more than half were active during the days of the Revolution.[22] In relation to the adult population of the county (325,000) the figure represents roughly one in thirty. However, if we add the informers working for the militia, whose numbers have not been released, the percentage would rise considerably.

In 1972, Major-General Costandache, the coordinator of the Centre for Information and Documentation of the then Council for State Security (CSS), sent all the county inspectorates of the CSS standard forms on which details of the sources of information of the Securitate were to be entered. This information remained stored in the computer banks of the Criminal Investigation Department. The informers were classified in four categories: hosts (*gazde*), collaborators (*colaboratori*), informers *(informatori)* and residents (*rezidenţi*). The first category comprised those who, willingly or not, placed their homes at the disposal of the Securitate officer to enable meeting the source in secret. The proportion of hosts to the other types of informers was one in twenty. The second group, the collaborators, represented almost half the informers. These met officers from time to time and provided them with information, which they signed. The third category, those who agreed to give information on a regular basis signed an undertaking to this effect (*angajament*). They were then given a cover name. The last group, the residents, was made up of people whose social position gave them the possibility of building up their own small network of informers. Many of them were retired Securitate officers.

Party members who served as informers formed a separate group. They could only be used with the permission of the local Party secretary and their collaboration had to be requested by the head of the Securitate inspectorate. A list of such informers was kept by the municipal Party secretary or by the deputy county secretary. All information, except that obtained by Directorate VI for penal investigation, was remunerated after its value was assessed by the bureau for analysis. The reasons for collaboration have been outlined above but during the period 1968–73, that is, after the Soviet invasion of Czechoslovakia, the numbers who did so from conviction increased. After that date, such altruism waned and by 1988 some Securitate officers stooped to the most abject form of blackmail in order to meet their target of recruits. They were to be found everywhere, even in old people's homes and schools: in the Securitate records in Sibiu, the names of ninety-eight children between the ages of nine and sixteen were found.[23]

The personality cult

Ceauşescu's protest at the Soviet-led invasion of Czechoslovakia on 21 August 1968 led him to discover that appeals to national sentiment could be an efficient mechanism of social control and personal dictatorship. It persuaded him of the rewards to be gained by lending emphasis to national symbols and to his own position in Romania. The huge rally in Bucharest on 21 August and its acclamation of Ceaușescu's denunciation of the occupation proved to be his finest hour, which whetted his appetite for the establishment of a personality cult. This was reflected in the increasingly ubiquitous appearance of slogans such as *Ceaușescu și Poporul* (Ceaușescu and the People), *Epoca de Aur: Nicolae Ceaușescu* (The Golden Age: Nicolae Ceaușescu), and *Nicolae Ceaușescu: Campion al Păcii Mondiale* (Nicolae Ceaușescu: Champion of World Peace). Ceaușescu's reaction to the Soviet-led invasion of Czechoslovakia drew its political justification from the Romanian Central Committee declaration of 1964 which remained throughout the period of Ceaușescu's rule the fundamental premise upon which Romanian autonomy within the Warsaw Pact and the Council for Mutual Economic Assistance (CMEA) was based.[24] Romanian foreign policy under Ceaușescu thus showed a continuity after 1968 which, by contrast, domestic policy lacked.

How seriously the threat of a Warsaw Pact invasion was taken by Ceaușescu can be gauged from two decisions: his announcement on 21 August 1968 of the setting up of the Patriotic Guards, a workers' militia, in which the majority of adult men and women was mobilised, and his secret order from the same time that an escape plan for him be drawn up by the CSS. Work on the plan started immediately in Directorate XI (Technical Directorate) of the CSS and was completed in 1970. The main thrust of the plan, codenamed Rovine-IS-70, was that in the event of an invasion, the CSS should organise armed resistance on a nationwide scale involving the whole population.[25] If this failed, then Ceaușescu would flee to a foreign country. Over the years the plan was continually modified, in particular, when Ceaușescu was told by the Directorate of Foreign Intelligence (Serviciul de Informații Externe; SIE) of the Soviet plot, codenamed Dnestr, to replace him with a leader more sympathetic to Moscow.

A fellow communist who shared a cell with Ceaușescu before the war detected in him, even at this early age, 'an unlimited confidence in himself which was nurtured by his equally unlimited lack of confidence in everyone else and especially in those to whom he was professionally subordinated'.[26] That lack of confidence became manifest in his refusal to accept advice, a refusal which meant that he would accept only sycophants around him and these appeared in increasing numbers throughout the 1970s and 1980s. His intolerance of others drew him closer to his wife, Elena, a woman of unbounded ambition and vindictiveness, who exploited her husband's growing paranoia, thereby encouraging him to give rein to his prejudices and pretensions. Her pernicious influence was most manifest in the preposterous personality cult which was generated around her husband.

The lengths to which the absurd could be taken by writers was most evident in the propagation of the personality cult. A significant body conspired in the concoction of the new truths demanded by the cult. New gods were created in the poems of Adrian Păunescu (1943–2010) and the paintings of Sabin Bălașa (1932–2008). The insular society of Ceaușescu's Romania provided fertile ground for the development of a cult providing a focus for people's attention. Initially, the president was projected as that focus, but by the early 1980s it was extended to Elena.

After Ceaușescu's denunciation of the Warsaw Pact invasion of Czechoslovakia in August 1968, a growing identification of Romania with a single figure can be detected in the editorials in the Party press, and in the statements of officials. At the same time, the intellectual elite was called upon to add its voice to the appreciation of the leader.[27] Birthday anniversary volumes containing poetry and prose in honour of Ceaușescu and his wife were published annually in the 1980s.[28] An anthology of some of the titles conferred on Ceaușescu in the Romanian media in the 1980s, together with their authors, was compiled by Dan Ionescu and included 'architect', 'celestial body' (Mihai Beniuc), 'fir-tree' (Ion Manole), 'genius' (Eugen Barbu), 'god' (Corneliu Vadim Tudor), 'morning star' (Vasile Andronache), 'navigator' (Victor Nistea), 'Prince Charming' (Ion Manole), 'saint' (Eugen Barbu), 'saviour' (Niculae Stoian), 'sun' (Alexandru Andrițoiu), 'titan' (Ion Potopin) and 'visionary' (Viorel Cozma).[29]

In summer 1971, Ceaușescu visited China and North Korea. The experience aroused in him an admiration for the cultural revolution and for the grandiose spectacles dedicated to the personality cult. The stage-managed adulation of Mao and Kim Il-sung, so meticulously choreographed, fired Ceaușescu's imagination and he demanded the same upon his return to Romania. Stubbornness and capriciousness became the hallmarks of Ceaușescu's rule. It not only humiliated the Romanians but also robbed them of their dignity in their everyday lives and reduced them in the 1980s to an animal state, concerned only with the problems of day-to-day survival.

Religious life

A major obstacle to the imposition of the Soviet model of communism after the Second World War was the Church. The Securitate was called upon to remove it. Yet in tackling this problem the Romanian Communist Party did not follow to the letter the Soviet solution. Both the Romanian Orthodox Church and the Uniate or Greek Catholic Church in Transylvania had been vital in preserving a sense of national cohesion and identity during the eighteenth and nineteenth centuries, and both retained the allegiance of millions of

Romanians. If both Churches could be manipulated to serve the regime's ends, then there was no point in destroying them. The Orthodox Church had been declared the dominant faith under the 1923 Constitution and had been given special privileges, such as the payment of its clergy's salaries by the state, and the Communist Party was to use this dependence to bring the Orthodox hierarchy under its control. The Uniate Church presented a different problem. It had been created at the beginning of the seventeenth century as a result of the conversion by Jesuits of many Orthodox Romanians in Transylvania to accept certain articles of the Catholic faith, among them the primacy of the Pope. As long as authority over the Church resided in Rome, it would be difficult for the new regime to bring it to heel. Thus, the Romanian Communist Party, while officially condemning religious worship, nevertheless tolerated it within certain bounds prescribed by law. In this respect it was more lenient than the Soviet regime. Tolerance of the recognised Churches required their subservience to the Party and their sonorous validation of the Party's policies, whether domestic or foreign. This remained the position under Nicolae Ceaușescu.

The limits imposed on the Churches' freedom of action had been laid out in the Law on Religious Confessions, enacted on 4 August 1948. Under the previous law of 1928, some sixty religious denominations had been recognised; under the new law this figure was reduced to fourteen. Control of the affairs of all Churches in the country was vested in the Ministry of Religious Confessions (reorganised in 1957 as the Department of Religious Confessions). While asserting from the very outset a guarantee of 'freedom of conscience and religion' (Article 1), it severely circumscribed that freedom by qualifying it with the open-ended provision that the religion practised was in harmony with the Constitution, internal security, public order and general morality (Articles 6 and 7). Legal recognition of a denomination could be revoked at any time when considered justified (Article 13). Similar restrictions were implicit in Article 32, which stated that 'ministers of religious faiths who express anti-democratic attitudes may be deprived temporarily or permanently of their salary, which is provided by the state'. All confessions were required to submit for approval to the Ministry of Religious Confessions a statute regulating their activities in accordance with the laws of the state; in return, the Ministry would pay the stipends of clergy from recognised confessions.

The Orthodox Holy Synod and the National Church Council were stuffed with Communist Party members. Key positions in the Church were thus entrusted to tools of the regime who were completely unknown to the population. By stripping the Church of its assets, the regime removed its scope for independent action and made it reliant upon the favour of the state. Any Church contribution to the creation of a civil society was thus stifled at a stroke. All the estates and funds of the Orthodox Church were nationalised, and thus its dependence upon state support became vital. Under the education law of 3 August 1948, its teaching institutions were either taken over by the state or closed, in number 2,300 primary schools, 24 secondary schools, 8 chapters' schools, 13 seminaries and an academy of church music.

Religious worship, then, was not to be outlawed by the Party, it was to be discouraged. Efforts made by the regime to inhibit religious practice included a ban on the conduct of baptisms and church weddings, and on the public celebration of Christmas and Easter. Party members were instructed not to attend church services, as were army officers and soldiers. Civil marriage ceremonies were the only ones recognised by the state, even after the ban on church weddings was removed under Ceaușescu. Denied religious education in schools, the family, whatever their faith, played a vital role in transmitting it.

Control by the Communist government of the Roman Catholic and Greek Catholic (Uniate) Churches met with greater resistance. This was partly because the close links they had with the West made them more resilient, but it is also the case that their bishops displayed remarkable dignity, courage and fidelity to their creed. There was, however, a major difference in the treatment of the two Churches at the hands of the regime: the Uniate Church was suppressed, the Roman Catholic was not, although it did not escape persecution. The explanation lies in the fact that most of the Roman Catholic faithful were Hungarians, and the Romanian regime was guided in policy towards the Church by the need to avoid actions that might be interpreted by its fraternal neighbour as directed specifically against the Hungarian minority. Consequently, the Communist Party's policy towards the Roman Catholic Church was not to abolish it, but to manipulate it by replacing control from the Vatican with control from Bucharest. It was only a partial success. Although the regime severed the Church's links with Rome, it was never able to impose its own authority on the Church. Throughout the communist era the Roman Catholic Church was held in the ambiguous position of being tolerated, but unrecognised. Agreement was never reached with the Ministry of Religious Confessions over the Church's legal standing within the 1948 law on confessions and so the second-largest surviving Church in Romania remained effectively illegal.

The Uniates' fidelity to their Church resulted in a brutal campaign to destroy it. The last figures available before suppression indicated that there were one-and-a-half million Uniates, with 1,725 churches served by 1,594 priests, 34 canons and 75 prelates. The union with Rome was branded in official publications throughout the communist period as 'anti-national and anti-historical' since it had split the unity of the Romanian people. The regime manipulated the merger of the Uniate and Orthodox Churches in 1948 with the help of the Orthodox Church and in this process the Securitate was used to extract the consent of the Uniate clergy. Those who opposed the union became targets of the Securitate. Uniate churches were handed over to the Orthodox Church, while the monasteries were closed. The legal existence of the Uniate Church was terminated on 1 December 1948; its dioceses and institutions were abolished, and its buildings entrusted to the Orthodox Church. The historical arguments were regularly revived during the Ceaușescu years as his ultranationalist postures demanded the mobilisation by his propaganda machine of an undivided, 'unitary nation, assembled behind its unique son', as an Orthodox priest put it to me in the 1970s. It was no accident that Orthodox prelates played the dummy to the ventriloquist Ceaușescu, especially the successive metropolitan bishops of Transylvania, whose diocese had been awarded the confiscated Uniate churches and other property not nationalised in 1948, and whose congregations had been swelled by the hundreds of thousands of Uniates denied their own churches in which to worship.

In a sad dereliction of moral leadership, the prelates of the Orthodox Church failed their faithful during the Ceaușescu years. Their compliance with the regime can be explained by the privileged position and the freedom to worship that they enjoyed, and they expressed their gratitude for that privilege in the ritual adulation of Ceaușescu. Sycophancy towards Ceaușescu became a commonplace amongst the Orthodox hierarchy, spawning declarations in which black was presented as white. Charity dictates that four examples suffice: one is the birthday telegram sent by Patriarch Teoctist to the Romanian President in January 1989 which gave thanks to him for creating 'the climate of complete religious liberty for all confessions in our country'.[30] The second is the congratulatory message sent by the Holy Synod to mark the fifteenth anniversary of Ceaușescu's 'election' on 28 March 1974 as president. The prelates expressed their thanks to the president for:

> your personal and constant concern for the unending growth of the country's economic strength [. . .] for the ardent activity which you, as the greatest and most brilliant hero of peace [. . .] carry out for the victory of mankind's ideals of freedom and progress [. . .] for the atmosphere of complete religious freedom which you have ensured for the religious groups of our homeland.[31]

While reprehensible in itself, this toadying to the regime was surpassed in its infamy by the silence of Orthodox prelates in the face of the destruction between 1984 and 1989 of eighteen churches as part of Ceaușescu's plan to rebuild the centre of Bucharest. If this silence was a hallmark of acquiescence to the regime, Patriarch Teoctist's telegram of support for Nicolae Ceaușescu, sent on 19 December 1989, just two days after the shooting by elements of the army and the Securitate of unarmed protesters in Timișoara, was an outrageous act of validation. The telegram congratulated Ceaușescu on his re-election as Party leader at the November Party Congress and praised his 'outstanding activity' and 'wise and far-seeing guidance'. It hailed the 'golden age which justifiably bears your name and its achievements which will endure for thousands of years'.[32] Needless to say, there were retrospective efforts to erase the record of the telegram for in the December 1989 issue of the official bulletin of the Patriarchate, printed some months later, there was no mention of it; instead there appeared a message from the Holy Synod of the Church denouncing the destruction of churches by 'the bulldozers of the tyrant Ceaușescu' expressing solidarity with the new National Salvation Front!form[33] Any grain of honour Teoctist might have gained on 18 January 1990 by bowing to public pressure and resigning was lost within two months when he was recalled, a sign that perhaps the Orthodox hierarchy was unable to find any prelate less compromised. Teoctist's reinstatement was proof of a poverty of morality and eloquent testimony to a Church badly compromised by total servility to a despot.

Public opposition

The first serious collective protest against Ceaușescu's policies was directed by miners in the Jiu Valley who went on strike in 1977 against economic measures. The strike was sparked off by legislation introduced in July 1977 discontinuing disability pensions for miners and raising the retirement age from fifty to fifty-five. Miners in the Lupeni mine decided to strike in protest at this decision. Ceaușescu hastily convened a government commission to deal with the crisis and it was decided to send Ilie Verdeț, the member of the Political Executive Committee responsible for the economy, Constantin Băbălău, the Minister of Mines, Clement Negruț, the mayor of Petroșani, and Ghinea, the mayor of Lupeni, to talk to the miners. They no doubt intended to persuade them to call off their strike, but they were not given the opportunity to do so. They were jostled by the miners and even punches were thrown as they tried to make their way to the mine manager's office. Verdeț was told that the miners had no confidence in him since he had deceived the Central Committee as to the true situation in the Jiu Valley and was instructed to contact Ceaușescu with the demand that the latter should come to Lupeni to discuss the miners' grievances directly with them. Under the supervision of a group of miners, Verdeț repeated on a secure line the words he had been told to say: 'Please come immediately, the situation is serious!' To prevent any further details being passed on, and to make Ceaușescu realise that Verdeț was effectively a prisoner, one of the miners in the escort hung up the receiver.

Ceaușescu arrived the same day in a convoy of black cars which tried to force a passage through the masses of miners. They failed and Ceaușescu was forced to get out of the car and make his way to the mine manager's office, amidst chants of 'Ceaușescu and the miners', 'Ceaușescu and the people'. Ceaușescu, according to an eyewitness, was totally taken aback by the sight of so many protesters. His eyes darted from right to left and he was clearly shaken by the scene. When Ceaușescu reached the mine manager's office the miners' grievances were read out in front of the strikers.

Ceaușescu then took the microphone and in a trembling voice declared: 'Comrades, this is not the way [. . .] this is a disgrace for the entire nation, a disgrace! I have taken note of your grievances'.[34] He went straight to the point of the demand for a shorter working day. In an attempt to distort the reasoning behind the decision to extend it, he claimed that it had in fact been the Party leadership which had resolved to reduce working hours but that this decision had met with opposition from the miners. This insult to the miners' intelligence prompted the reply: 'It is not us! Bandits, thieves!' Ceaușescu then proposed that the shorter programme be introduced gradually at the Lupeni mines and extended to other pits. This suggestion was met with the chant: 'a six-hour day from tomorrow'. Ceaușescu became visibly angered, surprised by the audacity of people who dared to express their point of view in his presence. He descended to the level of threats: 'If you do not go back to work, we'll have to stop pussyfooting around!' Prolonged booing and the cry of 'Down with Ceaușescu' met these menaces and the Romanian leader struck a more conciliatory note, conceding a reduction in the working day to six hours throughout the whole Jiu Valley, and agreeing to build factories that would offer work to miners' families. He promised that no retaliatory measures would be taken against those who had organised the strike, and that all of those who were to blame for the miners' discontent would be brought to account. After these promises were made the miners dispersed and some even returned to work on the evening shift of 3 August. But the next day, despite Ceaușescu's promises, the Jiu Valley was declared a 'restricted area', the army sent in, and the Securitate began their work of repression. An investigation was launched to discover where the core of support for the strike lay and, in the months following the strike, many miners were moved to other mining areas, while some were said to have been sent to labour camps on the Danube–Black Sea canal.

Behind the second major protest against Ceaușescu's policies lay the introduction of draconian measures designed to reduce food and energy consumption, and wage reductions. Yet instead of heeding the warning signs of increasing labour unrest, Ceaușescu plunged blindly forward with the same measures, seemingly indifferent to their consequences. A sign that the cup of privations had filled to overflowing came on 15 November 1987 in Brașov, the country's second-largest industrial centre. The trouble started only five days after the implementation of a decree of Ceaușescu reducing heating quotas for domestic consumption by 30 per cent and instituting punitive charges for exceeding the quotas. Coming on top of the imposition of wage cuts for the second consecutive month for failure to meet production targets (they could not be met because of a shortage of orders since the internal market was stagnant and there had been a drop in exports), and chronic food shortages, particularly of potatoes which were an essential part of the diet of Brașov's inhabitants, the heating restrictions were the last straw for the working population. Several thousand workers at the Steagul Roșu plant (with a workforce of 22,000) came off the night shift and assembled, ostensibly to vote in the local elections taking place across the country that day. They marched off from the plant at about 9 am in the direction of the Party headquarters in the centre of the city singing the anthem of the revolution of 1848 '*Deșteaptă-te, române*' ('Awake, Romania') and chanting 'Down with the dictatorship' and 'We want bread'. They were joined by workers from the Brașov Tractor Plant (workforce 25,000) and by many townspeople as they made their way to the city centre, where they forced their way into the Party headquarters. Those inside the building fled through the back of the building. The first sign of the crowd's frustration was the tearing down of the sign 'Brașov Party Headquarters'. There was a moment's quiet. The building remained silent. The workers attacked the ground-floor windows, smashing them in with stones and their flagpoles. Meanwhile, a group of fifty or so workers rammed the wooden gate until it broke open. Within minutes, the crowd was moving from floor to floor, smashing windows and throwing pictures, posters, radios, telephones, files and papers out into the crowd. A small group appeared by the gateway, bringing cheese, margarine and bread by the sackful, and began distributing them to the crowd. The crowd went wild. In theory, these foods were rationed, but they had, in fact, been quite unobtainable for months, even on ration cards. On the second floor a portrait of Ceaușescu could be seen in the bay of a window: a man used his body to rip up the canvas and shatter the frame. Behind him a fur-hatted worker's sweeping gestures motioned the crowd to go in; many did so. Pictures, office equipment and furniture from inside was set alight. Everything was burned. A number of arrests were made after the disturbances.[35]

The Brașov protests were also a reminder of the inability of the Western media to penetrate the fog of obfuscation with which the regime covered the event. News of the disturbances barely trickled out of Brașov at the time, much less beyond Romania's borders. As in the case of the miners' strike a decade earlier in the Jiu Valley the Romanian media remained silent. It was left to foreign print and broadcast media to alert the world – and through the Romanian section of Radio Free Europe and that of the BBC World Service – the

Romanians themselves of this breach between the Romanian Communist Party and the Romanian working class.[36] The fact that this protest took place in a major industrial centre whose production of lorries and tractors was largely for export, and whose workers were formerly amongst the best paid in Romania showed the depths to which discontent with Ceaușescu's policies had sunk.

Censorship

With the imposition of communism in Romania began an era in which the leadership of the Romanian Workers' Party would seek, and succeed to a large degree, in manipulating political and artistic expression for its own ends. Censorship provided the mechanism. The measure of that success was reflected in the subservience of the press and cultural activity to the dictates of the regime. A new censorship body, the General Directorate of Press and Printing (Direcția generală a presei și a tipăritorilor), replaced the censorship department of the Ministry of Arts and Information which was deemed incapable of 'assuring a proper activity in the fields of means of expression and public information'.[37] The new body was established by decree in May 1949 and was made responsible to the Council of Ministers, thereby giving it an increased authority. It was charged with overseeing the publication of all printed matter and the distribution of films and works of art as well as all forms of literature. Its creation can be considered the beginning of the institutionalisation of information-control in Communist Romania.[38]

The compliance that had characterised relations between the intelligentsia and the Romanian Workers' Party under Gheorghiu-Dej continued undisturbed after Ceaușescu's election as First Secretary in March 1965. This was largely due to the popularity of the anti-Soviet stance that the new leader developed into a national and nationalist brand of Marxism. A feature of this was the importance given to the nation in a socialist society, which found expression in Ceaușescu's report to the Ninth Congress of the Romanian Communist Party (to which title the Romanian Workers' Party reverted in June 1965) on 19 July 1965: 'For a long time to come, the nation and state will continue to be the basis of the development of Socialist society. The development of the nation, the consolidation of the socialist state, comply with the objective requirements of social life.'[39] The role assigned to literature in society was to continue 'shaping the new man's Socialist consciousness' by employing a new method: 'deep-going Socialist humanism should pervade literary and artistic creation, which mirrors the Party's policy and activity devoted to the prosperity of our homeland, to the people's welfare and man's happiness'.[40]

The Romanian Communist Party was depicted as leading the nation through socialism towards the fulfilment of its aspirations. By arguing that the

Party represented the entire nation, Ceaușescu could claim for the party and for himself legitimacy as the defender of the national interest. The corollary of this was that any criticism of the Party or its leader from Romanians, whether inside or outside the country, could be branded as treachery to the nation, a charge that was to be levelled in the early 1970s against dissenting voices, in particular that of the novelist Paul Goma (1935–2020).

There is little doubt that Ceaușescu's proposals for the 'political-ideological activity, the Marxist-Leninist education of Party members and of all the working people', presented at a meeting of the Executive Committee of the Romanian Communist Party on 6 July 1971 were a bolt from the blue.[41] Coming as they did in the wake of Ceaușescu's proposals, or 'theses' as they have popularly been dubbed, they have been elevated to the status of a mini-cultural revolution by most observers. Nevertheless, their effect was to lead creative writers to employ more frequently an Aesopian language. Novels developed more allusive formulae, such as the parable. Poetry had recourse to an entire symbolism stemming from the same strategy of circumlocution. The use of intertextual and the absurd were means of denying censors access to the main message. It was not surprising that in a country that under the Ceaușescu regime announced record grain harvests but where bread was rationed, which produced petrol but that too was rationed, which built thousands of flats but could not heat them, a literature of the absurd, exemplified by the poetry of Marin Sorescu (1936–96) should flourish.

The descent from utopia into dystopia

One analyst described Romania in the 1980s as being characterised by the descent of Ceaușescu into 'the demonic obsessiveness of a man possessed and blinded by a crazed sense of himself and his mission'.[42] Ceaușescu declared defiantly in December 1982 that he would pay off the country's foreign debt by 1990 – a target in fact reached in April 1989 according to the Romanian press – and to achieve this introduced a series of austerity measures unparalleled even in the bleak history of East-Central European Communist regimes. Rationing of bread, flour, sugar and milk was introduced in some provincial towns in early 1982, and in 1983 it was extended to most of the country, with the exception of the capital. The monthly personal rations were progressively reduced to the point where, on the eve of the 1989 Revolution, they were in some regions of the country one kilo of sugar, one kilo of flour, half a kilo of margarine, and five eggs. At the same time, heavy industry was also called upon to contribute to the export drive, but because its energy needs outstripped the country's generating capacity drastic energy-saving measures were introduced in 1981, which included a petrol ration of thirty litres (about seven gallons) per month for private car owners. Other strictures stipulated a maximum temperature of fourteen degrees Celsius in offices and periods of provision of hot water (normally one day a week in flats). In the winter of 1983, these restrictions were extended, causing the interruption of the electricity supply in major cities and reduction of gas pressure during the day so that meals could only be cooked at night. During the severe winter of 1984–5, it was calculated from medical sources in the capital's hospitals that over thirty children had died as a result of unannounced power cuts affecting incubators.

Citizens' lives were conducted around the daily need to secure basic foodstuffs and it was commonplace to see long queues in urban areas that not only tested patience but also sapped the morale of the population, especially during the harsh winters when the daytime temperature often fell to minus 20 degrees Celsius. Such challenges to life were addressed by family networks rather than by state structures.

Romanian television had been a window on the world. Sometimes it was wide open, at others barely so. Following the Second World War, after the imposition of communism, the introduction of a television service became part of the Communist Party's first five-year plan of 1951–5. The first broadcast was on New Year's Eve 1956 and featured an address by Petru Groza, the president of the communist 'parliament', the Grand National Assembly. In a closed society, in which only a tiny minority were allowed to cross the borders into the free world, television was an opening to what was happening outside the country. For most Romanians, it was not only the main window on the world, but it was also the only one. The editions of *Teleenciclopedia*, a universal cultural, historical and geographical digest, attracted a dedicated Saturday audience in the late 1960s while on the same evening episodes of *The Saint*, starring Roger Moore, left city streets empty. The American saga *Dallas* had the same effect in the early 1970s.[43] But by the 1980s television entertainment was increasingly giving way to the ideological manipulation engendered by a stultifying personality cult.

The attitude of many Romanians under the final years of Ceaușescu's rule was summed up by a young theatre director in 1988:

> What most people want to do under a dictatorship is to forget about it, get on with their lives and enjoy themselves as best they can. Thus when Romanian TV was reduced to four hours of transmission per day in 1984 many citizens of Bucharest and the major cities acquired video recorders and cassettes with Western films. The import of these items was not banned, probably because amongst the users were Party and Securitate officials who did not alert Ceaușescu to the trend.[44]

Conclusion

The violent manner of Ceaușescu's demise set Romania's experience of political change apart from that of the other Central and East European states and was itself an indication that in Romania the peaceful overthrow of dictatorship was impossible. The obvious question arises: why was this so? One analyst has eloquently and concisely observed that Ceaușescu's 'once sturdy patriotism had become a deranged nationalism'.[45] His successful appeal to nationalism allowed him to tyrannise his people and allowed the people themselves to be tyrannised. Overt challenges to communist rule in Romania were uncommon and none threatened to overthrow the regime.[46] Sycophancy and participation in Ceaușescu's pervasive personality cult within all strata of Romanian society fed his megalomania. Ceaușescu's protest at the Warsaw Pact invasion of Czechoslovakia in August 1968 led him to discover that appeals to national sentiment could be an efficient mechanism of social control and personal dictatorship. It persuaded him of the rewards to be gained by lending emphasis to national symbols and to his own position in Romania.

Many in the population looked to their Christian faith for spiritual sustenance. In maintaining this they drew upon inexhaustible reserves of patience. Standing in queues for basic foodstuffs became a daily ritual. In tolerating the debasement of their dignity, citizens received little guidance from the Orthodox Church whose prelates, with very few exceptions, failed them. Following the suppression in 1948 of the Uniate (Greek Catholic) Church, which derived its authority from Rome, the Orthodox Church could claim to represent the spiritual needs of the great majority of Romanians, but its direction was entirely subordinated to the interests of the Communist Party. Despite this, it was commonplace to see churches filled to capacity on Sundays, notably by women of all ages.

The most remarkable Romanian dissident was Doina Cornea (1929–2018). At the heart of Cornea's messages stood the belief that every individual should feel responsible for their actions and should recognise that any failure to act responsibly had repercussions for society at large. She argued that Romanians had become 'a people without a scale of moral and spiritual values, a people fed solely on slogans', and this process of 'spiritual draining' lay behind all the inadequacies of life. Cornea depicted herself and her fellow intellectuals as 'passive onlookers at a regrettable perversion of consciences', which had led to the replacement of moral values by material ones. This situation could only be reversed by a return to the 'spiritual', which she defined as 'the highest value, one which generated intelligence, ethics, culture, liberty and responsibility'. She called upon her fellow teachers to cease teaching things which neither they nor their students and pupils believed in: 'accustom them to thinking more freely, more courageously, more conscientiously, and more generously'.[47] The downfall of Ceaușescu allowed the younger generation to do just that.

Notes

1 Such a multifaceted examination of Communism in Romania is presented in the three volumes authored by P. Cernat, I. Manolescu, A. Mitchievici and I. Stanomir, *Explorări în comunismul românesc* (Iași, 2005–6).

2 Bessarabia, the territory between the rivers Prut and Dniester, with a majority population of Romanians, had been annexed by Russia in 1812. In April 1918, the National Council of Bessarabia, composed of representatives of the peoples in the province, proclaimed the region's union with Romania. In June 1940, following an ultimatum from the Soviet Union, Romania withdrew its army and administration from Bessarabia and their place was taken by Soviet authorities. Although Soviet forces were driven out of the province by invading German and Romanian forces in July 1941, the Red Army reconquered the area in February–August 1944, and it was reincorporated into the Soviet Union as the Moldovan Soviet Socialist Republic. In the period of the Ceaușescu regime Soviet rule of the Moldovan SSR was a running sore in Soviet–Romanian relations and at the Romanian Communist Party's final conference in November 1989, Ceaușescu raised the issue of Bessarbia, denouncing the Molotov–Ribbentrop Pact of August 1939 and by implication calling for the region's restoration to Romania.

3 A. Heinen, *Legiunea 'Arhanghelul Mihail'. O contribuție la problema fascismului internațional [The Legion of the Archangel Michael: A Contribution to the Problem of International Fascism]* (Bucharest, 1999), 32, n5.

4 The figures are:

	1955	1960	1965	1970	1975
Washing machines	0	31,000	84,000	109,000	149,000
Refrigerators	0	7,000	117,000	144,000	260,000
TVs	0	25,000	159,000	242,000	395,000

(*Anuarul Statistic 1976*, Bucharest: Direcția Centrală de Statistică, 369).

5 https://web.archive.org/web/20200203203112/http://www.mnstarfire.com/ww2/history/economic/GDP1938.html (accessed 17 May 2022) and https://countryeconomy.com/gdp/greece?year=1989 (accessed 25 February 2020). See also P. Dobrescu and F. Durach, 'Unable to Stop Inequality from Rising: Evidence from Romania', in *Development in Turbulent Times: The Many Faces of Inequality Within Europe*, ed. P. Dobrescu (Cham, 2019), 93; see also L. Voinea (ed.), *Un Veac de Sinceritate: Recuperarea Memoriei Pierdute a*

Economiei Româneşti 1918–2018 [A Century of Sincerity. The Retrieval of the Lost Memory of the Romanian Economy] (Bucharest, 2018), 27–9.

6 *Organizarea şi funcţionarea Organelor Ministerului de Interne de la înfiinţare pînă în prezent* [The Organising and Functioning of the Ministry of Internal Affairs] (Bucharest: Ministerul de Interne, 1978), 106.

7 For comprehensive details of the organisation of the Securitate, see D. Deletant, *Ceauşescu and the Securitate: Coercion and Dissent in Romania, 1965–89* (London, 1995).

8 D. Aspinall [D. Deletant], 'Romania: Queues and Personality Cults', *Soviet Analyst* 13, no. 10 (16 May 1984): 4.

9 Information conveyed to me verbally by Dr Livia Stigleţ in October 1988.

10 P. Stephenson, M. Wagner, M. Badea and F. Serbanescu, 'The Public Health Consequences of Restricted Induced Abortion – Lessons from Romania', *American Journal of Public Health* 28, no. 2 (1992): 1328–31.

11 *Orizont*, 6 January 1984.

12 The degree to which Ceauşescu succeeded in mobilising support for his regime from cultural intellectuals and the reasons for that success are the subject of Katherine Verdery's path-breaking study of identity and cultural politics titled *National Ideology Under Socialism: Identity and Cultural Politics in Ceauşescu's Romania* (Berkeley, 1991).

13 M. Shafir, *Romania: Politics, Economics and Society – Political Stagnation and Simulated Change* (London, 1985), 146.

14 When asked what she despised, the poet Ana Blandiana replied 'Opportunism'; see 'Un chestionar pentru Ana Blandiana', *Cartea Românească. Exemplar de Semnal*, no. 2 (1984): 11.

15 For example, appointment as a university lecturer was conditional upon Party membership. There were, however, exceptions. My own father-in-law, Andrei Caracostea, professor of constructions at Bucharest Polytechnic, was exempted from this requirement when appointed in 1952, shortly after his release from a two-year spell in a labour camp – on the charge, never brought before a court, that he was the son of a pre-war minister – since his expertise was need by the regime for construction projects.

16 Shafir, *Romania: Politics*, 140–1.

17 This situation was evident from this author's contacts with peasants throughout the 1970s and 1980s, with the exception of those Hungarian villagers in Transylvania who received visiting relatives from Hungary.

18 J.W. Cole, 'Family, Farm and Factory: Rural Workers in Contemporary Romania', in *Romania in the 1980s*, ed. D.N. Nelson (Boulder, 1981), 91.

19 M. Vulcănescu, 'The Romanian Dimension of Existence: A Phenomenological Sketch', *Romanian Sources* 1, no. 1 (1975): 5–34. This is an abridged version of the original Romanian text which was published in the author's *Izvoare de filosofie* (Bucharest, 1943). Vulcănescu served in the government of pro-Nazi dictator Ion Antonescu from 27 January 1941 until 23 August 1944. He was arrested on 30 August 1946 on a charge of 'war crimes', convicted on 9 October, and sentenced to eight years' hard labour. He died in Aiud prison on 28 October 1952.

20 D. Deletant, *Romania Under Communism: Paradox and Degeneration* (Abingdon, 2019), 559.
21 *Cuvântul*, 18–24 August 1992. In discussion with this author (16 August 1993), Dr Măgureanu told me that he believed about 170,000 were active at the time of the Revolution.
22 Author's discussion with Dr Măgureanu, 16 August 1993.
23 Ibid.
24 The CMEA, also known as Comecon, was the trading bloc set up by the Soviet Union in 1949 to coordinate economic development among the communist states of Eastern Europe. It was dissolved in 1991.
25 For a discussion of Rovine-IS-70, see R. Hall, 'Nicolae Ceaușescu, Evacuarea din CC-ul, Soarele, Tîrgoviste, și Rezistența' at https://romanianrevolutionofdecember1989.com/nicolae-ceausescu-evacuarea-din-cc-ul-soarele-tirgoviste-si-rezistenta/ (accessed 25 March 2020).
26 P. Câmpeanu, 'Pe marginea unei recenzii. Mistere și pseudo-mistere din istoria PCR', *Revista 22* no. 34 (1995): 12: 'Chiar la 20 de ani, când, deținut fiind, nu avea nici o putere, încrederea lui [Ceaușescu] nelimitată în sine se hrănea din neîncrederea la fel de nelimitată în toți ceilalți și mai ales în cei cărora le era ierarhic subordonat'.
27 A host of examples from 1971 to 1973 are to be found in 'Antologia Rușinii', *Ethos* 1 (1973): 290–317; and *Ethos* 2 (1975): 331–68.
28 See for example, the collections (no editors named) *Din fiecare inimă a țării* [*From Every Heart in the Country*] (Bucharest, 1983); *Pentru cel ales* [*For the Chosen One*] (Bucharest, 1985); and *Prinos de sărbătoare* [*Festival Homage*] (Bucharest, 1985).
29 'An A to Z of the Personality Cult in Romania', *Radio Free Europe*, SR/1 (2 February 1989), 9–14. A shortened version is reproduced by J. Sweeney, *The Life and Evil Times of Nicolae Ceaușescu* (London, 1991), 181.
30 'Telegramă', *Biserica Ortodoxă Română*, Year CVII, nos. 1–2 (January–February 1989), 4.
31 V. Zelinsky, K. Szo, I. Tōkés, D. Cornea, E. Paian, L. Lukas, P. Neamtu and Elöre, 'Documents', *Religion in Communist Lands* 17, no. 4 (1989): 340–65, 365.
32 'Telegramă', *România liberă*, 20 December 1989.
33 *Biserica Ortodoxă Română*, Year CVII, nos. 11–12 (November–December 1989), 4.
34 All quotations in this paragraph come from K. Csalog, *Borton volt a hazam: Hosszu Istvan Beszel* (Budapest, 1989).
35 M. Oprea, *Ziua care nu se uită: 15 noiembrie 1987, Brașov* [*The Day We Won't Forget, 15 November 1987*] (Bucharest, 2002) and this author's interviews with participants in the protests, September 2001.
36 I was interviewed at the time by BBC TV. My knowledge of the disturbances came from the BBC, and their information came from second-hand accounts. There were no BBC correspondents based in Bucharest – not to mention

Brașov – and the town had been virtually sealed off after 16 November. The scale of the protests and its repercussions were a mystery to me, as was the fate of protesters. Since the BBC interviewer, from our pre-discussion off-camera, realised that I could not bring information on these points, he questioned me about the possible consequences for the regime.

37 B. Ficeac, *Cenzura comunistă și formarea 'Omului Nou'* [*Communist Censorship and the Forming of the 'New Man'*] (Bucharest, 1999), 34. For further reading on censorship during the period of communist rule in Romania see T. Troncotă, *România comunistă: Propagandă și cenzură* [*Communist Romania. Propaganda and Censorship*] (Bucharest, 2006); B. Nedelcovici, *Scriitorul, Cenzura și Securitatea* [*The Writer, Censorship and the Securitate*] (Bucharest, 2009); E. Șercan, *Cultul secretului: Mecanismele cenzurii în presa comunistă* [*The Cult of the Secret: The Mechanisms of Censorship in the Communist Press*] (Bucharest, 2015).

38 Ficeac, *Cenzura*, 34. The General Directorate's attributes were extended to include supervision of television broadcasts in resolution no. 267 of 23 February 1954 issued by the Council of Ministers. Its head between 1951 and 1973 was Iosif Ardeleanu, a veteran communist, who was notorious for his dogmatism and intolerance. V. Tismăneanu, D. Dobrincu, C. Vasile et al. (eds), *Comisia Prezidențială pentru Analiza Dictaturii Comuniste din România, Raport Final* [*The Presidential Commission's Analysis of the Communist Dictatorship in Romania, Final Report*] (Bucharest, 2007), 786.

39 Quoted from G. Schöpflin, 'Rumanian Nationalism', *Survey*, nos. 2–3 (1974): 77–104, 92. See also *Scînteia*, 20 July 1965.

40 N. Ceaușescu, *Romania in the Way of Completing Socialist Construction: Reports, Speeches, Articles, July 1965–September 1966* (Bucharest, 1969), 89.

41 This is the translated title of a speech given by Ceaușescu in Romanian, commonly known as the 'July theses'. It was published by Editura Politică in Bucharest in the same year.

42 J.F. Brown, *Surge to Freedom: The End of Communist Rule in Eastern Europe* (Twickenham, 1991), 202.

43 A. Cioroianu, 'O singură fereastră și mai multe povești', in A. Matei, *O Tribună Captivantă: Televiziune, ideologie, societate în România socialistă (1965–1983)* [*A Captivating Tribune: Television, Ideology, Society in Socialist Romania (1965–1983)*] (Bucharest, 2013), 7–8.

44 Author's conversation with Alexandru Darie, 2 October 1988. Video cassettes of American and British films dubbed in Romanian by a number of bold technicians, notably Irina Margareta Nistor, circulated widely on the black market.

45 Brown, *Surge to Freedom*, 209.

46 For a broader presentation and analysis of resistance, protest and dissent in Romania, see Deletant, *Romania Under Communism*, Chapters 8, 14 and 15.

47 D. Cornea, *Scrisori deschise și alte texte* [*Open Letters and Other Texts*] (Bucharest, 1991), 13–14.

Select bibliography

Abraham, F. *Romania Since the Second World War: A Political, Social and Economic History*. London, 2017.

Brown, J.F. *Surge to Freedom: The End of Communist Rule in Eastern Europe*. Twickenham, 1991.

Deletant, D. *Romania Under Communism: Paradox and Degeneration*. Abingdon, 2019.

Fischer, M.E. *Nicolae Ceaușescu: A Study in Political Leadership*. Boulder, CO, 1989.

Freedom House. *Romania: A Case of 'Dynastic' Communism*. New York, 1989.

Giurescu, D.C. *The Razing of Romania's Past*. Washington DC, 1989.

Hitchins, K. *A Concise History of Romania*. Cambridge, 2014.

Ioanid, R. *The Ransom of the Jews: The Extraordinary Secret Bargain Between Romania and Israel*. Chicago, 2005.

Joó, R. *The Hungarian Minority's Situation in Ceaușescu's Romania*. New York, 1994.

Kirk, R. and Răceanu, M. *Romania Versus the United States: Diplomacy of the Absurd, 1985–1989*. New York, 1994.

Kligman, G. *The Politics of Duplicity: Controlling Reproduction in Ceausescu's Romania*. Berkeley, 1998.

Manea, N. *On Clowns: The Dictator and the Artist*. London, 1994.

Oprea, M. *The Day We Won't Forget: 15 November 1987, Brașov*. Iași, 2003.

Pacepa, I.M. *Red Horizons: The True Story of Nicolae and Elena Ceausescus' Crimes, Lifestyle, and Corruption*. London, 1988.

Petrescu, C. *From Robin Hood to Don Quixote: Resistance and Dissent in Communist Romania*. Bucharest, 2013.

Shafir, M. *Romania: Politics, Economics and Society – Political Stagnation and Simulated Change*. London, 1985.

Tănase, S. *At Home There's Only Speaking in a Whisper: File and Diary Recording the Late Years of the Romanian Dictatorship*, translated from the Romanian by Sorana Corneanu. Boulder, CO, 2007.

Tismăneanu, V. *Stalinism for All Seasons: A Political History of Romanian Communism*. Berkeley, 2003.

Tismăneanu, V., Dobrincu, D., Vasile, C. et al. (eds). *Comisia Prezidențială pentru Analiza Dictaturii Comuniste din România, Raport Final*. Bucharest, 2007.

Verdery, K. *National Ideology Under Socialism: Identity and Cultural Politics in Ceaușescu's Romania*. Berkeley, 1991.

8

Between barbed wire and country garden idyll: Dictatorship and everyday life in the German Democratic Republic (GDR)

Stefan Wolle

Introduction

A novel about the GDR must start on a Sunday afternoon; on one of those melancholic and depressingly beautiful summer afternoons that you do not want to end, and which you believe you have experienced before: once in a dream, or a long time ago. Even work in the arbours ceased, and the industrious brigades of workers at the weekend allowed themselves some time off. The whine of the circular saw, screeching in short, rhythmical intervals, and the monotonous clatter of the concrete mixer fell silent. The smell of home-made coffee and cake hung in the air above the gardens. Crockery rattled. Everyone gathered for the sacred hour of partaking in afternoon coffee. Bits of muffled conversation could be heard over the garden fence, '. . . another piece of plum tart? . . . another cup of coffee? . . . Do you fancy a drop of cream for your coffee? . . . Oh. Real cream!'

Cream for coffee in the small, orange-coloured individual portions was hard to get hold of. In an emergency, you could decant the long-life milk out of the big blue carton. But this was also scarce at the weekend. So the housewives had to queue up in front of the supermarket on Thursday at the latest, or you brought the cream for the coffee with you from Berlin. 'Oh yeah, Berlin. They stock it up from the very front to the back of the shelf for them. Have you heard the latest joke yet? New road signs are now being put up on the outskirts of Berlin: a banana with a line through it. It means the end . . . of the supply zone.' Everyone knew the joke. Nevertheless, everyone laughed. They were now on a never-ending topic, '. . . ran around because of a roll of roofing felt . . . five-year wait . . . we should write an entry for it . . . perhaps my brother-in-law could have a look at work . . .'.

Everything was in short supply, and everything was available in superfluous amounts. The lack of goods and services resulted primarily in a permanent waste of resources and capabilities. Everyone was unhappy because there was always something unavailable to buy, and everyone was happy because there was always a lot to hunt down. People worried about the important things; they tried to get through and to make the best out of the situation. They got by; they knew the rules of the game. The state and the Party with their claims, their slogans and their ideology were completely out of the picture on Sunday afternoons like this. If problems transpired at all, they were apparently accounted for as mere problems of supply.

Was there nothing but the lower-middle class as far as the eye could see? Was the conformist, humble, petite bourgeoisie made up of fearful subjects who fared well in the small country behind the barbed wire? Did the totalitarian system at the garden fence border on its limits, or did the wire fence around the weekend plot constitute the limit of the imperceptible cage of bondage? Did the slight happiness of the middle class manifest as an opposite reality to the dictatorship of the *Sozialistische Einheitspartei Deutschlands* (SED – the Socialist Unity Party of Germany, also known as the East German Communist Party), or was it a part of it? Was the GDR a society of willing subjects who had entered into a secret social contract with their state, or was the retreat into privacy a form of resistance? Was being part of the petite bourgeoisie, derided and reviled, the only way to exist and survive for people in the socialist state, and which ultimately triumphed over all ideologies and utopian thought?

Images of the GDR can be broken down in an extreme manner. On the one hand, the idyll of both power and protection is presented, symbolised by the ownership of a second home in the countryside, the protection of the devoted father state, social security and full employment. On the other hand, we see images and stories of people being shot at the Berlin Wall, the ever-present surveillance undertaken by the Stasi, the many political prisoners and, finally, as a closing image, the mass of demonstrators and the fall of the Berlin Wall. How can these images be put back together again? To answer this question, the notion that there were good and bad sides of the SED dictatorship, that could be offset against each other, must be rejected. Instead, the system must be understood as a dialectical set of interdependent conditions. This explanation should be explored with the aid of the key terms from the system.

The double security of dictatorship

The concept of security is one of the key words for understanding the SED system. The term had a strange but noteworthy semantic ambiguity in the GDR. First, security meant the *Ministerium für Staatssicherheit* (Ministry of State Security), abbreviated to MfS and commonly called the Stasi. In official language, when the term *Sicherheitsorgan* ('security organ') was used, the abbreviation MfS was to be avoided.[1] Officials from the SED used the turn of phrase '*Genossen von der Sicherheit*' ('comrades from the Security') whenever they referred to colleagues from the MfS. The officer liaising with the MfS in the district and provincial administration offices of the SED was called the *Sicherheitsbeauftragter* (Security Representative). As a rule, they were referred to as *Offiziere im besonderen Einsatz* (OibE; officers on special assignment). They were responsible for the security of events, national gatherings and state visits, carrying out security checks to determine whether everything was *sicherheitsmäßig* (in order from a safety perspective). People often whispered that a particular colleague was their *Sicherheitsnadel* (safety pin).

The pair of terms *Ordnung und Sicherheit* (order and safety) was related to this, which included a third key concept: *Sauberkeit* (cleanliness). Every line manager, in fact every citizen, was responsible for this.[2] It involved workplace, roads and fire safety etc. Every employee in uniform, even an employee of German Rail or the Post Office, was a representative of 'order and safety'; they had to educate their fellow citizens about it, consider criminal charges and lead them back to the path of public virtue. In the same way as the term 'security' was ambiguous, so was the term 'cleanliness'. It meant cleanliness in the street, which was often non-existent, as well as moral cleanliness. Erich Honecker coined the memorable phrase, '*Unsere DDR ist ein sauberer Staat*' ('our GDR is a clean state'), in 1965, at the height of the struggle against the capitalist lack of culture.[3] In his statement, he meant that the GDR was a state devoid of dropouts, beat music, drugs and sexual promiscuity. This applied at all times to the dutiful citizen.

'Security and cleanliness', therefore, constituted protection from drugs, criminality and prostitution in the eyes of the citizens. The GDR propaganda was successful in its attempts to positively highlight this form of public security against the insecurity in the West. Murders, sexual abuse and other serious crimes were consistently concealed in public. This was how the image of a safe state emerged. All in all, the West appeared as a morally corrupt society, the East as a paragon of virtue and decency: a petit-bourgeois idyll of nuclear families, happy babies and friendly neighbours tending the green spaces together at the weekend.

'Security', however, also meant *soziale Sicherheit* (social security), in particular, the security of employment and nursery places.[4] The media in the

GDR deliberately juxtaposed this form of security with the insecurity in the West. While the number of applications for emigration to the West increased after the 1970s, the television audience in the GDR was provided with images of how miserable the unemployed and homeless from the Federal Republic of Germany (FRG) were. The fourth semantic dimension of the term 'security' was closely related to this. It was the security policy of the Soviet Union and the socialist community of states. This security policy, or peace policy, stopped the warmongers and revanchists in the West. In this respect, security constituted, above all, peace. With the exception of the national coat of arms, the most frequently used political symbol of the GDR era did not in fact originate from communist symbolism but from the Old Testament. It was the dove of peace, in its different guises, the most common of which created by Pablo Picasso in 1947, that featured throughout the socialist iconography and topology. In such a way, the levels of world peace mixed with the peaceful life under the protection of the socialist society, and the social freedom of the classless, economic order free from exploitation. Thus, the key concepts of tranquillity, order, security, cleanliness, protection and peace created a system of positively regarded feelings that was internalised deeply by many people and characterised the memory of the GDR.

The Wall as a way of life

The reason why this idyll was surrounded with bars could neither be explained meaningfully at the time by the propaganda from the State, nor by those who explain the SED dictatorship today. The awareness of living in a cage and of never being able to leave it, as far as is humanly possible, shaped everyday life, the mentality of the citizens and their relationship with the power of the state. The barriers separating East and West consumed a good part of the imagination and creativity of the subjects. They were looking for ways to overcome the barriers, and the state authorities considered measures to stop them. Overall, the *Staatsgrenze der DDR* (state border of the GDR) formed an iron grip that held the unstable system together by force.[5] The Wall was everywhere, and in this respect, it was not only a construction, but also a state of mind reflected in the public and private sphere too, as an ever-present neurosis towards the barrier. Peace, and thus the protection of the people, order and security were saved by the GDR on 13 August 1961, according to the state-official view of history.[6] Workers and farmers wearing uniforms belonging to the combat groups prevented the German Armed Forces from '*mit klingendem Spiel durch das Brandenburger Tor zu ziehen*' ('marching through the Brandenburg Gate accompanied by the noise of beating drums'). This strange topos was repeated ad nauseum.[7]

The Wall's construction began in the following months and was perfected more and more up to 9 November 1989. *Abgrenzung* ('separation') was one of the favourite words in GDR propaganda.[8] It primarily meant disassociation from the imperialist FRG. Nothing was to connect the people with the state belonging to the revanchists from Bonn. Since the beginning of the 1970s, the common language served as an incidental relic of history. Even history offered nothing in common, but division above all else. From the historical perspective of the SED, the German division was the continuation of the irreconcilable struggle between the reactionary exploiting class and the progressive working class. Of course, there were changes and distinctions in this Manichaean explanatory model of the world over the years, but the central theme of SED propaganda was separation from everything associated with the West. The *politische Gegner* (political opponent) was constantly present like the devil in the medieval view of the world. It penetrated into the living rooms of the socialist state via radio waves and television channels, and into the hearts and minds of the people just as a commonly used expression would. As a result, people had to be alert, to recognise the intentions of the enemy and to thwart them at the right time. Everyone was called upon to do so.

In the GDR, the West did not simply constitute a cardinal direction. First and foremost, it was synonymous with West Germany, the name given to the other German state in the first two decades of the separation, or the Federal Republic of Germany, which was articulated reluctantly by officials along with a grim expression. Instead, the abbreviation FRG was used. Prescribed by its use in the media, this combination of letters was to be enunciated in a clipped manner with deliberate breaks between the letters themselves. The chief commentator of television in the GDR, Karl-Eduard von Schnitzler, mastered this particularly well. The abbreviation was therefore limited almost exclusively to official use. In everyday language, people just used to say, 'the West'.

If a *politisch komplizierte Situation* (politically complicated situation) reared its head, even dutiful comrades tuned in their radios or television sets in order to listen to *was der Westen sagt* (what the West said). It was not just the receiving devices and antennae though; even people were *westlich eingestellt* (tuned-in to the West), a common phrase in the vernacular, especially in the 1950s and 1960s. In harmless cases, they enjoyed listening to the hit pop songs from the West; in more serious cases, they were open to *Westargumenten* (arguments from the West). Everybody was waiting for the sought-after *Westpakete* (parcel from the West) or for the *Westbesuch* (visitor from the West) who would hopefully bring along some *Westgeld* (money from the West) or at least some *Westschokolade* (chocolate from the West) and some *Westseife* ('soap from the West').[9] Such *Westkontakte* (contacts in the West) could be complicated for some people because they had to be registered at the district office, and secret contacts were prohibited. Worse still were

Westverwandte (relatives in the West). The material blessings from over there were so sought after that a *Westbruder* (brother from the West) or a *Westschwester* (sister from the West) could negatively affect one's career in the Party or state machine.

True bilingualism may be referred to in the GDR. The different editions of the Duden dictionary in the GDR cite around three dozen compound nouns between the entries of West Africa and West Virginia. However, they do not reference any compound nouns beginning with the word 'West' that are regularly used in everyday language. Even so, the *Handwörterbuch der deutschen Gegenwartssprache* (*Pocket Dictionary of German Contemporary Language*), published in 1984 by the Institut für Sprachwissenschaft der Akademie der Wissenschaft (The Institute of Linguistics at the Academy of Sciences), recorded the entries *Westmark* and *Westfernsehen* (television from the West). In the dictionary, the *Westmark* is defined as an 'outdated, colloquial designation for the currency of the FRG', and *Westfernsehen* is translated as a 'colloquial designation for broadcasted television programmes in the FRG'.

For almost half a century, the electronic media, i.e. television and radio, had the most significant grip on the Germans in their two enemy states.[10] The sky over Germany may have been divided, as implied in the famous novel by Christa Wolf.[11] The metaphor of a divided sky indeed referred to the sphere of political ideals and dreams, even though this was strange amid the officially prescribed dialectical materialism. In this allegorical sense, the German sky may have been divided. However, in the actual realm of electromagnetic waves, between the frequency range of long and ultra-short wave, a medial nation of radio listeners and television viewers emerged. For four decades, a communicative space of a peculiar, inner contradictory nature existed amidst the flickering and crackling of the borderless airwaves. This space did not do away with the SED dictatorship, but it did undermine public opinion of the Party every single day. The society of the GDR was a room with *geschlossenen Türen* (closed doors), in the words of Jean-Paul Sartre. The windows were wide open even when they were barred up. There was never a *Tal der Ahnungslosen* ('valley of the clueless') in the GDR. In those regions that did not receive television from the FRG – the district of Dresden and the eastern part of the Baltic district of Rostock – they listened intensively to *Deutschlandfunk* (German Radio), Radio Luxembourg, RIAS, *Rundfunk im amerikanischen Sektor* (Radio in the American Sector) and other programmes broadcast on medium-wave radio.

For the GDR, the West reflected all fears of threat, hope and desire; the Federal Republic was always represented as the standard of comparison, the mirror image, the *tertium comparationis* (third comparison), the dialectical equivalent of what darkness is to light. Between the demonisation and the exaltation of the FRG, there was a whole manner of conceivable variations and distinctions. Nothing is more incorrect than the assumption that the GDR citizens were naive and had been badly informed. It was rare to be able to get past an almost neurotic fixation. Like conjoined twins, the Germans were not able to separate themselves in their four decades of division.

Work as myth and reality

The national coat of arms of the GDR, in use since 1953, which also decorated the national flag from 1959, consisted of a hammer, a compass and a ring of rye. The three symbols stood for the working class, the intelligentsia and the peasant class respectively. The entire bank of images and word usage of the East German state is permeated by symbols and concepts from the world of work. Calls for increased work productivity featured at the forefront of its rhetoric in all stages of development. These were often linked with military imagery. Battles of production became the rhetoric; the workplace was to be the battlefield for peace, and demonstrations took place on high days and holidays. In these verbal battles, imperialism was largely defeated, at least from a moral perspective. But within *Brigaden* (work groups), school classes and military units, they fought each other to win the battle of performance and to win the title. In the end, references were made to the term brigade, for example, the *Brigade der sozialistischen Arbeit* (Brigade for Socialist Work) or the *Brigade der Deutsch–Sowjetischen Freundschaft* (Brigade for German–Soviet Friendship).[12] It was not a coincidence that the term brigade also originated from the military. Work, in particular, heavy physical work, was surrounded by the aura of heroism. Every year, on the *Tag der Republik* (Republic Day), and on 1 May, the *Internationale Kampftag der Arbeiterklasse* (International Workers' Day), working people were honoured as heroes of socialist work.

Work was not simply a goal-oriented, valuable activity to ensure one's livelihood, but was surrounded by a mythical aureole. Labour was a central category in the Marxist interpretation of history. Friedrich Engels, the son of a factory owner raised in the tradition of Calvinism, equated labour to being human. One of the chapters in the *Dialectics of Nature* deals with the 'Part Played by Labour in the Transition from Ape to Man'. When the ancestors of humans stood up in order to walk on two legs, their hands became free for work. In this way, the industrious apes became humans whereas the lazy ones remained true to their species. The entire history of the world, according to Marx and Engels, revolved around the creation of value through labour and the appropriation of the surplus product by the owners of the means of production. In socialism, labour finally took on a new character. 'The socialist relations of production, cooperation among comrades, and mutual support, as well as the socialist cooperation of labour, lead to a new attitude towards labour itself; it becomes a matter of honour for every member of socialist society fit to work.'[13]

Stratification of society into social classes resulted from ownership of the means of production. Membership to a class was therefore given objectively. According to Marx, Engels and Lenin, one was a good or bad person by the grace of the right birth. To question the origin of these theorists – all three of whom originated from the middle class and the upper echelons of state service – was considered improper in the GDR. A thoroughly momentous theory for the reality of life in communist countries came into force from 1917. The fairy-tale world of socialism had a precisely defined ensemble of characters. The brilliant and invincible hero was the worker. In overalls smeared with oil, wearing his worker's cap or his helmet, with his safety glasses pushed onto his forehead, soaked in sweat, holding a tool in his powerful hands, he stood smiling good-naturedly or with a serious or humble expression, in bronze and marble on the plinth of the monuments. He strode powerfully through the political, visual propaganda of the socialist regime, and mastered the ideological rhetoric, art and literature of the socialist reality. At his side was the farmer: politically not as important, but indispensable. Even the farmer's wife appeared regularly. Standing next to the farmer, they created an image of chastity like the famous sculpture in the Soviet Pavilion at the Paris International Exposition in 1937, which was subsequently seen for decades in the opening credits of the films produced by the Mosfilm studio. Even the employee from the intelligentsia featured amongst the images of socialism. The cultural and spiritual creator of the socialist regime presented himself with a serious and cool expression contemplating a test-tube sample, in the control centre of a nuclear power station, or as an artist in discussion with the workers. There was a small but significant difference between the employee from the intelligentsia and the intellectual. The term intellectual related exclusively to the past or to the Western hemisphere. Remains of mistrust and contempt lingered there. From a socially economic perspective, the intellectual was perceived as a petit bourgeois, who had succeeded, at best, in rising above class barriers to become an ally of the proletariat.

Despite the petit bourgeois way of life being heavily criticised, the basic spirit of the SED upper class was completely petit bourgeois.[14] Here, the class theory of Marx and Lenin revealed itself as an empty bubble of propaganda. The terms member of the petite bourgeoisie, petit bourgeois and petite bourgeoisie were ideological slogans with a specifically defined network of meaning. Members of the petite bourgeoisie had not understood the severity of the class struggle. They were prone to radical phrases. They seesawed between the front lines. They were prone to thoughts of acquiring goods and services, opportunism and careerism. When the poison of a petit-bourgeois way of thinking had set in, the class enemy had an easy time of it. In particular, all appearances of reconciliation, dilution of ideological principles, and infiltration had their roots in the petit-bourgeois social environment. All efforts to secure a state of socialism in a peaceful manner, and to reconcile democracy and socialism were illusions characteristic of the petite bourgeoisie. In this respect, the petite bourgeoisie and social democracy were inextricably linked. Lenin taught that its economic situation incites in the petite bourgeoisie the profoundly contradictory efforts to free itself from the yoke of capitalism and to consolidate its position as a small property owner, and that this unavoidably and inevitably makes it fluctuate between revolution and counter-revolution.

In this particular instance, the criticism of the petite bourgeoisie was a killer argument; it made the individual defenceless. After all, every counterargument merely provided new evidence that the indictment was correct. It was precisely the dogmatic insistence on a false argument that was typical of the petite bourgeoisie. The petite bourgeoisie, in particular the petit bourgeois intellectual, had a propensity for anarchy, and for overestimation of individual opinion with regard to the wisdom of the collective because he had not firmly established himself in society. The victim was particularly defenceless against criticism of his social origin. In the field of education, there was systematic and targeted discrimination against the children of independent craftsmen. Entry to secondary school and university was not blocked, in principle, but it was made considerably more difficult. Even those having to demonstrate a purely proletarian lineage were not immune to suspicion of being from the petite bourgeoisie. Every average graduate of an educational course run by the Party knew that the petite bourgeoisie would often and willingly worm themselves into the ranks of the *Partei der Arbeiterklasse* (Party of the Working Class).

Bewährung in der Produktion (Probation in Production) was a popular form of education for dissidents of socialist ideology. The reasons could be varied; often they were *ideologische Unklarheiten* (ideological ambiguities).[15] In such cases, students or intellectuals had to subject themselves to rituals of criticism and self-criticism. The clever ones did not try to defend themselves; instead, they accused themselves and others of moral or ideological transgressions. In this way, they proved that they could better themselves, and got the chance to undergo a probation. At the end of such rituals, the offenders were pushed down by the ruling class. In the bosom of the working class, they were to challenge their convictions: a grotesque aberration. Those who still had illusions about the system were thoroughly cured by the proletariat. At that time, that original spirit of anti-communism prevailed, which was hardly found in university circles anymore. Still spoken about as if it were yesterday,

17 June 1953 was the day when the SED bigwigs were taught about fear. People raved uncontrollably about the time before the construction of the Wall, when you could still go to a jazz concert or to the cinema in Berlin. At best, there was complete indifference to the Party's slogans. If that working-class instinct existed, as often suggested, it was directed entirely against the SED regime.

Full employment, half the availability of goods

The significance of work, particularly heavy, physical work, was very high. The communist culture of the worker as the hero and the Protestant work ethic combined, due to the fact that Prussianism and socialism had many points in common. Pictures of the best workers were hung up in the factory yard. On *Frauentag* (Women's Day), 1 May (International Day of Struggle and Celebration of the Workers for Peace and Socialism) and Republic Day, there were bonuses, medals and red carnations for individual and collective performance. Of course, a widening gulf separated theory from practice. This mystification of labour stood in strange contrast to notions such as lack of motivation, and sloppiness, which stemmed from socialist economics. In practice, all the larger companies were the property of the state and operated according to directives from the top. The result was a top-heavy administration, unclear responsibilities, a reluctance to perform to targets, and minimal motivation to take responsibility within a company.[16] No one needed to fear for their job, however, provided they did not become embroiled in political conflict.

There was not only full employment in the GDR, but also a permanent shortage of personnel. 'No people. No people,' was the proverbial groan uttered by all the economic leaders in the GDR. The shortage of staff was the universal reason for poor service in retail and other outlets of goods and services in the socialist state. 'My colleague's coming now,' was constantly on people's lips. Hearing this in the gastronomic establishments was usually the clue that the impatient guests were becoming rather demanding. Outlets providing goods and services were often closed due to a lack of staff. Even the manufacturing companies often experienced delivery problems for this reason. A sign hung on every company entrance stating: 'We are looking for staff from the unemployed population'. This was the prescribed wording, although an unemployed population did not actually exist at all. Poaching employees from other companies or institutions was prohibited. The above-mentioned stereotypical wording was therefore displayed right at the top of the sign. It was then followed by a list of offers of employment. The rule of thumb was that the lower the qualification of the workers, the greater the need. Graduates sometimes had difficulties finding a job appropriate to their qualifications. Unskilled workers never had this problem. Even secretaries, cleaning staff, drivers and other transport workers were like gold dust in the state-owned economy. Unskilled workers often earned more than the company bosses and even the chartered engineers or scientists.

The consequences of this often huge imbalance were felt everywhere. The lower level of the proletariat allowed little to be said to them by their superiors. Alcohol consumption was often significant, especially during the night shift, and work discipline left a lot to be desired. It was considered normal to disappear in the direction of the shower a quarter of an hour before the shift change. At the end of the working day, the workers wanted to be at the factory gate at least. Shifts often failed to be realised because a particular colleague did not turn up in the morning. At the worst, there was a deduction from the employee's wages, or they were obliged to work the time back. Serious penalties were only threatened in the event of the situation happening again. Even recording of illness was administered rather liberally.

Whatever you needed at home, or at your second home in the country, you took from the company, joking that it was the property of the people, and everyone could take their share. Or you could joke: 'Erich Honecker did say that we could still get much more out of our companies'. In fact, an employee could not be blamed for securing tools, wooden boards or building material at work. Things were hard to get hold of in the retail outlets of the socialist state. Thus, it became customary that the boss would write on a slip of paper, to protect the company, that the wooden boards or replacement parts taken by the colleague were in fact overstock and could be removed from the premises. As a general rule, there was a consensus between workers and middle management not to exaggerate things. Then you could turn a blind eye. And everything ran its correct course in the socialist regime.

The high proportion of women in the workforce reinforced the vicious circle of the shortage economy and inefficiency in the workplace.[17] Doing the shopping and dealing with official business had to be done as the shops were often empty after the close of business, doctors' appointments and hair appointments were booked up and the offices of the state authorities were closed. The universal excuse was sick children. However, in this case, there was no continued pay in many companies. The constitutionally guaranteed right of work went hand in hand with a de facto obligation to work. Both were governed by the Constitution. The refusal to work was considered asocial and subject to penalties. In reality, the police controlled whether people complied with their obligation to work. Sometimes, the community police officer, similar to a district police officer, would ring the doorbell and ask a person who had aroused suspicion to provide information about his workplace. If it transpired that the person did not have a job, he was requested one last time to take up employment by the start of the month. Otherwise, legal action would be taken as a result of living an asocial way of life. This statement was often used with recalcitrant artists, musicians and other members of the independent workforce. If they were not members of an association of artists, and did not have a tax identification number, they would be met with court summons, intimidation and legal penalties. Even excuses like having saved up enough money to be able to devote themselves fully to their art did not wash. Of course, there were ways and means to slip through the net of the state authorities. In the very last years of the GDR, a grey area of the demographic developed; people who made their living from semi-legal or prohibited businesses.

From the cradle to the grave

The obligation to work resulted from economic reasons. It was also motivated by the fundamental need of the state from a pedagogical perspective. The authorities reluctantly tolerated it if a member of society failed to adhere to the strict rules of the world of work. As a whole, society was characterised by a marked propensity towards uniformity and inflexibility. The latter was both vertical and horizontal, and affected the entire educational curriculum and working life. In principle, people were free to choose where they worked, but significant difficulties were put in the way of one moving to another city or to another company. The basic procedure was as simple as it was effective. Without a permanent job, it was impossible to apply for housing. And without a permanent residence, it was usually impossible to get work. These obstacles were not insurmountable, but still very difficult to overcome.

Many citizens, therefore, in the GDR spent their entire working life in one company. The company became their second home and their colleagues became their second family. Companies were not solely responsible for providing vocational training, which was even combined to some extent with the German equivalent of A-level qualifications. They supported optimistic cohorts to study at university or technical institutes, taking them on after they had graduated. People had a much better chance of finding a home through their workplace than at the regular housing office. Employers had their own allocation of homes that they could assign to their employees. The Party and the Armed Forces were at the top of this hierarchy. The Ministry of National Education and the Ministry of Health also had homes to distribute. Membership of the Arbeiterwohnungsbaugenossenschaft (AWG; Workers' Housing Cooperative) was, as a rule, linked to a certain length of service to a company.

Sales outlets were set up inside the factories, where the choice of goods was significantly better than what could be found at home. In the bigger factories, there were even bookshops where many black market items could be found on the counter, as the employees there had little taste for literary treasures. Furthermore, companies had cultural institutions, health facilities, crèches and kindergartens, as well as holiday homes, at their disposal. The latter were mostly finished to a better standard than the homes of those belonging to the FDGB-Feriendienst (Free German Trade Union Federation Holiday Service). The price for this, of course, was being under the control of the workplace, even during the meagre holiday period. The financial contribution of the workers was very low in company-owned homes as well as in union-owned homes. The problem was that it was difficult to get one during the school holidays. It was particularly difficult to get a place on the Baltic coast unless one appreciated the charm of the bitter coast in winter or loved rambling through the forest in Thuringia in the November mist.

Love in the time of socialism

'The family is the smallest cell (i.e. unit) in society.' This striking sentence is found at the start of the *Familiengesetzbuch der DDR* (*Family Code of the GDR*) in 1975. Of course, this sentence provided cause for many jokes. On their wedding day, the bride and groom were tormented with comments such as: 'Get into the smallest cell! And stay there for the rest of your life!' Nevertheless, the introductory sentence of the preamble to the *Family Code* was meant quite seriously. A definition of the family followed: 'It is based on marriage for life, and on the particularly close bond which results from the emotional relationship between man and woman, and the relationship of mutual love and respect, and of mutual trust between all family members.' The emphasis on purely intangible themes in the midst of a material culture was supposed to raise the profile of marriage as understood in socialist terms, as opposed to the particular marital relationships in the petit bourgeois class, determined by economic forces. The legal basis of a marital relationship or a relationship between partners was thoroughly petit bourgeois even in the socialist state. The GDR had left the experiments of the early Soviet era far behind. In these experiments, marriage was rejected as an institution of the petite bourgeoisie. Even the revolutionary enthusiasm customary during the time of Stalin, which solely paid homage publicly to the love of the fatherland and the Party, was ultimately a thing of the past from the mid-1960s.

'*Echte Liebe gehört zur Jugend*' ('True love belongs to the young people') was the statement in the SED's communiqué on youth in 1963:

> Love between two people is often represented as a circumstantial phenomenon, where people have very little to say about it. In fact, problems associated with love and marriage affect all areas of society; every leader

ought to be clear about this. Loveless relationships can stop the development of a young person for a long time; those full of love inspire him or her.[18]

After years of peculiar petit-bourgeois proletarian puritanism, the state finally allowed the notion of love to be spoken about publicly after the communiqué on youth. From 1963, a column entitled '*Unter vier Augen gesagt . . .*' ('In Private . . .') appeared in *Junge Welt* (*Young World*), the newspaper of the Freie Deutsche Jugend (FDJ; Free German Youth) movement. In this column, well-known sexual experts, such as Professor Klaus Trummer, answered questions from young people. In one letter, a female young person asked whether a romantic relationship in the workplace could have negative consequences on team morale. Professor Trummer denied this emphatically.

> The dictates of socialist morals and ethics demand every person in our society to live a clean and reputable way of life. Does this demand contradict the relationships which develop between people in the socialist process of production? Does this mean that friendly relationships between the sexes i.e. between girls and boys in the company are 'immoral'? Not at all. I would even like to say that in relationships such as these, genuine ideals and high goals transpire to a far greater extent than in many other friendships. The way in which the socialist community operates, where new relationships develop between people, allows, in many respects, new standards of behaviour to arise in relationships between the sexes. This affects other areas of life as well as relationships on the production line, and changes people to the core of their personality.[19]

Such maxims did not just herald the sexual revolution but allowed romantic relationships in the workplace without the fear of reprisals from middle management. The individual member of the team was allowed a private life. Individual freedom in society began to increase slowly.

As was the case in the West, the introduction of the contraceptive pill signified an important watershed moment in social history and in the history of the mind.[20] In the West as in the East, it is easy to recognise when the pill kicked in through demographic graphs. However, there was a significant difference, which had its causes in the political environment. In the GDR, the term contraceptive pill was not used in official language. Turning the term on its head, so to speak, to make it sound more positive, it was called the pill for the wanted child. The prevention of pregnancy was not paramount, but the planned and conscious desire for a child was. The right time and circumstances for children to be born were to be included in plans for education and employment. This related to individual life planning as well as the design of social and economic policy.

The pill, whether described as the pill for the wanted child, or the contraceptive pill, suited the social planners in the GDR well in its concept. In the FRG, it was available from 1961, and it was also prescribed in exceptional cases from this time in the GDR. Those with the right contacts could get hold of it from the West. In 1965, Ovosiston, the first hormonal contraceptive manufactured in the GDR, was available in pharmacies. It was manufactured in the *Volkseigener Betrieb* (VEB; Politically Owned Enterprise) called Jenapharm, the only company in the GDR that developed and manufactured hormone medication. Ovosiston was awarded a gold medal at the Leipzig Spring Exhibition in 1965 for being 'a product of excellent work quality'. One pack, equivalent to a month's supply, cost almost 3.50 marks in the GDR. It consisted of a small glass tube containing twenty-one green pills as well as seven placebos so that the tablets could be taken continuously.[21] Less than a million packs were prescribed or, rather, sold from 1965 to 1967. In 1968, this increased to 2.5 million packs, in 1969, to 4 million packs, and in 1970, to 5 million packs. This rose further and faster to 13 million packs in 1972.[22] In other words, around 10 per cent of women in the corresponding age group took the pill in 1968. One year later, it was as high as 20 per cent in Berlin.

In the book called *Wunschkinder?* (*Wanted Children?*) by Karl-Heinz Mehlan, which was published in 1969, we read:

> Science and technology have already provided the ways and means for practical contraception [. . .] We consider the liberation of the human being from all trials of nature, and in doing so, from the permanent link of his or her sexuality with unwanted reproduction, as a human right. The hopelessness in which numerous women find themselves for fear of unwanted pregnancies is not compatible with striving for humanity from our perspective [. . .] Every night before going to sleep, over 20 million women take the pill for a wanted child, incorrectly named the contraceptive pill. The contraceptive freed millions of women from the permanent fear of an unwanted pregnancy. It aroused a new sexual feeling. A new freedom was realised for women. For the first time, the woman was able to have sexual intercourse as an equal sexual partner to the man from a physical sense. The dividing curtain, which the former methods established between procreation and sexual freedom, is now noticeable; everything plays out as if no contraception were used at all. All the woman's functions remain intact. She has subordinated one, however, to her will: that of conception.[23]

The chemical control of fertility proved to be an intrinsic part of the general utopia experienced by the new generation. Science and technology seemed to allow families to be free of planning. Medical, social and ethical considerations were brushed aside. Humankind had apparently come one step closer on its path of self-development. In reality, however, it was acting heteronomously in its decision-making as a result of constraints in employment, education, housing conditions and consumer habits, a situation, of course, which differed only slightly between East and West.

The perfect world of babies

The GDR saw itself as a child-friendly and family-friendly country. *Muttis* (mummies) beaming happily with healthy babies in their arms were part of the most beloved images in socialist propaganda. The planned demographic policy in the GDR was successful in part, although the birth rate trended downwards as a whole, in an uneven manner. Between the two periods of 1950–5, and 1959–65, two *Geburtengipfel* (peaks in the birth rate) can be identified; they were not to be seen again in the time that followed. After 1965, the birth rate began to decline. In 1974, it reached the lowest figure of 10.5 births per 1,000 people; the lowest figure ever to be recorded in the history of the GDR. After this, it increased again for a short time, reaching a peak of 14.6 births per 1,000 people in 1980.[24] From this point onwards, it decreased on a continual basis.

Despite a fundamental change in social behaviour, which influenced the population's desire for children, the social policy measures that had been introduced did not have a demographic impact. The *Fruchtbarkeitsziffer* (fertility rate) i.e. the number of births in one year per 1,000 women of childbearing age (15–45 years) increased significantly as a result of the incentives that had been introduced to raise it.[25] The general tendency was for women to have their first child at a relatively young age; the majority of the women were between 20 and 25 years of age. This trend was related to women adapting to having children while still being able to work. However, the average age of mothers increased in the 1980s. Between 1970 and 1989, it had risen by one year for the birth of the first child, and by four months for the birth of the second. In the final year of the GDR, it had risen to 22.9 years for the birth of the first child, 26.3 years for the second, and 29.3 years for the third.[26] Conversely but interestingly, the trend for two, three and even four children increased in the 1980s. This was the case in other industrial states, not just the GDR. It was probably partly associated with wanting to return to *private Glück* (private happiness: happiness in the family unit) and partly because economic considerations, such as plans to finance education, had a limited effect on the decision to have several children.

To keep women in work, the SED leadership implemented a whole series of social policies over time. The most significant of these were the possibility for an abortion, as well as full provision of nursery and kindergarten places, and after-school care. The proportion of children attending nursery increased continually until its peak at 81.1 per cent in 1986, remaining at 80.2 per cent three years later.[27] Even more children attended kindergarten where the admission rate was consistently well above 90 per cent and at its peak in 1989, it was 95.1 per cent. In primary school, around 80 per cent of schoolchildren used the after-school care provision.

Pedagogical ideals

The rate of female employment in the GDR at that time was obviously far higher than that in the FRG. In the 1960s, it was approximately 85 per cent; in 1989, and including apprentices and students, it was 90.1 per cent at the end of the GDR.[28] On one hand, this corresponded to the demand for equal rights in the workplace, and on the other hand, it was also an economic necessity. Wages and salaries in the GDR were so low that the father's income was not sufficient to support the family's standard of living as a general rule. Thus, the family in which both parents worked became the norm in the GDR. The consequences of this situation were extremely far-reaching and had a long-lasting effect on society. Over 90 per cent of children in the GDR passed through the institutions set up to raising children from a collective perspective i.e. crèches, kindergarten and after-school care, with all the consequences of being separated in such a way from their parents.

What was everyday life really like for 'mummy', a term people even liked to use in official German, in the GDR? As a general rule, 'mummies' worked. The working day began early in the GDR, usually at seven or eight o'clock in the office and as early as six o'clock in the factories. It was therefore still dark for many months when the children were woken up in the mornings. They then had to be dressed and fed. The children, still half asleep, were handed over to one of the care facilities. This had to be done quickly so that there were no discussions or arguments from the children. The subsequent journey to work was often long. Only a few young people had cars, so travelling to work had to be done on public transport, which was unreliable, overcrowded and not heated in the winter. When the need arose, a few tasks unrelated to work were carried out during the working day. Wherever practically possible, working women did the shopping, went to doctors' appointments and carried out official errands during their lunch break or during the working day. There were often queues at the shops, and the doctors' waiting rooms and waiting areas at official institutions were always overcrowded. The female workers therefore had to rely on the goodwill of their managers and frequently had to take the afternoon off. At the end of the day, the whole process took place again but in the reverse order. At around five or six o'clock in the afternoon, the children were picked up. They were a lively and exuberant group who had been moved from pillar to post the entire day. Correspondingly, they were often overwrought. In spite of this, they still had to accompany 'mummy' to the shops, or to see a tradesman. There was a lot of standing around in queues, bad tempers and excitement. The children misbehaved, starting a downwards spiral of moaning, typical of children, that caused their parents significant stress. There was still just enough time for tea while watching *Sandmännchen* (*Little Sandman*) on television.

According to sociological surveys, fathers were far less involved in this cycle than they would have people believe. Still, they dealt with repairs, sourcing material for home renovations and the like as tradesmen's services were in significantly short supply in the socialist economy. Traditional gender roles remained unchanged in many respects despite all proclamations to the contrary. Time spent at school became even more problematic from a practical perspective as the schools only usually opened when teaching began. Care provision in the morning did exist in some schools, but it was nothing more than a drop-off facility for children. This led to the fact that many children got up to an empty house in the morning and got ready for school by themselves. Even homework was seldom checked by parents which resulted in a bitter wake-up call for them when the school reports were sent home to them for sign off. The great ideals of socialist pedagogy fell by the wayside as was the case with the much-lauded equal rights for women. Of course, there were parents who could organise their work better. There were grandparents who were on hand in the case of emergencies. Some parents could even afford to pay for childcare. Nevertheless, the worst-case scenario of the social paradigm outlined above was typical throughout the state.

Living conditions and free time

The change from Walter Ulbricht to Erich Honecker brought about a further change in construction policy. Instead of large-scale construction, residential areas were to be built from the ground up. Solving the housing problem was at the core of the SED's attempts at social policy reform until the 1990s.[29] Every new housing estate was built from this premise; after the *Wende* (turning point), they became an architectural symbol of the GDR. Living in the *Platte* (the 'prefabs', that is, the large-panel prefabricated buildings used as housing stock) in the GDR was both a blessing and a nightmare. The *Platte*, the succinct name given to the blocks of flats built from industrially manufactured parts, represented freedom from cramped and uncomfortable living conditions for many people. Anyone who knows the horrors of the separate toilet up half a flight of stairs, cold kitchens with simple windows in

FIGURE 8.1 *Prefabricated buildings in Berlin.* © *Getty Images.*

the winter, the inconvenience of a flat without bath and shower, the daily dirt from the ash bucket, the sight of crumbling facades of buildings from damp, the gloom in the backyards, the need to shovel coal on Sundays and many other travails, will not find it difficult to understand that people who were allocated a luxuriously comfortable flat saw it as a godsend. Moving in was celebrated with a family party, and all the relatives and work colleagues helped with the move. All too often however, prior to this happy day, years of hard work, weekly visits to the authorities, writing out personal details to all and sundry, and other laborious tasks had been carried out. Now, at last, the children could be bathed every day. The hot water came out of a tap and what was more, it did not cost anything. The flat was already warm and cosy in the morning without having to lift a finger. The supermarket, childcare services, playground, school, outpatient or primary care clinic, and a whole array of other goods and services were located within walking distance. In addition, there was a space to park the car in front of the block of flats. Everything was well planned, standardised, simple and convenient. Was this a success story in housing policy then?

People constantly moaned about the monotonous appearance of these neighbourhoods. The blocks of flats were vilified as *Arbeiterschließfächer* (workers' footlockers) or as *Schnarchsilos* (snoring silos). The pejorative phrase *fernbeheizten Fickzellen* (remotely-heated cells to fuck in) is attributed to the poet Heiner Müller. The loss of community was clear. There was nowhere for people to go for a walk, nowhere to hang out, nowhere to relax where you could take your eyes off the children for a moment and be safe in the knowledge that they would not run off. In later years, large, colourful may beetles, teddy bears or crocodiles were painted on the entrances to the blocks of flats. It was a long time before any new buildings were erected or steps put in place to create green spaces. Even the transport connections were terrible in many cases. Giant puddles and mountains of sand collected between the blocks of flats. Although they had a certain charm as adventure playgrounds, many inhabitants considered them unsightly. That was not the only issue, however. In Berlin, the town planners took it upon themselves to appease the most uncouth complaints from the people. *Fresswürfel* (cuboids for eating: huge cafeterias) appeared, built from concrete in a standardised construction where people could relax comfortably at the end of the day. These places, where you could recharge, were even given romantic names. Restaurants owned by the Handelsorganisation (Trading Organisation) were located in the middle of the new-build wasteland. They had names like *Zu den drei Linden* (The Three Lime Trees) or similar, although there were neither lime trees nor any other types of trees as far as the eye could see.

The lucky ones had a small balcony and made their four or five square metres into a nook of individual creativity. The residents' imagination was boundless. They decorated the walls with jolly characters or paintings, and they fixed iron chains to the ceiling, where they hung ceramic bowls with creeper plants. Some put up wood panelling, cartwheels or horses' bridles. Imitations of timber framing were particularly popular, giving the concrete a distinctively individual touch. The balcony culture of the GDR was famous. From time to time, newspapers or SED organisations based in the residential area carried out competitions. Standardisation of life and provincial insularity but also social security and the touchingly homely attempts to gradually establish a level of happiness in one's private life beyond politics, was expressed to perfection in the *Vollkomfort-Wohnungen* (luxuriously comfortable flats) such as the WBS 70. The housing programme in the 1970s and 1980s was the centrepiece of Erich Honecker's social policy and at the same time the most significant manifestation of its failure.[30] The seventy-nine square metres of a four-room luxuriously comfortable flat conformed to a meticulously standardised programme of interior design.

Die Schrankwand (wall storage system) has been a symbol of interior design in the GDR for a long time. Its standardised components fitted exactly into the prefabricated flats belonging to the WBS 70 series. Crucially, a space slightly away from the centre was left for the television. Glasses for schnaps and wine were stored behind glass in a cabinet, as well as a few souvenirs from travels to other communist states and other knick-knacks. There was also a very modest place to store books, and significant room for storage in drawers and compartments. Armchairs or a settee with soft fabric or leather upholstery was positioned in front of the television. On the table, which could be adjusted with a few handles, a vase containing an arrangement of dried flowers was placed on a tablecloth; freshly cut flowers were difficult to acquire. An opening had been left in the wall to be used to pass items through to the kitchen. This could be closed with a curtain according to need. The room also contained an upright lamp, an artificial plant or other household plants, lots of cushions, covers, curtains, net curtains embellished with patterns and carpets. Art prints decorated the walls. The entire ensemble was framed by floral wallpaper in bright colours including gold and silver if possible. The typical living room in the GDR was complete: insular, standardised and planned to the last square metre, readily interchangeable and aesthetically uniform until it became a thoroughly faceless affair.

A modern and contemporary conception of interior design, dating back to the 1920s, was realised in the GDR; it became the norm and was consequently misinterpreted. Its original aesthetic clarity, expressed in precious natural materials and clean lines, was destroyed repeatedly by the production line of traditional furniture. To fulfil customer demand and to comply with the export requirements of the planned economy, furniture with gold and silver fittings, highly polished wood veneers, Baroque ornamentation and other fashionable adornments were produced. First, this was difficult to get hold of in the furniture shops. Second, it was very expensive. A wall storage system in the higher price bracket would cost three to four thousand marks. This amount of money equated to three or four months' salary for a well-paid skilled worker or scientist. Many customers were willing and able to pay these prices. This is why people today do not consider the standard design to look cheap, aesthetically speaking, or boring but symbolic of a certain prosperity, as was the case if a Trabant was parked in front of the house. Coming home to this environment, one could sit back happily, serve up some nibbles from the expensive delicatessen, and turn on the television from the West.

The summer house as symbol and reality

Die Datsche (the summer house) is one of the few GDR terms that remained in the lexicon of the German language, after the *Wende*. The Russian word is on its way to replace the Anglo-Saxon term bungalow, as well as the old-fashioned German term arbour, and the term allotment garden in the German vocabulary. In Russian, *datscha* means a summer house on the outskirts of the city. During the hot and dry summers in central Russia, half of the Moscow population would escape to these small wooden houses surrounded by gardens. Here, the Russian spirit was able to unwind from the pressures of big city life. The foreign visitor, working in the Soviet Union on official business, was also welcomed here. Somehow, the term infiltrated the GDR. It became symbolic with the phenomenon of many people fleeing the city to enjoy a private life. Away from the demands of society, fulfilment was found in life's little pleasures.

According to the statistics, there were 855,000 small garden plots in the GDR. In addition, there were the summer cottage owners who had their permanent residence in the countryside. Despite all the difficulties of comparison, it would be possible to assume a top European position with regard to the number of summer houses. The allotment garden had been part of the proletarian lifestyle since the nineteenth century. The idyll was certainly ridiculed, for example, by the communist agitprop writer Erich Weinert, who wrote a lyrical epitaph to the *Postbeamten Emil Pelle und seiner Laubenlandparzelle* (Post Office clerk Emil Pelle and his allotment) in 1930. However, during the war and the post-war period, produce from the allotments was important in the fight for survival. Opinion from the SED regarding the exodus to the countryside was split. The provision of fruit and vegetables from the allotment gardeners was essential to the economy. On the other hand, people always turned up their noses with regard to the middle-class idyll behind the garden fences of the staunch SED officials.

Fleeing the city for their summer houses was always preferable to fleeing to the West or taking part in activities organised by citizens' rights groups opposed to the policies of the state. The Party leadership surmised that whoever spent the entire weekend working on their allotment had less time to come up with stupid thoughts. Consequently, the allocation of plots of land had been systematically encouraged in the 1980s. Yet, one plot of land would not be sufficient. The new allotment gardeners brought wooden boards, garden fences, plants, paving stones, equipment and much more. It was not possible to get hold of much of this in legal ways. As a result, the black market flourished, the state economy continued to be damaged and activities were increasingly transferred to the private sector. Many people acquiesced in the short term as a result of their crippling social passivity.

Shopping in the state-owned retail trade

From as early as the 1960s, the GDR had increasingly developed into a socialist consumer society. This was connected to a furtive withdrawal from the utopia of communism, which was in fact welcomed by the people, and which stabilised the system. If, in the conglomerates sector *Waren täglicher Bedarf* (large-scale business entities), abbreviated to WtB in official German, certain customer requirements were not fulfilled, the effort to take the consumer wishes of the citizens seriously was noticeable. To a certain extent, objective and future-oriented criticism in the media was permitted and even desired. Buyers were supposed to be given a certain selection of items so a discussion could take place at the shop counter to decide upon the quality of a product. This was to be reflected in the manufacturer's balance sheet, thus affecting profit and loss, and to have certain consequences on remuneration for the work.

Product advertising and political propaganda formed a strange amalgam. The system was identified, indeed, it was categorically defined by its capacity to perform on an industrial level. A product was not simply a commodity whose value was realised by supply and demand, but a 'fetish' in terms of Marxist theory, a projection screen for the performance capability of the socialist system. The other side of this obsession of identification was that the inadequacies of the domestic products were attributed to the system by the buyers. The SED leadership tried to promote itself in a commercial landscape where it was difficult to beat the West. Even in the 1960s, the SED leadership propagated a form of consumer ideology, accepted the Western illusion of the constant demand for new products, and the internal rationality of an irrational production system that aimed to satisfy endlessly new requirements.

Admittedly, in the 1960s, there were still tentative attempts to counteract the intrinsic logic of the goods production in the West. In the fashion industry, styles that were easy to clean, crease-resistant and breathable were promoted. Clothes were supposed to be suitable for the working woman, and mother: practical, edifying and simple to wash. Non-iron products from synthetic fibres were advocated to save time. Clothes should not have to be changed frequently and they were supposed to be used as part of an overall capsule wardrobe in order to create different looks from the same pieces. Synthetic materials were promoted as a great achievement. Aside from the practical benefits, the state economy wanted to ensure that imported cotton was unnecessary. It was planning to extract the synthetic fibres from cheap Soviet oil. In the 1970s, in the attempt to fulfil all customer wishes comprehensively, a new dimension was reached. Consumer aesthetics and consumer ideology were now dominated purely by the West. The national economy of the GDR had embarked on playing catch-up; an initiative that it had to lose. It provided no rational alternative to the oversupply of goods and ever-increasing consumption, both tenets of Western economic philosophy. The GDR produced nothing other than substitutes and cheaper replacements. It became a prosperous society without prosperity. The planned economy was not in a position to convincingly imitate the colourful assortment of goods manufactured in a capitalist society. The GDR did little to develop a stable alternative, however. The consumer industry remained the problem child for the state leadership until the bitter end, the main reason for dissatisfaction and disaffection from the state, and the most important reason why many

FIGURE 8.2 *Queue at a food shop in East Berlin, 1982.* © *Getty Images.*

people retreated to the private sector where they looked for ways and means to fulfil their consumer demands.

The administrators of the shortages

Article 1 in the GDR Constitution assigned the role of leadership to the *marxistisch-leninistischen Partei* (Marxist-Leninist Party).[31] Critics of the system believed that power lay in the hands of a small group of officials or even with the General Secretary of the SED alone, who exerted his authority in a quasi-dictatorial manner. In the reality of everyday life in the GDR, a group dominated by contrast, which could be described as the *Verwalter des Mangels* (Administrators of the Shortages). Anyone with excess availability of any product or service that was in short supply belonged to this group, in particular tradesmen, waiters and vendors, but also administrative staff or employees from the Post Office. Its power did not result from the availability of the products per se, but from its position in the complex system of distributing goods and services. These could be tropical fruits, telephone sockets, wooden boards, spare parts for cars, means of transport, holidays abroad, tradesmen's services, specialised knowledge, theatre tickets, flats or rock music records from the West. The 'Administrators of the Shortages' exerted a form of power unrelated to economics over the exchangeable value of the goods and services, which was not only incompatible with the authority of the state but also contradicted its economic ideology and intentions. In the event of an oversupply of goods and services, the customer was king. On the other hand, in the event of a permanent shortage of goods and services, it was the distributor who reigned supreme. In addition to the political hierarchy – illegitimate by its nature, however firmly established – there was consequently an indiscernible social hierarchy in the GDR, where head waiters in fine restaurants or owners of tiling businesses could be positioned well above the middle ranks of the SED apparatus. Indeed, the excesses of the *Verteilungsmacht* (distribution power) were repeatedly criticised publicly, and occasionally contested by administrative means, but every state regulation regarding distribution in the longer term strengthened the shortages and, as a result, the administrators' influence.

The Gaststättenkollektive (Food Department of the Central Trading Organisation) controlled the gastronomic establishments. This led to strange traditions, some of which still exist. As a rule, a sign adorned the entrance to the restaurant stating '*Sie werden platziert*' ('Please wait to be seated'). Customers had to wait in front of the sign until a waiter came and showed them to their seats. This ritual even took place when there were enough free tables available. Customers were occasionally shown to a table that was already occupied even if it was uncomfortable for the diners who were already seated there. So, the customer had some understanding as to what was going on. It was not recommended to enter the restaurant pompously, going against the specific instruction on the sign, and to take one's seat at a table. In such cases, it was possible that the waiter chased the uninvited customer back to the entrance with comments such as '*Sie können wohl nicht lesen?*' ('Can't you read?') or '*Was bilden Sie sich denn ein, wer Sie sind?*' ('Who on earth do you think you are?') This did not suffice, however. Whoever had stood out, unpleasantly, like this, had to be educated about the rules and was then permitted to wait, but for a particularly long time. Rebellious protests against the waiters' instructions even ran the risk of being ejected from the premises, and the demand for the customer complaints book Der Gast hat das Wort (The Customer Has His Say), theoretically available in all restaurants, was frequently met with derision.

Another practice relating to the supply of goods relates to the strange rule that GDR citizens were not allowed to book a hotel room in the area where they lived. Whether this happened out of concern for public morality or to ease the burden of limited availability remains one of the many mysteries that have yet to come to light. In any case, it was a rare stroke of luck to be able to book a night without having to organise it weeks in advance. The hotel receptionists took the completion of registration forms very seriously, compared the details provided with the personal identification documents and refused customers who did not have the corresponding paperwork. Unmarried couples were either turned away or they were imposed with a booking of two single rooms. No legal basis existed for this; the *Kuppelei-Paragraf* (sexual intercourse outside of marriage which was punishable by law) had been abolished a long time ago.[32] But you could count yourself lucky to get a room at all, and to have the objection waived.

In the event of doubt, the 'Administrator of the Shortages' was always right. Petitions and complaints were taken seriously in the GDR. They almost created a literary genre of their own. But the letters of apology from the companies and authorities were, at best, a delayed form of gratification. Within these grey areas of the economy, tips played an important role of course, and turned seamlessly into bribery and corruption. It would be wrong, however, to accept the dictate of the distributor as a purely economic relationship of *Herrschafts- und Knechtschaftsverhältnis* (lordship and bondage) in the sense of Karl Marx. Not only did the value of the special financial payments and the provision of beer, coffee, cakes and lunch play a role for the tradesmen and employees in other service roles, but so did the *seelische Betreuung* (spiritual care). During repair work in the flat, the customer had to try to be a gofer, acting like the apprentice being taught, and laughing at tradesmen's jokes, even when it was at their own expense. In any case, after a tradesman had finished a job, his customer knew about the condition of his health and his marital problems. Reports about the last day of the fifth division football league, or world politics were also very welcome. There was enough time to discuss these topics while eating and drinking coffee. In principle, it was the customer's responsibility to procure the material for the work. In the event that a tool was missing, for example, a bucket, step ladder or screwdriver, this could lead to stern instruction from the tradesman. In such cases, the customer ran off to get hold of the missing items, not without setting up the coffee table for the team of tradesmen beforehand. Naturally, the rubbish remained on the floor in the flat. You could be happy if the work had been completed successfully.

The power of the 'Administrators of the Shortages' had varying consequences. One of these could be described as bad publicity. While advertising, since the emergence of the commodity–money relationship, served the purpose of tempting people who were eager to buy, bad publicity served to keep customers away or to protect the staff from troublesome enquiries. At the entrance of sales outlets or restaurants, signs advised the customer of the products that were unavailable or prohibited. They often informed customers about additional closures or days off. Vendors also made efforts to reduce their opening hours as much as possible. Although retail outlets in East Berlin were supposed to be open in general from ten o'clock to one o'clock and from three o'clock to seven o'clock, with retail outlets outside of the city operating similarly but advancing their hours earlier by an hour, there were often additional times when they were closed. Reasons could include deliveries of goods, necessary repairs or lack of staff. In any case, the sales outlets opened at least several minutes after the specified time but closed several minutes earlier. At least a quarter of an hour before the shop closed, a disgruntled employee would block the entrance and dismiss the last customers with unfriendly comments. The *Zivil-Gesetzbuch der DDR* (Civil Code of the GDR) in the same way as the *Bürgerliche Gesetzbuch* (Civil Law Book of the FRG) stipulated that every customer entering a shop before closing time still had the right to be served. However, a different customary law was applied as was the case in other areas.

The social equality of the GDR was based, above all, on the principle that everyone was equal because everyone had to queue at shops, go on a waiting list for cars or building materials, and deal with arrogant waiters and shameless tradesmen. In this area, there were of course those who were even more equal. The GDR was transformed into a society of hunter-gatherers. People were constantly on the hunt for products or services that were in short supply. It was the norm to always take a shopping bag with you in case you *dazu kam* (came across it), somewhere. *Dazu kam* was the colloquial phrase. If a queue formed somewhere, people would join it quickly and then enquire about what was being sold. That was not the only issue, however. The monetary value of goods was replaced by its exchangeable value as a result of subsidies. Bartering became increasingly common in society: the owner of a repair company was not paid for his services but received goods that were in short supply or other services instead. It therefore became increasingly important to know as many people as possible. An extensive network of relationships was necessary in the fight for survival. A brother-in-law with contacts in the supply of telephones, or a nephew working at the housing office could be worth their weight in gold. Still, there were not many doctors who would prescribe time off work. Even an artisan, who could get hold of ceramic pots or nutcrackers from the Erzgebirge (Ore Mountains) had a purpose. However, the academics had little to offer in this subsistence economy. Consequently, GDR society adopted more and more features of a tribal society. Maintaining relationships with relatives and acquaintances out of economic necessity was one of the reasons for the much-lauded goodwill between people in the GDR.

Years of change

The year 1989 was one of the most remarkable and most eventful years in recent history. It was clear at the end of the 1980s that the world east of the Iron Curtain had changed irrevocably. However, the reactionary forces still appeared very strong. The ruling communists had continuously preached that there could be no compromises in the question of power. The *revolutionäre Arbeiterklasse* (revolutionary working class) would never relinquish power. It had demonstrated often enough that only the strongest battalions counted at the critical moment of decision-making. Again and again, people had to learn the hard way that fighting tanks with bare hands alone was not possible, as had been the case on 17 June 1953 in the GDR, in November 1956 in Hungary, in August 1968 in Czechoslovakia and in December 1981 in Poland.

At the same time, however, the latent domestic political crisis gained momentum. Increasing numbers of GDR citizens tried to force their way out via the German Federal agencies in Prague and Budapest. Those people, especially, who no longer believed in the situation changing in the GDR, and who wanted to turn their back on their home forever, provided the impetus for the long overdue advent of democracy. For a long time, a prayer for peace was read in the St Nicholas Church in Leipzig every Monday. Applicants requesting to leave the GDR used this service to subsequently march together through the narrow streets of the city centre to the central station, and once there, they loudly expressed their desire to leave. The choir responded to their cry of *'Wir wollen raus!'* ('We want to get out!'), for the first time on 4 September 1989 by singing: *'Wir bleiben hier!'* ('We're staying here!'). Resignation was juxtaposed to hope. 'We're staying here!' meant '*Wir glauben an Veränderung*' ('We believe in change'). That was the open declaration of war against the SED system. On 10 September 1989, a political movement named Neues Forum (New Forum) was brought before the public. In its founding proclamation, it demanded nothing more than an open dialogue in society. Everything else was left open in the proclamation document and therein lay its explosive force. The start of something new quickly took on the momentum of an avalanche. Day by day, more people overcame their lethargy and fear, signed the founding proclamation, handed it out to others, and hung it on the walls which companies and offices had set up for news items appropriate to the ideology of the state. Apprehensive and surprised by their own courage, people who had never met each other before gathered in churches and other places and began to intervene in their own affairs. A fever of political change raged. Increasing numbers of political movements were brought before the public. Despite the fact that refugees had applied for exit permits at the embassies in Prague and Budapest, the corridors of the embassy were full again. In Dresden, the passage of refugee trains led to violent riots around the central station.

Meanwhile, preparations for the fortieth anniversary of the GDR continued as if nothing was happening. The situation became grotesque. The ageing SED leadership celebrated the festivities for the birthday of the Republic in the usual way on 7 October 1989. In the afternoon, demonstrations had begun in Berlin, Leipzig, Potsdam and other cities, where the demonstrators were violently clubbed by the authorities to break them up. On the following day, the situation from the previous evening was repeated in Berlin. Many people were physically abused at the demonstration sites or brought before the courts in a much quicker process than normal. There was a trace of civil war sentiment over the country. The demonstrations in Leipzig on 9 October 1989 brought about the change. Faced with approximately 70,000 demonstrators, the state power capitulated and did not dare to give orders for its forces to go into action. As a result, the SED had abandoned its exertion of totalitarian power. It now settled for dialogue and consensus: the most important buzzwords of those days. Suddenly, there was much talk about trust, as if it were able to be won back. But it was too late for the SED. Even the change at the top of the party leadership on 18 October did not have the desired effect. Egon Krenz was too deeply involved in the system to be credible. Power disintegrated from the SED's hands. Every day, there were resignations at all levels, the opposition parties gained ground, and became more radical in their demands. On 4 November, the largest mass demonstration in the history of the GDR took place at Alexanderplatz in Berlin. This day marked the culmination of the democratic mass movement and at the same time, the historical moment of increasing differentiation. The speeches and slogans still focused on a democratic renewal of socialism and on changes within the GDR. At the same time, however, many people wanted to go further, and questioned the very existence of the system.

On the evening of 9 November 1989, an unsuccessful press release led to people gathering at the border crossings in Berlin. Finally, those on duty at the border crossing points bowed gradually to the peaceful pressure of the masses, and the people surged towards West Berlin, cheering. The iron grip which had held the GDR together until now was broken apart. This was the actual end of the GDR and the division of Germany. A return to the old situation appeared impossible. Within just a few days, a fundamental spirit of change had arisen. It was now just a question of time and terms until both German states would be united. Even governments in Moscow, Paris and London had to take this fact into account. If the principle of self-determination of the people was taken seriously, unity, demanded by a growing majority, especially in the East, could not be denied to the Germans. Unification finally resulted from the *Zwei-plus-vier-Vertrages* ('Two Plus Four Agreement') which was eventually signed 12 September 1990 in Moscow. Beforehand, both German parliaments renounced all territorial rights they had in Poland and the Soviet Union, ensuring that this agreed with the NATO membership of the unified Germany. The strength of the German military was reduced to 370,000 men and the withdrawal of the victorious powers was agreed within four years. As a result, this marked the end of the post-war period and the Cold War.

Entropy

If the current political debates are followed in Germany, one could almost get the impression that two different states existed in parallel under the name of the GDR. On the one hand, there is a vibrant and thriving commemorative culture oriented towards everyday life. Recipes from the GDR era can be found on the internet, and old films are shown on television, in particular on the regional channel, Mitteldeutscher Rundfunk MDR, operated by the three states formerly part of the GDR: Saxony, Saxony-Anhalt and Thuringia. There are also fan clubs for the Trabant, the most popular car in the GDR, and many other clubs as well. For some time, the term *Ostalgie* has been used, a word coined from *Ost* (east) and *Nostalgie* (nostalgia) which was originally conceived by a cabaret artist. Political repression, persecution of those opposed to the system, travel restrictions and even the shortages in the economy continue to be blocked out, or only perceived as a result of their ridiculous and grotesque side. On the other hand, the repressive characteristics of the system have been highlighted by both research and documentary films, as well as feature films and works of literature.[33] Research has concentrated very intensively on the resistance against the SED system.[34] There are also numerous memorials and museums in former prisons and Stasi headquarters that commemorate the victims of oppression.[35]

Public debates and private conversations repeatedly lead to the same questions. Was it possible to live a happy life in the dictatorship? What was the final assessment? Social security imposed by the state led to a loss of motivation and initiative resulting in the absence of technological innovation. The GDR continued to lag behind the West. To make up for this deficit, resources were overexploited. Basic research, infrastructure, the protection of the environment and the upkeep of cultural monuments were wantonly ignored. This only worked when each and every public criticism was punishable by law. An opinion of dissent was perceived as, at best, a cognitive aberration and at worst, as a crime. In the end, it resulted in entropy, when expressed physically. The incapacitation of the people, including their own supporters, by the jurisdiction of the Party, led to the loss of responsibility. By establishing a monopoly of truth where power was protected, the ability to exchange information and opinion in the public space was destroyed. Society needed this in the same way as the body is dependent on its blood circulatory system.

The constant demand from the state to nurture its people kept them in an infant state; they were provided with everything as long as they were obedient. The rest was achieved by the removal of their freedom, as a result of the Berlin Wall and the Stasi. A collective developed that was in part necessity, in part emergency association and in part refuge. This functioned through the shortage society, which stabilised the system in the short term but paralysed it in the long term and deprived it of its defences. The state could get the population, at times, to even accept the loss of freedom by means of insufficiently financed social gifts. In the long term, however, the social and economic consequences were disastrous. The system thus developed in a downwards spiral. Whenever the possibilities of new social benefits were exhausted, the state was forced to tighten the screw of repression. In an economically networked world, as was the case in 1980s Europe, that was hardly possible. A system built on command and obedience can create in the short term, perhaps for a period of several decades even, a kind of deathly silence. If the orders from above failed to materialise, the puffed-up and bureaucratic security system decayed into a state of shock, resulting in immobility. This is what happened in autumn 1989, when the morally unsuccessful and economically bankrupt SED system was removed, pathetically and uncomfortably, from the annals of history. Socialism foundered – it did not fail by its imperfections, but by its achievements.

Notes

1. J. Gieseke, *Mielke-Konzern: Die Geschichte der Stasi, 1945–1990* (Munich, 2001); I.-S. Kowalczuk, *Stasi konkret: Überwachung und Repression in der DDR* (Munich, 2013).
2. S. Wolle, 'Sehnsucht nach der Diktatur? Die heile Welt des Sozialismus als Erinnerung und Wirklichkeit', in *Der Schein der Normalität – Alltag und Herrschaft in der SED-Diktatur*, ed. C. Vollnhals and J. Weber (Munich, 2002), 17–39.
3. G. Decker, *1965: Der kurze Sommer der DDR* (Munich, 2015), 284 et passim.
4. G. Winkler, *Geschichte der Sozialpolitik der DDR, 1945–1985* (Berlin, 1989).
5. H. Harrison, *Driving the Soviets up the Wall: Soviet–East German Relations, 1953–1961* (Princeton, NJ, 2003).
6. H. Mehls and E. Mehls, *13 August (Illustrierte historische Hefte, no. 17)* (Berlin, 1979).
7. *Neues Deutschland*, 8 September 1962.
8. For example, 'Beißen sich Abgrenzung und Koexistenz?', in *Berliner Zeitung*, 2 April 1973.
9. C. Härtel and P. Kabus (eds), *Das Westpaket: Geschenksendung, keine Handelsware*, 2nd edn (Berlin, 2001).
10. J. Staadt, T. Voigt and S. Wolle, *Operation Fernsehen: Die Stasi und die Medien in Ost und West* (Göttingen, 2008).
11. C. Wolf, *Der geteilte Himmel* (Halle, 1963).
12. J. Behrends, *Die erfundene Freundschaft: Propaganda für die Sowjetunion in Polen und in der DDR* (Köln, 2006).
13. *Wörterbuch der Ökonomie: Sozialismus*, 2nd edn (Berlin, 1969), 45.
14. S. Wolle, 'Sozialistisches Biedermeier als Lebensform: Vernichtung, Auferstehung und Apotheose des Kleinbürgertums in der DDR', in *Kleinbürger: Zur Kulturgeschichte des begrenzten Bewußtseins*, ed. T. Althaus (Tübingen, 2001), 313–31.
15. S. Wolle, '"Sicherheitspolitische Bedenken": Das MfS und die Personalpolitik an der Humboldt-Universität', in *Unter Hammer und Zirkel: Repression, Opposition und Widerstand an den Hochschulen der SBZ/DDR*, ed. B. Schröder and J. Staadt (Frankfurt am Main, 2011), 319–26.
16. A. Steiner, *Von Plan zu Plan: Eine Wirtschaftsgeschichte der DDR* (Munich, 2004).
17. A. Kaminsky, *Frauen in der DDR* (Berlin, 2016).
18. *Neues Deutschland*, 21 September 1963.
19. K. Trummer (ed.), *Unter vier Augen gesagt: Fragen und Antworten über Freundschaft und Liebe* (Berlin, 1966), 71.
20. G. Winkler (ed.), *Sozialreport '90: Daten und Fakten zur sozialen Lage in der DDR* (Berlin, 1990).
21. G. Winkler (ed.), *Frauenreport '90* (Berlin, 1990); Dr Annette Leo, *Die 'Wunschkindpille'* (2018) in Digitales Deutsches Frauenarchiv. Available online:

https://www.digitales-deutsches-frauenarchiv.de/themen/die-wunschkindpille (accessed 17 May 2022).

22 S. Wolle, *Die heile Welt der Diktatur, 1971–1989*, 4th edn (Berlin, 2013), 231.
23 K.-H. Mehlan, *Wunschkinder? Familienplanung, Antikonzeption u. Abortbekämpfung in unserer Zeit* (Berlin, 1969), 110.
24 *Statistisches Jahrbuch der DDR 1980* (Berlin, 1981), 355.
25 Mehlan, *Wunschkinder?*, 25.
26 Winkler, *Frauenreport '90*, 28.
27 Wolle, *Die heile Welt der Diktatur, 1971–1989*, 236.
28 Winkler, *Frauenreport '90*, 62.
29 C. Hannemann, *Die Platte: Industrialisierter Wohnungsbau in der DDR* (Berlin, 2004).
30 P. Meuser, *Vom seriellen Plattenbau zur komplexen Großsiedlung: Industrieller Wohnungsbau in der DDR 1953–1990, Teil 2: Neue Städte, Großsiedlungen und Ersatzneubauten* (Berlin, 2021).
31 *Verfassung der Deutschen Demokratischen Republik* (Berlin, 1974), 9.
32 *Strafgesetzbuch (StGB) sowie angrenzende Gesetze und Bestimmungen*, 5th edn (Berlin, 1981).
33 K. Schröder, *Der SED-Staat: Partei, Staat und Gesellschaft 1949–1990* (Berlin, 1998).
34 H.-J. Veen (ed.), *Lexikon Opposition und Widerstand in der SED-Diktatur* (Munich, 2000).
35 A. Kaminsky (ed.), *Orte des Erinnerns: Gedenkzeichen, Gedenkstätten und Museen zur Diktatur in der Sowjetischen Besatzungszone (SBZ) und DDR*, 3rd edn (Berlin, 2016).

Select bibliography

Adelmann, Q., von Godin, G., Marotz, S., Sieber, E., and Wolle, S. *DDR Guide: A Companion to the Permanent Exhibition of the DDR Museum*. Berlin, 2017.
Badstübner, E. *Befremdlich anders: Leben in der DDR*. Berlin, 2000.
Behling, K. *Leben in der DDR: Alles, was man wissen muss*. Berlin, 2018.
Dokumentationszentrum Alltagskultur der DDR. *Alltag: DDR – Geschichten, Fotos, Objekte*. Berlin, 2014.
Engler, W. *Die Ostdeutschen: Kunde von einem verlorenen Land*, 2nd edn. Berlin, 2019.
Fulbrook, M. *The People's State: East German Society from Hitler to Honecker*. New Haven, CT, 2005.
Hantke, I. *Im Konsum gibts Bananen: Alltagsgeschichten aus der DDR, 1946–1989*. Berlin, 2017.
Hertle, H.-H. and Wolle, S. *Damals in der DDR: Der Alltag im Arbeiter- und Bauernstaat* [book to a ten-episode television series of the same name]. Munich, 2004.

Kaminsky, A. *Frauen in der DDR*. Berlin, 2016.
Kleßmann, C. *Arbeiter im 'Arbeiterstaat' DDR: Deutsche Traditionen, sowjetisches Modell, westdeutsches Magnetfeld (1945 bis 1971)*. Bonn, 2007.
Schröder, K. *Der SED-Staat: Partei Staat und Gesellschaft 1949–1990*. Berlin, 1998.
Sommer, S. *Lexikon des DDR-Alltags: von 'Altstoffsammlung' bis 'Zirkel schreibender Arbeiter'*. Berlin, 1999.
Winkler, G. (ed.). *Frauenreport '90*. Berlin, 1990.
Winkler, G. *Geschichte der Sozialpolitik der DDR, 1945–1985*. Berlin, 1989.
Winkler, G. (ed.). *Sozialreport '90: Daten und Fakten zur sozialen Lage in der DDR*. Berlin, 1990.
Wolle, S. *Die heile Welt der Diktatur, Alltag und Herrschaft in der DDR*, in three parts: *Der große Plan, 1949–1961*; *Aufbruch nach Utopia, 1961–1971*, 2nd edn; *Die heile Welt der Diktatur, 1971–1989*, 4th edn. Berlin, 2013.
Wolle, S. *The Ideal World of Dictatorship: Daily Life and Party Rule in the GDR 1971–89*. Berlin, 2019.

Conclusion

Lisa Pine

Each chapter in this book has illuminated the nature of lived experiences in dictatorial regimes in twentieth-century Europe. An analysis of the circumstances of daily life has highlighted significant commonalities, as well as some important distinctions. One of the key differences pertains to the length of time for which the dictatorship remained in power. Some lasted for a short number of years – Ulmanis in Latvia for example, from 1934 to 1940. At the other end of the timescale, the Iberian dictatorships of both Franco and Salazar extended over a period of several decades. In addition to that, some regimes of shorter duration, especially Hitler's Third Reich, from 1933 to 1945, brought about the most radical and far-reaching changes quickly and with devastating consequences, both internally and beyond their borders. Many of these autocratic governments promised modernity and progress, perhaps exemplified by Stalin's efforts and demands to transform the USSR into an industrial giant through his series of five-year plans. Others, including Ulmanis's, harked back to idylls of the past and found their expression of the nation through those traditions. Some combined the two – backward-looking and conservative in some respects, radical and modernising in others. The Italian Fascist regime and the Third Reich were characteristic of this approach.

In all these autocratic regimes, the people somehow, wherever and as much as possible, went on with their lives, sometimes eking out a very precarious existence that was a matter of day-to-day survival. In the circumstances, what does that say about the ideologies that underpinned these regimes – whether Fascist, Nazi or Communist? Ideas and ideals proven erroneous; promises broken; policies imposed 'from above'; the strong arm of fearful state institutions and police systems to ensure compliance; corruption and hypocrisy among those high in Party positions; a cult of personality surrounding the leader; the repression of liberties and rights; and the censorship of news and information. And what of the people and their responses to and relationships with these dictatorial regimes? Most simply tried to get on with everyday life – but that often entailed changes of behaviour. With the fear of secret police forces and their informers, people had to be extremely careful about what they said and to whom. Others took advantage of the system in order to procure personal or professional advancement in a variety of ways through Party-promoted clientelism, as illustrated in the cases of Portugal and Spain, to name just two examples. Others still became acclimatised or used to the system – it became part of daily life and was somehow normalised. Many liked the order imposed by these regimes and were system-supportive, often caught up in the leadership cult. The angle 'from below' then is crucial too.

In Fascist Italy, it was precisely in everyday settings, such as factories and other workplaces, leisure time and activities – as well as interactions with family members, friends and neighbours – that the lived experience of Mussolini's regime was constituted. In addition, the institutions of repression and persuasion worked in overlapping ways and reinforced each other. The Fascist government purposefully created an interplay between consensus-building and coercion, exemplified by the control of the press, the regulation of cultural life and state intervention into people's leisure time. The fact that the number of state-imposed executions was lower than in some of the other regimes we have looked at, most notably Hitler's Germany or Stalin's USSR, did not make Mussolini's rule – characterised by the violence of fascist squads from the very earliest days of the movement even before it attained power – benign.

Opposition or dissent could be very dangerous, and there remained, throughout the Fascist period in Italy, a popular perception of surveillance and fear of state violence. But the role of state terror and the climate of repression was complex. Criticism or nonconformist behaviour was restricted to private familial or intimate friendship circles or spaces. And indeed, many Italians liked the state of order kept by the regime and this often accounted for their acceptance of it or acquiescence to it. There was even some popular approval of violence against 'others'. In addition, the role of the mass formations and the Opera Nazionale Dopolavoro (OND) were significant in forging popular consensus for the regime. The Fascist groups for boys and girls and for Italian women aimed to inculcate their members with fascist ideals as well as to give them an opportunity for belonging to the formation and engaging in its activities. The OND, with its multitude of events and activities, was an effective way in which the regime could intervene in people's free time. The administration effectively utilised leisure to create a 'culture of consent', but consent was as much constructed 'from below' as it was orchestrated 'from above'. Yet the regime's policies did not achieve uniform appeal across Italian society, and especially among the wealthier middle class and upper class they had less impact. The cult surrounding Mussolini – vaunted in fascist propaganda with images of Il Duce shown digging at the land reclamation scheme at the Pontine marshes or making a powerful speech to the nation – had an obvious role in the creation of consensus and support for the regime. Yet, in another way, it could serve to allow Italians to express dissatisfaction with the regime or the policies of the Party, with the oft-used term and sentiment that if only Mussolini knew about an unpopular or unpalatable policy, he would put a stop to it. This leadership cult then also encapsulated a sense that the leader himself was somehow distanced from and disassociated with disliked policies. This was certainly the case in regard to the leadership myths that surrounded Hitler and Stalin too.

Hence, in various nuanced ways, it was possible to delineate room for manoeuvre and evasion, despite the repressive nature of the Italian Fascist regime and the limitations and restrictions it placed upon people's daily lives. Particularly in domestic spheres, for example, in regard to alimentary policies, with its emphasis on frugality and autarky, people found ways to circumvent these at times, and the same was true in the case of Nazi Germany as well. In the spaces of intimacy and behind closed doors, in family and kinship groups, or even with close friends, the intersections of everyday life and experiences of the dictatorship took place. There people negotiated their relationships with each other and with the regime too, whether of support, accommodation or evasion. To be sure, the Fascist government knew this and tried to infiltrate private areas and spaces, including the home and the family. Indeed, in a system in which the family was regarded as the basic cell of the state, it could not, from the administration's point of view, be left 'outside' the state and this was, of course, the main reason for intrusion into the family unit. For example, as in the Third Reich too, schools and youth groups were utilised to circumvent the role and influence of parents and to impose state control and ideology upon the youth. Furthermore, the concern with the birth rate and the desire to create a strong population for the nation and its overseas empire profoundly impacted demographic and pronatalist policies, which in turn affected Italian families. Yet the reaction to state intrusion into family life was also ambivalent, and the family could be a place of compliance or dissent from the goals of the Italian Fascist regime.

Daily life and the policies that affected its conduct in the Third Reich were also layered with complexity. The relationship between the Hitler regime and its people was not as straightforward as it might appear on the surface. In a dictatorship which lasted twelve years – six in peacetime and six at war – Hitler government's put into place a vast number of policies and enacted legislation across a wide array of areas that impacted the lived experiences of the German population – and differently, too, for distinctive groups within it and indeed beyond it – and with tremendous speed. The result was staggering and Nazi policies and institutions deeply influenced people's daily lives.

Like the Italian Fascist government, the Nazi dictatorship tried to create conformity and consensus for its rule in a variety of ways, including the use of propaganda and the development of a range of associations, not least the German Labour Front, the Nazi women's formations and the youth groups, to bind people to the Party and to imbue them with its ideology. The Nazi government aimed at autarky and implemented alimentary policies that affected the eating habits of the German people. In addition, after-work and leisure activities as well as touristic opportunities provided by the KdF played their part in influencing people's daily lives. Simultaneously, the apparatus of terror, surveillance, control and punishment permeated everyday life, in particular in the form of the Gestapo and the concentration camp system. Whilst the Gestapo was in reality not as pervasive as people thought at the time, it certainly instilled fear among the German populace, especially because of its use of a network of informers, which enabled its repressive work. In addition, the concentration camps were no secret in Nazi society, and it was widely known that 'enemies', undesirables or anyone who fell foul of the regime for a whole variety of reasons (not just on political or racial grounds), could be and were interned in them. This enhanced the climate of fear and had a direct effect upon people's behaviour.

Whilst in the case of Fascist Italy, as we have seen, mechanisms of consensus-building and repression overlapped and reinforced each other, in the Third Reich, terror and fear underpinned policies aimed at the creation of consensus. In both the Italian Fascist and the Nazi regimes, the cult of the leader and popular responses to Mussolini and Hitler respectively, were broadly similar. In Nazi Germany, the myth that if only the Führer knew about unpopular policies, he would put an end to them chimed with that of the Italians and their Duce. And here too, the leader cult was as much created by people 'from below' as placed upon them 'from above'. In addition, this concept allowed ordinary Germans to grumble, joke or complain about an aspect of the Party or a particular policy, whilst still supporting the system and, importantly, showing loyalty to Hitler.

In the Third Reich too, with its pronatalist policies and its concern to raise the nation's birth rate, the family was an institution into which the state intervened. This intrusion into family life and into private and domestic spaces was a crucial aspect of everyday life in Nazi Germany. Population policies, eugenics and racial policies drastically impacted the daily lives and family lives of Germans under Hitler. Depending upon the regime's assessment of a person's value or lack of value to the *Volksgemeinschaft* (national community), concepts of 'selection' and 'eradication' permeated many aspects of life in the Third Reich, from education to sterilisation, 'euthanasia' and ultimately genocide. In Hitler's Germany, living under dictatorship often necessitated a situation of outward compliance and conformity, sometimes offset by internally expressed or unexpressed dissatisfaction or dissent. The term 'beefsteak Nazis' (brown or Nazi on the outside; red or Communist on the inside) encapsulates this ambivalence well. Added to the complexity was that often people liked the order brought about by the regime, and approved of the repression, removal or even incarceration of 'enemies' and other groups including 'asocials', Jews, Sinti and Roma, homosexuals or political dissenters, especially communists and socialists. Hence, many layers of complexity characterised both everyday life in the Third Reich and the relationship between the German people and the Hitler regime.

In Franco's Spain, terror was existent throughout the period, although it reduced in intensity over time. Continued high rates of illiteracy and poverty, as well as lack of food in the two decades after the end of the Civil War, meant that great inequalities in society persisted. The role of the Falange in monitoring the mass of the population, for example through its youth groups and control of the press, was significant. The clientelist system in the Falange worked to the advantage of those with political contacts and simultaneously created a dependency or clientele among those at the lower levels. The complex and nuanced relationship with the Catholic Church, which was close to the Franco government, the near-suppression of civil society and the cult of personality that surrounded Franco himself also impacted daily life and people's experiences of the regime. Franco's great popularity meant that people blamed his officials, the Falange or even the army for policies they disliked, and – similarly to Hitler in Germany – the leader was detached from the worst aspects of life and was associated only with the better ones in the popular imagination. Opposition was too dangerous for those who had supported the Republic and there were many exiles. There was some dissent from separatists – Catalan, Galician and Basque – from Franco's concept of Spain. In terms of family life and daily life, the key objectives were work and survival, without much opportunity for leisure. The position of women regressed after the gains of the Republican era, for example, in girls' education, women's legal rights and the role of women as wives and mothers. The persecution and criminalisation of homosexuality was another significant facet of life under Franco's rule. Social inequality, corruption, recourse to the black market and bartering also featured throughout this regime. Internal migration from the countryside to the cities, where the industrial and service economy provided better employment opportunities, engendered the development of neighbourhood associations in the 1960s and 1970s, which were tolerated by the government as long as they appeared, and remained, apolitical. People kept their views close to themselves within the circle of their family and close friends.

Most preferred not to take part in either pro- or anti-regime politics. Certainly, if they did engage in any dissent, it was with great care not to be discovered. By the early 1970s, some – although still very limited sectors of Spanish society – opposed the regime; others embraced a new consumerism and thus society started to change and modernise. Life was better for most Spaniards than it had been in previous decades, but it was still hard. The Franco regime used violence against opposition or calls for reform. Whilst society was not progressive in the first decades of the Franco dictatorship, some modernisation occurred in the latter years.

In neighbouring Portugal, under a regime with a similar ideology and longevity, an apparatus of repression and inculcation saw a normalisation of Salazarist rule by much of the population. People assimilated the autocratic institutions as part of the framework of their daily lives. Salazar's conservative authoritarian regime intended to realign the Portuguese with their perceived socio-historical trajectory, by force if necessary. The mechanisms of repression and value system of the Salazar government formed significant aspects of the everyday lives of the Portuguese. Salazar's rule was founded on a single party, the National Union, with its core values 'God, Fatherland, Family and Work'. This traditional structure, together with the implementation of censorship and political repression, was intended to keep any potential resistance in check. The PIDE formed the basis of the apparatus of control, and similarly to the Gestapo in Nazi Germany, used informers to assist in its activities. In addition, by means of a small number of political murders and arrests, the Salazar regime succeeded in politically atomising the Portuguese population and paralysing any serious perceived or actual opposition.

Ideological inculcation was similar to that in both Franco's Spain and Mussolini's Italy, with reading material and school textbooks closely monitored and censored. Portraits of Salazar hung in school classrooms, with a strong presence too of crucifixes as important symbols of Christianity, to counter and indeed silence any Moorish influence. Furthermore, Salazar popularised the idea of national regeneration through empire and colonies (similarly to Mussolini) and put forward a new vision of the nation. National consciousness was encouraged with initiatives such as 'the most Portuguese village in Portugal competition'. Salazar's ideology of traditionalist nationalism meant that modernisation was not a key aim for Portuguese society.

Similarly to the situation in Franco's Spain, daily life for most Portuguese who lived in rural areas did not change much. They were still landless agricultural workers, or small landowners or land renters. Hence, life was mainly about subsistence. Poverty, together with malnourishment, continued high illiteracy rates (as in Spain), basic provisions, amenities and housing, including a lack of electricity, signified the lack of progress and modernisation during Salazar's rule. In addition, the rigid hierarchical social order for the average rural labourer continued. Indeed, the New State reinforced and perpetuated established tiered social structures. In the National Union too – similarly to the Falange in Spain – clientelism meant that power cliques favoured influential nobles and strengthened *caciquismo* and the power of local elites over Portuguese rural and agricultural workers. And most of them submitted, fearing physical violence on the part of the state for any resistance or rebellion. Small acts of daily resistance, such as feigning ignorance of laws or stealing a few acorns or olives, took place, but not much more than this.

The regime's glorification of rural life and agricultural labour meant that in reality the conditions of the rural masses would not improve and, from the late 1950s until the early 1970s, internal migration from the countryside to the cities occurred – in like manner to Spain – as people tried to improve their lives; emigration abroad also took place for the same reason. This urbanisation led to fast economic growth between 1960 and 1973, and an increase in consumer items, including radio and television sets, throughout the 1960s. But individual politicisation or active opposition remained very small. The political police stifled any active opposition. The population had grown accustomed to political disengagement. Steering clear of politics meant that people could go about their daily lives without fear of the political police. The longevity of the Salazar regime was in no small measure due to the normalisation and routinisation of it, and the way in which the population had adapted to it. For example, the political police force was an accepted part of the framework of everyday life. There was perhaps some slim room for manoeuvre towards the end of the Salazar era, among elites whose influence remained very limited and would not ignite opposition among the masses. But pervasive conformity persisted overall.

Many aspects of life in Salazar's Portugal resembled those in both Franco's Spain and Mussolini's Italy – including the indoctrination of youth through party youth groups. The subordination of women was similar to that in Spain under Franco, with women's roles comparable to those proposed in Nazi Germany and Fascist Italy too. The system of social control and repression by the new state and its organs, the rigid, hierarchical social order strengthened by the conservatism and Catholicism of the Estado Novo and the National Union, together with a cult of the leader that surrounded Salazar, all worked together to create a political demobilisation, except in very small urban elites which would not spread and were therefore pragmatically accepted by the regime. Overall, for the Portuguese, a normalisation of the institutions imposed by the system on their daily lives engendered a lack of opposition and an acceptance of Salazar's rule.

In Latvia, between 1934 and 1940, the Ulmanis regime sought to cultivate a new totalitarian public consciousness. As Vadonis, Ulmanis held much the same status to the autocratic rulers in the cases of regimes in Italy, Germany,

Spain and Portugal that we have noted so far. The cult that surrounded him was similar to those of Mussolini, Hitler, Franco and Salazar. His government was characterised by conservative ultra-nationalism. He conceptualised his rule as not a government of parties or even of a single party, which differentiated it somewhat from those other regimes. In his role and his interaction with his people he sought a distinction from that of others – that each nation appropriated totalitarianism in its unique way (not necessarily mimicking or mirroring Italian Fascism or German National Socialism), a concept of transnational totalitarianism, although his rule displayed similarities to both.

The idea of palingenesis or rebirth of the nation – epitomised by 15 May 1934 as the day of 'renewed Latvia' – surely borrowed from Italian Fascism. The censorship of the press, and the closure of left-wing presses and publications, as well as the corporative chamber system, also bore distinct similarities to the Italian Fascist model. Under Ulmanis, everyday life revolved around ideology and spectacle. Mass participation in public events – in particular, Harvest Celebrations and Victory Clearing – was utilised to build consensus and conformity. These occasions promoted the values of this regime – unity, modernism (unlike in Franco's Spain and Salazar's Portugal for the most part) and efficiency. The harvest celebrations held in 1935, 1936 and 1937 were week-long events, culminating in a speech by Ulmanis. They were significant and powerful representations of a 'renewed Latvia', organised by the state and intended for all citizens. The unity of the nation and complete belief in the leader were the key ideological aspects. The positive response to this renewed Latvian truth was demonstrated by high levels of attendance. Participants cheered and waved as Ulmanis passed by them because they regarded him as a patriarch and as father of the nation. Ulmanis's speeches were about joy and gratitude, with a nationalistic view that overturned 'foreign influence' and promoted 'Latvianisation'. He extolled national unity and the eradication of political parties. He spoke of the responsibilities and the duties of Latvian citizens to 'love our nation and state' and to act in accordance with that love.

The Victory Clearings brought about the transformation of marshland into farmland. This was linked to the idea of the renewal of the ancient past of the land and its spirit. Broadcast over the radio too, these events included renditions of the national anthem and were carried out with pomp and ceremony. The great national 'leader' formally placed a cornerstone of the first farmhouse. This was an ideological, nationalist project, showing the regime helping Latvian farmers to settle on formerly unusable land (and bearing much similarity to Mussolini's land reclamation schemes in Italy) and simultaneously using a charitable initiative to encourage and urge Latvians to donate money to schools, institutions and other worthy projects. Victory Clearing was very much a modernisation initiative, to reconquer marshes that had dominated particular areas for centuries, exemplifying a claim and a demand for a new Latvian consciousness, with the aim of national renewal and regeneration in all aspects.

Whilst Stalin's totalitarian regime in the USSR bore many resemblances in terms of the cult of the leader, the one-party state, and the use of political education and propaganda to the Italian Fascist and Nazi governments, it was distinctive from them too, not only because of its diametrically opposed communist ideology, but also because of the vast territorial space of the USSR and the tremendous number of lives lost under Stalin between 1929 and 1953 in peacetime and in war. The complete lack of civil society and heavy mechanisms of control over the population were absolute on paper, but the size of the land meant that lived experiences were different. The Gulag system became a characteristic part of life in Stalin's USSR, with perhaps as many as 18 million passing through them during his rule. The secret police and use of informers also had a large impact on people's lives and behaviour. In addition, the show trials of 'enemies of the people' were intended to have a deterrent effect upon any opposition to Stalinist rule. Stalin was regarded as a great leader who brought modernity to the USSR and who led the country in the darkest hours of the war. But in reality, not many became convinced *homines Sovietici* either.

Stalin's five-year plans between 1929 and 1941 aimed to modernise the USSR into a powerful industrial country. Many people migrated to the urban and industrial areas. Collective farms were intended to create greater efficiency in agriculture too. Famine and terror pervaded much of life. The period of the Great Patriotic War (1941–5) saw not only a great death toll of soldiers, but also a massive destruction of housing, transport and infrastructure. In the final phase of Stalin's rule, from 1945 to 1953, reconstruction took place, with the added key priority of attaining a nuclear bomb. In terms of everyday life, however, the means of control had limits in a land as large as the USSR. In the countryside, many learned to adapt their behaviour to the demands of the state. In the cities, token enthusiasm for the regime was displayed because this could enhance career prospects. Loyalty had to be shown in order to thrive, prosper and rise up in the Party.

Gender equality improved in some ways for women, but that was in large part due to the necessity for women to work, as families could not exist on one income. Women tended to be lower paid and attain lower positions, even in the professions. Healthcare and access to it were poor in the countryside. Although abortions were illegal, rates were high in the urban areas, partly because housing conditions in the cities made it very difficult to have more than two children. Educational opportunities for children improved. Whilst religion was repressed, some religious traditions and activities continued in the countryside out of the line of sight of the authorities. In reality, the regime's control over people's daily lives remained far from absolute, even if it appeared otherwise and the mechanisms of control looked to be complete. After the war, workers and farmers carved out a private space – spending time with family and friends, engaged in swimming, fishing or sporting activities – although in the countryside there was often less time available for leisure. Overall, everyday life in the USSR under Stalin was a bleak affair, often a genuine struggle for survival on a daily basis, and with the constant backdrop of famine, arrests and violent deaths. Stalin's attempt to modernise the USSR and the means with which he carried this out came at a tremendous cost to the people who lived (and died) under his rule.

In Romania, Ceaușescu's communist regime too was marked by a personality cult of the leader, repressive single party rule and the use of the political police force, the Securitate, to maintain the Communist Party in power and to eradicate opposition. A pervasive fear of the Securitate became a part of everyday life in the late 1940s and the 1950s. Conversations became whispered, there were no open discussions and people spoke in coded messages. As the years went by, with a rise in living standards in the late 1960s and early 1970s, demonstrated by an increase in consumer goods, such as cars and television sets, Ceaușescu was still willing to resort to those earlier Securitate practices, if necessary, in order to secure his continued dominance and power, especially when the economy declined again at the end of the 1970s.

A key feature of Ceaușescu's regime in terms of its tangible impact on the daily lives and private lives of its people was its intrusion into family life and family planning. As the birth rate fell in 1966 to fourteen births per 1,000 people, a new law was passed which permitted abortion only to women over the age of forty, mothers of four or more children, victims of rape and incest and for cases of potential foetal abnormality. As contraception was unavailable, many women used abortion – albeit now illegally – as a method of birth control. From the point of view of the Ceaușescu regime, breeding was a woman's 'patriotic duty'. The birth rate increased to twenty-one live births per 1,000 people in 1969, but declined again thereafter, down to six births per 1,000 people in 1981. There was a dramatic rise in backstreet and self-induced abortions, especially among young working women, sometimes with fatalities. During the twenty-three years of the duration of this abortion law, it is estimated that at least 10,000 women died from unsafe, illegal abortions, from haemorrhaging or blood poisoning.

In general terms, Romanian citizens not only tolerated the Ceaușescu regime, but also supported it. There was a great degree of compliance and a virtual absence of intellectual or ideological dissent. This was often motivated by opportunism – as we have seen in like manner in other cases – as compliance created chances for self-betterment and career advancement.

Party membership was needed for job security and for promotion. The system of patronage could be powerful too, with the habitual use of connections with Party officials. In addition, there was a sense of futility about resisting the authority of the regime and submission was commonplace. Fear of the Securitate and its informers continued. 'Block caretakers' in flats, not only maintained the physical upkeep of the buildings, but also kept an eye on the activities of its residents and any visitors. From the point of view of the Securitate, a reliable network of informers existed, which grew steadily over the years (similar to the modus operandi of the Gestapo in Nazi Germany). The use of violence and surveillance persisted as key features of Ceaușescu's regime throughout its existence.

Whilst the status and power of the Church were largely removed, these were not completely destroyed. Officially, the Communist Party condemned religious worship, but it tolerated the Churches to some extent and was more lenient than the USSR in this respect. In return, the Churches had to validate the Party's policies. However, this compliance and sycophancy towards Ceaușescu signified a dereliction of moral duty and the Church was compromised by its servility to the dictatorship. And the control of information and system of repression in Ceaușescu's Romania made access to knowledge difficult and popular protest uncommon. A collective protest by miners in the Jiu Valley in 1977 was met by a strong response from the Securitate. In 1987, at Brașov, there was another major protest because of wage cuts and chronic food shortages. This too was followed by a high number of arrests. Censorship and the subversion of the press and cultural activity to the dictates of the regime meant that any depiction of the Romanian Communist Party glorified it entirely. The Party was shown as leading the nation. Through socialism and the fulfilment of its aspirations, the Communist Party, with Ceaușescu at its head, defined the national interest. A personality cult surrounded Ceaușescu and later encompassed his wife Elena too.

Life in the German Democratic Republic (GDR) entailed a constant ambivalence – with items either unavailable or overabundant. Whilst people might have been unhappy with the shortages, they were happy at the same time because there was always a lot to hunt down in terms of goods or provisions. They concerned themselves with the important things and tried to get through and make the best out of their situation. The state offered social security, protection and full employment yet, simultaneously, it was based on a pervasive surveillance system by means of the Stasi. Citizens had to fall into line with the regime and its norms – for example, 'order and safety' and 'cleanliness'. The GDR was portrayed as a paragon of virtue and decency – in contrast to West Germany, which was regarded as a morally corrupt society – characterised by a lower-middle-class ideal of nuclear families, happy babies and friendly neighbours enjoying their country gardens at the weekend. And this concept of prevailing tranquillity, order, security, sobriety and protection engendered positive sentiments towards the state, both at the time and in the popular memory of the GDR.

But at the same time the restrictions on life – concretised by the Berlin Wall between 1961 and 1969 – shaped everyday activities, the ethos of GDR citizens and their relationship with the state and its representatives. Indeed, the German Federal Republic was demonised throughout the four decades of the division of Germany and yet, for the people, the sense of connection to 'the other Germany', West Germany, was inescapable. Work was central to life in the GDR, as the embodiment of communist ideology, not just as an activity to ensure people's livelihoods. The creation of value through labour remained crucial in the GDR. The worker and the farmer were idealised, the petite bourgeoisie was heavily criticised; and yet the basic spirit of the SED Party's upper echelons was completely middle class. Hence, there were inevitable tensions evident in the Party and in society in the GDR. Whilst the status accorded to workers and the significance of work remained very high, another key tension or ambivalence was that despite full employment in the GDR, there was also a permanent shortage of personnel. Shops and services were often closed due to a lack of staff. In addition, the right to work and the obligation to work – for women as well as for men – went hand in hand. And economic necessity underpinned this situation. It was impossible to apply for housing without a permanent job and vice versa. And so, many GDR citizens spent their entire working lives in one company. This had manifold advantages, in terms of access not only to company-owned housing, but also to the availability of goods.

The family was an institution of great significance to the GDR system – as it had been under the Nazi dictatorship – as the 'smallest cell' or the building block of society. Although the advent of the contraceptive pill changed a key feature of reproductive life, the GDR intruded in the private sphere and introduced policies aimed to match the propaganda image of socialist happy families, because of its aims to raise the nation's birth rate. The provision of childcare by the state in the form of kindergartens and after-school care was intended to enable women both to continue to work and to have families. But these institutions and the separation of children from their parents in childcare for long hours each day had consequences for daily and family life. Women's lives were full – getting their children ready at the start of the day, doing their day's work and trying to fit in medical appointments for themselves and their family members, errands and shopping, which often entailed long queues. At the other end of the day came picking up the children, feeding them, watching television and putting them to bed. It was a relentless and repetitive daily existence.

Whilst housing improved under Honecker with the development of prefabricated blocks of flats, simultaneously this brought a loss of community and a sterility along with the standardisation of life, as the flats and their components were entirely uniform. The summer house allowed some private life and leisure time away from the city and away from the demands of society and the state. Small pleasures could be enjoyed. Garden plots and allotments suited the regime because the Party leadership believed that people working on their allotments at weekends had less time to engage in subversive behaviour or to develop dissenting ideas. Greater consumerism was also accepted by the regime as a way of keeping the population happy enough not to make trouble. Consumers were even given a certain amount of choice of items, but as the GDR produced inferior or substitute products, dissatisfaction and disaffection from the state grew, and this was exacerbated by constant shortages of goods. People were always on the hunt for products or services that were in short supply. In fact, the exchange of goods and services became increasingly common in GDR society, and personal connections became crucial in terms of acquiring provisions and services. Indeed, the maintenance of relationships towards relations and acquaintances out of economic necessity was part of the reason for people's goodwill towards each other. But, as have seen, state surveillance played an important role in ensuring people's behaviour met with the requirements of the dictatorship too.

Whilst much has been written about the dictators themselves or the nature of the regimes and their mechanisms of control and repression, this book has analysed the experiences of the people who lived through these eight dictatorships. It has examined choice and agency – people's decisions about how to go about their daily lives within the parameters of a very restricted lifestyle imposed upon them by these governments. We have examined the lived experiences of dictatorship in eight separate regimes in Europe in the twentieth century. We have seen both the similarities and the differences. The similarities are clear, in terms of the autocratic nature of rule and the subjugation of individual citizens to the state. We have reflected upon the personality cult that surrounded many of the leaders and the impact of their policies and their organs of repression upon the lives of their populations. Control of information, censorship of publications, and usually the rule of a single party characterised these regimes whether their durations were long or short, whether their ideologies were Fascist, National Socialist or Communist. They displayed a staggering disregard for democracy and civil society. They forthrightly intruded into the lives of the people, beyond their work into their leisure time, and even into the private realm of the family unit. Their policies – whether reactionary or modernising – had wide-ranging ramifications for their populations and additionally had distinctive implications for people in different groups of society, for example, by class, gender or for those living in rural or urban areas. The differences (apart from the obvious ideological ones) are perhaps more nuanced, depending on the circumstances present in each regime, geographically and temporally. Their ideological imperatives and the impact on their societies were far-reaching, always intrusive and demanding, sometimes with catastrophic consequences for their citizens.

Index

Page numbers in **bold** refer to figures.

abortion, 37–8, 59, 66–7, 115, 166, 181–3
actually existing fascist dictatorship, 15
agitprop, 152
agricultural production, 29–30, 31
Akhmatova, Anna, 171
Albanese, Giulia, 21
Alexopoulos, Golfo, 150–1
alimentary sovereignty, 29
Amendola, Giovanni, 126–7
American culture, 27, 43
Andropov, Yuri, 173
Arendt, H., 14n1, 124, 125
Arnould, Vana, 37
arrests, 20
autarky, 29–32, 78, 81
authoritarianism, 129–30

Backe, Herbert, 65
Baehr, Peter, 126
Barcelona, 90
Basque Country, 90
Basso, Lelio, 127
beautification campaigns, 55
Ben-Ghiat, Ruth, 124
Berghoff, Hartmut, 63
Berlin, 205–6, 233, 234
Berlin Wall, 12, 206, 208–11, 250
Bessel, Richard, 4
biopolitics, 58
Birznieks, Jānis, 139–40
black market, 87
Blackbourn, David, 138
Blandiana, Ana, 183, 201n14
Bologna, 40
Boterbloem, Kees, 11–2
Bottai, Giuseppe, 47n85

Brezhnev, Leonid, 173
Brzezinski, Z., 13–4n1, 124
Burleigh, Michael, 68

Caetano, Marcello, 104, 114
car ownership, 54–5
Carmona, General Óscar, 102–3
Catholic Action, 90, 91, 105
Cattalini, Lina, 40
Cazorla-Sánchez, Antonio, 7–9
Ceausescu, Elena, 183, 188, 189
Ceausescu, Nicolae, 12, 179, 248–9
    birth control policy, 182
    Church support, 192–3
    demonic obsessiveness, 197
    downfall, 199–200
    economic policies, 181
    final years of rule, 197–8
    legitimacy, 197
    opposition, 193–6
    personality cult, 187–9
    religious policy, 190
    support, 183, 201n12
    theses, 197
    Warsaw Pact, 188
censorship, 3, 8, 9, 10, 21–2, 103, 112, 128, 196–7, 251
children, 34–6, **36**, 220-1, 250
China, 189
Church, the, 8, 77–8, 79–80, 88–90, 91–2, 105, 107–8, 113
cinema, 27–9, 43
circumstances, 1–2
civil society, 3, 11–2, 77
clientelism, 82, 108, 115, 240
cocktails, 27
coercion and persuasion, Italy, 17–24, 42

INDEX

Cold War, end of, 14n1
collective identity, 138
collusion, 4
colonial context, 16–7
Comecon, 202n24
communism, 179
Communist Youth League (Komsomol), 163–4
compliance, 183–7, 196–7
compromise, 125
concentration camps, 7, 51, 57
Confederazione Fascista dei Commercianti Italiani, 29
conformity, 6
consensus, 6–7, 241
    building, 51, 52–7, **54**, 130–40, 242
consent, 10–1, 17, 38–41
    cultures of, 25–7
conservative authoritarianism, 9–10
Consiglio Nazionale delle Ricerche (CNR), 30
consumer-combatants, 30
Conti, Conti, 61
Cornea, Doina, 199–200
Corner, Paul, 4–5, 20, 22
corruption, 9, 94
Costa Pinto, António, 9–10
coverage, 2–3
Cremona, the, 39
Croce, Benedetto, 124
cronyism, 94
cultural despair, 124
cultural life, 53
cultural traditions, 168–9
Czechoslovakia, Soviet invasion of, 187–8, 189

Dachau concentration camp, 57
dancing, 25, **26**
day-to-day survival, 239–40
de Grazia, Victoria, 25–6, 48n107
death penalty, 19–20
Deletant, Dennis, 12
Delgado, General Humberto, 104
democracy, 8, 92
denunciations, 56–7, 149
depoliticisation, 111
discontent, 20
Dišlers, Kārlis, 129–30, 140

dissent and dissident behaviour, 38–9, 55, 85–6, 92–3, 111–2, 115, 160–1, 168, 183, 193–6, 197, 199–200, 203n36, 240–1, 244
double security, 207–8
Dunham, Vera Sandomirsky, 172

Ebner, Michael, 20
education, 10, 35, 77–8, 107–8, 163–5, **163**, 247–8
education discourse, 66
elections, non-competitive, 103
Engels, Friedrich, 211–2
Enlightenment, the, 1–2
Ente Opera Assistenziale, 17
entertainment, public, 10
ETA, 94, 94–5, 96
Ethiopian War, 17
Eufémia, Catarina, murder of, 109
eugenics, 51–2, 65–9
euthanasia, 7, 65, 66, 68, 242–3
evasion, 4
executions, 19–20
exiles, 86
experience, scales of, 6
experiences, transmission of, 7–8

Falange, the, 80–1, 85, 94, 243
family and familial relationships, 7, 13, 32–41, **36**, 43, 51, 241, 248
    ambiguity in relation to power, 40–1
    GDR, 217–21, 249–50
    health visitors, 33
    intrusions, 33–7, 40–1
    mediations, 38–41
    Nazi Germany, 58–60, **59**
    oppositional familism, 48n107
    parenting practices, 34–7
    roles and relationships, 33–4
    Spain, 87
    USSR, 166
Farinacci, Roberto, 39
fear, 7, 185–6, 240, 248
Federal Republic of Germany, 208, 209, 250
Ferris, Kate, 5–6
fertility control, 37–8, 58–60, **59, 66–7, 242–3**
First World War, 2

Fitzpatrick, Sheila, 4, 48n107
FNAT (National Foundation for Joy at Work), 10
food and food policy, 29–32, 51, 60–5
force, threat of, 3
France, Spanish exiles, 86
Franco, Francisco 8,, 75, 76, **89**, 149, 239
   autarky, 78, 81
   Church support, 79–80
   death, 94–6
   peace myth, 85
   personality cult, 82–4
   political system, 80–1
   power, 81
   and Second World War, 84
   in Seville, **80**
   succession, 95
   use of terror, 76–7
free time and leisure, 24–9, **26**, 43, 47n70, 53–5, **54**, 172–3
Friedrich, Carl, 124
Fulbrook, Mary, 111

Gellately, Robert, 56, 57
gender relations, USSR, 161–2, 247
gender submission, 113–5
Gentile, Giovanni, 124
geographical extent, 2
Gerhard, Gesine, 61
German Communist Party, 58
German Democratic Republic, 12–3, 205–35, 249–51
   Administrators of the Shortages, 229–32
   allotments, 226–7
   bilingualism, 210
   borders, 208
   childcare, 220–1, 250
   Constitution, 229
   consumer industry, 228–9
   dissident education, 213–4
   fall of, 232–4
   family and familial relationships, 217–21, 249–50
   Family Code, 217
   family planning, 218–20
   fashion industry, 227–8
   female employment, 221–2
   final assessment, 235
   fortieth anniversary preparations, 233
   historiography, 4
   housing, 222, **223**, 224–6, 251
   images of, 205–6
   living conditions, 222, **223**, 224–6
   monopoly of truth, 235
   pedagogical perspective, 216–7
   radio, 210
   romantic relationships, 217–8
   scarcity, 205–6, 229–32, 235
   security, 207–8
   separation from the West, 208–11
   shopping, 227–9, **228**, 251
   significance of work, 211–4, 214
   social equality, 231–2
   social security, 207–8
   standard of living, 221
   standardisation of life, 225
   summer houses, 226–7
   surveillance, 206, 249, 251
   television, 209
   Westkontakte, 209–10
   workforce, 214–6
   working life, 13, 216–7, 250
Gestapo, 6–7, 51, 56–7
Geyer, Michael, 4
Ghana, 4
Ginsborg, Paul, 58
Gissi, Alessandra, 38
Gleason, Abbott, 127
Goma, Paul, 197
Gorbachev, Mikhail, 168
Gramsci, Antonio, 20
Greece, 180–1
Grossman, Vasily, 11, 171
Groza, Petru, 198
gulags, 152–3, 247

habit, 101
Hanovs, Deniss, 141
health and welfare, 165–6, 167
Helstosky, Carol, 29, 32
Hess, Rudolf, 60
historiography, 3–5
Hitler, Adolf, 10, 52, 125, 128, 149
Hitler Youth 52

HOAC (Hermandad Obrera de Acción Católica), 8
Hofmann, Reto, 129
Hollywood, 27, 28, 43
homosexuality, 34, 90
Honecker, Erich 13, 207, 215, 222, 225
human weakness, 186

identity, collective, 138
ideological imperatives, 251–2
illiteracy, 114
imperialism, 16–7, 29
individualism, 124
information, intragenerational transmission of, 8
informers, 11, 186–7
Italian Fascism, 4–6
Italy, Fascist, 15–43, 33, 140, 240
   March on Rome, 18
   abolition of trade unions, 20–1
   abortions, 37–8
   actually existing fascist dictatorship, 15
   agricultural production, 29–30, 31
   Alfieri Law, 28
   apparatus of repression, 18–24
   arrests, 20
   autarky project, 29–32
   authority, 18
   cinema, 27–9, 43
   coercion and persuasion, 17–24, 42
   dancing, 25, **26**
   dissent and dissident behaviour, 240–1
   economic privation, 47n85
   executions, 19–20
   family and familial relationships, 32–41, **36**, 43, 48n107
   fertility control, 37–8
   food policy, 29–32, 43
   free time and leisure, 24–9, **26**, 43, 47n70
   health visitors, 33
   imperialism, 16–7, 29
   limits, 42–3
   mediations, 38–41, 43
   national regeneration, 15
   outlawing of political parties, 20
   paternalism, 26
   penal system, 19
   police and policing, 18–9
   political religion, 23
   scales of experience, 6
   schooling system, 35
   Second World War, 16
   totalising project, 5–6, 15–6, 41–3
   violence, 5–6, 17, 42

Japan, 129
jazz, 27
Jews, 53
JOC (Juventud Obrera Católica), 8

Kershaw, Ian, 52
Khrushchev, Nikita, 150, 173
Kogon, Eugen, 57
Korea, 4
Kuck, Jordan T., 10–1
Kühl, Stefan, 68
Kyiv, 160–1

Latvia, 10–1, 123–42, 239, 245–7
   censorship, 128
   collective identity, 138
   consensus building, 130–40
   constitution, 125
   fascist totalitarianism, 123–5
   foreign influence, 134
   Harvest Celebrations, 131–6, **131**, 141, 246
   Lake Lubāns amelioration work, 146n62
   morality, 124
   national renewal, 140–1, 246
   new consciousness, 140
   transnational totalitarianism, 125, 130–40
   Ulmanis regime, 125–6, 140–2
   Ulmanis's coup, 128
   Victory Clearing, 136–40, **137**, 140, 246–7
League of German Girls 52
League of Militant Atheists, 169
Legião Portuguesa, 10
Leipzig, 233
Lenin, V. I., 149, 150, 152, 212
Leningrad, siege of, 157
Liepiņš, Roberts, 134

limited pluralism, 104–5
Lisbon, 105, 110, 115
lived experiences, 1
loyalty, fake, 11
Lüdtke, Alf, 4, 119n59

Madrid, 90
Mallmann, Klaus-Michael, 56
Marinetti, Filippo, 27
Marris, Henry, 101
Martins, Hermínio, 104–5
Marx, Karl, 156, 164, 211–4
Mazpulki, 10–1
mediations, 38–41, 43
Mehlan, Karl-Heinz, 218–20
misery, 87–8
Mocidade Portuguesa, 10
Molotov, V.M., 158
Molotov–Ribbentrop Pact, 156
moral regeneration, 108
morality, 124
Morocco, 96
Müller, Heinrich, 56
Mussolini, Benito, 126, 127, 128, 140, 149
   March on Rome, 18
   and cinema, 27–8
   outlawing of political parties, 20
   paternalism, 26
   personality cult, 23–4, 43, 241
   totalising project, 5–6, 15–6, 41–3
MVSN (Voluntary Militia for National Security), 18

national cohesion, 189
national community, 51, 52, 53–4
national histories, 1–2
national identity, 86
national myths, 76
national renewal and regeneration, 15, 105–6, 132, 140–1, 246
nationalism, 2
Nazi Germany, 51–69, 149, 239
   Auslese and *Ausmerze*, 51–2, 65–9
   beautification campaigns, 55
   car ownership, 54–5
   concentration camps, 7, 51, 57
   consensus building, 6–7, 51, 52–7, **54**, 242

   cultural life, 53
   denunciations, 56–7
   dissent and dissident behaviour, 55, 241
   education discourse, 66
   eugenics, 65–9
   euthanasia campaign, 7, 52, 65, 66, 68, 242–3
   family and familial relationships, 7, 51, 58–60, **59**, 241
   food policies, 7
   food policy, 51, 60–5
   free time and leisure, 53–5, **54**
   historiography, 4
   invasion of USSR, 156–8
   and Jews, 53
   Kraft durch Freude (KdF), 53–5, **54**
   population policy, 58–60, **59**, 66–7, 242–3
   propaganda, 6
   sterilisation programme, 67–8
   use of terror, 52, 56–7
   Volksgemeinschaft, 51, 57, 58, 68, 69, 242–3
   whole-grain bread campaign, 61
   women's magazine, 62
   youth organisations, 52
New Left, the, 93
NKVD, 153
nonconformity, 32
North Korea, 189
NSDAP, 52–3

one-party state, 3
Opera Nazionale Balilla , 22, 35
Opera Nazionale Dopolavoro, 18, 24–7, 27–8, 240–1
Opera Nazionale Maternità e Infanzia, 17
oppositional familism, 48n107
Ostalgie, 234–5
OVRA, 18, 19

parenting practices, 34–7
Paris, 27
Passerini, Luisa, 21, 38, 40
Pasternak, Boris, 11, 171
paternalism, 26
patronage, 22, 108, 249

INDEX

Paul, Gerhard, 56
Paul VI, Pope, 92
penal system, 19
personality cults, 3, 242, 251
    Ceausescu, 187–9
    Franco, 82–4
    Hitler, 52
    Mussolini, 23–4, 43, 241
    Stalin, 11–2, 166–8, 172, 247
petite bourgeoisie, criticism of, 212–3
Peukert, Detlev, 46n68, 55
Picasso, Pablo, 208
Pine, Lisa, 6–7
police and policing, 18–9, 103–4, 181, 245
political persuasion, 3
political religion, 23
political repression, 9
Portugal, 9–10, 84, 101–15, **102**, 244–5
    the Carnation Revolution, 110
    censorship, 103
    Christianisation, 105–6, 107–8, 113–4
    the Church, 105, 107–8, 113
    Constitution, 1933, 103
    dictatorship overthrown, 102
    dissent, 111–2, 115
    economic growth, 110
    Estado Novo, 101, 102, 102–5, 108–9, 111–3, 115
    franchise, 114, 117n32
    institutions, 103–5
    internal migration, 110, 245
    limited pluralism, 104–5
    migration, 109–10
    National Propaganda Secretariat, 106
    national regeneration, 105–6
    National Republican Guard, 109
    National Union, 103
    non-competitive elections, 103
    police and policing, 103, 245
    poverty, 107–9
    proletarianisation, 110–1
    purges, 104
    rural subsistence, 106–10, **107**, 115, 245
    schooling system, 107–8
    subordination of women, 113, 113–5
    the *Trente Glorieuses*, 110
    urban life, 110–3
    urbanisation, 110
    value system, 105–6
Portuguese Communist Party, 104, 115
Portuguese Youth (Mocidade Portuguesa), 113
poverty, 107–9
pragmatic acceptance, 39
Preto, Rolão, 103
private life, 7
private sphere, the, 8
proletarianisation, 110–1
propaganda, 3, 6, 8, 9, 30, 56, 139, 152
public consciousness building, 130–40
public sphere, the, 5, 8

racism, ?
radio, 47n70, 55, 210
Reagin, N., 63, 65
Reiter, Hans, 61, 64
religion, 156, 169–70, **170**, 189–93, 199, 249
repression, 17, 18–24
Roberts, David D., 126, 130
Romania, 12, 179–200, **180**, 248–9
    abortion-related mortality rate, 182–3
    abortions, 181–3
    birth rate, 181–2
    Brasov protests, 194–5, 203n36
    censorship, 196–7
    compliance, 183–7, 196
    descent into dystopia, 197–8
    dissent and dissident behaviour, 183, 193–6, 197, 199–200, 203n36
    economic achievements, 179–81, 200n4
    family and familial relationships, 248
    fear, 185–6
    General Directorate of Press and Printing, 196–7
    gross domestic product, 180–1

infant mortality, 180
informers, 186–7
Law on Religious Confessions, 190
opposition, 193–6
Party membership, 183
personality cult, 187–9
political police, 181
population, 179–80
religion, 189–93, 199, 249
rural workers, 184–5, **184**
the Securitate, 181, 185–7, 192, 248
television, 198, 203n38
urban workers, 184–5
Romanian Communist Party, 196–7

Salazar, António de Oliveira, 84, 101, **102**, 103, 104, 105, 108, 114, 239, 244–5
Schnitzler, Karl-Eduard von, 209
schooling system, 35, 77–8, 107–8
Scott, James C., 109
Second World War, 16, 83–5, 151, 156–8, 159, 167, 171, 247
security, 207–8
Segreteria Particolare del Duce, 23
self-preservation, 11
Seville, **80**
sexism, 88–90
shared experiences, 131
silence, cultures of, 21–2
Simpson, Duncan, 9–10
Skubin‚š, Vil‚ums, 132
Soares, Mário, 104
social capital, 40–1
social equality, 229–30
social justice, 92
social networks, 33
social peace, 105
social security, 207–8
socialisation, 163–5, **163**
socialisation agencies, 8
socialist iconography, 208
Socialist Unity Party of Germany, 206, 207, 209, 214, 226, 227, 233–4, 250
socialist-realist prose, 154
sociocultural change, 9
socio-economic status, 25

Solzhenitsyn, Aleksandr, 153
Sorescu, Marin, 197
Soviet ideals, 161
Spain, 7–9, 75–96, **80**
 Army, 78, 82
 autarky, 78, 81
 black market, 87
 the Church, 8
 and the Church, 77–8, 79–80, 88–90, 91–2
 civil society, 77
 Civil War impacts, 75–6, 78, 82–3
 clientelist system, 82
 Communist Party, 85–6
 corruption, 9
 democratization, 96
 dissent and dissident behaviour, 85–6, 92–3, 244
 economic decline, 78
 elections, 1977, 96
 end of dictatorship, 94–6
 exiles, 86
 factors affecting, 8–9
 the Falange, 80–1, 85, 94, 243
 family and familial relationships, 87
 fascist victory, 75
 GDP, 93
 internal migration, 90–2
 misery, 87–8
 municipal governments, 91
 neighbourhood associations, 92
 peculiar peace, 76–7
 political system, 80–1
 rationing, 79
 school system, 77–8
 and Second World War, 83–5
 sexism, 88–90
 social change, 75–9
 social system, 79–88
 social values, 88–93, **89**
 sociocultural change, 9
 Stabilisation Plan, 93
 starvation, 78–9
 tax system, 91
 use of terror, 76–7, 243
 wealth distribution system, 91
 welfare system, 82
 women's legal rights, 243
Spanish Civil War, 8, 75–6, 78, 82–3

Stalin, Josef, 10, 11–2, 126, 149, 150, 171, 239
  death, 160, 167, 167–8
  grand Ukrainian famine, 78–9
  Great Patriotic War, 156–8, 159, 167
  Great Terror, 156
  Great Turn, 152, 154–6
  personality cult, 11–2, 166–8, 172, 247–8
  post-war, 159–60
  regime, 150
  secret police, 152–4
  use of terror, 150–1
Stalinism
  context of daily life, 150–2
  historiography, 4
Stargardt, Nicholas, 58
starvation, 78–9
Stasi, 12, 206, 249
state, the, relationship with individuals, 38–41
sterilisation, 67–8
Stern, Fritz, 124
Stoltzfus, Nathan, 55, 125
Stranga, Aivars, 10, 123–5, 141
surgical violence, 18–9
surveillance, 20, 34, **36**, 57, 206, 249, 251

technological development, 3
terror, 7
  use of, 52, 56–7, 76–7, 150–1, 242, 243
terrorism, 94, 96
Timpe, J., 55
torture, 104, 111
totalitarianism
  definition, 123–5, 126–30
  historiography, 4–5
  vanishing of, 14n1
trade unions, 20–1
transnational fascism, 125
transnational totalitarianism, 125, 130–40
Trummer, Klaus, 218
Turati, Augusto, 33, 40–1
Turkmenistan, 126

Ukraine, 154, 155, 157, 158, 160–1, 172
Ulmanis, Kārlis, 10–1, 239, 245–7
  consensus building, 130–40
  coup, 128
  fascist totalitarianism, 123–5
  Harvest Celebrations, 131–6, **131**, 141
  propaganda, 139
  regime, 125–6, 140–2
  and totalitarianism, 128–9
  transnational totalitarianism, 125, 130–40
  Victory Clearing, 136–40, **137**, 140
United Nations, 84, 85
United States of America, cultural hegemony, 27–8, 43
USSR, 149–74, 239, 247–8
  abortions, 166
  agitprop, 152
  citizen deaths, 150–1
  civic life, 168–9
  classless society, 161
  collective pastimes, 172–3
  collective-farm villages, 11
  collectivisation, 155
  context of daily life, 150–2
  cult of Stalin, 11–2, 166–8, 172, 247
  cultural revolution, 156
  cultural traditions, 168–9
  dissent and dissident behaviour, 160–1
  divorce, 165
  education, 163–5, **163**, 247–8
  ethnic deportations, 154–5
  everyday existence, 149
  fake loyalty, 11, 170–1
  family and familial relationships, 48n107, 166
  gender relations, 161–2, 247
  grand Ukrainian famine, 78–9
  Great Patriotic War, 151, 156, 156–8, 159, 167, 171, 247
  Great Terror, 156
  Great Turn, 152, 154–6
  gulags, 152–3, 247
  health and welfare, 165–6, 167

housing, 164
intelligentsia, 161, 170–1
invasion of Czechoslovakia, 187–9, 189
lack of a civil society, 11–2
level of control, 172
military training, 164
Nazi invasion, 11
popular and elite culture, 171–3
post-war, 159–60
production targets, 155–6
propaganda, 152
reconstruction, 160
religion, 156, 169–70, **170**
secret police, 152–4
socialisation, 163–5, **163**
Soviet ideals, 161
subversive behaviour, 168
summer houses, 226
territory, 151
totalitarianism, 150
Ukrainian famine, 155
Ukrainians, 154
use of terror, 150–1
women, 161–2
youth organisations, 163–4, **163**

Varusco, Luigia, 39–40
Venice, 32, 37
violence, 6, 17, 18–9, 20, 21–2, 42
Volksgemeinschaft, 51, 57, 58, 68, 69, 242–3

Wagner, Gerhard, 61, 68
Warsaw Pact, 188
Weinert, Erich, 226
welfare provision, 17, 82, 165–6, 167
Wolf, Christa, 210
Wolle, Stefan, 12–3
women, 13
  abortion-related mortality rate, 182–3
  bodily autonomy, 34
  familial obligations, 87
  fertility control, 37–8
  food policy and, 30–2
  gender submission, 113–5
  illiteracy, 114
  as mediators, 39–40
  migration, 90
  status, 34, 88–90, **89**, 243
  subordination of, 113, 113–5
  unmarried mothers, 34
  USSR, 161–2
  workforce, 215
women's magazine, 62
work, 13
  significance of, 211–4, 214, 250

Yekelchyk, Serhy, 160–1
Yeltsin, Boris, 168
Young, Glennys, 4
youth organisations, 52

Zhdanov, Andrei, 171
Zoshchenko, Mikhail, 171